THE
TEUTONIC KNIGHTS
STRIKE EAST

THE
TEUTONIC KNIGHTS
STRIKE EAST

The 14th-Century Crusades
in
Lithuania and Rus'

William Urban & Darius Baronas

Greenhill Books

The Teutonic Knights Strike East

First published in 2024 by
Greenhill Books,
c/o Pen & Sword Books Ltd,
George House, Unit 12 & 13,
Beevor Street, Off Pontefract Road,
Barnsley, South Yorkshire S71 1HN

www.greenhillbooks.com
contact@greenhillbooks.com

ISBN: 978–1–80500–054–9

CIP data records for this title are available from the British Library

Edited and designed by Donald Sommerville
Typeset in 10.5/13.1 pt. Minion Pro

Printed and bound by CPI Group (UK) Ltd, Croydon, CR0 4YY

Contents

Plates

(Colour Plates)

Marienburg castle. *William Urban collection*
Marienburg, river view. *Wikimedia Commons/DerHexer*
Siegfried of Feuchtwangen statue. *Wikimedia Commons/Lestat*
Painting of Siegfried of Feuchtwangen. *Wikimedia Commons*
John of Bohemia sculpture. *Wikimedia Commons/Packare*
Gediminas of Lithuania. *Wikimedia Commons*
Queen Jadwiga. *Wikimedia Commons*
Władysław II (Jagiełło), depicted in Wawel Cathedral.
   Wikimedia Commons
Cathedral in Königsberg. *A. Savin, Wikipedia*
Castle in Königsberg. *Wikimedia Commons*
Vilnius Upper Castle. *Courtesy of Gintautas Zabiela*
Castle site at Veliuona. *Courtesy of Gintautas Zabiela*
Kartupėnai hillfort. *Courtesy of Gintautas Zabiela*
Castle site at Medvėgalis. *Courtesy of Gintautas Zabiela*
Trakai Island Castle. *Courtesy of Gintautas Zabiela*
Kamianets-Podilskyi citadel. *Wikimedia Commons/*
   Grzegorz Gołębiowski

(Black and White Plates)

Martyrdom of St Adalbert. *Wikimedia Commons*
Prussian idol. *Wikimedia Commons/WereSpielChequers*
Winrich of Kniprode (1310–82), in a statue in Marienburg.
   Wikimedia Commons/Lestat
Marienburg after World War II. *Wikimedia Commons/*
   Daniel Widawski
A woodcut of Marienburg castle and town from 1696
   Wikimedia Commons
Ragnit, a modern view. *Wikimedia Commons/Julian Nyča*
Ragnit and its castle, an engraving of 1684. *Wikimedia Commons/*
   Rafael at ru.wikipedia
Seal of Ladislas I. *Wikimedia Commons*

Introduction

This volume is a much enlarged and totally revised edition of *The Samogitian Crusade* that was published in 1989 and updated in 2005 to reflect recent scholarship out of the Baltic States. Since then the number of publications has grown beyond previous imagining, especially in Lithuania and Poland. For this reason, it made sense for me to work with Lithuanian scholar Darius Baronas, who widens and deepens the narrative.

Norman Davies remarked in *God's Playground*, his provocative survey of Polish history, that the numerous changes in politics require historians constantly to revise or completely rewrite their histories. When I first began my studies in the 1960s, the recently exiled Baltic Germans and East Prussians were still trying to understand why fate had treated them so unfairly, while the exultant Russian and Polish communists were celebrating their liberation from centuries of perceived oppression. Thirty years later the fall of communism showed why history is an unreliable guide to the future, but is still important as a guide to the present.

In the past the state of the Teutonic Order in Prussia was often studied in isolation. However, in the fourteenth century the kingdom of Poland recovered from the Mongol invasions and the subsequent civil wars, Lithuania emerged from its tribal past to become a multinational empire, and the Mongol/Tatar hold on Russia began to weaken. Everything was in flux, everything seemed possible, and for western Europeans, it seemed like the crusade against paganism in Lithuania was the best opportunity they had for accomplishing something meaningful.

Standing in the way were endless dynastic wars, crises within the Church, and failed efforts to turn back the relentless advance of the Turks, then the Plague, popular heresies, fear of the Jews, revolts against centralised authority, and, amid the calls for leadership, incompetent kings and popes.

Nevertheless, there was one organisation that Germans (and for a while Bohemians, then French and English knights) could count on to restore pride and meaning to their lives. That was the Teutonic Knights, a military order dedicated to protecting Christianity from armed foes. That they had jealous enemies (sometimes with valid reasons) goes without saying. That the Order had limited resources is another given: it ruled over an isolated region with poor soil, vast swamps, dense forests, and harsh winters. However, that did not mean that neighbours did not wish to take it from them. The challenges were great, the outcome uncertain.

The Teutonic Order had established a base at Culm on the Vistula River (the Wisła in Polish, the Weichsel in German) in 1226 to shield the duchies of Kujavia (Kujawy) and Greater Poland (Wielkopolska) from Prussian raiders. When the Mongol invasion of Poland in 1240–1 almost fatally weakened the kingdom for seventy years, the Order advanced down the Vistula River and along the shore of the Baltic Sea, then inland towards Lithuania. When the Prussian Crusade came to a close either at 1283, a date specified by Peter of Dusburg, a prominent chronicler of the Teutonic Order, or 1309, when the Teutonic Order took advantage of a dispute over the inheritance of Pomerellia (known to Germans as West Preußen and to Poles as Pomorze Wschodnie) to occupy that territory, that provoked an easily roused Polish ruler to cease co-operating in the holy war.

By this time the crusade was less to force recalcitrant pagans to allow Christian missionaries to preach to them than to conquer the sandy coastal lands that lay between the Teutonic Knights' lands in Prussia and Livonia to ensure safe overland travel at all seasons. This involved conquering a densely wooded swampland with many slow-moving rivers. The region to the north of the Nemunas (Niemen, Memel) River was called Samogitia (Žemaitija) or the Lowlands. This would also open the way eastward into the Highlands (Aukštaitija), the heart of the emerging Lithuanian state. However, these tasks proved more difficult than the crusaders expected – the swamps, woods and hills were difficult to cross in summer, while winter expeditions moved too slowly to catch the villagers fleeing ahead of the invading armies; crusaders could move safely over the ice during the coldest weeks in December and January, but their chargers could not gallop through snow drifts. While the expeditions into Lithuanian lands involved volunteers from many lands, some past historians nevertheless identified them as representative of medieval German imperialism, a military aspect of that eastward migration known as the *Drang nach Osten*. This popular summary of complex and generally peaceful human migrations ignored the contemporaneous Polish move eastward and an equally important movement of Jews to newly founded cities on the frontier with Rus'. That would have complicated a story otherwise composed only of villains and victims, one that nationalists loved to exploit.

Readers who do not know German might easily confuse *Drang* (push or pressure) with *Eroberung* (military conquest). Similarly, those acquainted only with nineteenth- and twentieth-century history might misunderstand this aspect of population expansion in East Central Europe as a foreshadowing of modern nationalism. However, there was more going on in the Baltic than military operations and dynastic intrigues. There were profound shifts in technologies, economics, social status and political organisations.

Nils Blomkvist compared the medieval Westernisation process in the Baltic with modern globalisation, and the Christianisation–colonisation process that replaced diverse and eastward-looking societies with more self-confident and technologically advanced cultures tied to Germany and Scandinavia. Sometimes the weaker tribes traditionally dominated by aggressive neighbours accepted the Western systems willingly and sometimes they adapted to them, but those tribes which had lost power and prestige resisted – actively if that seemed likely to succeed, passively if not. In time, when all the tribes came to realise that the newcomers were exploiting them, there were few opportunities to reverse the loss of status. Only slaves and serfs were lower, and while slavery was rare, there were more serfs every year, because captives taken in raids were settled on lands emptied of the native population by pagan raiders.

The Baltic tribes initially impacted by the Western commercial-centred, hierarchical system adopted a variety of survival strategies to contend with the powerful combination of merchants, nobles, and churchmen. One of these was to form what Blomkvist called regimes of plunder and warfare. In short, they organised themselves for war and attacked their Christian neighbours, taking by force what they could not produce themselves. According to the Western chroniclers, the shamans encouraged this, proclaiming that the gods wanted their worshippers to take what they wanted from the followers of the false religion of Christ. When that happened in Prussia and Livonia, a combination of ecclesiastical and mercantile interests called on crusaders to intervene.

The Westerners were not without fault in this matter, but neither were the native peoples. If missionaries were intolerant, so were shamans who saw missionaries as a challenge to their religious monopoly. As for the empty lands, those were the homes of animals they hunted and the haunts of their ancestral gods. They did not want Polish or German immigrants moving in on them.

To complicate this story, the crusades could not be conducted effectively by volunteers who went home before winter arrived. Military orders, in contrast, had knights who would stay all year round and eventually could afford to hire mercenaries to assist them. The first to appear was the Order of Swordbrothers in Livonia, then the Teutonic Knights in Prussia, who absorbed the Swordbrothers in 1237.

But even a military order whose knights took vows of poverty needed money to buy food, clothing, weapons, and labour services. The Teutonic Knights, encouraged by the belief that military means were proper to the spread of Christianity, trade, and political power, had no interest in a purely defensive war. To conduct holy war successfully, they needed supplies and more warriors for offensive operations.

To repopulate areas devastated during the conquest and to make ancient forest barriers effective, they relocated natives from endangered frontiers, then brought peasants, burghers and knights from Germany, Pomerellia and Poland as settlers. Meanwhile, the crusade that had begun as a means of securing the communications route between Prussia and Livonia evolved into an effort to force the Lithuanians to accept Christianity. The question of the Teutonic Knights' territorial aspirations will perhaps always provoke a lively debate.

As Rasa Mažeika and Loïc Chollet demonstrate, efforts to apply modern standards to this crusade are misguided, especially the temptation to see the pagans as the Ultimate Other. In general, the farther away writers were from Prussia, the more likely they were to be fascinated by the seemingly strange customs of the pagans; the closer the writers, the more likely they were to accept those same customs as understandable and normal.

Although this crusade could have come to an end in 1387 with the conversion of Lithuania, it persisted until 1399, when the Samogitians surrendered, and was over on 15 June 1410, when the Battle of Tannenberg removed the Teutonic Knights from the struggle for regional hegemony. As important as were the changes in culture, language, and the economy in Prussia during the late Middle Ages, even more important today are the ways that Germans, Poles and Lithuanians think about their common history. Once nationalism became significant, historians on all sides exaggerated and distorted facts that were both glorious and cruel enough in the bare telling.

Poles saw themselves as victims of German aggression in the west, but as defenders of Western civilisation in the east, out of the wars against Russians and Tatars came the great Polish–Lithuanian Commonwealth, the Polish Renaissance, and the love of the chivalrous gesture. To appreciate the richness of this multi-cultural state, see the introduction to the special issue of *Central Europe* edited by Richard Butterwick-Pawlikowski.

Lithuanians, as Darius Baronas reminds us, were influenced by Romanticist historian-cum-fiction-writer Teodor Narbutt and others – despite their writing in Polish, a sore point for nationalists – to see their ancient homeland as a fairy-tale country, one filled with courageous and virtuous people who were brought close to nature by their gods and forests.

Those narratives tell us more about views common in the chroniclers' era than those farther back. Today scholars think that the medieval period has to be approached on its own terms, to be understood as best possible within its own limits. While some Franciscan friars argued that war was less likely to achieve conversions than peaceful approaches, it was not until the fifteenth century that anyone questioned the theoretical basis of this crusade. At that time the Polish scholar Paulus Vladimiri (Paweł Włodkowic, *c.* 1370–1435), one of the royal spokesmen at the Council of Constance, called for the utter destruction of the Teutonic Order, citing its numerous crimes against humanity, the crown of Poland and the people of Lithuania. However, when he went on to argue that no state could take lands that it had not been given by God at the beginning of time, he went too far. Hardly a European state had not taken neighbouring lands. Vladimiri was henceforth ignored by most of his contemporaries, but it was not so long ago that historians were advancing the same arguments that Vladimiri and his foes had made.

There was another, simpler explanation: Michael Howard argued that Christendom was a warrior society in which 'Ecclesiastical organisations and doctrine were subordinated to the needs of the warrior ruling class.' In short, nobles existed to make war, and make war they did.

Warriors were a necessity: without a military elite, every village and town was at the mercy of invaders or robbers. Although mercenaries were beginning to erode the military monopoly of the nobles, it was not until the development of regular armies in the early modern era that Western society could do without its hereditary warriors.

This was the justification that Polish and Lithuanian historians made in defence of their homelands' expansion towards the east.

Poland as the *Shield of the West* also justified the abandonment of important provinces in the west – no nation can do everything, and Polish contributions to holding off first steppe warriors, then Turks, and finally Russians became central to the patriotic message taught to generations of children.

Claims to national sovereignty reflected traditions based on dynastic foundations. Only slowly did people begin to think that nations existed because specific territories were occupied by people who shared a common language, culture and religion. That was because every group in the incredible ethnic and linguistic mix of early modern states impeded change by defending hard-won traditional privileges and exemptions.

Eventually, the consolidation of kingdoms, then the imposition of bureaucracies and mass education – all aspects of modernisation – divided the political world into those nations which made the necessary changes to survive and flourish and those which were remembered only in museums and history books; often this meant a division between states which were large enough to defend themselves and those too small to do so.

Only in the twentieth century, after conflicting claims to territory had been largely resolved by two terrible world wars and massive ethnic cleansing, was a new start possible. In these new circumstances historians in Poland, Germany, and the Baltic States no longer felt obliged to represent national interests. No longer must we see all crusaders as saints, all their enemies as Rousseau's noble savages. As Immanuel Kant put it, we have built our world with the crooked wood of humanity.

One cannot fight wars with saints alone in even the best of causes; and it is not always clear that the crusades were the best causes. Nevertheless, not only did crusaders become more like Prussians and Lithuanians in equipment and tactics, but these enemies came to resemble their Christian foes. The remarkable developments we see in fourteenth-century Lithuania occurred partly because of its compli-cated relationship with its German and Polish neighbours, adapting their attitudes and technologies, and eventually their religion. More important, perhaps, was the Lithuanians' relationship with their Slavic subjects, because in order to reconcile those peoples to an alien rule, the Lithuanians had to put aside traditional habits in favour of more sophisticated ones. Peaceful skills had to be acquired as well as military ones.

It was through governing the people of Rus', not through conquering them, that the Lithuanians became a great people. They came to see a world larger than the forests of their gods. As the Lithuanians concluded alliances with Russians and Poles, acquired modern weapons, and came to understand the mentality of their foreign enemies, they unwittingly undermined the foundations of their rural paganism; as they encountered Mongols, Tatars, and ultimately Turks, they met peoples utterly different in languages, religions, and mentalities. That their ultimate fate was to become Roman Christians associated with the Polish kingdom was not foreordained, but that process cannot be understood without reference to this long crusade.

Most inhabitants of Europe had once been pagans. They believed in a complex system of nature gods and natural forces, each of which could be influenced by rituals and prayers, sacrifices and ceremonies. Fourteenth-century Christians seem to have accepted Baltic religious practices as a valid effort to reach out to obviously real gods. They believed that shamans and magicians could foretell the future and influence the weather; their principal evil lay in preventing their believers from entering the Christian heaven. The Order's chroniclers seldom wasted valuable vellum denouncing the enemies of the Cross – every listener would have taken that for granted.

Neo-paganism is popular today, usually associating magic and mysticism with imaginative re-enactments of ancient ceremonies. In Lithuania it is characterised by anti-Catholic attitudes that merge with alternative religiosities, prehistoric feminism, diet and deities. Its most eloquent proponent, Marija Gimbutas, is now seldom mentioned.

There were also infidels, Muslims and Jews who represented a special challenge to the creation of a universal Christian society. The Jews were not a military threat, but some Christians argued that extreme measures were necessary to persuade them to convert, because only after that happened would the Second Coming be possible.

The Islamic world could not be dealt with so lightly. Most medieval Christians knew little about Islam; those who were moderately informed thought of Islam not as a competing religion, but as a heresy; common people, who were discouraged from discussing religious beliefs and practices, often did not know what pagans, heretics, Jews and Muslims really believed. The Teutonic Knights remained above such controversies – they were not trained in disputation, and moreover were sternly warned to leave preaching the gospel to priests, especially to Dominican friars who had studied the techniques most likely to be successful at converting the heathen. The knights and priests of the military order were proud of their simple faith in what the pope told them – unless the pope was 'misinformed' by the Order's enemies, at

xvi   *The Teutonic Knights Strike East*

which point they could be just as stubborn in resistance as they had been in obedience.

Nor, for that matter, did many Westerners know much about Russian Orthodox beliefs. Lithuanians learned much of their Christian vocabulary from Orthodox churchmen, but the rulers of Rus' were not enthusiastic about converting them, fearing that pagans would bring with them beliefs and practices that could dilute the faith required to support the True Church in a time when it was on the defensive every-where.

Western churchmen, though enthusiastic about mass conversions, were far from united on how to do it. Dominicans were famed preachers whose scholarship made them formidable debaters; Franciscans believed devoutly that only their more peaceful practices would make lasting conversions; and some churchmen were more interested in accumulating power, prestige and wealth than in saving souls.

The principal problems here were heretics and schismatics. For centuries heresies had grown naturally out of efforts to explain or express Christian doctrine in ways that reflected local cultural practices, philosophical traditions, or logic. Churchmen met in formal assemblies (councils) to identify heretical ideas, then authorised the civil authorities to arrest or exile those who stubbornly held to them, but language, culture, theological traditions and powerful personalities stood in the way. The Great East–West Schism of 1054 divided the Roman and Greek churches until 1965.

The Greek and Roman churches never completely overcame their mutual antagonism even when it was necessary to fight together against the enemies of the faith. As a result, Western Christians tended to call Orthodox believers schismatics, and even today Westerners must resist the tendency to equate the modern Roman Catholic Church with its medieval ancestor, and the medieval Roman Church with all of Christendom. This sometimes leads us to imagine that the schism was as serious at its origins as it became later. It wasn't. It was merely important.

In the Western tradition popes and ecumenical councils determined what steps were appropriate to protect believers from false beliefs that could imperil their immortal souls. But not every secular ruler was willing to defer to this authority; when they thought popes were abusing their power, they fought back. In 1328 the emperor-elect of the Holy Roman Empire, Louis IV, named a Spiritual Franciscan as an anti-pope and gave some heretics refuge at his court, among them the Italian Marsiglio of Padua (1275–1342), who advocated representative government for the church and the state. More traditional reformers, desperate to end the Great Schism that began in 1378, with feuding popes in Rome and Avignon, placed their hopes in a Church Council (this story is told in *The Last Years of the Teutonic Knights*).

Many historians see an eleventh-century shift from the western church's emphasis on pacifism and withdrawal from the world to engagement with society's problems, a shift that was partly expressed in the attitude towards knighthood called chivalry. Knights were henceforth identified as society's protector against pagans and Muslims, an identification that became even stronger after the First Crusade achieved the seemingly impossible re-conquest of Jerusalem. The elaborate rituals associated with taking the Cross and the crusade as pilgrimage were considered extraordinary even in an age that loved pageantry and display.

Chivalry was, as Maurice Keen noted, 'elusive of definition, tonal rather than precise in its implications'. This made it easy for the Western church to insert religious values into the secular concepts that are part of chivalry, then to encourage knights to go on crusade.

Source Materials

I wrote the first draft of *The Samogitian Crusade* on a sabbatical at the Johann-Gottfried-von-Herder-Institut in Marburg/Lahn, with financial assistance from the DAAD, the German bureau that supports foreign research. The Herder-Institut has an extraordinary collection of materials on East Central Europe and one of the friendliest staffs.

Source materials from this era are largely Western in origin. This reflects several facts. First, most surviving diplomatic correspondence was in Latin or perhaps German, only little in medieval Ruthenian. Secondly, Western chanceries saved more documents and later scholars collected and edited them. Thirdly, because Samogitia was in north-west Lithuania, it was often mentioned in Prussian and Livonian documents, but seldom in the Ruthenian ones.

A Note on Language

Years ago I followed the practice of the *Cambridge Medieval History* in using common English-language forms for well-recognised eastern European names whenever they exist. Władysław became Ladislas, Johann became John. 'Von' disappeared completely because it misleadingly suggested that everyone was a noble. Today, I do not anglicise as many names. I do not want to suggest that they were all misplaced Britons in a real-life Graustark or Ruritania.

When I first began to publish, it was virtually impossible to print special characters in Lithuanian and Polish, letters essential to names like *Kęstutis* and *Jagiełło*, beautiful names which convey nuances and memories that anglicised forms cannot. Still, my experience with above-average college students and editors is that some mellifluous names can be an obstacle to reading and understanding. In a story already complicated by personalities, political and religious disputes, and constant change, I feared to add unnecessary complications. Readers may wish to consult the acerbic comments on nomenclature by Norman Davies in *God's Playground: A History of Poland*. Nevertheless, the use of Polish, German and Lithuanian names underlines the ethnic realities that the individuals of the time were dealing with.

A special remark is in order regarding spelling. Some individuals and localities have borne many names. For example, the modern English name Samogitia is Žemaitija in Lithuanian, Žmudź in Polish, and Schamaiten in German. Rus', in contrast, is the name that many medieval historians use for Kyivan Russia to remind us that this medieval collection of states, with its rulers from the Rurik dynasty and its important mercantile foundations, was very different from the later unified nation created by the grand dukes of Moscow.

Pronunciation guides are widely available on the web, and alternative spellings of names as well as further information can be found there too.

Place Names

Almost every location has at least two names, and often three. I generally use the ones most familiar to English-language readers. The most important examples in Prussia are Danzig (Gdańsk), Thorn (Toruń), Culm (Chełmno), Marienwerder (Kwidzyn), Marienburg (Malbork), Elbing (Elbląg), and up the coast to Königsberg (Kaliningrad). Some names elsewhere, such as Cracow (Kraków), are similarly treated. Galicia is more difficult – it is a more modern name than Halich (Halych) and is easily identified with the later Austrian province, but it is so much more commonly used in the English-speaking world that we will use it here to refer to the region just east of Cracow.

Politics has a way of reminding us that the world changes, and that the names of cities and states do too. Thus, today Kyiv is preferred over Kiev, today's Lviv was formerly Lwów, Lvov and Lemberg.

Why No Footnotes

Footnotes are for scholars, but they take up space and do little for the growing number of non-professional readers. Popular history can inspire further reading and even draw some individuals into enjoyable and useful careers as teachers and scholars; it informs the general public about areas of the world and eras of the past that do not often make headlines, yet are important for understanding how those headlines come into being.

William L. Urban
Lee L. Morgan Professor Emeritus of History and International Studies
Monmouth College, IL

Chapter One

Between Crusades

Prussia and its People

In the Year of Our Lord 1309 most of the lands of the Teutonic Order in Prussia were at peace, as much as any area of northern Europe was in those days. For much of the previous century the native converts to Christianity and the Polish and German immigrants had fought terrible wars with Prussian and Lithuanian pagans. These wars were Roman Christendom's reaction to a pagan militarism that had taken booty and prisoners from the northern duchies of Poland and from Pomerellia; the long contest had ended with the conquest of the native tribes and begun the process of Christianisation, but there had been little cultural change.

Archeological studies confirm that, aside from language, before the crusades there was not much to distinguish Prussians from other tribal groups living along the shores of the Baltic Sea. Everyone employed the same methods for fishing, raised the same crops, and herded the same animals. Although there were differences in cult practices, in burials, and in the houses, their societies were usually divided into elites – military and religious (shamans), commoners (farmers and artisans), and slaves. The tribes were subdivided into clans, with elders holding considerable authority, but with military leaders elected for each campaign. This was an attractive semi-democratic political organisation, but in wartime it was less effective than a feudal hierarchy; also, it was unable to fuse the tribes together for united resistance to outside attack, so that the tribes fell one by one to the crusader armies.

The strongest of the tribes lived in Sambia (Samland) far from the fighting during the early years of the crusade. Their location was also better for trade, both in having harbours and being near two rivers – the Nemunas and the Pregel – that led towards Lithuania and Rus', and from time immemorial they had traded their amber to merchants who came from lands as distant as Egypt, Greece and Rome; they occasionally sold slaves – presumably taken in local wars. They were also lucky in that in 1255 they were conquered quickly and decisively by the Bohemian king, Ottokar II, for whom the city of Königsberg was subsequently named. Thus, Sambia was spared the destructive wars of attrition experienced by the other tribes.

The tribal societies were all disrupted by the conquest, but not completely transformed – the Teutonic Knights learned that it was best to ignore customs and land-holding practices that did not violate Christian principles; in fact, the Teutonic Knights were often criticised for their toleration of ancient practices, criticism that went so far as to accuse them of preventing the conversion of the native people; meanwhile, other critics complained that they were oppressing the natives. The critics generally stood to benefit from destroying the Order's state and taking its lands.

The Teutonic Order established in 'East Prussia' a base for holy wars against pagans in Lithuania which could support the semi-autonomous knights in Livonia in their wars; it even promised to aid the distant crusade to the Holy Land, in the event that crusaders managed to return there.

Yet the story was not altogether quite so simple and straightforward. The natives (often called Old Prussians to distinguish them from the German-speaking immigrants) had not been known as an aggressive people until 1147, when the Piast dynasty in Poland tried to collect tribute. Subsequent royal efforts to extort money aroused fierce resistance, after which the victorious Old Prussians took revenge in Masovia and Kujavia in Poland and the coastal duchy of Pomerellia, killing and kidnapping, rustling cattle, and burning homes and villages. Christian resistance was ineffective because the Polish kingdom was divided among feuding brothers who ruled in Masovia, Kujavia, Great Poland, Sandomierz, Little Poland, and Silesia. Pomerania and Pomerellia were Slavic states loosely tied to the Polish kingdom, but also to the closest German duchies and to the kingdom of Denmark.

The Old Prussians were able to enrich themselves by raids, and their shamans (pagan priests) mocked, then martyred the occasional missionary who dared to preach to them. In the course of time Old Prussian culture became increasingly militaristic and aggressive. This caused the rulers of Masovia and Pomerellia to look beyond the borders of Poland for help.

Enter the Teutonic Order

Innocent III (pope 1198–1216) seemed to believe that declaring a crusade was the proper answer to every challenge he faced, whether it was in the Holy Land, Byzantium, Spain or southern France. Innocent III also believed that papal sanctions were appropriate for reproving disobedient Christian monarchs such as the rulers of England, France and the Holy Roman Empire. He was usually successful.

Past efforts to Christianise the Prussian tribes by force had not been successful because the Prussians did not have one ruler who could be coerced or intimidated or persuaded into becoming a vassal prince. Thus, the results of the campaigns had always been the same – as long as the Polish armies were in Prussia, some natives promised to stop their raids, to pay tribute, and to listen to missionaries. However, because the feudal obligations of Polish knights did not extend to acting as an occupation force, and the resources of the duke of Masovia did not allow him to hire sufficient mercenaries as garrisons for the castles, as soon as the armies went home, the natives resumed their raids. It no longer mattered who had begun this cycle of attack and counter-attack – revenge for the last atrocity was all that counted.

In the 1220s the duke of Masovia invited Western military orders to defend the frontier, concentrating especially on the embattled region of Culm where some natives had accepted Christianity. Among those approached by the duke was that *Deutscher Orden* (literally, the German Order) which in English is called either the Teutonic Order or the Teutonic Knights. It was understood that those friar-knights would fight the Prussians on his behalf, their reward being heaven in the afterlife and a share of whatever lands and booty they could take, resources that would allow them to maintain garrisons in the castles, thereby making sure that the natives did not rebel again and providing protection from attacks by tribes that had not yet converted. The knights did not live in luxury and idleness. That came centuries later.

The founders of this military order had never imagined being called to the Baltic. Their order came into existence at Acre, in the Holy Land, to assist ill and impoverished German crusaders. By the 1220s they were attracting recruits and donations of property from burghers and nobles in the Holy Roman Empire who were distressed by the disintegration of imperial authority and societal values, but repeated truces in the Holy Land led the grandmaster to look for other places to employ his knights.

The Teutonic Knights flourished in Prussia to a degree probably surprising even to themselves, since they had to divide their resources between crusades in the Holy Land, Prussia and Livonia. They also had divided loyalties during the conflicts between Emperor Friedrich II (1194–1250) and the popes. For these reasons, the military order did not send many of its members to Prussia at first. Instead, it relied on lay volunteers from Poland and Germany who earned spiritual benefits called indulgences. Pious individuals could already earn indulgences by visiting shrines, going on pilgrimages, or assisting the Church in various ways, thereby shortening the time they would suffer in Purgatory. In contrast, the plenary indulgence earned by crusaders exempted the recipient from punishment for all past sins; in effect, this meant immediate entry into heaven if the crusader died in the service of the Church or lived a pious life afterwards. Although the popes normally limited the use of plenary indulgences, they believed the crusades in the Baltic were sufficiently important to award them to those who took the Cross in support of the Church in Prussia and Livonia.

Critics of the crusade have noted that the popes did not call for crusaders to join specific expeditions, as was common for the better-known crusades to the Holy Land. But there were no annual calls for crusades in Catalonia, Castile or Portugal either. Nor did contemporaries see anything odd in the northern crusades proceeding without regular papal involvement. Apparently, everyone realised that it was not practical for the pope to supervise warfare on a distant northern frontier. Whenever the presence of a papal legate was appropriate, the popes sent one. Eric Christiansen, whose *Northern Crusades* is highly regarded for its sensible insights, said that the Church had adopted a common-sense approach to 'perpetual Holy War'.

Piety was not the only motivation for young men to volunteer their services on behalf of the Cross and Lady Mary. Most crusaders were young of course, because that is the age when men are most enthusiastic for adventure and status and least concerned about death or injury, but there were individuals of middle age who sought fame or needed to perform penance or to fulfil a vow. A few were mercenaries rounding out a lord's entourage (a number that became larger as the century progressed) or served in the military order (presumably through the winter, when castle garrisons most needed reinforcement), and there were individuals seeking knighthood who could not otherwise have afforded the expensive ceremony, because it was the practice of the most prominent nobles present on each foray into the wilderness to honour worthy squires by dubbing them knights.

Most of the early crusaders came from Poland and Pomerellia, but there were also knights, merchants and commoners from the Holy Roman Empire who saw Prussia as an attractive place to fulfil their crusading vows: the journey to the Holy Land was expensive, time-consuming, and often frustrating because the numerous truces would send them home without having struck a blow. Moreover, Polish and Pomeranian rulers were trying to attract German farmers, artisans and knights into their lands, which was the quickest way, perhaps the only way, to populate deserted regions with taxpayers. The interest in eastward migration also made everyone more aware of the Prussian menace than might otherwise have been the case.

Recruiters, nevertheless, often found it difficult to raise armies. The attraction of Jerusalem was so strong that whenever the pope called for volunteers to fight in the Holy Land, most crusaders went there rather than to Prussia. Also, since a lord had priority on his vassals' military service, the Teutonic Knights could organise expeditions only when potential crusaders were not otherwise engaged. Consequently, the Teutonic Knights' conquest of Prussia was characterised by spasms of rapid expansion when large numbers of crusaders were present, and defeats when too few volunteers came forward. Above all, the Order's plans depended on relations among the Piast dukes, because they provided the largest contingents in the early crusading armies; if they were quarrelling, as was common, none of their subjects took the Cross.

This holy war eventually became a form of Christian militarism that some contemporaries believed equalled in horror the barbaric militarism it defeated; the most that historians can agree upon concerning the Prussian Crusade is that it greatly reduced the number of pagan raids into Poland and Pomerellia. As the holy war became a success, the Piast dukes began to lose their sense of urgency about prosecuting it. When their internal feuds came to take precedence over all other matters, the Teutonic Order of necessity replaced the Polish knights with whatever Germans and Czechs they could recruit. Since the crusaders from the Holy Roman Empire went home after each expedition without demanding a share of the conquests, the Teutonic Order was left with the fruits of victory: possession of Prussia east of the Vistula.

This success created jealousy. When the Teutonic Knights refused to turn over their possessions to the king, his nobles and his favoured churchmen, conflict followed.

The Government of Prussia

The Teutonic Order had divided itself into three branches to accommodate local interests and to make supervision easier – the Holy Roman Empire, Prussia and Livonia. The order's possessions in the Holy Land were directly under the grandmaster (*Hochmeister*), but for all practical purposes, those ceased to exist after the fall of Acre in 1291; henceforth, the estates and convents in the Holy Roman Empire were used to support the Livonian and Prussian masters and the military activities of the Holy Roman emperor.

Each branch reflected a combination of democratic and authoritarian practices. That is, each knight, priest, and half-brother took the vows of friars – poverty (not to possess private property), celibacy (not to marry), and obedience (to all officers right up to the emperor and pope). But the practical need to govern Prussia meant that the individual officers commanding districts called *Kommende* or *Komturei* were very important; in the Holy Roman Empire the *Komturei* were often gathered into administrative units called *Ballei* (bailiwick or province). In this book a *Komtur*, as these officers were known, will be called a commander (though castellan might be more accurate). The highest officers (*Großgebietiger*) met as the master's council.

The half-brothers were men-at-arms who fought in units of ten mounted warriors. Often called serving brothers or sergeants, they wore grey mantles, to distinguished them from the white-clad knights. Also, they did not serve for life, but presumably returned to lay life, married, and found a career where their administrative talents would be useful.

Over all was the master, originally called the *Landmeister*, who was elected by the members to serve as long as his health permitted or until he was removed. He consulted his council on important matters and the entire Prussian membership on important issues, but we know little about these men personally. Konrad Sack, master in 1302–6, is mentioned only in a few documents and the brief remarks of the chronicler Nicholaus of Jeroschin (*c.* 1290–*c.* 1341), who praised his pleasant personality, his fairness, and his piety. Konrad's successor, Siegfried von Schwarzburg, despite his obvious connection to one of the most prominent families in Thuringia, left even fewer records.

The Early Development of Prussia

Prussia was not a rich land. Lying on the southern coast of the cold Baltic Sea, its frequent rains drained well only along the shore. The interior was filled with lakes, forests and swamps. Bees flourished, as did wildlife generally, but the thick forests were almost devoid of human inhabitants.

The Lithuanians who lived to the east spoke a language related to Old Prussian and were devout pagans. Their numbers, their legendary height and their physical prowess combined with a love of battle to make them the foremost warriors of the region; they dominated weaker peoples wherever they found them – in Rus' (medieval Russia) and Livonia (modern Latvia and Estonia). They wore armour, were skilled at using crossbows and catapults, and employed infantry, mounted infantry and cavalry. This made them formidable enemies.

Despite the natural poverty of the land, the Teutonic Order found ways to exploit the resources it had. Although most Prussian farmers had farms only two-thirds the size of those allotted to immigrants, the Order favoured the rich *Witingen* – clan leaders and peasants who could afford good weapons and owned horses – by freeing them from taxes and labour duties and exempting them from trial under German laws; they were tried instead under native law in courts supervised by special officers of the Teutonic Order called *advocates*. The *Witingen* were not knights in the French or English sense, but neither were the *ministeriales* who made up most of the knightly class in Germany; their status was like that enjoyed by *turcopoles* in the Holy Land, native warriors whose weapons and tactics were appropriate to the region. By 1310 the main difference between the converted warriors and their pagan ancestors was their choice of victims: instead of raiding a comparatively rich Polish countryside, they fought in Samogitia, the swampy, wooded lowlands lying between Prussia and Livonia and along the Nemunas River.

Although many of the *Witingen* had supported the peasants in uprisings and even fled to Lithuania rather than surrender, those who remained saw the advantages of working with their new masters. (Ultimately, many would abandon their ancestral language and become incorporated into the lower nobility of Poland and Prussia.) Some Samogitians doing the same were not cowards or traitors, but they had seen no point to resisting the military incursions when a negotiated surrender, the acceptance of Christianity, and moving to Prussia to live on small fiefs guaranteed them an honourable exile; moreover, when their homeland was pacified, they expected to be granted large estates there.

These *Witingen* were auxiliaries when Teutonic Knights, local knights and gentry, and crusaders formed an army to defend the land or attack Lithuania or Poland, but for smaller operations they formed the main force. When combat was joined, they would watch the commander's banner or the crest on his helmet – sometimes feathers – to see where he led, then raise the battle cry. They were doughty warriors, but if they saw defeat likely, they would slip away into the woods to fight another day.

With Lithuanians making devastating retaliatory raids into the lands ruled by the Teutonic Order, nobody who saw their villages burned, their parents and children murdered, and wives, friends, relatives, and serfs herded away in shuffling columns of chained prisoners needed much encouragement to join the crusader armies. As a result, the conquered tribesmen fought as much for revenge as from any instinct for survival, and the Teutonic Order rewarded the most successful warriors handsomely.

The poorer farmers were less happy. They worked individual patches of land in their traditional manner, using wooden ploughs. Wherever there was sufficient land to allow half the fields to lie fallow each year, where sandy soil could be turned by a one-horse plough, and where cattle were a major part of the economy, the two-field system had real advantages. However, planting the same cereal crops year after year wore out the soil, and when the amount of grain harvested became barely sufficient for sustaining life, Prussian farmers found it difficult to raise any surplus for taxes or export.

The Teutonic Order had tried to force the farmers into villages and to adopt the more efficient three-field system based on co-operative ploughing and harvesting while retaining the ownership of individual plots. It had expected that diversifying and rotating the crops, and giving each family more land, would increase per-acre production so that higher taxes could be collected. However, its ruthless herding of the farmers into larger villages was combined with an unrealistic expectation that they would master the new technology and collective labour practices quickly. Whenever the Teutonic Order demanded that Prussians pay the same taxes per capita that German and Polish immigrants did, it provoked uprisings. For better or worse, the Prussian farmers chose to work their small plots individually and to pay the lower taxes.

This might not have been a foolish strategy. Jared Diamond, in *Guns, Germs, and Steel: The Fates of Human Societies,* noted that the small difference between barely enough and starvation discouraged subsistence farmers from taking risks. Although Blomkvist, in *Discovery of the Baltic,* suggested that slash and burn agriculture produced superior crops in the region, the master of the robes – the officer in charge of settling vacant lands – sent out *locators* to bring in farmers from Poland, Pomerellia and the Holy Roman Empire who understood the three-field system. Skilled at draining swamps and clearing forests, they willingly paid the taxes because these were lower than what they paid in their homelands. This provided the military order with ready money for food, clothing and equipment.

The numbers of immigrants grew rapidly after 1283, after the last insurrection of the native Prussians was put down. The first wave had come from northern German states and Holland – thus making Low German the dominant language of the towns and villages – but this era ended when plague came to the Holy Roman Empire in the mid-1300s, killing the surplus population that had once chosen to emigrate. The next wave was largely composed of the children and grandchildren of the earlier immigrants; these were joined by farmers and knights from Masovia and the northern Polish duchies, who moved into nearby regions. The last area settled was Sambia.

This pattern was not unusual, Germans had already moved eastward beyond the border of the Holy Roman Empire into Hungary, Bohemia and Moravia, and Poland, almost always settling as artisans and merchants in cities or in the countryside where their skills as miners, millers and in diking rivers were in demand. Shortly afterwards Jews followed them, also settling in the towns (but they were not welcomed in Prussia).

The Teutonic Order had founded towns at strategic locations as soon as possible, then required the burghers to serve in the militia – in the infantry or on horseback, depending on each individual's wealth – and to assist the garrisons with watch duty and patrol. The burghers were also middlemen for Hanseatic merchants. They bought grain, wax, honey, lumber and furs, thus making it possible for the peasants to pay some of their taxes in coin. They also purchased Polish grain, which came down the Vistula River from as far away as Cracow.

The Teutonic Order encouraged all these activities, each of which brought in some revenue. The end of the wars allowed its officers and the bishops to concentrate on building a solid economic base for their states, but it was still not easy, especially after the colder weather that set in about 1300 caused repeated crop failures. Nevertheless, because of peace and careful management of resources, the Teutonic Knights ultimately made Prussia rich beyond what the climate, the few natural products, and the small population led everyone to expect.

The conversion of the native peoples continued, but it made little impact on daily life. Polygamy was no longer practiced openly, but like Germans and Poles, the Prussians knew how to get around that prohibition; cremation of the dead was forbidden; and the last memories of paganism were evolving into folklore and superstition. But class structure and economic practices were left intact.

The Teutonic Order had almost no role in this, as the knights were forbidden to offer religious instruction. Dominican friars had dominated the mission in the early period, but later the four bishops (Culm, Pomesania, Ermland, and Sambia) established churches throughout their dioceses, hiring priests from Germany to live among the natives and immigrants. By 1360 they had established at least 735 parishes and endowed the churches with lands for the support of priests and supporting staff; but many parishes went empty – as was often the case in Germany. Although reduced to hiring incompetent priests who were otherwise unemployable, the bishops were reluctant to train native converts for the priesthood, lest they be too tolerant of the Old Religion's surviving practices or emulate the first young men taken to Germany to be trained as priests, who had led dangerous revolts.

Dominicans and Franciscan friars, who might have been effective substitutes, preferred to preach in cities where townsfolk understood German and Polish, and where guildsmen were eager to make arrangements for burials and masses. Despite these circumstances, the Christianisation of the natives had gone quite as well as could be expected. No one had ever believed that the older generation of Prussians would become enthusiastic about the new religion. It was enough that they no longer killed female babies or sold girls into slavery, that polygamy became the informal keeping of concubines, and that the open worship of the old deities ceased.

In 1300 it was still not clear who would prevail in the contest between Christianity and paganism. Lithuanians were still striking as deep into Prussia as Christburg. Chroniclers recounted two attacks in that year. One involved a diminutive knight who led nine men in pursuit of ten raiders, finally overhauling them deep in the forest. There he was so severely wounded that his intestines coiled out, but he continued to fight until he had liberated the captives. The women he had freed accompanied his body home, followed by two snow-white doves. The second episode involved Lithuanians who had killed 200 Prussians and taken many captives. The pursuers were perplexed when the raiders split into two groups, because they did not know which group contained the captives. Though it was more dangerous to divide their forces, they did. One group killed 65 raiders and freed 70 women and children; the other group found five orphans who had been abandoned in the hasty flight. The chroniclers reported that many Lithuanians drowned, starved or hanged themselves. That was perhaps wishful thinking, but it might reflect the real conditions of warfare in the wilderness.

Christianity did not strike deep roots among the Prussian tribes – most converts learned little beyond a few prayers, an appreciation of some saints and of the Virgin Mary, and knowledge of when to stand and when to kneel. That was judged sufficient even in Italy, which had been Christian for a thousand years, because it was believed that the laity, especially women, should not concern themselves with theology. Women were stubborn and conservative, but even they would understand the words, 'protect us from evil'. It was the native *Witingen* who concerned the Teutonic Knights; and their formal conversion seemed secure enough. The Christian god, the warriors saw, had more power than the pagan gods, because the crusaders had beaten their adherents in battle. Warriors had to respect that.

By 1310 Prussia was no longer the rural, isolated land which had existed eight decades before. It had become a Western-style state with numerous small cities, proud castles, international trade, and an undoubted if modest prosperity. A visitor who had heard how it had been before could not help but be impressed. The nobles, both the native *Witingen* and the immigrant Germans and Poles, were well-to-do. The farmers benefited from peace and order; the burghers – at least the most prosperous ones – were thriving behind their stout walls. Responsible for this were the wise policies of the Teutonic Knights. Prussia had one law, one centralised government (as long as the bishops co-operated), and one currency. It was free from civil strife and foreign invasion, still had vacant lands that attracted settlers and investments; and it was ruled by men of skill and vision.

Christian Neighbours to the South

As Stephen C. Rowell noted in *Lithuania Ascending*, this was a tumultuous era. Poland, Prussia's most important neighbour, was torn by civil war. The kings of Bohemia, Wenceslaus II and III, occupied the throne in 1300–6, but each died unexpectedly. Even so, no Piast duke was able to make himself fully master of the kingdom until Casimir the Great (1310–70) – his father, Ladislas the Short (Władysław Łokietek, *c.* 1260–1333), had to fight rivals and rebels until late in his reign. There was a fairy-tale quality to these years – vast foggy forests from which Lithuanian raiders would emerge without warning, complex hereditary claims to the crown, interventions by foreigners, and the ultimate happy ending.

Political confusion was a problem in Hungary, too, where Pope Boniface VIII (1235–1303) worked to end the contest for the crown of St Stephen. Boniface had begun his career in the Church as an advocate for the Angevin dynasty – as the descendants of Charles of Anjou (*c.* 1226–85) were known. Charles, the brother of the French king, St Louis (Louis IX), had seized power in Naples and Sicily by overthrowing the Hohenstaufen king at papal behest, then lost half that patrimony in 1282 in the complicated conspiracy/rebellion known as the Sicilian Vespers. That was a setback to the new king's ambitions to conquer the weak Byzantine Empire; as consolation, the dynasty now looked towards Hungary.

Boniface became pope in 1294 after removing his incompetent predecessor (a hermit who had been chosen after a long deadlock in the college of cardinals). When the throne of Hungary became vacant in 1301, he feared that the Bohemian monarch would fill it, thereby making himself master of east central Europe and then resist efforts to extend papal influence. In 1303 Boniface concluded that Charles Robert of Anjou (Károly Róbert; 1288–1342) would serve the Church's interests best, even though his claim came only from his grandmother having been the daughter of King Stephen V. He had no knowledge of the country or its language, and he was still a minor.

Boniface laid an interdict on the kingdom, forbidding marriages, burials and baptisms until all rebellions ceased. Since pious believers, and even the superstitious doubters, saw the interdict as an eternal death sentence, this worked until the Czech candidate died and Boniface himself passed away. Charles Robert had counted on aid from his uncle Albrecht, the Habsburg archduke of Austria and Styria (and Holy Roman emperor-elect), but he died in 1308. As a result, Charles Robert was unable to have a proper coronation until 1316, and the unrest lasted almost to the end of his reign in 1342.

Charles Robert might well have yearned to be back in the more attractive and richer kingdom of Naples – even with its own political unrest. What he did was to import Italian/French practices that made the Hungarian government more effective and introduced the nobles to the extravagant customs of chivalry, including its literature and its impractical dreams.

Papal Troubles

Boniface VIII persuaded himself that he could use the popularity of his Jubilee Year in 1300 to overawe all opposition, but Boniface misjudged the situation in France, where he demanded that the king, Philip IV (le Bel, 1268–1314), acknowledge that all Christian states were subject to the papacy, France included.

This was a claim that, if limited to matters of faith, all monarchs could agree to, but Boniface carried it right into the political arena. Boniface might have thought that his canonising the French crusader-king as St Louis (*d.* 1270), had won him royal friendship, but he was mistaken. Philip was a cold-blooded plotter whose ambitions equalled his the pope's. The king was determined to strengthen royal authority by striking down anyone he thought stood in his way – independent-minded nobles, clergy loyal to the pope, military orders, Jews or heretics. After all, Philip's propaganda had persuaded most French people that his dynasty was especially favoured by God, a claim that holy women were confirming. Moreover, Philip's guile surpassed anything even a pope known for sly underhanded dealings could imagine. In 1303, after Boniface renewed the excommunication of all enemies of the Church in France, among whom everyone understood the king to be numbered, then issued a second excommunication that specifically named the king, Philip quietly ordered the pope kidnapped.

Philip's hirelings, accompanied by Colonna family retainers, struck while Boniface was in his summer mountain retreat at Anagni. After a heated exchange among the kidnappers about whether to kill the pope outright or not, they held him without food or water for three days, hoping to starve him into cancelling the excommunication and in general abandoning his political programme. Boniface replied that he'd rather die. At that point local pride moved the citizens of Anagni to act – Boniface had been born and reared there. The townsfolk freed the shaken, aged pope, but Boniface soon developed a fever and took to his bed. A month later he was dead.

Dante had already placed the pope in Hell in his popular serial poem, *The Divine Comedy*. This was a thought that had cheered Ghibellines – as Italians who wanted a strong secular state were known. Many Ghibellines were in exile for having dared argue that the pope and emperor should be co-equal, sharing the governance of Italy for the benefit of everyone. However, the idea of having a strong pope was not popular even among the Ghibellines' enemies, the Guelphs. Nobody wanted to exchange one haughty ruler for another. Besides, Roman emperors had never shared power with clergymen.

The Teutonic Knights took the imperial side. The chronicler Jeroschin cited Pope Celestine, who had resigned the holy office in 1294 after having realised that a lifetime as a hermit was a poor preparation for dealing with the complicated intrigues and jealousies in the curia – the papal court – much less understanding the political rivalries in Italy and beyond. Celestine reportedly said to Boniface: 'You have achieved the honour of this prize by the cunning of a fox, and you are ruling like a lion; later you will be destroyed and will die like a dog.'

Within a few years the Church was so badly split between the Italian and French cardinals that the popes of the next decades – all French – withdrew to Avignon, then in the Holy Roman Empire, but on the border of France. This mean that papal interest in northern affairs diminished just as it was most needed.

Christian Neighbours to the North of Prussia

Scandinavia was sufficiently peaceful that Swedish nobles, merchants and even peasants were pushing eastward into Finland; rulers even dreamt of occupying the fur-trapping areas of Rus'. This was understandable, since to a considerable extent Swedish prosperity rested on trade with the regional power, Novgorod, and few Swedes had forgotten that not too long before Vikings had safely made their way to Byzantium and back. How difficult would it be to dominate that vast area's trade again, or at least the northern reaches, now that the Mongols had overrun most of Rus'? Novgorod was politically isolated, and although the Mongol khan encouraged commerce, he would not have objected if the last independent city ceased to be a symbol of successful resistance. Swedish offensives from Finland into the Neva River basin had implications for the branch of the Order in Livonia, because if they joined in that war, they could not help in Lithuania.

Modern preconceptions about the Catholic–Orthodox relationship are misleading. At this time there was more co-operation than conflict. There had been no significant Western interest in conquering northern Rus' since the 1242 defeat on the ice of Lake Peipus by Alexander Nevsky. Geography, climate, and the desire of the people and the Orthodox Church to decide their own fates made conquering Novgorod unlikely, and there was no money or popular enthusiasm for another war. Although historians from the late fifteenth century on have tended to see this frontier as one of continual conflict between competing Christian confessions, the years of peace vastly outnumbered the years of war, and disagreements were typically over trade. The Catholic–Orthodox relationship in the south was similarly hopeful.

Christian Neighbours to the South-East

The history of the lands known as Ruthenia was recorded in the *Hypatian Chronicle*, a detailed account of foreign wars and dynastic struggles that warned of the dangers of disunity and civil conflicts. Ruthenia – then composed of Galicia and Volhynia (Wołyń) – was vulnerable to aggression from every direction, except to a certain extent from through the Pripet (Pripyat) Marshes. The princely house had been extinguished by war, and now the nobles there felt threatened by Poles and Hungarians to the west, Lithuanians to the north and Tatars from the south-east.

To the east, Kyiv (Kiev) was at a crossroads for trade north and south, east and west, but that had been ruined by long and desperate civil wars, then the disastrous battle on the Kalka River against a Mongol–Tatar army. Renewed Mongol attacks began in 1237, conquering one Rus'ian city after another, culminating in 1240 in the destruction of Kyiv. The Mongols moved on to ravage Ruthenia, much of Poland and Hungary, then withdrew to the steppe again, warning the surviving princes to pay a heavy annual tribute and provide troops to Mongol armies, or else. All that remained of Kyiv's once glorious past was the metropolitan, the head of the Russian Orthodox Church, who left in 1299 and ultimately moved to Moscow.

Thus it was that a unified Roman Catholic Church faced a fractured Orthodox world whose secular rulers mistrusted or hated one another. The ancient dynasty of Rurik had been further weakened by the practice of inheritances passing to brothers rather than to sons, thereby guaranteeing that rulers would often be too old to lead armies and too unfamiliar with the people and geography of their new realms. Civil wars were common because each generation produced ambitious young men who were too impatient to await their turn.

The main residence of the dukes of Galicia–Volhynia was at the castle in Halich, which lay on the upper reaches of the Dniester River that flowed south to Moldavia and then to the Black Sea. East of the river was the vast Eurasian plain; to the west hills eventually merged with those of the kingdom of Poland; some steep outposts were topped by impressive castles, but with too few peasants to feed the garrisons. As Halich declined, Lviv (Lwów, Lvov, Lemberg) rose in importance. That city, which came to mark the division between Catholic and Orthodox Europe, was on a tributary of the Bug River that flowed north to the Narew River, where the stream turned west to pass through dense forests and empty into the Vistula near the future site of Warsaw. This did not mean a total abandonment of trade with the east or the Black Sea, because, the small boats of that era could approach tributaries of the Dniester, allowing merchants to transport their goods over short portages, then continue their journey.

The most important town on the northern Bug was Brest. Thanks to its having been conquered by the Lithuanians in 1319, its name eventually became Brest-Litovsk to avoid confusion with a similarly named town in Kujavia (Breść). Brest-Litovsk lay on the direct route between Poland and Moscow that ran just north of the vast Pripet marshes.

To the north-east of Brest-Litovsk lay Grodno (Hrodna, Gardinas, in modern Belarus) on the Nemunas River. The road eastward passed just north of the marshes – as every invader of Russia, including Napoleon and Hitler, understood – and westward lay the twisting, twining branches of the Narew that flowed towards the Vistula, and northward the Nemunas flowed into the Curonian Lagoon. Since numerous trade routes met at Grodno, every aspiring ruler wanted to control it. At the moment the Lithuanians held sway.

Most Polish merchants wanting to trade with the east left from Cracow, the city that Ladislas the Short had selected as his principal residence instead of a city in Silesia or Kujavia. They avoided the Pripet marshes by going through Galicia, via Lviv or Lutsk (Łuck). Thus, whatever happened in Galicia would have repercussions as far as Prussia.

When the Romanovich dynasty of Galicia–Volhynia became extinct – the last ruler of Volhynia dying in battle in 1321 and the brothers ruling Galicia falling two years later against the Tatars – that gave Ladislas a claim on those regions through an agreement with the Lithuanian ruler, Gediminas (*c*. 1275–1341), to install a young Masovian prince, Bolesław, as ruler, with Gediminas's brother Liubartas (*c*. 1300–85) watching over him from Volhynia.

Ladislas was too busy in the north of his kingdom to object to the growth of Lithuanian influence in Volhynia, but he must have followed developments in Galicia closely, where Lviv would have been a valuable and easy addition to his possessions. However, all he could do was to pass down that ambition to his son, Casimir.

Internal Conflicts in Prussia

In 1309 Grandmaster Siegfried of Feuchtwangen came to Marienburg, presumably on a conventional (if rare) visitation of the Order's northern possessions. While traditionally scholars have seen this as transferring the residence of the grandmaster from Venice, in 2014 Klaus Militzer suggested that it was something less dramatic. In 'Die Übersiedlung Siegfrieds von Feuchtwangen in die Marienburg' in *Ordines Militares*, he noted that Siegfried was almost completely inactive as grandmaster while in Prussia – he issued no formal documents, he allowed local commanders to make important decisions, and he relinquished further authority to a subordinate in Venice. This was right in the middle of disagreements over whether to concentrate on efforts to return to the Holy Land or put resources into the crusades in Prussia and Livonia. Peter of Dusburg, who began his chronicle in Marienburg while living witnesses of Siegfried's time were still present, had almost nothing to say about him.

This suggests that the transfer of his residence came only a decade or more later. He had to have watched the mock justice of the Templar trial in France in full knowledge that powerful enemies were seeking to subject his order to a similar judicial ordeal, but he had felt safe in Venice. His presence there, in a powerful state long committed to the crusade, was proof of his intent to return to the Holy Land.

In 1309, however, Venice ceased to be safe. When Pope Clement V (pope 1305–14) declared a crusade against the city for having occupied Ferrara, that made every ally of the Venetians into an enemy of the Church. It may be that, to avoid giving any appearance of supporting the Venetians, as Feuchtwangen's presence in the city would imply, he had decided to remain in the north; if he had gone to a nearby Italian city, he would have offended the Venetians whose help would be needed in any future crusade, and the pope might ask why he was not serving in the papal army. As it happened, Clement was so successful in recruiting volunteers to wage war against his secular Christian opponents that the political crusade was confirmed as a means of implementing papal policy.

The knights in Prussia favoured bringing the grandmaster north, but the knights living in the Holy Roman Empire, with their numerous convents, churches and hospitals, seemed to believe this would demote them to collectors of gifts, solicitors of bequests and donations, and recruiters of novices and crusaders. The result was a conflict between the knights in Germany and their brethren in Prussia over who should be the bearers of the crusading tradition.

This quarrel was not new. Earlier, in 1302, Gottfried of Hohenlohe (1265–1310) had come through Prussia en route to Riga to take fifty knights to reinforce the brethren in Livonia. When he returned to Prussia, he discovered that the knights there refused to obey his orders. He summoned representatives from all the convents to Elbing for an assembly called a general chapter, where he hoped to win a majority to his side. When that failed (perhaps because the Prussian knights so greatly outnumbered the rest), he resigned his office and rode back to Germany. While the grandmaster claimed to exercise authority over the membership, the knights in Prussia insisted that their military order was essentially democratic, and therefore the grandmaster should not act without their advice and consent. This attitude reflected conflicts over authority common to the Western feudal world.

At the next general chapter, held in Elbing in 1303, the electors chose as grandmaster Siegfried of Feuchtwangen, the German master (*Deutschmeister*). He was related to a recent grandmaster, but perhaps more importantly, he was from Franconia and knew Nuremberg well, a city closely associated with imperial power – the powerful office of *Burggraf* was possessed by the Hohenzollern family, imperial diets were held here, and Holy Roman emperors often resided in the high castle. Siegfried apparently went to Prussia to participate in the discussions that had led to Hohenlohe's resignation. Wisely, perhaps, he avoided a confrontation by departing for Venice and leaving local matters in the hands of the Prussian officials. He maintained that attitude after returning to Prussia in 1309.

In contrast, the next grandmaster, Karl of Trier (1265–1324), insisted that a grandmaster should do more than preside – he should rule. He had been the chief officer in Venice, tasked with reviving the crusade to the Holy Land, but had met with little success, because the Hospitallers, with their strongly fortified islands in the eastern Mediterranean and their fleet, had become the leaders of Christian resistance to the Muslims. Also, Karl's relatively modest birth to patrician parents – that is, rich but not noble – did not inspire awe, nor did his meagre military experience. (He had supervised the Order's properties in the French-speaking provinces nearest Trier.) Nevertheless, at a meeting in Marienburg in 1311, the electors chose him over the leading Prussian candidate. Six years later, outraged with the resistance to his efforts to limit commercial activity in Prussia to officers he appointed, he called a general chapter meeting to discuss that matter. When the assembled knights, half-brothers and priests asked him to resign and give up his seal, he did so, then left for Germany, where the members of his Order tended to agree with his policies; a year later, thanks to the intervention of the pope, Karl was re-elected grandmaster at a general chapter in Erfurt.

The Livonian Knights and Riga

The knights in Livonia, like their brethren in Prussia, were semi-autonomous. That is, they were under the authority of the grandmaster and general chapter meetings, but in practice were self-governing, with their own master and high officers. They differed from the rest of the Teutonic Order mainly in that their members spoke Low German. They supported the actions of the grandmaster in Lithuania, but they had to watch their neighbours to the east – Pskov and Novgorod. Like the Prussian knights, they sent representatives to elections and general chapters, and the knights stationed in the Holy Roman Empire, who knew and trusted them, agreed that they should be the dominant power in Livonia.

This viewpoint was the source of difficulty with the archbishops of Riga, the bishops and abbots, the local nobility, and the citizens of Riga who had repeatedly challenged the Livonian masters for hegemony. Archbishop Johannes III of Schwerin (c. 1267–1300) had known Boniface VIII well, having obtained the confirmation of his own election in 1294 against the strong resistance of the Order's knights in

Livonia by renouncing the right of his canons to elect his successors in favour of papal nominations.

By the time Johannes III had made his way to Riga, a violent conflict had broken out between the citizens and the Livonian master over a bridge that the citizens were using to transport building materials for a new levee intended to prevent springtime floods; however, since the bridge cut off the Order's access to the sea, rendering them dependent on the citizens' goodwill to obtain supplies and reinforcements, the Livonian master was alarmed when the citizens announced that they would not remove the bridge when the project was completed. When the Rigans persisted in their plans, he tore it down.

In 1296 the citizens employed their trade relationship with Lithuania to obtain military aid in besieging the Order's castle in Riga. Johannes III initially tried to mediate the dispute, then joined the citizens. In 1298 the Rigans and Lithuanians defeated the Livonian master, killing him and about twenty knights. But soon afterwards the Order's knights captured the archbishop and then, reinforced from Prussia, inflicted a decisive defeat on the Rigan–Lithuanian army and captured Riga. Only in 1300, at the request of Pope Boniface VIII, did they release the archbishop, who went into exile at the papal court, where he died.

Johannes's successors followed the peregrinations of the curia and saw to it that each pontiff was aware of every dispute involving the Teutonic Order's knights in Livonia or the grandmaster. The alliance of an archbishop in exile, the citizens of Riga, and the dukes of Lithuania became so dangerous to the Livonian branch of the Teutonic Order that the knights in Prussia found it necessary to send men and money north even when hard pressed in their own wars.

What presented the greatest difficulty in defending Livonia was its isolation for six months of each year. Ice and storms made travel by sea impossible or fearfully dangerous during the winter and, therefore, communication between Prussia and Livonia was possible only via the castle at Memel (Klaipėda), whence travellers could go along the beach to Kurland. Even this was not safe. A better and more direct route to Riga would be a road through the heart of Samogitia, but that lowland province was inhabited by the most warlike and most determinedly pagan tribes in all Lithuania.

The Samogitian Crusade

One reason for conquering Samogitia was to secure a land bridge to Livonia, but it was also hoped that persuading/forcing the Lithuanians to become Roman Catholics would resolve numerous regional problems.

However, when the coastal tribes withdrew into the interior, their fields and pastures became a wilderness so dense that neither side could easily get at the other. As the grandmasters came to realise that the Lowlands were not much of a prize in themselves, they turned their interest to the valleys of the Nemunas and Neris (Vilija) Rivers that led into the richer Highlands of Lithuania.

German merchants from Riga and other cities had already searched out the best routes into the interior of Rus', Lithuania and Black Russia. Travelling by ship during summer and by sled over the ice in winter, they had learned which waterways were navigable, how friendly the various native peoples were, and what possibilities existed for commercial exchange. This information had always been useful to the crusaders, who also profited by the willingness of merchants to take the Cross and employ their vessels in the service of the Church.

Throughout the thirteenth century, both in Prussia and in Livonia, the Teutonic Knights had used naval power effectively in advancing along the coasts and up the rivers, building earth and log forts at strategic points. Whenever possible, the Teutonic Knights avoided overland treks because of the difficulty of carrying supplies and war materiel. While they could use the backs of native warriors and their stout ponies, hills, swamps and woods were such formidable obstacles they preferred to travel on the rivers – across the ice in winter and by boat in summer. Three rivers – the Nemunas, the Šešupė (Scheschupe), the Jūra – became one near Ragnit (Nemen) before it split into multiple mouths emptying into the 'Wild Gulf' (the Curonian Lagoon). This made Ragnit one of the most important bases for offensive operations. Ships crossing the Baltic could stop in Memel, then make their way to one of the shallow routes through the Nemunas delta until they reached what Lithuanians called the father of waters. The castle at Ragnit was large enough to store the supplies that armies would need for campaigns up the winding Nemunas River.

As it happened, however, neither the Narew nor the Nemunas were as suitable for navigation as the Vistula in Poland or the Daugava (Düna, Dvina) in Livonia had been. The twisting Nemunas had natural obstacles that prevented sea-going cogs from reaching the heartland of Lithuania at Vilnius (Wilna) and Grodno, and somewhat inland – between those key fortresses – the castles at Trakai (Tracken).

Merchants using the Narew to reach Lithuania first sailed from the Vistula east up the Bug, then entered the slow-moving Narew with its multiple channels and islands. This was the most sparsely populated part of Masovia, bordered on the north by the even more desolate Masurian

Lake district. But only shallow tributaries connected the Narew to small rivers that fed into the Nemunas, so portages were necessary.

This was also partly true for poorly developed routes from the Pregel and Alle rivers in Prussia to the Lake District. Depending on the season and weather, travellers could find themselves in a wilderness where streams were often indistinguishable from swamps. At that point, unless they were sailing in very small boats, they often had to carry their cargo overland. If lucky, they could tow their lightened vessel over the portage, then reload the cargo and proceed to their destination.

Grodno was more of a military outpost than a commercial centre, but it had been important before the Lithuanians took over; now, however, after numerous attacks by the Teutonic Knights, it was in decline. Crusader raiders had burned and plundered the countryside as far as Vilnius, partly in retaliation for attacks on Prussia, partly to strike at the many Old Prussian exiles who had resettled there, and partly in hope of surrounding the Lithuanian Highlands. This war had become more deadly in early 1305 when German crusaders set villages ablaze as far as the eye could see. The next year, according to the chroniclers, when the Prussian master heard that Lithuanians were raiding Poland, he sent militiamen to see if they could take advantage of the situation. Attacking under the cover of a thunderstorm, Prussian militia destroyed much of the town, but refrained from a direct attack on the citadel – Prussians were good fighters in the forests, but they recoiled from hand-to-hand combat. A second force included knights skilled at storm tactics. However, by then the Lithuanian army had returned, so the fighting was fierce, toe-to-toe, back-and-forth, before the attackers gave up. Still, the repeated destruction of the commercial district and the capture of merchants and artisans – including, most likely, many Rus'ians – must have hurt the mercantile community greatly.

Travel along the Nemunas route remained possible for merchants, though very dangerous: there were numerous islands, sandbars and logjams that made navigation difficult. Upstream of the confluence with the Neris impassable rapids required time-consuming portages, and even on the lower river the channel twisted between bluffs and among islands in ways that permitted defenders to build obstructions which could slow down the progress of any hostile fleet. Here and there Samogitian forts protected the obstacles.

The Teutonic Knights, having been on the Samogitian frontier since the 1250s, were aware of the difficulties they faced. Still, they were well-prepared. Estimates of manpower available vary wildly – 400 to 1,000 knights, with most scholars favouring something above 800 once the aged and infirm are counted – but the armies were always smaller than one might imagine. There may have been 3,200 men-at-arms, 4,900 vassals, 1,200 episcopal vassals, and 850 well-trained men from the city militias. About half could be used for any offensive operation, the rest kept back to defend the castles and cities. To these they added the crusaders, whose number varied wildly, depending on the political situation in their homelands. Lastly, there were the native militias, enthusiastic when attacking, but easily panicked; many were probably employed carrying supplies, tents and war machines. Altogether, this was a sufficient force for an advance into the Lithuanian heartland that would cause the pagans to take the offer of conversion seriously; larger numbers would have created difficulties for the quartermasters.

The grandmasters knew better than to underestimate their opponents, but their principal advantage came not from wealth or numbers, but from superior organisation. Swords and stout hearts could only do so much. The bases at Ragnit and nearby Tilsit (Sovetsk) held storehouses for the supplies and siege equipment necessary for an offensive; in addition, they had castles to the west and north of Samogitia – at Memel, Goldingen, Mitau, Riga, Kokenhusen, and Dünaburg. This allowed them to attack swiftly, destroy villages and burn crops until they had weakened the tribes sufficiently that they could besiege and capture their strongholds. This strategy had worked in Prussia and Livonia. The Teutonic Order believed it would work again.

The natives, of course, were not without resources. They knew the land, they had allies, and they were fighting for home and hearth, their freedom and their gods.

Brandenburg's Ambitions to Occupy Pomerellia

Between 1290 and 1309 most crusader attacks on Lithuania were against Grodno. In 1309, however, a radical change in the relationship of the military order and the Polish crown developed when Ladislas the Short, duke of Kujavia and Great Poland and uncontested but uncrowned king of Poland, quarrelled with the Teutonic Knights over possession of Pomerellia. This would cause the dukes of Masovia to turn their attention to an enemy who also had designs on Silesia – the historic heartland of Poland.

Brandenburg lay just to the west of Pomerellia, across the strategic territory of the Neumark. Over generations the margraves of Brandenburg had increased their power by marriage and war. They were violent men who in 1296 had sent mercenaries to kidnap the Polish king,

Przemysł II, when he had paused to spend the night in a village and they had mourned little when their thugs bungled the job, killing him.

They had been moved to act because shortly before, when Mestwin II of Pomerellia (Mściwój II or Mszczuj II, *c.* 1220–94), realised that his health was failing, he left his lands to the crown of Poland, hoping thereby to keep them out of the hands of the margraves of Brandenburg or the Teutonic Knights. After Przemysł attended the funeral in Danzig, he intended to return to Great Poland, apparently believing that he had successfully brought Pomerellia under royal control. This is what had led to the failed kidnapping – the margraves of Brandenburg seemed to have hoped to extort concessions from him regarding Pomerellia.

Długosz (1415–80), the greatest Polish chronicler of the Middle Ages, described this murder in detail – the assault on the sleeping king, overpowering him only after a lengthy fight, then finishing him off with dagger blows.

This whole affair must have puzzled some contemporary observers. Przemysł had relied on his alliance with Brandenburg to offset the power of his principal rival, the king of Bohemia. He had reason to think that this would be the basis of a powerful alliance against his many enemies. However, Polish nobles who feared him had welcomed the Bohemian king, assuming that a distant foreign monarch would be unable to dominate them. Thus was Poland torn asunder by rivalries and ambitions that modern readers find confusing and boring.

This, however, was only the latest act of aggression by a dynasty that intended to conquer all the lands to the north and east, especially the strategic city of Danzig. Brandenburg itself had little to offer. Its sandy soil and numerous streams were not conducive to farming, and merchants had little interest in settling there. (Berlin was probably not named for a 'bear', as is suggested at times, but from a Slavic word meaning swamp.) Danzig was altogether another matter – its prominence in the young Hanseatic League was based on its merchants selling Polish and Prussian grain to German merchants and western products to Poles and Prussians, and to its connections to Scandinavia, Livonia, and even Rus'. It had perhaps 2,000–3,000 inhabitants of various ethnicities – Kashubians (a Slavic group living at the mouth of the Vistula, closely related to the Poles), then Pomerellians, and finally Germans.

The Bohemian Interlude

Długosz found much to criticise about King Ladislas – he imposed crushing taxes, ravished noble maidens, and failed to control his violent temper. The king, mocked as 'elbow-high' (*Łokietek*), had a long history of failures, the most recent, in 1300, causing him to flee into exile. Ladislas had gone to Hungary, then torn by civil war, afterwards heading to Rome, where Pope Boniface had promised him help. When he returned to Hungary, nobles opposed to Bohemian rule aided him in returning to Poland. In 1306, after a long campaign that gathered strength after the death of the Czech king, he captured Cracow.

He was a lucky ruler in that his brothers had died young and his chief rival, Wenceslaus III of Bohemia (1289–1306), had encountered difficulties in all three of the realms he had claim to – Bohemia, Hungary and Poland. But uncertainty and unrest were nothing new – Wenceslaus's father, Wenceslaus II (1271–1305), had assembled his own empire only after the unexpected deaths of the kings of Poland and Hungary.

The Bohemian kings' ability to finance foreign adventures rested greatly on the revenues of the silver mines at Kutná Hora in central Bohemia. German miners – some of those energetic immigrants who were beginning to dominate the Czech cities – were producing coins in such quantity that generations of Czech monarchs would have the resources to fund their domestic projects and foreign wars.

Wenceslaus II had made the Prague *Groschen* into the principal currency of regional trade. By announcing plans for a university in Prague (a project that his successor, Charles IV, achieved in 1348), he was laying the intellectual foundation for an empire that would reach from the Baltic to the Adriatic. However, tuberculosis first slowed him down, then killed him.

There was an immediate crisis. Wenceslaus III, though only sixteen, succeeded in crowning himself king of Bohemia, but he failed to do the same in Poland and Hungary. Wenceslaus was leading his army towards Cracow in August 1306, when he decided to spend a night in the house of the dean of the Olomouc (Olmütz, Ołomuniec) cathedral. There he was stabbed to death. No assassin was ever identified, but there were suspects aplenty and one was slaughtered before he could be interrogated. As the Bohemian foreign policy fell apart, the Polish nobles and clergy recognised Przemysł as their legitimate king.

Przemysł immediately moved against his rivals, starting with the most prominent duke in Silesia and then moving to solidify his control of Pomerania. This war, however, created an opportunity for the Lithuanians to attack through Masovia. Penetrating as far as Kalisz (Kalisch) in Great Poland, they drove home thousands of captives. No one dared challenge them because, as Długosz phrased it, everyone was terrified by the very name Lithuanian.

This chain of events was so unpredictable, yet so characteristic of Polish history over the centuries, that Norman Davies chose the provocative title *God's Playground* for his history of Poland to suggest that only divine whims could explain much of what happened.

The Pomerellian Crisis of 1308–11

As mentioned earlier, Mestwin II had left his lands to the Polish crown in his will, and a Polish governor had been installed in Danzig. Mestwin's father, Swietopelk (*c.* 1195–1266), had, like the neighbouring dukes of Pomerania, taken advantage of Polish weakness to make himself independent in all but name. Until then, it had not been clear who would dominate the long Baltic coastline that the Poles called Pomorze – the Danes, the margraves in Brandenburg, the dukes in Great Poland or those in Kujavia – but now it was clear that the mouth of the Vistula River, a marshy area inhabited by Kasubians, belonged to Swietopelk.

He had made himself master of the lands west of the Vistula, together with the multi-ethnic town at Danzig, but he was not secure in holding these or various territories in Pomerania until 1227, when he ambushed and murdered the king of Poland as he travelled to attend a regional meeting of lords. This so appalled the duke of Masovia that when Prussian attacks became intolerable, he did not ask Swietopelk to lead the Christian forces but invited the Teutonic Knights to protect Culm and northern Poland.

Swietopelk might nevertheless have become master of Prussia, if in the years that followed the Teutonic Knights had not moved down the Vistula, cutting him off from the lands he had hoped to conquer. Changing tactics, he reached out to the Prussians, promising to allow them more self-government than his competitors. This effort failed because the pagans understood that Christianity would bring unwelcome changes no matter who introduced it; moreover, they had no reason to trust him.

The collapse of the Polish state under Mongol attack in 1241 and the ensuing civil wars provided Swietopelk with new opportunities to become a regional strongman, but his wars with the Teutonic Knights ended in defeat.

Mestwin never forgave the Teutonic Order for frustrating his family's ambition. But he also hated the margraves of Brandenburg who had promised to help him win lands in Pomerania if he became their vassal. They failed to deliver on their pledge, then refused to withdraw their garrisons when the war ended. Only by calling on Ladislas had he been able to preserve his independence. It was logical, therefore, that he named Ladislas his heir.

The margraves of Brandenburg-Stendal, sensing that this would upset the regional balance of power, promptly invaded Pomerellia. Their very title, margrave, was shared only with the dynasty ruling eastern Austria; it indicated a frontier ruler who was expected to expand the boundaries of the Holy Roman Empire eastward. Margrave Waldemar, later known as Waldemar the Great (1280–1319), was determined to live up to this expectation. When the powerful Swienca (Święca) family called upon him to protect them, he leapt at the chance, joined at first by his uncle, Otto IV (1239–1308/9), one of the most colourful figures in a colourful age – how many rulers were famed for their chivalry, their ability to play chess, and for walking around for a year with an arrow in their head?

Otto had been the late duke's feudal overlord since 1269, and, as Waldemar and Otto saw it, only they had any right to dispose of the land when Mestwin died without direct heirs, leaving two neighbours with competing valid claims to inherit his lands – Ladislas the Short (his designated heir) and themselves (his feudal overlords).

Długosz gave many pages to this Pomerellian crisis – it was central to his general theme that Poland had been robbed of its best provinces by Germans. He was thinking primarily of Silesia, the home of the Piast dynasty that ruled Poland through the fourteenth century, but Prussia and Pomerellia were never far from his active mind – Długosz was a canon in the Cracow cathedral, a scholar, and a diplomat, but foremost he was a Polish patriot through and through.

The Pomerellian inheritance was, even for contemporaries, a complicated business. Przemysł had been overlord until his murder in 1296 after which Wenceslaus II had appointed the powerful family of the Swiencas as governors. In 1307, after Ladislas was generally acknowledged to be king, he moved to reverse that decision. The Swencas, angry that the king's officials had refused to repay their expenses for defending the land, called on the margraves of Brandenburg for protection.

Ladislas succeeded in imprisoning the head of the Swienca clan but released him after his brothers agreed to become hostages in his place. Soon afterwards, the brothers escaped, the clan rebelled, and the margraves captured Danzig. Because Ladislas was fully occupied in his eastern lands, he asked his advisors what to do. One suggested that he ask the Prussian master, Heinrich of Plötzke, to drive out the invaders and restore order. This was awkward. Ladislas's past behaviour was well known to the Teutonic Knights, who responded with due caution, obtaining a promise to reimburse all their expenses – a promise sealed with a formal treaty. This led to, in Długosz's words, the 'cunning and perverse' Heinrich of Plötzke incorporating Pomerellia into the lands of his military order.

Meanwhile, as Lithuanians once more crossed Masovia into Great Poland, the weak response of the king was obvious to everyone. Therefore, Ladislas had to act decisively when Pomerellia presented yet another challenge to his prestige.

Heinrich of Plötzke

Ladislas may not have been powerful, but he was still dangerous. Moreover, he was angry. Nobody appreciated this more than Heinrich of Plötzke. The son of a ministerial vassal of the Anhalt duke who at that time possessed Brandenburg, born about 1264, he entered the military order when he was about twenty-two years old. Following an initial posting to Thuringia, about 1300 he was transferred to Prussia, and in 1306 was elected master.

Heinrich was initially reluctant to become involved in the Pomerellian crisis. He knew how important margraves were in German politics, and how many crusaders crossed Brandenburg to come to Prussia. Going to war with a secular state, especially a traditional ally, was sure to be controversial. However, when Ladislas promised to pay the Teutonic Knights for their support and to give them a fort near Danzig, those scruples fell away. Besides, who knew how far east the Brandenburgers planned to go? They were already on the Vistula.

The decisive voice now may have been that of Siegfried of Feuchtwangen, who sent a few hundred horsemen under Günther of Schwarzburg to join the Polish forces in driving the Brandenburgers out of Pomerellia. Information is too meagre to determine what the internal politics of the military order were, but it seems that Siegfried was willing to allow Heinrich free rein in local affairs – which he obviously understood better than the grandmaster – just as he allowed his representative in Venice, Karl of Trier, to manage affairs in the Holy Roman Empire. Feuchtwangen seems to have avoided difficulties with the knights of his order by concentrating on uncontroversial activities such as tearing down the old castle at Zantir and replacing it with a new one that would come to symbolize the power and pride of his order – Marienburg.

His only other act that the chronicler Jeroschin thought worth mentioning was his requiring brothers to recite the prayer '*Salve Regina*', and for lay brethren to say the 'Hail Mary'. Strikingly, when

Feuchtwangen died in 1311, he was not buried in Marienburg, but in the cathedral of the bishop of Culm in Löbau. His successor, Karl of Trier, was chosen by the electors in Marienburg, but it was clear that the losing candidate, Heinrich of Plötzke, held the real power in Prussia – all the centralising reforms proposed by Karl of Trier were rejected.

But that was later, after the war in Pomerellia was over. In the autumn of 1308 Ladislas declined to honour his governor's agreement – or so the Prussian master claimed, while Długosz blamed the 'treacherous' Prussian master, Heinrich of Plötzke. The caused the intervention to take a direction perhaps nobody had anticipated – there were threats of war. We do not know what was said, but neither side was known for soft words and offers of concessions. The Teutonic Knights had the advantage of being nearest the contested land, while Ladislas had to tend to problems in the south of his kingdom. Still, the king was a survivor – several times in the past it had appeared that he would lose both his lands and his life, but he had always prevailed. Ruthless and vindictive, now that he had finally reunited Poland, he was also ambitious. Would he move against Prussia?

To forestall this Heinrich went further than Ladislas anticipated: after expelling the last Brandenburg forces, in November 1308 he drove out the Polish garrison of Danzig as well. What may have begun with complaints about sharing the crowded castle and not being paid ended with the Teutonic Knights killing ('slaughtering' was the term used in the many lawsuits that resulted) knights, citizens, and even women and children. The number 10,000 was mentioned by the pope in his denunciation, a figure which meant 'an awful lot' and was impossible in a town that had at best a third of that number; most likely sixteen men from the garrison living in the city were killed – as Paul Knoll notes in his careful analysis of the sources, the grandmaster called them robbers. The number of citizens slain varies – eyewitnesses testifying in papal investigations said 'many'. Modern Polish historians say 60–100, but nobody really knows. What is uncontested is that much of the city went up in flames. One might expect this from wood buildings with thatched roofs or wooden shingles.

This was a moment that was literally burned into the collective memory of the inhabitants. After the city was rebuilt, it had a German-speaking majority. Many were probably immigrants from other Hanseatic cities.

Master Heinrich now had a problem. A ruined city was not worth much, and he had lost men and horses. He was ready to turn the city over to the king, once he was reimbursed for his expenses, but Ladislas did not see much value in a ruined city, either. By refusing to pay an exorbitant fee – 100,000 marks, which was indeed a great sum – for such a poorly conducted rescue operation, Ladislas set in motion events that were to affect the history of his country and Prussia as well for centuries to come. Hoping that he would persuade or overawe Heinrich in a personal meeting, he arranged for a conference at Breść in Kujavia.

At the conference Ladislas accused the master of lacking gratitude for Polish help in the past and of having killed or exiled from Pomerellia all royalist supporters. According to Długosz, Heinrich rejected arbitration, then offered to buy the territory and pay damages and expenses, on the condition that the king would formally sign a bill of sale. In addition, he would endow a monastery for any religious order that the king named, with income to support forty monks. Then he would return some disputed border territories and provide forty warriors for the king's use at the Order's expense. Ladislas rejected the proposals and stomped out in anger. Długosz thoroughly sympathised with the king – his descriptions of the crimes and cruelty of the Teutonic Knights would never be forgotten by any Polish patriot.

What to do? Heinrich apparently believed that if he backed down now, he would only be given another ultimatum, then another. Therefore, he decided to keep Pomerellia in lieu of payment, asserting that the duchy had never been a territory of the Polish crown, but was subject to Brandenburg alone, and the margraves were willing to acknowledge the Teutonic Order as the legitimate ruler of the land.

By signing the Treaty of Soldin with Margrave Waldemar in 1309, Heinrich acquired the Brandenburg claims to most of Pomerellia. (The lands associated with the Swienca dynasty were retained by Brandenburg.) Adding the 85,000 people of Pomerellia to Prussia's 200,000 inhabitants would considerably strengthen the military order; and the king knew it.

The weakness of Heinrich's argument lay in his having intervened in Pomerellia on behalf of Ladislas, not the margraves of Brandenburg. Yet now he chose to believe that paying Waldemar 10,000 silver marks would satisfy everyone who understood German feudal law. More importantly, Heinrich had possession of the duchy and could defend it against the worst Ladislas could do. Surely at some future date they could work out some mutually acceptable arrangement.

Unfortunately for Heinrich's plans, technical legal forms have less ultimate value than public sentiment. The Polish king, the Polish nobles, and eventually the Polish people were persuaded that

Pomerellia had been stolen. When Ladislas asserted that any Slavic-speaking state along the shore of the Baltic Sea that paid Peter's Pence (a tax for the pope) was a part of his kingdom, it did not take long for him to include Culm in his claims as well. This exaggeration ultimately complicated negotiations, since Culm was the oldest land held by the Order, and the one to which the Teutonic Knights had the most secure title (but which some Polish historians have contended was falsified). However, many of the peasants there spoke Polish. A chronicler noted that in 1303 or thereabouts Lithuanian raiders striking Löbau (the seat of the bishop of Culm) sent one of their number who spoke Polish to inquire about the defences of the country – presumably, some of the raiders would have spoken Prussian, but the peasants would not have understood them.

When Grandmaster Feuchtwangen arrived on the scene in 1309, he chose to ignore the Polish protests, believing perhaps that it was more dangerous to give *West Prussia* (as we will henceforth call Pomerellia) to a known enemy than to risk his wrath by keeping it; moreover, he wanted a secure land route between the Holy Roman Empire and Prussia, and he hoped to summon West Prussian knights to serve in the crusade. If his decision was a mistake, it did not become obvious quickly. The only adverse consequence, as Heinrich must have seen it, was that he was demoted to grand commander; that lasted until 1312, when he became marshal. His successor as grand commander was Werner of Orseln (c. 1280–1330), the former commander of Ragnit. More important in many eyes was Friedrich of Wildenberg (Fryderyk, d. 1330), who became Prussian master in 1317, assuming the duties of Grandmaster Karl of Trier when he was in the Holy Roman Empire or at Avignon. Friedrich had been commander of Ragnit, hospitaller, and later grand commander.

The question of West Prussia was discussed in both the imperial and papal courts, but it was little more than a temporary embarrassment to the grandmasters who were summoned to give testimony. The Teutonic Knights had experience in both courts, and among the knights were a few from important families who knew how to make their order's voice heard. When rank did not count, money did. The emperor-elect was Heinrich VII of Luxemburg (1275–1313), who was principally interested in recovering Italy for the Holy Roman Empire. After spending most of his reign there, Heinrich VII died of malaria shortly after having himself crowned in a Rome seething with feuding factions and enemies. His second interest lay in securing the vacant throne of Bohemia for his fourteen-year-old son, John (Johann, 1296–1346), by marrying him to the equally young sister of the late Wenceslaus III, then leading an army into Bohemia to capture Prague. These were all extremely expensive projects, so the Order's contributions were very welcome; moreover, the Order possessed estates in Bohemia and Moravia, a fact that helped to offset John's unpopularity with the Czech nobility.

The Teutonic Order was happy to support imperial plans because Bohemia had been a traditional source of crusaders to Prussia, because strong Holy Roman emperors had been dependable friends of the crusading movement, and because, only a few years before, friendly Bohemian monarchs had been kings of Poland. In this light, the Order's occupation of West Prussia was a patriotic act, because the Luxemburg hopes for Bohemia were opposed by King Ladislas, who wanted to recover Silesian lands that had become Bohemian possessions (as some are even today). Not unexpectedly, when Ladislas appealed to the pope for justice, he sought more than the return of Danzig and West Prussia. He wanted to ruin the Teutonic Knights.

Relations with the Papacy

In 1309 the papal court was in Avignon, which at that time was within the Holy Roman Empire, on the east bank of the Rhône River. It was not yet thoroughly corrupt and cynical, but the signs of future difficulties were already present. Until recently the popes had been able to balance France against Naples and Germany; now, however, Clement V, was in exile from Italy and increasingly under the influence of the ambitious French king, Philip IV, whose relatives already ruled in Naples and Hungary. Germans were unable to offer the pope much support or even protect German territories from French inroads, but they did elect Heinrich VII as German king and emperor-elect rather than the French king's brother.

Pope Clement V was closely following the trial of the Templar Order, whose members had been arrested *en masse* by the king of France. The military orders had been in widespread disrepute before the fall of Acre, but now their shameful quarrels were widely blamed for contributing to the loss of the Holy Land. The Templars, in addition, were hated for their wealth and arrogance.

The situation, in short, was favourable to enemies of the Teutonic Knights. If Ladislas could persuade the pope and his cardinals that their misdeeds were worse than those of the Templars, he might be able to duplicate the French feat of confiscating their lands and wealth. He found a willing ally in the archbishop of Riga, who spread claims that the Teutonic Knights had slaughtered 10,000 citizens of Danzig.

A papal legate, Francis of Moliano, investigated the accusations and, like many talented men of low birth, was repelled by the aristocratic dismissal of his inquiry. In 1312 he forwarded to the pope a detailed report on his interviews with local witnesses. Only a few mentioned the massacre, and almost none were eyewitnesses. Nevertheless, it was a momentary sensation. Only when calmer minds recognised that the process was biased, were his recommendations reconsidered, then ignored. As a result, those who thought that their complaints were legitimate nursed them carefully for future use.

Polish churchmen, for their part, imposed an interdict on the lands of the Teutonic Knights, and especially on Pomerellia, because the Order had ceased to deliver tithes to Polish churchmen in kind (grain, for the most part), but sent them hard cash. The Polish churchmen were furious, believing that they would be better off selling the produce themselves. The Teutonic Knights, knowing the cost of delivering the grain across the border, then seeing it brought back to sell in cities like Danzig, probably thought that they were being frugal as well as wanting to profit from price fluctuations.

The Teutonic Knights may have, as Długosz wrote, laughed at the Polish churchmen, because they knew that the papal court did not want to see a second military order destroyed. Pope Clement V was angry at the crusaders' actions, but he was also aware that only a few years before this a French king had sent men to kidnap Boniface VIII. No one had to point out to him the implications of that for his own safety and the independence of the Church: with Rome too turbulent for him to live there and the Knights Templar no longer available to serve him, he had reasons to feel unsafe. Consequently, even if the charges were true – which he may have doubted – the pope refused to take actions that would have made it difficult to revive the crusading movement.

Nor were the cardinals and papal officials eager to have an important military order ruined. To make certain that doubtful loyalties at the curia did not change, however, the procurator-general (the Order's supervisor of lay lawyers) had money for whoever seemed in need of help. Money made friends. This was a low period for the papacy, but it was not yet the abyss it would become. In the years to come the procurator-general would profit from the decline in moral standards to buy protection for his employer, the Teutonic Order.

On the other hand, because the kingdom of Poland paid Peter's Pence, the king generally received a respectful hearing for each of his complaints.

The Prussian Church

The grandmaster had no troubles with Prussian churchmen. His relationship with convents and friaries of other orders was also excellent, thanks partly to his displaying real sympathy with their needs and wishes, and partly to policies which prevented anyone challenging his authority. That was less true in Livonia, where the archbishops believed that they should govern the entire land. They had been frustrated, however, by a papal legate, William of Modena (Gullielmus, 1184–1251), who had divided the church lands in 1225/6 to guarantee that the Order of Swordbrothers remained dominant; and that arrangement continued after the Teutonic Knights absorbed the Swordbrothers. Although the archbishops of Riga later often challenged the Livonian master, the minor bishops rarely supported him.

Later, in 1236, William of Modena did the same in Prussia. The bishops in Pomesania, Culm, and Sambia were poorer than the bishop of Ermland (Warmia), who was consequently the leader in art, architecture, education, and in the settlement of peasants on vacant lands. The three smaller dioceses were essentially convents of Order priests who functioned as canons; the supervision of diocesan property, normally a major function of canons, was performed by the Order's advocates. While the relationship of the grandmaster with these cathedral chapters was close, Ermland was an exception – the selection of each new bishop alternated between the canons and the pope, and the canons came from varied religious backgrounds; thus, they felt free to behave much like their colleagues in the Holy Roman Empire.

The bishops sent priests to preach to the native converts through translators. Later they trained a handful of native boys as priests, and although they worried about their secretly preaching pagan beliefs, they made some native-born priests into canons in their cathedral chapters, and in 1344 one became bishop of Sambia. In any case, the bishops were unable to pay much attention to their cathedral schools, because they lacked sufficient income from tithes and gifts to staff their chapters properly or even support priests in all the parishes. Until they had their financial problems under control, they had to concentrate more on attracting immigrants to their dioceses than on training priests; German and Polish farmers and artisans didn't need to be taught the rudiments of Christianity.

There were various other religious orders in Prussia, most notably the Dominicans and the Franciscans; this undoubtedly helped in preaching the crusade, for those orders were both very influential in Germany, especially in the cities where the commercial classes gave alms for support of the armed mission and even became crusaders themselves. The Cistercians, once the leading order on the frontier, were essentially confined to a small holding around Oliva because they still nursed an ancient claim to govern all Prussia.

Recruiting Crusaders

The overriding concern of the moment was for more warriors. The number of knights in the Teutonic Order has never been precisely calculated – accurate data just isn't there – but it was never very large. There were probably 800–1,000 in Prussia and perhaps only 500 in Livonia, including those past the age of military usefulness. To these could be added the secular knights and militia of German and Polish origin and the native *Witingen* and militia.

Half-brothers were far more numerous than knights. Since these men traditionally followed a knight's flag, each resulting unit was called a banner. Such units could make up a wedge formation (*Keil*) in battle, with the leading edge five horses wide, the second line seven, then nine, then eleven and so forth until an almost unstoppable mass was created. Sometimes the half-brothers were equipped with heavy armour and rode a trained warhorse, but lighter equipment was more appropriate for scouting duties and raiding. The half-brothers were of common birth and usually Germans though, unlike the knights, they might have been born in Prussia or Livonia, and they served for fixed terms. Advancement into the ranks of the knights was extremely rare, but they were represented in the assemblies and elections. They ate and slept in their own barracks but observed the same daily religious services as the knights and priests.

Although these numbers were adequate for manning the castles along the frontier and for coping with raiders, they were insufficient for great offensives. To keep the knights and sergeants in training and to harass the pagans as much as possible, the Teutonic Order sent them across the border wilderness accompanied by small bodies of native militia, to burn and loot. Such raids, though destructive of lives and property, were not considered particularly unusual, because raiding was the principal means of conducting medieval warfare everywhere. Raids served both sides as a means of training, of weakening the enemy, and of winning a great reputation.

It is difficult to establish exact figures before 1410, after which 'crusaders' were often actually mercenaries, but Werner Paravicini's careful studies show that volunteers from the Lower Rhine in 1304 were among the first to come to Prussia after a pause of almost two decades. The numbers grew swiftly.

At first religious motivation was very important, as was to be expected in a time when spiritual fervour was strong. However, zeal alone was insufficient. New incentives were necessary, ones that could persuade knights and burghers to overlook the failure of the crusades in the Holy Land, then travel to a frontier region, to fight in sacred woods inhabited by devils and magicians. Moreover, many of the military expeditions were in the dead of winter, in a desolate region known for its inclement weather and dearth of likely booty, with the unseen enemy screaming wildly each night outside the closely guarded camps. Recruiting volunteers required preachers of great ability and proper training – the type of people who are never available in great numbers.

Those who took up this task were of diverse origin. Often, they were Dominicans, traditional preachers of the crusades and rivals of the Franciscans (who tended to reject the concept of holy war), but the knights or priests of the Teutonic Order stationed in the Holy Roman Empire were also important, because they could use their offices to spread the word among subjects, friends and relatives. Some recruiters were ordinary priests who read translated letters from popes and bishops urging loyal Christians to hasten to the aid of oppressed brethren in the east, but sometimes they were visiting bishops from Livonia and Prussia, asking for help to conquer or recover their sees from the pagans. All had the same message. They emphasised the duty to protect Christians, to crush heathenism, and to earn the favour of God and His saints; they told of atrocities, such as butchering children, raping virgins, spitting on altars, and burning captured crusaders on iron grills or tied to their warhorses on elevated pyres.

Perhaps even more important were stories told by former crusaders: how one would find in Prussia a combination of piety, feasting, hunting and adventure, all in the company of famous men. A crusade to Samogitia, such as was described in 1377 by the Austrian poet, Peter Suchenwirt (1320–95), was an exciting journey that no red-blooded knight or blue-blooded noble would ever forget. Stories of warfare against proud and dangerous pagans inspired listeners to take the Cross.

From 1307 on, such an expedition was called a *Reise* (journey), a medieval euphemism for a military venture. This avoidance of the technical term, crusade, has led to some misunderstandings and perhaps to undervaluing their significance. Until recently most scholars argued that only military expeditions intended to liberate Jerusalem could be called crusades, but now most agree with Jonathan Riley-Smith, that the criteria for a crusade include papal authorisation, vows taken by participants, guarantees of protection of family and property while on crusade, and the promise of an indulgence equal to those enjoyed by those who took the Cross for the Holy Land. The wars of the Teutonic Knights qualify.

The Order's wars were noteworthy for discipline and tactics that had been learned in the Holy Land and brought to a high degree of perfection through continual training and practice. Young knights on crusade could learn much by observation and participation, then take the lessons home for their own use. They could observe the infantry and knights singing as they advanced against the foe, see how to direct an army with flag signals and horn calls, and, not least, understand how important it was to reward good counsel and valour. The Order celebrated its deeds in chronicles written in both Latin and German, the latter certainly for the edification and encouragement of the knights, squires and priests, and perhaps for the entertainment of guests. For time out of mind historians believed that these chronicles were read aloud at mealtimes, but more recently Alan Murray, in *Crusade and Conversion*, has argued that rather than inspiring knights with past deeds of valour, they were more useful in recruiting volunteers. Peter of Dusburg's *Chronicon terrae Prussiae* was written in Latin, which would have been suitable for influencing churchmen. However, when translated into German, it would have been effective for recruiting crusaders and for persuading members of the Order in Germany to use their resources in Prussia rather than wait until they could return to Acre and Jerusalem.

These exciting accounts not only restated traditional arguments for holy war but added to them popular secular ideals. With little question, the Teutonic Knights had developed new ways of thinking about their vocation.

The Order's officers demanded strictest discipline while on campaign, both from their own men and from 'guests' (crusaders). By aligning the crusaders under the banners of St George or St Mary, they lessened their identification with their own lands and heightened the feeling that they were all part of one large Christian army. This made the crusade unlike the earlier hard-fought conquest of Prussia, unlike the almost unknown defensive war in cold and lonely Livonia, and it had little of the religious content or exotic experiences of the crusades to the Holy Land. Nor was it a war that benefited any family or dynasty, as did the crusades in Spain and Greece and Cyprus. It was an international war, one supported by both emperor and pope, joined by men of diverse nations who perhaps had fought one another for generations past and who would fight again for generations to come; but for a winter or a summer those burghers, knights and nobles would strive together to serve Christianity against its enemies. At least that was the reason they gave for coming on crusade.

Lithuanians had a different view of these actions, but they had their own religious conceptions, some of which were perhaps even stranger to us than are those of the crusaders.

The Samogitians

The Samogitians were among the last true pagans in Europe, their religion echoing the general concepts of the Celtic, Germanic and Scandinavian peoples in past centuries. Tacitus' account of Germanic paganism would have been recognised by most Samogitians, even though it did not fit their practices exactly. Their beliefs had certainly undergone modification through contacts with Vikings, Byzantine missionaries, Rus'ian churchmen, and untold thousands of Orthodox Christian and Roman Christian prisoners of war who were part of Lithuanian society as slaves, wives and concubines, but we can only guess at what these were. There is no fully satisfactory description of the pagan practices, although some aspects of the worship are well known. Christian onlookers were fascinated by the sacrifice of animals (and the rare human being), but they had no interest in the philosophy. It was a woodland religion that thrived in the mists of dense forests, but weakened when brought onto ploughed fields, then died in cities. Military and economic changes were making this presumed idyllic forest paradise a fond memory.

Paganism was tolerant in comparison to Roman Catholic and Russian Orthodox Christianity, each of which claimed to have a monopoly on truth. It had served well the tribes that lived in relatively remote forests, then had partially given way after Mindaugas (c. 1203–63) converted to Roman Christianity about 1251. Three years later, with the assistance of the master of the Livonian Order, he was crowned king of Lithuania, ending any justification for further crusades against his people. Although some areas, such as Samogitia, refused to recognise his authority and remained militantly pagan (while others remained under Tatar influence), it seemed that Mindaugas had brought most of his people into the Roman Christian world. However, opposition among the warriors became so strong that he returned to paganism in 1261, then two years later was assassinated. Unity was restored only in

1295 by Vytenis, who made himself supreme over the surviving regional dukes. We know relatively little about him or his pagan beliefs other than that he attributed his successful wars to the favour of the gods and that he was very practical in allowing Roman and Orthodox Christians to practise their religion if they did not attempt to make conversions among his people.

The Samogitians were less tolerant. Surrounded by enemies, they considered the Lithuanian grand duke almost as dangerous to their freedom as the Christians, and they viewed his tolerance as a ploy to extend his power over other peoples. They emphasised the military aspects of their ancient religion, just as the Prussians had done in the previous century: shamans used casting bones to predict the outcome of campaigns; prisoners were sacrificed to obtain omens, particularly the spurting of the blood; the appearance of birds could turn an army in its tracks; and rich booty was burned to repay the gods for their aid. Christian priests and monks were more than mere competitors: conversion to Christianity would have taken away many aspects of life they loved. Christianity meant the end of honourable war, stolen brides and horses, a shortage of slaves for work and sale, a halt to the ceremonial drinking bouts, and the substitution of a dull heaven for the eternal life of a warrior in their equivalent of Valhalla. Moreover, it meant changing all the holidays and ceremonies that had given reason to their lives for centuries and marked the events of birth, manhood, marriage, harvest, victory and death. Consequently, the *Witingen* of Samogitia dealt with the representatives of Christianity ruthlessly: they delighted in burning churches and torturing priests. Among the exceptions was respect for military prowess, especially that of Teutonic Knights, giving them a warrior's death by fire or torture, or by individual combat against a picked champion, or they offered them for ransom or in exchange for prisoners. On the other hand, pagan warriors believed that Christian peasants hardly counted as human beings: they were but two-footed cattle, suitable for rape, sale and work. They valued priests even less, being useless for war, sex or labour; and they knew that some Teutonic Knights privately shared their attitude.

Life was simple in the forest clearings. The wooden houses were small, as befitted an economy based on cattle and the hunt; the agricultural methods often produced crops so meagre that crusaders did not consider them worth burning. Nevertheless, not even the common folk lacked sustenance. Lithuanians were big, strong people, accustomed to military victories; they celebrated festivals lustily and bathed in saunas. When beset by bad weather, illness or personal crisis, they took offerings to the shrines of their gods in the forests. Wilhelm Mannhardt has collected every extant reference to these practices in their original language in *Letto-Preußische Götterlehre*, and Stephen C. Rowell has summarised them effectively in *Lithuania Ascending*.

Simple in its practices and without a complicated priesthood, Baltic paganism was nevertheless loaded with many ancient traditions and superstitions whose origins are lost. Only by comparing Lithuanian beliefs with those nearby and related pagans (such as Estonians and Old Prussians) and studying statements by Christians (who misunderstood or misrepresented their theology) can we grasp its essential features. First and foremost, it was a fertility religion (Christian missionaries to Old Prussia were expelled because the offended gods had withheld good harvests so long as the new religion was tolerated). It was a forest religion, with forest gods and sylvan groves. Over extensive stretches of Lithuania oaks formed a canopy high above the shadowy fern-covered ground. Where giant trees had fallen, saplings and firs struggled towards the light. Wolves stalked wary prey; werewolves stalked men. The forests were thickest and least penetrated in Samogitia and the region just to the south, Sudovia (Yotvingia), and the gods were the strongest there.

Religious observances were based on folk rituals. The gods lived from sacrifices offered by believers at the many ceremonies of season and celebration, especially at births, marriages and deaths. They believed that the ghosts of unburied warriors haunted the night alongside the unhappy shades of criminals who were punished by being denied funeral rites. A proper funeral began with the cremation of the body, then burning items the deceased would need in the afterlife: weapons, tools, clothing, and, in the case of a prominent warrior, his steed.

There seem to have been a variety of religious practices. A snake cult was prominent in Samogitia, the sacred serpents being cared for and fed in a manner reminiscent of the ancient Mediterranean. Virgin priestesses may once have tended sacred fires. Shamans conducted ceremonies under ancient oaks, young people dancing round the trees hand in hand. The most prominent god was Perkunas, who made his presence known by hurling lightning bolts from the sky.

Merely cataloguing these beliefs was enough to make a Christian shudder, for almost everyone believed that pagans possessed magic powers. Not to believe so would be to doubt the statements of powerful churchmen and the traditions of popular Christianity. There were few Christians who did not believe that the great force of the Evil One stood behind paganism, each god and fairy doing devilish service, seeking the destruction of Christianity and the damnation of all mankind.

The warrior-friars of the Teutonic Order accepted this without explanation. In fact, they wanted no explanation. On matters of belief, they were not trained to investigate, and they were forbidden to instruct. Their duty was solely to strike anyone who would harm or hinder the priests responsible for converting the pagans. They sought out presumed pagan centres relentlessly, raiding even the most remote ones to destroy them with sword and fire. They forbade converts to cremate the dead, to carry flowers and fruit to the graves, or to practise polygamy. Customs they did not consider dangerous, such as the sweat baths, they adopted themselves.

The crusaders saw that many superficial aspects of pagan life were abominations but nevertheless easily understood. Naturally, the life of a warrior was war; a noble should rule over peasants and win booty and glory. That pagans drank to excess was no exception to the rule that a noble should live nobly, and that he should have access to many women was a law of nature. That the Teutonic Knights fasted, prayed and lived in chastity was, in a sense, testimony to the normalcy of the pagan attitudes – abstinence, especially virginity, gave power! The knights did not doubt for a moment that strange gods existed. The world was inexplicable, with aspects visible and invisible, powers great and small. If the heavens could be read by signs, if the zodiac predicted one's destiny, and if dreams foretold the future, why could not livers and birds and dice do the same? Saints appeared to individual knights in their dreams. Why could not pagan gods speak to their followers? The difference was that the Christian God had come to supplant these older ones and to bring order and justice into this chaotic world. Moreover, Christianity offered a true salvation in place of the hellfire into which the pagan warriors, confidently expecting to enter a glorious afterlife, would doubtlessly be cast.

It was not necessary for the Samogitians and other Lithuanians to change much, the Christians thought. Only to recognise the power of their God, to worship the Holy Trinity, honour Mary, pray to the saints, and cease attacking the lands of the Teutonic Order and its allies. Of course, they had to pay taxes and tithes like other Christian folk.

This, ultimately, was getting to the heart of the matter. The Samogitians detested taxes more than most rural people. It was not so much that they were poor (although they were), it was that paying tribute, taxes or tithes would acknowledge their inferior status. More than anything else, the Samogitians worshipped honour; and honour required absolute freedom. This was not unlike the exaggerated concept of nobility in the Germanic past: taxes meant subservience; subservience meant slavery. There was no middle ground. No Samogitian *Witingen* was ready to give up his freedom in this way. He would not lower himself to the status of his slaves, to herd cattle and work on a small plot of unproductive cropland surrounded by swamps and woods. He would rather fight to the death. Or, so he said. In practice, compromise was possible, at least temporarily.

One might surmise that the pagans understood as little about Christianity as Christians did about paganism. They were all superstitious in different ways, believed in magic and visions, and put their trust in prayers, rituals, and ceremonies. In this the Christians had the advantage of Judeo-Roman traditions that were wider and deeper than pagan beliefs which were handed down orally, and of the scholastic methods taught in the convents and the new universities.

The Samogitian frontier was quiet in 1309, but that would not last.

Chapter Two

The Teutonic Order

An Organisation Undergoing Change

This story is partly about how a military order's values were transformed from puritan to cavalier, from stoic to epicurean, from religious to chivalric. The historian working through the original sources sees this transformation occurring over the fourteenth century, first slowly, then with increasing speed. The anonymity cloaking the process of decision-making in the thirteenth century was successful because the monkish disdain of worldly fame was not confined to those clerics who conducted the correspondence and wrote the chronicles of the Teutonic Order. There was a consensus that all of the Order's knights should aspire to be ideal warrior-friars who lived in poverty and fought against odds so hopeless that only the Virgin Mary could give them victories over both their local pagan enemies and the temptations of Satan.

The message these records convey as late as 1310 is that the Teutonic Knights still identified with the struggles against loneliness and isolation, poverty and disease, and fierce enemies in the cold forests and swamps of the north. Their churches and castles reflected an ethos of self-denial and self-sacrifice, of fights to the death and preparation for future conflicts. After 1310 this was to change. Poverty was giving way to a modest prosperity, thanks to having freed the interior provinces of Prussia from fear of attack and to wise domestic policies. The austere combativeness of fanatic religiosity succumbed to chivalric pageantry as young recruits from the Holy Roman Empire rose through the ranks into positions of authority.

At the head of the Order was the grandmaster. Subject jointly to the pope and the Holy Roman emperor, whose predecessors had long ago established the military order, he was elected in a general chapter representing all classes of membership. First, they selected one elector, who then submitted a second name for confirmation; the two then recommended a third, and so forth until there were thirteen electors (one priest, eight knights, and four half-brothers). The electors retired into secret session to discuss the merits of the various candidates, emerging perhaps days later with a name (usually a member of the late grandmaster's council, mature in years, experienced in war, and conventionally pious).

That the office was elective had both advantages and disadvantages. In contrast to any secular state, the Teutonic Order never had a minor as ruler, never feared that its military commander would lack intelligence, bravery or experience, and never worried about connubial strife, mistresses or arranging marriages for children. On the other hand, the grandmaster could not win friends or disarm enemies by suggesting a marital alliance. His social life lacked any feminine influence or charm. His was a life of business, prayer, government and war.

From the time of Siegfried of Feuchtwangen (1303–11), the grandmaster was considered a sovereign prince. Though his authority was theoretically limited by his obligations to the pope and the emperor, he conducted war and diplomacy without consulting either one, and when the pope or emperor disapproved, he sometimes went ahead anyway. Outsiders viewed him as an absolute monarch. He possessed the symbols of office, an ancient ring and a seal bearing the figure of Mary with the Christ child that only he could impress upon his special black wax. He alone wore capes and habits of expensive imported cloth and bore as his insignia a lily-bedecked gold-bordered black cross with the golden single-headed imperial eagle in the centre. He was unique in having private sleeping quarters, with a private chaplain, and at meals he received four bowls of fish or meat, so that he could share his repast with those knights who were doing penance. These distinctions often persuaded him to think of himself as an autocrat.

In reality, his authority was limited. In Prussia he could do little without the consent of his council and the commanders. Livonia was distant and difficult to visit. The convents in the Holy Roman Empire were so widely scattered that regular personal inspections were not practical. Also, he had to be mindful of the wishes of neighbouring powers – he had to keep the routes to Germany open for trade and crusaders; although the routes through northern Poland were the shortest, it was essential to have access through Brandenburg and Pomerania available; and the sea lanes were open only in summer and only if the newly founded Hanseatic League was friendly.

Feuchtwangen selected the small castle at Marienburg as his seat, thus distancing himself from the Prussian master in Elbing. It lay on a tributary to the Vistula River and was not far from Danzig. Presumably he personally laid the foundations for the new castle that would eventually be one of the most spectacular in medieval Europe.

Difficulties with the Papacy

The Teutonic Knights always had important matters pending at the curia. In 1310 the most serious was the report of the papal legate, Francis of Moliano, who had come north to investigate charges that the knights of the Order in Livonia were preventing the conversion of pagans and Rus'ians, oppressing prelates and free cities, and depriving the natives of their liberty. The legate reported only the hostile allegations because the knights had boycotted every stage of the hearings, contending that the process was unfair and illegal. The legate, angry and frustrated by the knights' attitude, had issued a general excommunication, and delivered a damning report to the pope.

The Teutonic Knights were represented by two officials at the curia (the papal court). The first was a cardinal-protector (each religious order was supposed to be represented by a cardinal). The second, the procurator-general, was primarily responsible for hiring lawyers. He was also a *de facto* diplomatic representative to the pope. Some scholars say that the procurator-general cannot be considered a diplomat, because diplomats can be exchanged only between sovereign states, and the Teutonic Knights were subordinate to the popes; moreover, no European state had real diplomats as yet (the institution was only in its formative stages). Nevertheless, he performed important diplomatic functions.

The procurator-general's most important task was to speak to those individuals who influenced papal policy, asking who else could protect the lands of Prussia and Livonia against pagans. This rhetorical question was effective with worldly-wise clerics and knowledgeable nobles because King Ladislas and the archbishop of Riga could not argue plausibly that they could carry out the Order's responsibilities better. He could not ward off all danger, however, because the charges against the Order were well-founded and Pope Clement V was determined to punish anyone who ignored or defied his authority.

The conclave of cardinals had taken a year to elect Clement, because not only had Rome been in such turmoil that the cardinals were unable to meet there, but the Italian and French cardinals had been unable to agree upon anything. Eventually, someone proposed that they look for a distant outsider, and their eyes fell on the archbishop of Bordeaux. That was a mistake that the Italians would quickly regret. Clement chose to have his coronation in Lyon rather than Rome, then immediately named nine new French cardinals to cement his control of the Church.

In an effort to revive the crusades Clement called upon the Knights Templar and the Hospitallers to unite their orders – the Teutonic Knights were too unimportant to merit consideration – and when they refused, he made few efforts to restrain the king of France when he decided to rid himself of debts to Templars (who were close at hand), and not the Hospitallers, who were less important as bankers and, moreover, were actually fighting the Muslims. In 1307 Philip IV arrested the Templar grandmaster and many of the knights on implausible charges of heresy and treason, then tortured them until they said whatever their captors wanted them to say.

The pope protested, but after the captive grandmaster and his knights renounced their early confessions, he allowed the king to burn them at the stake as lapsed heretics, then confiscate their properties; soon other monarchs followed suit. This was a signal that no military order was safe.

In 1309, after his officials in Rome were frightened by street riots and intimidated by ambitious local families, Clement decided to settle in Avignon, a papal territory on the Rhône, but in the Holy Roman Empire and therefore not subject to the king of France. With his Italian incomes needed for armies it Italy, he had few resources; nevertheless, he became a nepotist without peer.

Pope Clement was a complicated man. At one time he was harsh and exacting, at another weak and conciliatory, at yet another friendly and accommodating. Not only did he represent a Church in exile, but his efforts were designed, first, to cope with immediate crises, then to reassert control over institutions and individuals that had been unresponsive to papal wishes. He was particularly interested in recovering authority over religious orders which had become practically autonomous. Obviously, military orders had to feel threatened.

The pope and his officers also wanted to exert influence on political decisions in the Holy Roman Empire. The Teutonic Knights being an important German institution, the curia wanted to make them into a more responsive and co-operative organisation. Unfortunately for his plans, Pope Clement became victim of a debilitating illness that made it difficult for him to conduct business personally, thus delaying important decisions or assigning the problem to relatively low levels of the bureaucracy. For those matters which required papal attention (such as the complaints about Danzig and Riga), only a few interviews could be scheduled each day. These enabled court officials to demand exorbitant bribes from petitioners who could not wait their turn (or who wanted their case postponed).

Even before the move to Avignon, access to the pope had been difficult, but after curial officers stripped the procurator-general of minor offices such as doorkeeper, and the pope confiscated his comfortable residences (Santa Maria in Domenica in Rome, and at Viterbo and Montefiascone), this made matters worse. The procurator-general followed the pope as he moved from one city to another, lived in rented lodgings, begged for interviews, and presented his Order's defence to anyone who would listen. As he lingered outside the doors of important men, he had watched the archbishop of Riga, the papal legates, and the Polish representatives sweep past him on their way into the papal chambers. Under the circumstances, it was not surprising that he was unable to prevent the pope from excommunicating the Order's principal officers. However, he knew excommunications came and went (some of the best people in society had been placed under the Church's ban). He was more concerned about Clement's confiscating Santa Maria in Domenica and presenting it to a favourite nephew. (Clement made five nephews into cardinals.) That was the way church politics operated. Confiscations, in contrast to bans, tended to be permanent.

The procurator-general was more successful in dealing with the excommunication by persuading churchmen that it might discourage potential crusaders who could protect converts on Christendom's frontiers, but it was less easy to explain why it was important to replace deceased bishops in Livonia and Prussia with clerics friendly to his employer. Moreover, barred from presenting his arguments directly, he had to hire more lawyers and distribute money more lavishly to important officials. He bribed the cardinal of Albano, Peter Colonna, Cardinal Raymund de Fargis (a papal nephew), and even Clement V (with 4,000 florins), to suspend the excommunication until further hearings could be conducted. Then he staved off vigorous prosecution of the matter until Pope Clement's death in 1314, after which the case had to be postponed until a new pontiff was elected. Since it was not until 1316 that Pope John XXII (1244–1334) took office, the matter was temporally set aside by the press of deferred business. The next pope, however, never forgot it.

The Grandmaster's Council

The grandmaster's residence lay roughly in the centre of the Order's possessions, easily reached by land or water. Marienburg was too great a complex for the knights and half-brothers to operate by themselves. Many workers – from cooks to bakers, from janitors to guards – were civilians, and the farmers and herders in the surrounding countryside provided food for perhaps 3,000 people working there. The necessary bureaucracy was supervised by the five officers who, together with commanders and respected knights who happened to be present, formed the grandmaster's council.

The grand commander (*Großkomtur*) was the most important officer. The title originally belonged to the head of the military order in the Holy Land, who governed there while the grandmaster was in the Holy Roman Empire, but the last holder of the title there had died when Acre fell in 1291. It was given to the former Prussian master, Heinrich of Plötzke, in 1311.

The marshal (*Marschall*) was based in Königsberg, close to the eastern frontier. He usually led the field armies, although when the grandmaster or grand commander were present, he deferred to them and took command of the cavalry. Most crusading armies assembled in Königsberg, where the participants visited the cathedral and the churches of St George and St Anthony; some crusaders painted their coat-of-arms in the cathedral, and some were buried there.

The commander of the hospital (*Spitler*) was theoretically responsible for medical care, though in practice his duties were much like those of the other high officers. The title reflected history – the Order had been founded as a hospital unit in 1190 and maintained many hospitals in the Holy Roman Empire. However, the knights themselves knew little about medicine and did no nursing personally: they were warrior-friars with a tradition dating from 1197, when the hospital of St Mary of the Germans in Jerusalem was founded anew as a military order. The hospital was supervised by a sub-commander, who had a separate budget, with special farms, stables, and other sources of income. The medical staff provided herbal medicines and primitive surgery (bleeding and fasting were standard cures), but most healers of wounds and broken bones resembled modern athletic trainers. Their cures came from the combination of clean bedding, good food, and care, to which were added religious consolations appropriate to the spiritual needs of the stricken. Fast days also contributed to physical well-being by keeping Order members slim.

The real duty of the commander of the hospital was to govern the convent at Elbing. However, he was much more than an ordinary commander – his territory was extensive and wealthy, and Elbing itself was, after Danzig, the second-largest city in Prussia; this meant that he bore a significant responsibility for any matter involving commerce, especially the relationship of the Order and the Hanseatic League.

There were a small number of nuns in the Order, most if not all associated with the hospitals maintained in the major convents. We know very little about them, but it is unlikely that they were specialists in herbal treatments, as some modern scholars have suggested.

The master of the robes (*Trapier*) held an honorary role, since the actual procurement and distribution of supplies was managed by the wardrobe officials at Marienburg. Often a half-brother, he was nominally the general manager of the Order's affairs and quartermaster-general. He commanded the convent at Christburg, just south-east of Marienburg, and was responsible for settling immigrants on vacant lands, a practical arrangement due to the fact that central Prussia was a sparsely populated region.

The treasurer (*Treßler*) resided at Marienburg, supervising the great iron vault in the High Castle where the bullion of the Order was stored. Only he, the grand commander, and the grandmaster knew exactly how many silver coins were there, but everyone believed that it was a fabulous sum. The uniform currency of the Prussian lands, the reliable taxes, and the abundant trade were bringing wealth into the coffers, wealth envied by neighbours. The treasurer's bookkeepers tallied payments and debts carefully.

These officers were honoured but not otherwise separated from the other knightly members of the Order. They wore simple clothes, ate at the common table, and slept in the dormitory. The grandmaster had other minor officers, too: a chaplain, a secretary, a chancellor and so forth. However, many of these were priest brothers, who had less influence than the knights on the formation of policy and military strategy.

Periodically the grandmaster called the commanders and advocates to general chapter meetings, usually at Elbing. Since all major subjects, including matters important only in the Empire, were discussed at such meetings, the grandmaster annually summoned representatives from near and far. (Lithuanians learned to stage invasions at these times.)

Local Governance

The government was complex, as was common elsewhere. Cities were largely self-governing, monasteries and convents also, and the bishops had varying degrees of independence. The native peoples were allowed significant self-governance but were closely supervised by advocates appointed by the grandmaster and priests appointed by the nearest bishop.

Most convents were castellanies, territorial divisions governed by each convent's officers: a commander, a marshal, a quartermaster, a cellar master, a kitchen master, a mill master, a building master, a treasurer, a tax collector and a chaplain. Some of these officers were half-brothers, especially at the lower level where most of the work was done. Occasionally the records show some nuns and visitors and even some married couples living in the convent, though those were less common than in the Holy Roman Empire. The grandmasters sent inspectors to supervise life in the convents and their business operations, but they had to be careful in exercising their powers of appointment and removal – the power of the commanders in the general chapter assemblies was formidable enough to cause grandmasters to resign.

Borderland territories, native tribal districts and some episcopal lands were governed by advocates (from the Latin *advocatus*). The German title was *Vogt*, which implies a supervisor or manager who oversaw the collection of taxes, the militia, the system of justice and anything where the lives of Germans and Prussians intersected. Only religious life was beyond his responsibilities. That duty fell to the priests – recruited from Germany and often lonely and unhappy with life among recent converts – who were supervised by canons from the cathedral chapters. The advocates were directly responsible to the grandmaster. While they frequently lived in castles, their duties were different from those of the commanders, for they often had to govern vast stretches of wilderness where orderly administration was impossible, and they did not have a convent of knights to assist them. They presided over the native courts, trained the militia for war, and apparently spent considerable time among the native Prussians. Therefore, it was essential for advocates to know the Prussian and Polish languages and customs.

Knowledge of foreign languages was not uncommon. Since the knights joined the Order only as adults, many grew up in regions where languages other than German were spoken; and the dialects in some parts of Germany were often incomprehensible to outsiders.

Convent Life

Each of the thirty-three convents was located in a strong castle. Originally these had been earth and log forts (motte and bailey castles), but in the fourteenth century these were rebuilt in brick. The knights' living quarters usually abutted an outer wall and consisted of two large rooms, one for dining, one for sleeping; examples are known of 14.6 × 7.3 metres up to 24.6 × 11.9 metres (48 × 24 ft. to 81 × 39 ft.). The dining room was filled with tables and benches; the dormitory was divided into individual cubicles open to general view, with the knights sleeping under blankets on sacks filled with straw. Nearby were a chapel, a chapter room, a hospital, a kitchen and many storage rooms. Across the courtyard were stables, workshops and facilities for the servants and half-brothers.

Generally, one knight was in charge of fishing – a major source of food for consumption and sale, obtained from local streams and ponds; another supervised the woods – for lumber, firewood, beekeeping and hunting; yet another oversaw the care and breeding of the horses, and another the hospital, and others the weapons and military supplies; one – presumably a brother with a burgher upbringing – dealt with merchants; a priest likely conducted the correspondence.

They were allowed to spend part of each day in the clerestory, conversing or playing games of chance and skill (so long as no one dallied over the game when called to prayer). Since knights were not supposed to have private possessions, theoretically, gambling would be impossible. However, because knights varied in size, each had to have his own clothing, armour, weapons and horses, as well as his own servants and half-brothers. The Order struggled manfully against the multiplication of objects possessed by knights and priests, legislating against gifts and bequests, but without permanent success.

The knights spent much time outdoors. In good weather they went afield to hunt, using a crossbow for small game and a spear for larger animals. In bad weather they practised less exciting drills, mastering military skills that made them superior to the militiamen, native *Witingen*, and even to experienced Lithuanians in full battle gear. They were professionals of the Church Militant, without the distractions of secular life, watched by strict disciplinarians who took pride in the military efficiency of their units. Their entire existence centred on preparation for holy war.

There were few amenities, but those few were significant. Prussia was a cold land, so castles had to be well heated. Some had central heating from a great furnace in the basement. In addition, there were the newly invented free-standing ovens and the traditional fireplaces.

Separate heating facilities supplied the baths with hot water – perhaps using the heat from the bakeries. The weekly bath was an opportunity for bleeding and sweating, both of which were believed to relieve the body of impurities and assure good health. Fresh water was always available from deep, stone-lined wells.

The toilet facilities were cold but hygienic. Each castle had a latrine, often in a freestanding tower outside the walls that could be reached by a covered walkway high above the ground. Presumably, most higher-status men preferred to use chamber pots which would be emptied by servants. Whatever was precipitated from the toilet fell into a collecting tank and shattered into liquid. The tank was not unlike a modern disposal pond; the bacteria prevented the accumulation of foul matter or unpleasant odours.

This does not mean that the garrison was healthy. Despite the constant exercise and frequent fasting, the diet had too few vegetables and fruit, too much meat, and too much alcohol. Constipation must have been a major problem. Being constantly on horseback and riding recklessly while hunting would have led to arthritis, broken bones, concussions and hernias. The medical care often emphasised bleeding, even in situations that today would call for blood transfusions. It was a different world, where more help was expected from saints than from medical treatment.

Each convent obtained locally almost everything the knights, half-brothers and servants required. Native peasants paid part of their taxes in grain and were required to carry it to the castles themselves. Half-brothers raised barley and produced malt on manors, using native labour as much as the treaties permitted (usually a few days in the spring and autumn). The manors were more important for animal husbandry. One count later in the fourteenth century revealed that the Order owned 13,000 horses, 10,000 cattle, 19,000 pigs and 61,000 sheep. In one year the garrison at Danzig, about 200 men, ate 90 oxen, 100 sheep, and 300 pigs. Presumably they feasted on these huge quantities of meat when visiting crusaders were present, because their daily diet was largely vegetarian. They stored thousands of tons of rye, wheat and malted grain against famine and siege. Beer was more common than wine, but it did not have the alcohol content of modern brews; also, it probably tasted better than well water and may have been safer. Mead, made from the local honey, and wine, imported from the homeland – good Rhenish and Mosel wines – were limited to quantities that would easily satisfy modern men.

The knights did not spend every day drinking and feasting. Three days of the week they had two meals with meat or fish, three days they had two meals of milk and eggs, and Friday was a fast day. This was true except for the fast days of the church calendar: 120 days of the year, most of them concentrated during Lent and Advent. This alternation of Spartan and Lucullan habits reinforced tendencies towards the excesses that characterised medieval life.

Like their political counterparts today, the grandmaster and his officers spent considerable time in necessary but unexciting meetings, large and small, formal and informal, which required reflection and debate. A strong bladder and hard rump were as vital to an administrative career as a grasp of essentials and sound judgement. Detailed knowledge was not always required – that could be left to the scribes and secretaries, some of whom were priests in training for higher posts in the Order, men who hoped to become a bishop, procurator-general or perhaps chancellor. In formal meetings the grandmaster and his officers were seated, while the other knights and priests stood. (This was a practical matter, since furnishings were very sparse, but it also honoured the officers.) Petitioners stood before the grandmaster until a decision was reached and were then dismissed formally, perhaps to leave, perhaps to melt into the crowd. Hours and hours could be spent in this fashion, sometimes to little effect, sometimes accomplishing much. However, no petitioner wanted to leave without being heard fully. Such was the concept of honour in those days that being heard was almost as important as obtaining the petition. Moments spent praising visitors or consoling the disappointed were important. The officer who was brusque or rude soon heard complaints about his behaviour, and records show citizens protesting about insulting remarks and a failure to give their wishes serious attention. Burghers and secular knights were limited in what they could do, but they were not servile: they voiced their opinions in the regional assemblies.

Formal and Informal Entertainment

Political discussions almost always involved formal entertainment. Banquets were necessary both to show respect to the guests and to vary the tempo and seriousness of the talks. For the knights of the convents and the officers alike this was a welcome respite from the spartan diet required by the rules, and not least because meals could be filled with conversation rather than the silence necessary to listen to a priest read a Bible text or a history of the Order. Of course, if critics are to be believed, that silence may not have been practised faithfully – instead, discussions of politics, war, and money were heard where the lives of saints and pious thoughts should have been foremost. The presence of guests lifted these restrictions. Meat, drink and music became abundant.

Men of that era preferred outdoor entertainment to indoor. Like secular nobles, the Teutonic Knights had a passion for the hunt. The grandmasters even inserted clauses into treaties and truces with the Lithuanians that safeguarded all hunting parties in the wilderness. While the chase was forbidden to other crusading orders, the Teutonic Knights were permitted to hunt as a means of maintaining good physical condition, exercising their horses, and becoming acquainted with the countryside and the natives. Naturally, the guests, who at home practically lived on horseback when the weather was good, were enchanted by the spectacularly wild country in Prussia, so unlike their more civilised and well-hunted woods. They had never seen aurochs and European bison, nor elk so large. They were impressed by the numbers of wild pigs and deer and the variety of game birds; and if they wanted to hunt birds and smaller animals with falcons, their hosts would provide them. Prussian falcons, in fact, were so popular that grandmasters forbade their export. This was to prevent the birds from being exterminated by private hunters and to allow grandmasters to curry favour with supporters. Falconry was the true sport of kings, and no gift of money or jewellery would impress a monarch as much as a gigantic bird.

Lastly, there was religious devotion. Mass being a form of entertainment as well as a duty, men were accustomed to long and frequent religious services. The Teutonic Order required its knights to participate in the eight divine services of the day, one every three hours. They complied with this even on campaign, as much as practicality allowed, daylight being very short in the winter. It was a routine that few thought unusual. The rite was that of the Dominicans, involving psalms, hymns, and readings. The role of the knights who did not know basic Latin was limited to reciting seven to thirteen '*Pater Nosters*'. Some knights knew enough Latin to participate in the chants, but others had great difficulty in memorising the '*Pater Noster*' and '*Ave Maria*'. (Each knight had a year and a half to learn these on pain of being expelled from the Order.) Many knights were pious; some were exceptionally so, like Hartung of Sonnenborn, a master of the robes who had obtained his wife's consent to enter the religious life.

Chapter Three

The Early Years of the Crusade

By 1300 Christian and pagan raiders had been hitting each other's settlements in mutual retaliations for at least a decade, making the frontier regions so dangerous that many villagers withdrew to safer locations. Darius Baronas noted in a 2015 article in *Rocznik Lituanistyczny* that neither the Teutonic Knights nor the Lithuanian dukes had much control over these raiders – the raids were conducted by paramilitary bands that ignored whatever agreements their lords made about stopping cross-border robberies. The best the grandmasters could do was to patrol the Prussian frontier and authorise similar raids across the wilderness to keep some pagans at home to guard their villages and fields.

The main base for patrols was at Ragnit, on the left bank of the Nemunas about 100 kilometres (60 miles) from the river's mouth and almost equidistant from Königsberg and the castle at Memel. Supported by another strong castle at Tilsit downstream, the garrison at Ragnit bore the brunt of the border war. For attacks across the wilderness, the commander at Ragnit called on the advocates of Sambia and Natangia (a district south-east of Königsberg) and their native militias to steal cattle, burn homes and crops, and kidnap everyone who did not hide or die in resisting capture. This was the only practical strategy in an era when fortifications were almost impregnable, and troops had to be paid in booty. Like the pagans, the crusaders justified whatever brutal acts they and their subjects committed as necessary to achieve a worthy goal.

Preachers recruiting for the Prussian and Livonian crusades told large audiences that the enemies of the Cross were foes of both God and man. Moreover, they suggested that pagans, Saracens, schismatics and heretics had no rights except those that Christian rulers might choose to grant them. As long as those foes were independent, they were a danger to Christendom and had to be destroyed, like sheep infected with disease, to save the healthy ones.

Whatever doubts may have persisted after such a sermon were quickly stilled by churchmen who declared that any war between Christians and infidels was a just war, a proper means of protecting and expanding Christendom. Citing St Augustine, they declared that the entire life of pagans was sinful, regardless of the goodness or evil of their actions, because everything they did was done without knowledge of the eternal truths of God. To be sure, pagans should not be *forced* to accept Christianity. They were to be permitted to survive, like the Jews, in hope that they or their descendants might eventually be converted and saved. In the meantime, pagans should not be permitted any role in society that might cause Christians to admire them. Therefore, Christians should strip them of property and power, of pride and prestige.

While the pagans were still dangerous, preachers assured potential volunteers that once they had cut down the enemies of God, then Christ himself would hurl their souls into hellfire. Of course, it was easier to preach the crusade than it was to reach the Samogitians to kill them. Most Samogitians lived in the interior, surrounded by mosquito-filled swamps and dense forests. This wilderness was almost untouched by humans, thanks to their religious beliefs, which incorporated forest gods and spirits into a wider pantheon, and to ancient fears of attack from Prussia, Kurland, Semigallia (in modern Latvia) and Livonia which had caused them to hew down giant trees across possible paths. This wilderness along the entire Prussian frontier grew ever denser as untilled fields became part of the forest. The only winners were the wild animals. Aurochs and European bison found refuge here, and stags grew to impressive size.

As the battlefields moved away from the populated regions of Prussia, city councils began to complain about being summoned to perform military service on far-away frontiers. Elbing councilmen even went so far in 1300 as to write the University of Paris, the foremost law school north of the Alps, to ask whether they could be compelled to perform such service. This was the first time we know of that Roman law was cited in support of such a case. However, although the response favoured the city's interpretation, nothing came of it. Common sense seems to have prevailed – victories often only last until the enemy gets an inspired leader.

Vytenis of Lithuania

Vytenis, the Grand Duke of Lithuania, was called a king by his followers and the chroniclers of the Teutonic Knights, but he could not be recognised as such by the pope or emperor because they reserved royal titles to Christians. He was a capable ruler and a wily commander, who led a combination of Lithuanians and exiled Prussians in daring incursions into Prussia and Livonia. These attacks would have been even more destructive if he had not been distracted by wars in Ruthenia and by *Witingen* in Samogitia who disliked taking orders from anyone, even when it was in their best interests – as manning the new forts on the borders clearly was. Often, he himself would lead one army and send out small forces as diversions so that the Teutonic Knights had to guess where he would strike with his main force; and they usually guessed wrong. Vytenis had Christian allies in the burghers and archbishop of Riga, and for their sake he occasionally made a pretence of seeking conversion. Franciscan friars at his court in Vilnius made his gestures credible. Though allowing his subjects and visitors freedom of worship, he was personally a devout pagan.

In February 1311 he gave the Teutonic Knights a demonstration of his prowess, breaking into Sambia and Natangia with 4,000 men, killing many villagers and taking 500 captives. Although Heinrich of Plötzke was far away in Marienburg, where the grandmaster was lying ill, he knew that the retreating pagans would be slowed by their prisoners and booty sufficiently that pursuers might be able to catch them. Indeed, Marshal Friedrich of Wildenberg was able to attack while some pagans were feasting and dividing up their gains. His victory (at an unknown location) was among the greatest of this era. It was the beginning of his brilliant career.

Meanwhile, another force, mainly of Prussians, had gone straight for Grodno, probably hoping to catch raiders who had returned separately to their homes. The Christian pursuers got lost in the marshes, so they arrived late, but this was not bad luck – the raiders were so thoroughly drunk from celebrating their success, that the Prussians were able to kill many of them and lead others off to a life of serfdom.

This threw Vytenis into a fury. As soon as his warriors had rested, the king led them through the lake wilderness into Ermland, evading patrols sent out by the Teutonic Knights and the dukes of Masovia. The modern estimate of invaders is 4,000 men, compared to 8,000 by the chronicler who tended to exaggerate pagan numbers. It was April and the snow and ice were just melting, so the attack came as a surprise. Vytenis's forces captured every castle they attacked except one, and every town except one. As they swept through the diocese almost to the coast, Vytenis paused at the castle at Braunsberg (Braniewo) to yell insults at the bishop on the ramparts before destroying every settlement within sight and taking 1,200 prisoners, mostly women. (The men were presumably either slain or had escaped into the woods to join the militia.) According to the Christian reports, he made churches a special target of his wrath, desecrating altars, tearing down crucifixes and trampling on them, handling and spitting on the consecrated wafers of the host, and then burning the buildings. The chroniclers lamented that mothers had to witness the rape of their daughters, and the daughters that of their mothers. As Vytenis led away the captives, bound and fettered, he taunted them, asking, 'Where is your God? Why did he not help you, as our gods help us now and at other times?'

If that quote is accurate, Vytenis was rejoicing too soon. His forces were in great danger. The deeper he had led his men into Prussia, the more time he gave the Christian militias to assemble. At that very moment Heinrich of Plötzke was gathering a large army to follow Vytenis's slow-moving, booty-laden raiders out of the country.

Heinrich had dreamt of an opportunity like this for many of his fifty years. Now he had a force of eighty knights and thousands of militiamen in position to overtake the Lithuanian army. With luck he could destroy the invading force and perhaps kill or capture the king.

At first, fortune did not seem to be with him. When Vytenis saw the Christian army approaching, he ordered his men to form their ranks on a hill near Wopławki, about three kilometers east of the future site of Rastenburg (Kętrzyn). He surrounded the crown of the hill with an improvised wall of hedges and felled trees, and he apparently planned to wait there as long as necessary. After all, he had the Christians' cattle for food, while the Christians had brought few supplies with them; however, he had only seen the Christians' advance guard.

Heinrich would have preferred a battlefield where he could use his heavy cavalry more effectively, but he was ready to fight on foot, if necessary, even on ground chosen by the enemy. Unless he could force the pagans to fight now, they might slip away. Moreover, his Prussian militiamen would not have understood allowing the enemy to escape with their captive friends and relatives. Therefore, he ordered Günther of Arnstein, the most heroic knight of his generation, to lead an immediate assault with the forces on hand. Günther retreated quickly, leaving behind forty to sixty dead, but he had learned the location and strength of Vytenis's forces. As soon as Heinrich heard his report, he ordered an attack on the most vulnerable part of the defences.

A crusader poet tells us that this was a moving scene: there were cries from captive women and children, the shouts of their relatives in the militia, yells by desperate men in the fury of battle. Such passages, emphasising knightly deeds, courage, fairness, pity for the unfortunate, and service to the Church and Lady Mary, give us valuable insights into the mind of the crusading knight. Unfortunately, we lack a Lithuanian equivalent of this: the pagan tradition was oral, not written, and it has largely vanished.

When the full force of Christians came up, Vytenis saw all the flags and banners for the first time. Only then did he realise who his opponents were, and how many there were. Success in arms, he knew, was not a question of numbers alone, but also of quality. The gay banners of the commanders and the great black cross on a white field told knowledgeable pagans that they were facing the best the Teutonic Knights had; and there were a lot of them. Consequently, as the attackers approached, then broke through the pagan lines so that the Order's banner fluttered in their midst, the less bold Lithuanians (or, at least, the most discreet and prudent) began to seek their horses. Meanwhile, some female captives broke loose from their bonds and caused confusion in the rear. Vytenis disappeared (and escaped, badly wounded, with three companions), while thousands of his followers fell in the hand-to-hand fighting. The pursuit continued right to Grodno, the Christians slaying those pagans too exhausted to flee farther and driving others into the swamps. Only when Heinrich sensed the danger of ambush, did he turn back towards home – after, according to Długosz, hanging or drowning all the prisoners.

At a later peace conference, Vytenis asked to meet the knight who had almost killed him. Introduced to him (perhaps the future grand-master, Heinrich Dusemer), he said, 'You almost killed me with your sharp sword.' The knight responded that he would have if Vytenis had waited around.

The Christians took 2,800 horses and thousands of spears and swords, reclaimed the Lithuanians' plunder, liberated the women and children, and captured Vytenis's chamberlain. One chronicler wrote a hymn of victory, 'Oh, noble knights of God, God must honour you on earth and in heaven.' Heinrich commemorated the day by founding a nunnery at Thorn.

Stalemate

The impact of the crusader victory was small, however, because the Teutonic Knights could not exploit it. Vytenis regrouped his forces, encouraged them to defend their forts resolutely, and ordered everyone to refrain from taking risks. Somewhat later, when a young commander, Gerhard of Mansfeld, boldly rode into Lithuania, the pagans followed his small army out of their country. Fearing an ambush, they refused his offer of battle, but they asked his name and warned him that he would not live long if he again entered their country with so few men.

The officers of the Order realised that significant advances could be made only by building castles in strategic locations – capturing a fort by siege so ruined the site that it could not be held, while a Christian force that erected a log and earth fort along the Nemunas could supply themselves by ship. The only way to take a Lithuanian castle intact was by ransom or by treason.

This had led Heinrich to believe that Vytenis's chamberlain, who had been taken prisoner in the recent battle, could deliver Grodno to him. The official had promised that, rather than pay ransom or surrender prisoners, he would arrange to surrender that strategic fortress. However, it was necessary for him to be released immediately, so that he could explain his late return as the result of hiding in the woods. Though sceptical, Heinrich released his prisoner. Indeed, the chamberlain 'betrayed' the Christians by telling Vytenis and arranging for an ambush of the Prussian forces as they approached Grodno.

It could have been a Christian disaster, but Heinrich's scouts came upon an old man, who must have aroused their suspicions. When they put him to torture, he revealed that Lithuanians were lurking at a river, waiting for half of the Christian army to cross over before attacking. Heinrich spared the old man, as promised, and fled to safety with his army.

In late May 1311 Heinrich called up 140 knights, a larger number of half-brothers, and a strong force of native *Witingen* and mounted militia, perhaps 2,000 men in all, then crossed the Lake District on boats. After remounting their steeds, they approached Grodno through a thick forest. Coming upon four scouts, they killed three and learned from the fourth that nobody was aware of their approach. Quite the contrary: Vytenis was feeling so secure that he had ordered a hunting camp set up nearby. Heinrich annihilated the fifty men there, then crossed the Nemunas. Leaving twelve knights and the foot soldiers to guard the boats, he sent his men on a rampage through the countryside, sparing neither age nor sex. The raiders took 700 prisoners, and of the dead they left behind, 'only God knows the number'.

Modern nationalist historians sometimes forget the mutual hostility of the native tribes. This desire to take revenge, to harm one's traditional foes, and to gain wealth and reputation made it easy to raise armies, to organise raids, and to summon labourers for work on fortifications. The terrible atrocities also made defection to the enemy less likely.

Unrest in Poland and the Empire

King Ladislas faced the same problems as his neighbours in Bohemia, Hungary, and the Holy Roman Empire – to suppress unrest and banditry, intimidate rebellious vassals, and fend off foreign rivals. He raised money by methods that provoked unrest and rebellion, and his fierce temper made his subjects fear him. Churchmen disapproved, too, when he demanded ever more money from them. In 1312, after a riot in Cracow, the king had the instigators dragged through the streets before torturing them to death on the wheel. He then confiscated the property of merchants and artisans, imprisoned the bishop and seized his property, and built towers around the city from which his garrison could crush any future resistance.

The Holy Roman emperor, Heinrich VII of Luxemburg, died in Italy in 1313, perhaps of poison in a communion wafer given to him by a Dominican friar, perhaps of malaria. Rumours ran rampant, each reflecting political interests in the contest between the empire and the papacy. This led to another period of instability, since Heinrich VII's son, John, was considered too young to be emperor. In any case, there was the usual indecision among the electors, who wanted an emperor strong enough to protect their interests, but too weak to threaten them. The divided election led to civil war.

A pattern was developing; Henrich VII had died while trying to restore order in Italy, His predecessor, Albrecht I, had been murdered while trying to bring order to his territories on the Rhine. Albrecht's father, Rudolph of Habsburg, had been mocked by Dante for being so weak. It appeared that Germany would remain disunited, and the Holy Roman Empire merely a dream that always disappointed.

These were the circumstances in which the Teutonic Knights had to work. It is not surprising that they came to believe that God would protect those who loved and served him, but kings could not be relied on. Those who even half-listened to the sermons knew Psalm 146: 3: 'Put not your trust in princes.'

A New Grandmaster

Although Heinrich of Plötzke's impressive victories had made him a strong candidate to succeed Siegfried of Feuchtwangen in 1313, the electors chose Karl of Trier instead. That may have been a rebuke of Heinrich's domineering ways, but the new grandmaster recognised political realities – he made Heinrich grand commander and later marshal.

Karl of Trier made a tour of Prussia, inspecting the castles and discussing strategies, after which he ordered the attacks on Grodno suspended in favour of occupying western Samogitia, hoping that this would secure a shorter land route to Riga and end devastating attacks on Kurland and Semigallia. He also introduced the ceremony of dubbing knights that would become a popular part of each crusading expedition, with the honour bestowed by the most prominent noble present as soon as each candidate performed some deed of valour. He invited the most valiant warriors to sit at a Table of Honour modelled after King Arthur's Round Table and awarded distinctions to the most outstanding knights.

In April 1313 Karl loaded ships in Königsberg with supplies, war equipment and men, and sent them to the Nemunas via the Baltic. Other forces went overland to Ragnit. Despite losing four knights and 400 men at sea, with a vast amount of supplies, and building materials for a new castle, the grandmaster marched his forces 50 km. (30 miles) upriver, where he built a bridge of boats across the wide stream. When the bridge was completed, priests led a great procession over it and held a festive mass before the craftsmen started work on a great castle of logs and earth that he named Christmemel. The chroniclers reported that the Lithuanians were more amazed by the bridge than by anything else the Christians had ever done.

Christmemel, lying about halfway from Ragnit to Kaunas, was to be the base for Karl's attacks into the heart of Samogitia. We have good information on the routes that the raiders took. *Die Litauischen Wegeberichte*, compiled between 1384 and 1402, when the war was reaching its conclusion, described a hundred routes across the wilderness, giving the names of the men leading the attacks, the distances between potential camps where horses could graze, the locations of swamps and forests, and difficulties that might be encountered.

In the summer of 1313 Heinrich moved against the castles immediately upstream. He personally led the army to Bisenė, sending some troops by land and others by water, then using a bridge of boats to bring siege weapons to bear on the earth and log walls. Unsuccessful, he returned in the autumn with Prussian militia, managing to burn some of the outer works, but not the central fortress. This was disappointing, because thirty years earlier a winter expedition had been able to cross the ice to burn it.

Meanwhile, according to the chroniclers, the commander of Ragnit sailed to Veliuona (Welun) a hilltop castle near the mouth of the Dubysa River. His plan was to assault the walls directly from a gigantic warship. However, a strong burst of wind drove his entire fleet ashore as he approached the castle. Only after desperate fighting were the crews able to get their vessels back into mid-stream and return to Ragnit.

Vytenis was stirred into action by these attacks. He was especially worried about the large warship, because it threatened every riverside castle along the Nemunas. Therefore, he ordered one of his vassals to destroy it as quickly as possible.

The Lithuanian commander ordered 100 horsemen to make their way to Ragnit, while 600 men went downriver in a hundred small boats. These forces were observed by Christian scouts and lookouts, but the current enabled the small boats to move so swiftly that they arrived at Ragnit ahead of any warning. The rest of the plan was not so easy to accomplish. Although the pagans found the great warship anchored in mid-stream with only four bowmen on board, the vessel was so huge that they could not scale the sides (especially while the archers were shooting them down one after the other). In fact, the attackers might have been massacred if the archers had been reinforced. However, the Lithuanian cavalry prevented a sortie from Ragnit until the anchor rope was cut, after which the ship glided down the river, followed by the host of small boats. When the vessel ran aground, the Lithuanians were able to set it ablaze. The four bowmen died, but it was reported that so many pagans had been wounded that 350 died on the retreat.

The grandmaster did not replace the warship. Apparently, he had concluded it was not practical even in summer; and in winter all vessels would be icebound – and easily attacked.

Brutal Warfare

We know from the sources how cruel warriors of this era could be. Polish witnesses testifying to papal legates in 1320 and 1339 indicated that when the Teutonic Knights and their allies assaulted Polish villages, they tortured and massacred prisoners, slaughtered innocent civilians, stripped women, abused clerics, and destroyed houses, fields and churches.

Wiesław Sieradzan noted that such denunciations had become stereotypical in this era, but that after the hearsay and conventional outrage were set aside, some claims remained that were more specific and plausible. Even these cases, however, were not as clear-cut as they first appeared. Since the Teutonic Knights burned every village they reached, the destruction of the parish church would not necessarily have been intentional. There would have been looting, of course – everything made of silver, everything that could be sold (books, paintings), and even clothing (which might explain the 'stripping of women') would have been stolen. Rapes undoubtedly occurred, but the suggestion that the Order's knights had violated their vows is less plausible than attributing this to the militia. Civilians who took refuge in churches and cemeteries seem to have been largely – but not completely – spared.

However, the churchmen who read the report must have asked themselves, if that was happening in Christian Poland, how were potential converts in Samogitia being treated? The papal investigators had attempted to get at the truth by hearing testimony privately, and asking each witness a detailed list of questions, but the Order's refusal to co-operate predisposed the judges to believe the most extreme accusations. The pope, hearing the reports of misdeeds and atrocities, summoned the high officials of the Order to appear before him.

The lawyers defending the Teutonic Knights denied some charges and explained that others were exaggerated or misrepresented. The Order's relationship with Poles, for example, was not uniformly bad. The bishop of Płock had even given the Teutonic Order the castellany of Michelau to protect that frontier of his diocese. The fear of pagan attack also made the dukes of Masovia friendly; and the dukes in Pomerania and Silesia were seeking allies against Ladislas. (Długosz wrote that nobody hated him as much as the Silesian dukes.) Nor were the Poles without fault in the dispute. Years earlier, when the Council of Vienne ordered the Polish bishops to pay a special crusading tax to support the Teutonic Order, the bishops ignored them. King Ladislas prevented his subjects from participating in the crusade, one exception being in 1324, when the duke of Masovia signed a treaty of alliance with the Teutonic Knights, promising that if an army of 'Saracens' should try to cross his territories, he would send a warning.

The investigations did not produce an uncontestable condemnation of the Teutonic Order, but they were ample testimony to the cruelty of fourteenth-century warfare. Moreover, this cruelty was confirmed by historians who wrote in praise of the crusade – as Paravicini noted in *Preussenreise*, the campaigns in Lithuania were much like those elsewhere in Europe; Sven Ekdahl noted the same for the treatment of prisoners of war.

Principles of Frontier Warfare

The descriptions of raids across the wilderness allow us to analyse the strategy which lay behind them. Even today, it is a principle that attempting to defend everything means defending nothing – the forces would be stretched too thin, and in any case, farmers and herders had work to tend to. The best that could be done was to employ scouts and watchmen, so that the villagers could seek refuge while the militia hurried to its assembly points. When an army had gathered, it would pursue the intruders even though raiders were usually gone by then.

Much of the year mud could be a major problem for invaders, but there were two periods when travel was practical – deep winter and high summer. February, June, and November were especially good for horsemen: in February the frozen rivers could still be used as highways and the pagans could not hide in ambush easily; June was good because men were available since ploughing was finished, and the harvest hadn't started; and by November the militia had brought in the crops and the snow was not yet too deep.

The expeditions were well organised. Unable to live off the land in the wilderness, raiders carried their supplies with them, often leaving them at a rendezvous site, sometimes guarding them, sometimes burying them, and sometimes simply hiding them. Castles served as depots and resting places, and ships transported food and equipment when surprise was not important.

Raiders generally divided into striking forces, each plundering all day and meeting at a pre-determined location where they would find the camp pitched. A strong detachment there would protect the booty and be ready to assist against any threat that appeared. The army moved each day to a new location, often proceeding in a zig-zag pattern, some-times hurrying forward, and sometimes returning to a district in hope of catching the inhabitants as they emerged from concealment. Occasionally small forces were sent ahead with the intention of retreating hurriedly and leading pursuers into an ambush. This instilled such caution among defenders that very small parties were able to make daring raids deep into the heart of the enemy countryside and escape unharmed. Christian and pagan alike employed the same tactics because they were practical for wearing the enemy down.

The Death of Vytenis

Vytenis did not allow the crusaders free run of his country. He was a skilful and determined warrior who had capable men in his service. One, David of Grodno (Dovydas Gardiniškis, 1283–1326), was long thought to be the son-in-law of Gediminas (Vytenis's successor), but Stephen C. Rowell, the foremost specialist in Lithuanian ducal genealogy, says that David was almost certainly the heir of Daumantis, duke of Nalšia, an important district bordering on Livonia and Pskov, and a hero to both pagan Lithuanians and Orthodox Christians. David first appears in

Western chronicles for 1314, when he destroys supplies left by Heinrich during a September raid near Navahrudak (in Belarus), the base for Lithuanian expansion into Slavic lands. That Heinrich would raid the environs of an impregnable fortress on a high hill so far from Prussia shows how daring he was. When David saw that the crusader force was too great to challenge, he gathered his men and looked for the camp the raiders would return to with their booty; finding it, he killed the guards, burned the foodstuffs, and stole 500 horses,

When Heinrich saw the empty underground store, he realised he could not take his planned route back to Prussia, because the enemy would be waiting for him and if he were blocked at any point, his men would have nothing to eat. Therefore, he made a detour through the wilderness towards a second food depot. It, however, was empty, too – the guards, having assumed from the delay that the army was not coming, had carried the supplies away or destroyed them. Desperate now, Heinrich ordered his men to split up and return home as best they could. Some rode so swiftly that they exhausted their horses, others got lost. Some men dug for roots, others ate their exhausted and starving horses, and many died in their tracks. Those who managed to escape were ill from their ordeal, and some ate so greedily upon returning home that they died. Without any fighting, David of Grodno caused Heinrich to suspend further raids deep into Lithuania that might have brought an end to attacks on Volhynia, Galicia and Masovia. The initiative now belonged to the pagans.

In August 1315 Samogitians slipped up to Ragnit unnoticed and were on the walls before the alarm was given. The startled garrison, presumably asleep, hurried into the keep, a strong tower tall enough to serve as a lookout and almost impossible to assault directly. The entrance was hardly more than a door, high above the ground and reached by a narrow staircase and solidly barred from within, but the base had no entrances or windows, and the stone wall was protected against undermining by barrages of heavy stones thrown from sixty or eighty feet above, and showers of crossbow bolts. Even wounded and exhausted men could defend such a post for several days. Therefore, the Samogitians did not even try an assault, but hurried home after burning the fields ready for harvest.

Six weeks later Vytenis appeared at Christmemel. He set up two hurling machines, brought up a multitude of Rus'ian archers, and put his men to work cutting wood and piling it to dry. His plan was to throw so much wood and brush into the dry moat that fire would destroy the wall and perhaps generate enough smoke to suffocate the garrison.

When Karl of Trier heard this, he summoned his forces. Although he could not start off himself until his army was fully assembled, he sent ten knights and 150 men ahead on ships. When the van of Heinrich's army approached the castle on the seventeenth day of the siege, Vytenis was not yet ready to attack, but this being his only chance to take Christmemel, he gave the order to throw the wood and straw into the moat, then set fire to it. Thousands of men rushed towards the castle, their arms filled with wood, while his archers covered them by firing volleys of arrows at the ramparts.

The garrison, however, was well protected; they rose up after each reloading, firing their crossbows as rapidly as possible, striking down so many Lithuanians that Vytenis stopped the attack, burned his siege machines, and led his army away.

This was the last the crusaders heard of Vytenis. No one knows what happened to him. Legend has it that he died when struck by lightning, but that seems to be a mistranslation of the name of his successor, Gediminas. So little is known of the genealogies of the Lithuanian rulers that historians long believed that Gediminas was Vytenis's son, whereas they were apparently cousins. Vytenis was almost certainly not killed by Gediminas – that story may have been a later effort by the grand dukes of Moscow to stain Gediminas's reputation. But if Vytenis was mortally wounded at the siege of Christmemel, the Teutonic Knights did not realise it – they would certainly have reported such a triumph. However, a tradition connected to a burial mound at Veliuona says that he was buried there. This would make sense if he had been borne away, only to die a few days later. Archeologists have not excavated the mound, but there might not be much to find besides charred jewellery, weapons and bits for his horse. Even though Vytenis's funeral would have involved great ceremony, the fire would have destroyed everything else.

Vytenis was a great man, an authentic national hero. Perhaps it is no coincidence that the first Lithuanian coins bore the symbol of a mounted rider called Vytis. That figure could well have been a canting reference to the grand duke.

Supreme Duke Gediminas Presses Eastward

There seems to have been no dispute about who the next ruler should be – Gediminas (c. 1275–December 1341). Although his early life was typically obscure, Gediminas must have impressed his contemporaries, because he was able to persuade them that the fight over Samogitia was not worth their full attention, not when the situation to Lithuania's east and south was so promising for exploitation. Indeed, Rus'ian princes, nobles, and burghers were willing to accept any overlord who would protect them. For three-quarters of a century Tatar khans of the Golden Horde had collected a heavy tribute from each prince and city in their empire, punishing those who refused or could not collect the funds, or who failed to deliver tribute personally when summoned. Their devastating raids destroyed villages and towns, carrying away thousands of prisoners for sale across the Black Sea, and their cruelty was as legendary as was their military prowess. This 'Tatar Yoke' – more accurately a Mongol–Tatar Yoke – referred to the way that the Rus'ians were treated as plough horses in the period between 1240 and 1480. It was the most elementary consideration of every prince in the region, and never forgotten by the descendants of the people so long terrorised by it.

The Tatars were a complex people, mostly nomads, some traders, all warriors. Their leaders took pride in being descendants of Genghis Khan, but most warriors were Turkic. The most important had felt tents carried on large wagons that they drove from one pasturage to another; all hated farmers who, they thought, were ruining the vast grazing lands of the steppe. Each Tatar was proud of his tribe and his ancestry and resentful of insults real or implied. This made them difficult to govern, and conflicts over pastures and prestige easily grew into civil wars. Few khans died of old age.

Uzbeg (Mohammed Öz-Beg, 1282–1341) became the Great Khan of the Golden Horde in 1313. Not content with titular authority, he set out to subdue his rivals permanently. He used Islam to reduce the religious diversity among the nomads in his wide empire because he believed that Shamanism and Buddhism had reinforced tribal desires for independence; towards Christians and pagans, however – lesser peoples – he was very tolerant if they were submissive. He established his court in Sarai on the Volga River and spent years seeking to make himself head of all the Turkic people to the south, into the Middle East and into China's westernmost province; he led huge armies against Bulgaria, Byzantium and even Serbia. This preoccupation caused him to neglect the Rus'ian princes except to reward those who were most servile and to punish the rest.

His tyranny caused Rus'ian princes and cities to contemplate ways of freeing themselves. Of course, before any prince considered rebellion, he cautiously looked about for protection; and some princes who had reluctantly agreed to go to the distant camp of the Great Khan had been beheaded seemingly to warn the others to obey without hesitation.

Now, however, some Rus'ians had begun to see the Lithuanian pagans as potential liberators.

When the princes of Galicia–Volhynia had sought aid first from the pope, then from Poland and Hungary, they received little beyond cautious encouragement; no western ruler could send a large force to the steppes. Since the Teutonic Knights were old allies, they even approached Karl of Trier, but because of the distance his men would have to travel, he was unable to assist. The Rus'ians then turned to Gediminas, who was, after all, related by marriage to some of their rulers. As it happened, it was a brilliant resolution of a complex problem. The Westerners were too far away, had other pressing concerns, and were demanding a church union on Roman terms. The Byzantines and Balkan states were far too weak. Gediminas was relatively close by, was ready to give full attention to their problems, and was tolerant in matters of religion.

The Tatars were willing to allow distant Lithuanians to rule some Rus'ian cities, so long as that kept Rus' divided and prevented a potentially stronger power, such as Poland, from moving in. Uzbeg had little interest in Ruthenians. Only once, in 1337 (or 1341), did he require their military assistance – in a twelve-day siege of Lublin – but little is known about that.

Meanwhile, the Great Khan was satisfied to maintain the traditional relationship: Rus'ian princes would take the census and collect the tax, then bring it to him and renew the formal declaration of submission. The prince would also maintain the courier system and send military forces when summoned. Serfdom and slavery were the fates of commoners who failed to pay taxes or to pay promptly, death the fate of nobles.

Gediminas took advantage of this situation. Once he proved that he could protect his clients, the trickle of men coming to him became a torrent. Gediminas often allowed his new subjects to retain their offices and he always permitted them to live by their traditional laws and customs. He especially respected the Orthodox Church and its leaders; they, in turn, urged their people to be loyal to him.

Soon Gediminas was signing his letters, 'King of the Lithuanians and many Rus'ians'. He gave his brothers Fiodor (Teodoras, *d.* after 1362) and Vainius (Voin, *d.* after 1338–42) Kyiv and Polotsk, and his son Algirdas (Olgierd, *c.* 1304–77) Vitebsk. Later, in 1322, he arranged for David of Grodno to become governor of Pskov, the post his father had held. Gediminas used marriage alliances win over the princes of Moscow, Ruthenia, Masovia and the kingdom of Poland. So successful was he that by 1358 his successor could declare that 'all Russia should belong to the Lithuanians'.

This allowed Gediminas to provide his *Witingen* with appointments in his Rus'ian client states, so that even if their estates were ravaged by crusaders, they did not have to choose between surrender and starvation. Realising that his military technology was inferior to that of the crusaders, Gediminas sought to attract merchants and artisans from the West, men who knew how to make or acquire the equipment he needed. German merchants in Riga, still angry at the Teutonic Order knights in Livonia, welcomed the opportunity to expand their trade network while weakening the Teutonic Knights. Their sole hesitation came from knowing that if they allied themselves with a pagan monarch against crusaders, violating a strongly held religious code, they would undermine their standing with the pope and emperor. This fear was allayed when Franciscan friars at Gediminas's court in Vilnius assured Catholic churchmen that the Lithuanians were ready for conversion, if only the crusaders would cease their attacks.

There was almost no chance that Gediminas would join the Roman Church, but he allowed Western visitors to imagine what they wished. Gediminas wanted to create an empire which included all faiths – Roman and Orthodox churches, Muslim Tatars, and pagans. He permitted each group to practise its own religion as long as they kept their heads down and mouths shut, but when they threatened his power, he would unleash his ferocious temper.

Karl of Trier at Avignon

While Gediminas was unifying western Rus', the knights in Prussia were dividing the Teutonic Order by quarrelling with the grandmaster. The origins of the disagreement were twofold, as we have seen earlier – the German knights wanted to use the Order's resources to support the Holy Roman emperor in his Italian campaign, while the Prussian and Livonian knights wanted reinforcements.

Meanwhile, the charges raised by the archbishop of Riga and the king of Poland had been so forcefully substantiated by two papal legates that the procurator-general worried that lands would have to be surrendered, huge sums paid for damages, and the crusade abandoned. Because the split seemed to prove that the Order's knights were indeed out of control, it was necessary to have the grandmaster argue that it was hardly more than a typical internal monastic quarrel, and then address the charges. That was why, late in 1318, Karl of Trier went to Avignon.

This situation was perfectly suited for an ambitious pope who knew how to profit from it. John XXII had plans to restore papal authority, but he needed money. There were papal taxes which had not been collected in recent years, or even never. Among these was Peter's Pence, a tax on each person in lands subject to the pope, England and Poland being the most important. On the advice of the archbishop of Riga, the pope adopted a Polish suggestion to include some territories of the Teutonic Knights in 'the ancient borders of Poland', implying that both West Prussia and Culm were parts of the Polish kingdom; this would not only make the grandmaster responsible for collecting a large sum from citizens already complaining about taxes but would also make him subject to the king of Poland.

The grandmaster had to persuade an impoverished but ambitious pope to give up a potentially rich source of income, as well as to ignore the reports of legates and the complaints of prelates and monarchs. Not an easy task.

When John XXII took office at the age of seventy-two, after the cardinals had been deadlocked for two years, he resumed Clement V's efforts to make the papacy strong again. John XXII was an excellent administrator, though his choice of Avignon as his seat meant that offices, assembly halls and housing were scarce. Visitors complained about high rent, the difficulty of getting a hearing and the need to offer 'gifts' to officials. The pope also had expensive tastes.

The papacy had been in financial trouble as far back as the eleventh century Investiture Controversy, when critics had argued that the only way to purify the Church was to strip it of secular power and the temptations of wealth. This idea had risen again and again, most notably in the Albigensian heresy and among the Waldensians. Now the 'Spiritual Franciscans' wanted the Church to return to the age of the apostles, holy men who had taken seriously Christ's admonition to walk barefoot from town to town preaching the gospel, with no possessions of their own, staying with those who invited them, but when rejected, to shake the dust off their feet as they left so they took nothing away with them. This concept of absolute poverty had been one of the most charming eccentricities of St Francis, and now many of his followers were demanding 'apostolic poverty' of the entire Church, beginning with the pope.

Practical men and women saw that this would dismantle the system that brought religious instruction and comfort to the masses, make it difficult to provide for the poor, the hungry, the orphans and aged, and eliminate the system of education that trained scholars in civil and canon law, philosophy and medicine. The pope would be unable to reach out to oppressed believers who currently could petition him for help; there would be no papal legates with authority to censure evildoers. Nevertheless, the idea was popular. Everyone could see church-men spending money on magnificent churches, lavish lifestyles, and occasionally on women and boys. Moreover, most high churchmen – bishops and abbots – were of noble birth, and many had taken office at very young ages, promoted ahead of their experience (and often their abilities) by families determined to control the wealth and political power of the Church in their neighbourhoods.

Even doctrine was in dispute. Was the Church a monarchy ruled by a pope chosen by divine inspiration or was it a democracy administered by a pope elected by his peers? Did a pious Christian enter heaven (or at least have a vision of it) instantly upon death, or did that happen after the Last Judgement? Dante became important in this debate, having made Hell, Purgatory and Heaven places that anyone could imagine.

Then there was witchcraft, which John XXII believed existed because the Bible said so. Most Christians believed in witches, too. After all, if evil did not exist, why fight it so hard? Such was the thought of those who believed in the crusade, including the Teutonic Knights, who saw it practised by shamans in Lithuania, who claimed to predict the future by casting bones or observing the flight of birds.

Lastly, there was the challenge of the Holy Roman Empire. In 1314 the disputed election between Louis IV of Bavaria (Ludwig, 1282–1347) and Friedrich of Habsburg, archduke of Austria, was complicated by two of the seven electors' lands being disputed. Thus, one vote went 4–0 for Louis, the other 5–0 for Friedrich. When Pope John XXII decreed that the throne was vacant and would remain so until he gave his consent to a coronation, he was, in effect, annulling the election.

When the Teutonic Knights joined their countrymen of both parties in protest, Pope John noted the fact. He took revenge in 1320 by appointing several Polish prelates to render a judgment regarding the ownership of West Prussia, rejecting all protests that the judges were prejudiced. Moreover, he denied the procurator-general admission to the papal palace while the issue was under discussion.

When the head of the Polish delegation ordered the Teutonic Knights to pay heavy damages within three days, surrender Culm and West Prussia to Ladislas and recompense him for lost incomes, and furthermore, pay all the expenses of the legation, or face the immediate imposition of ecclesiastical penalties, he provided the grandmaster a valid ground for appealing the entire verdict.

Karl of Trier was an excellent diplomat. His fluent French and Latin made it possible for him to communicate with Pope John XXII and his cardinals without an interpreter; moreover, he was personally charming. He was exactly the person to refute charges that the Teutonic Knights were arrogant, overbearing, obstinate criminals, and he was backed by an impressive retinue. In July 1319 he persuaded John XXII to order a long list of archbishops and bishops to act as protectors of the interests of the Teutonic Knights until the lawsuits could be resolved. Though the pope sympathised with the complaints of the Poles and Rigans, he was not willing to do more than order a new investigation; after all, the military order had not presented its defence of the charges. Still, this allowed the Teutonic Knights to rest more easily, as they had time on their side.

Although papal legates went to the east in 1319 and 1320, none met with full co-operation from the knights in Prussia or Livonia. Furthermore, although each delegation returned with armloads of parchments filled with accusations, the procurator-general had been operating quietly but effectively to counteract their reports, using secret means (usually money) to delay or sidetrack the process. Because delay is always the friend of the weaker party, this allowed the Teutonic Order to win the assistance of King John of Bohemia, who aided them by claiming the crown of Poland and recognising the crusaders' rights in West Prussia and Culm. It also helped that by 1323 Louis IV had won the civil war – for twenty years he had been the margrave of Brandenburg and a dependable supporter of their crusade.

Years of Frustration for the Crusaders

After the arrival of Western crusaders in 1316, a string of victories followed that so emboldened Heinrich of Plötzke that in July 1320 he took a large army up the Nemunas, then overland past Vilnius, right past the heart of Lithuania into Volhynia. While his men were ravaging the countryside, defenders gathered at the possible routes of retreat, cutting down trees to hamper any escape. As Heinrich made his way back, he drove prisoners and cattle before him, hoping to spring any ambush before his own forces came into danger.

The Lithuanians, however, lying in wait at a narrow passage in the forest, remained quiet until the van had passed. When they struck, the Prussian militia fled into the forest – that was an ancient tradition, one that had helped their ancestors survive even the worst ambushes. The heavily armoured knights could not do the same, practically or honourably. They had to stand and fight. The combat lasted for hours, until the weight of the armour exhausted both men and horses. As the knights became too tired to lift their arms, they perished one by one. A few escaped, but twenty-nine knights died. Among them was 'the lion-like' Heinrich of Plötzke, who was reputed to have fought to the end.

The captives were little better off than the fallen. The advocate of Sambia, who had led the Prussian militia, was tied to a horse tethered between four poles; then, after wood was stacked high around him, he and the horse were burned alive.

This battle resolved some of the remaining questions about governance in the military order. With the passing of Heinrich of Plötzke, the opposition to the grandmaster was greatly weakened. It also indicated that the Teutonic Knights could no longer safely venture deep into the pagan heartland.

In February 1322 two Silesian dukes along with Rhinelanders, Swabians and Austrians joined the crusade, but it was the Bohemians led by King John who were most important. The knights and militia of Culm came as well (perhaps to replace the decimated Sambians). One chronicler estimated 20,000 were in the army. Although that was probably an exaggeration, it indicated the presence of a very large force.

The army marched from Königsberg to the Nemunas, then struck into the interior provinces of Samogitia with overwhelming force. The crusaders reported to their friends at home that they had met and bested worthy foes, thereby increasing both their own reputation and that of King John, then becoming the foremost knight-errant of his generation – with three large white feathers decorating his helmet, he was unmistakable on the battlefield. His fame transferred to the Teutonic Knights, who were seeking to relieve the pressure on Livonia, where Gediminas had been rampaging in an effort to rescue his allies in Riga from the Livonian Knights. Now, he would have to fight in the Nemunas valley to keep the Christians from establishing bases for attacks on the heart of his empire.

As it happened, Gediminas was saved by the weather. The winter of 1323 was so cold that the Baltic froze over, and the master was unwilling to lead the Rhenish and Bohemian knights out of Königsberg, lest they perish in the bitter weather. The Teutonic Knights could do no more than entertain their guests and thank them for their good intentions.

The Samogitians were not affected as much by the cold, since their clothing and weapons were well adapted to the climate, and they could wait comfortably at home for a break in the weather. In March 1323, as soon as the crusaders went home, they struck at Memel, capturing the city, three local refuges for the native population, and a nearby castle. They could not take the keep at Memel, but they cast doubt on the crusaders' ability to maintain this vital point on the coastal route to Livonia. In

August they struck Sambia, and in September Kurland, sacking a town, killing seven monks and sixty young men studying for the priesthood, and carrying away huge numbers of prisoners. While medieval figures were usually highly exaggerated, the Teutonic Knights kept detailed tax records, and therefore the chronicler's estimate of 20,000 dead and missing must be considered within the realm of possibility.

Soon afterwards David of Grodno led an army into Estonia, then a Danish possession. Sacking even Reval (Tallinn), he left a trail of burned monasteries and churches behind him as he rounded up 5,000 captives, mostly women and children, then drove them home, most likely to Pskov. The previous year Lithuanians had hit the bishopric of Dorpat (Tartu), taking 5,000 captives.

Another devastating pagan raid hit the Masovian villages on the north bank of the Vistula west of Płock, burning ten churches. According to Jeroschin, they killed or captured 6,000 people in the countryside, then 2,000 in the city of Dobrzyń (Dobrin), and another 1,000 as they left the duchy, driving off all the livestock and carrying away everything worth stealing. However, the Lithuanians had barely returned home with their captives before they were struck by two armies of Teutonic Knights, who burned the raiders' villages and freed many of the prisoners. Nevertheless, the damage had been done. The next year the Lithuanians returned to Dobrzyń and Płock, destroying 130 villages and 30 churches.

This was a hard blow to Wenceslaus (Wacław, *c.* 1297–1336), the youngest of the three Piast princes who had divided Masovia between them; and it complicated the calculations of all three dukes: who could best protect their lands: themselves, the king or the grandmaster?

There was a new grandmaster now, Werner of Orseln, a former commander of Ragnit and grand commander. Born near Frankfurt am Main about 1280, he had entered the Order in his early twenties. During the recent turmoil he joined Karl of Trier in the Holy Roman Empire and when he returned to Prussia to represent him, he successfully restored discipline. Although he was an enthusiastic proponent of war against the pagans, there was little fighting in the next three years. That was because Louis IV and John XXII were at war, and neither wanted his supporters to leave the country.

Native Prussians at War

The Teutonic Knights found some Western techniques of war unsuited to the climate and terrain of the Samogitian wilderness. Heavily armoured knights were invincible if they could bring their massed forces to bear on pagan armies, but since Lithuanians were reluctant to fight on those terms, the crusaders adjusted, using more infantry. The result was that there was more searching for hidden cattle and people than combat, and more ambushes than enemies blocking fords.

The Teutonic Knights were helped in this unfamiliar warfare by native warriors who served as scouts and screening forces, who found paths and discovered ambushes. These were men who could enter Lithuania by obscure trails, operate for ten days on the supplies they carried, and be satisfied with a small fief and an occasional gift for their services.

The most illustrious of the native Prussian warriors was an Ermlander named Prewilte, better known as 'Mucke' (horsefly), who enriched his men with prisoners, weapons, cattle and horses. These were small-scale attacks, often with only twenty or so men, but that made them difficult for the frontier guards to detect. Mucke's special gift was slipping into the camps of raiders after dark, then, after slaughtering them while asleep or as they struggled to awaken, stealing their horses and possessions.

The nature of the heavily forested land with its many marshes and creeks also allowed larger forces to slip over the frontier undetected. In 1324 the commander of Ragnit took 40 knights and 400 native Prussians to attack Vilnius, burning the outer works. At that time Vilnius was little more than a small hill-top castle, with communities of merchants at its base, the German quarter being probably about an acre and the Orthodox quarter no larger. Few Lithuanians wanted to move into crowded urban centres.

All these incidents also show how important was the prospect of booty for native *Witingen*. The cattle, prisoners and stolen goods gave many Prussians a start in life, and the most successful could anticipate employment as guides for crusader armies or make a career of free-booting. This helped guarantee the loyalty of the native Prussians, although their hatred of the Lithuanians was probably just as important.

The pagan concept of honour was demonstrated in the summer of 1324 when 400 Lithuanians attempted to capture Christmemel by surprise, only to learn that the Christians – warned by a native fisherman – were crouched silently behind the ramparts, crossbows at the ready. When the Lithuanians emerged from the forest and began climbing the walls, the knights rose up and fired volleys of arrows, cutting down a number of warriors and their young leader. The attackers fled, but soon returned for the corpse of their chief. Groups came forward again and again, defying the volleys of arrows, each dragging the body a bit farther before they were cut down. Such devotion could be shown by the Prussians towards their chiefs, too, and even to individual knights of the Teutonic Order.

This loyalty coexisted with betrayals. Human characteristics are complex, and concepts of duty and obligation struggled with offended pride, revenge, ambition and opportunism. Inconsistencies of behaviour abounded then as now, and it was a wise ruler indeed who knew what his subjects really thought. Moreover, a betrayal was always most successful when it was least expected.

New Problems and Opportunities

In 1323, letters arrived in Avignon seeming to promise Gediminas's conversion. When John XXII ordered a truce be signed so that legates could travel to Vilnius to discuss this, the Teutonic Knights were outraged. They had recruited crusaders to serve Lady Mary and St George and they were not going to send them home to spread the word that journeys to Prussia were a waste of time. That October, though, after the knights in Livonia signed a truce with Gediminas, warfare ceased from Memel to Narva. Delegates from Riga, accompanied by suspicious Teutonic Knights, went to Gediminas's court and marvelled. They later reported that the supreme duke was surrounded by courtiers from Lithuania and Rus', that he allowed freedom of religion, and that he permitted a small group of Franciscans to conduct the Roman mass for foreign Christians; there was freedom to talk and no danger to the lives of Christian residents. The visitors listened to Lithuanian complaints against the Teutonic Order, complaints that angered the crusaders as much as they pleased their Rigan companions. They then signed another truce, one which included the grandmaster in Prussia.

Werner of Orseln ignored this interference in his business because he had already prepared a great expedition for that winter. However, when the crusaders from Bohemia and the Rhineland arrived, the cold was so severe that the grandmaster cancelled the raid, fearing that the knights were not properly clothed to avoid frostbite or freezing. Indeed, fruit trees were killed, and the salt sea between Denmark and Lübeck froze so solidly that horsemen could ride upon it.

This weather was, nevertheless, perfect for raiders. Because Rus' was not included in the truce, David of Grodno could legally strike from Pskov into Danish Estonia. The desecration of Roman Catholic churches left it unclear whether the army was made up of Orthodox citizens of Pskov or the duke's Lithuanian mercenaries. But clearly the border defences could not stop attacks from Pskov, and protests to Novgorod, the great mercantile city that protected Pskov, were ineffective.

Thus, the gigantic chasm of religion was still swallowing many who attempted to make the leap from one civilisation to the other. And neither pagans nor Christians could imagine anything like modern secular toleration. Western Christians insisted on permission to preach the gospel and make individual converts. Eastern Christians and pagans saw that as leading to religious totalitarianism – they preferred to retain group identities, with each minority led by its own religious leaders. Conversions reflected a community choice, a process led by political and religious figures. These were not principles that could be compromised.

Under new leadership the two old enemies prepared to face each other. Each was confident of victory.

Chapter Four

Lithuanian Naval Warfare

Medieval Lithuania was inhabited by people of Baltic origin we can divide into Lowland and Highland Lithuanians. One of the first to describe this land of forest, swamp and marsh was Bartholomew the Englishman, author of an encyclopaedia *De proprietatibus rerum* ('On the Properties of Things', *c.* 1240). As early as the late fourteenth century his work was available in English, here in John Trevisa's translation:

> Lectonia is a prouince of Scithia. The men thereof be called Lectini, and be men of comely stature, strong warriours and fierce. The soile of the country of Lectonia beareth wel corne and fruit, and is full of moores and marreis in diuerse places, with many woods and riuers, waters, and beasts wilde and tame, and is strengthened with woodes, moores, and marreis, and hath little other strength but woods, moores, and marreis. Therefore vnneth that land may be assailed in summer, but in winter when waters and riuers be froze.

Later historians wrote the phrase 'woods, moores, and marreis [marshes]' often enough to prove that the image stuck. The Lithuanian Herodotus, Simonas Daukantas (1793–1864), the first author to write a history of Lithuania in Lithuanian, was also a poet of the virgin forest. He said that the woods were a very special ecological niche, offering shelter, food and security to sturdy forest dwellers, but it was difficult to reach Novgorod in the north-east, and to penetrate deep into Polish and Ruthenian lands in the west and south-west by foot alone. For trade or war, they had to use the waterways. That is why historians Henryk Paszkiewicz and Edvardus Gudavičius were fond of calling medieval Lithuanians 'landbound Vikings'. However strongly these woodland roamers were initially tied to roads and paths, great changes were already under way that would require them to use boats. As Eric Christiansen noted, for centuries the peoples along the shores of the Baltic Sea made few attempts to conquer their neighbours until the late twelfth century, when the spirit of crusading augmented the desire for profit. After Hanseatic merchants and their military supporters had elbowed aside the less enterprising merchants of Gotland, they established themselves in the lower Daugava River region, with Bishop Albert of Buxhoeveden founding his see at Riga in 1201. Within a few decades the combination of Christian missionaries, conquest, and taxation would change the geopolitical landscape beyond recognition, with a colonial patchwork of Western-style lordships covering Livonia, a state which lasted into the early modern period.

Almost concurrently, to the south there was a stand-off between Prussians and Poles until the Polish dukes asked the Teutonic Knights for help in the early 1230s. This started that military order's conquest of Prussia, which ended in 1283, extending their dominion from the Vistula in the west to the Nemunas in the north-east. Then they embarked on the conquest or Christianisation of Lithuania.

As the Order's chronicler Peter of Dusburg wrote,

Fifty-three years had flowed since the war was begun against the Prussian nation, and all nations in the said land had been beaten and exterminated so that not one survived which did not humbly bend the neck to the holy Roman Church, the aforesaid brethren of the German House initiated the war against that mighty people, most hard of neck and well-versed in war, which is neighbour to the land of Prussia dwelling beyond the Nemunas river in the land of Lithuania.

Five decades later, the successes enjoyed in Prussia had not repeated themselves. Why? This is a big question that may be answered by a 'big answer' – in contrast to Prussia, with its feuding pagan tribes falling one by one to a unified Christian military order, by the middle of the thirteenth century Lithuanians had formed a state that could put up a prolonged resistance. This truism is plain but rather unhelpful. There are many examples in history of powerful states collapsing in the face of onslaughts, and it simply tells us too little about the actual events on the ground that decide victory and defeat.

One general observation must be kept in mind in studying the numerous campaigns, raids, battles, sieges, ambushes – the whole plethora of active violence in these wars – is that Lithuania was a society organised for war. That permitted its people to survive the most adverse conditions, even attacks from all sides by foes more numerous and armed with the latest in military technology. In short, for Lithuania peace was the exception, war was the rule. If we keep this in mind, we will not be surprised by the frequency and violence of the military activities conducted on and along the Nemunas.

Nowadays it is hard to imagine that this calm river was once the scene of heavy fighting. As the longest and largest river flowing across

Lithuania, its overall length extending 937 km. (almost 600 miles), the communities living on its banks or close to it had been involved in the slave trade at least from the late Roman period, and there was always an interest in amber. There are some archaeological traces of Scandinavian presence dating from the tenth or eleventh centuries, but they are too scanty to suggest that Viking adventurers had ever carved out a substantial dominion there. In its middle course the Nemunas posed major navigation difficulties, a problem that persisted well into the early modern period. Even if travellers sailing upstream successfully negotiated the boulders in its meandering flow, there were no easy portages to reach tributaries heading down to the Pripet Marshes to reach the Dnieper River and Kyiv. Consequently, the role of the Nemunas in the history of East Central Europe was far more modest than rivers like the Oder, Vistula, Daugava (Western Dvina), Volga, Don, or the Dnieper. Nevertheless, the Nemunas still served as a corridor for some traffic from the Baltic Sea to the interior, and living on its banks was a mixed blessing.

When the Teutonic Knights reached the Nemunas in 1283, this river instantly became a frontier line between them and Lithuania, the river also assuming the role of a mental zone separating 'us' from 'them'. This eventful coexistence persisted right up to the Great War of 1409–11, a conflict that pitted in mortal embrace the Teutonic Order on the one hand and Poland and Lithuania on the other. After the 1410 Battle of Tannenberg, the Teutonic Order was compelled to fall back on a defensive position for good. After the parties concluded the Melno treaty in 1422, the Nemunas reverted to its peaceful role by becoming once again an artery of trade, and the border became one of the most stable in Europe, delineating the eastern frontier of Prussia until 1919, after the First World War.

Campaigning along the Nemunas (1283–1410)

This story of this period of confrontations between the Teutonic Order and Lithuania must be reconstructed through the chronicles produced in Prussia by Peter of Dusburg, Wigand of Marburg, Johann von Posilge, and the author of the *Annalista Thorunensis*. When the coverage of the chronicles becomes meagre and patchy in the late fourteenth and early fifteenth centuries, we must rely on correspondence between the Teutonic Order, the kingdom of Poland, the papacy and other interested powers.

The Nemunas was less convenient for Teutonic Knights than for their Lithuanian adversaries since they had to sail upstream, and their forces included Prussian militia and crusaders from distant lands. The two parties mounted no fewer than 162 military campaigns along the Nemunas in this period, and some were unrecorded. For example, it is known that in the late thirteenth century the commander of Ragnit castle, Ludwig von Libenzele, conducted numerous raids as far upstream as the Nemunas's confluence with its tributary, the Neris, where in the early 1360s a Lithuanian stone castle would be built at Kaunas. The impact of these raids was telling enough to persuade numerous Lowland (Žemaitija) *Witingen* in the region to switch sides in favour of the Teutonic Knights.

A conservative estimate of military campaigns is that the Teutonic Order made 133 raids, and Lithuanians 29. Of course, it must be borne in mind that the Nemunas was a corridor leading to Lithuania's interior, but the reverse led only to the sparsely populated borderlands of Prussia; thus, strategically, control of this corridor was much more important to the Teutonic Order than to its Lithuanian enemies. In addition, the strong castles around Ragnit and smaller motte-and-bailey fortifications along the Nemunas further east (Christmemel, Georgenburg, Bayernburg, Marienburg am Memel, Gotteswerder and others) acted as disincentives for Lithuanian military operations. Even allowing for these two considerations, the difference in the number of raids and campaigns undertaken by Teutonic Knights and Lithuanian warriors is stark, more than four times as many being undertaken by the former, a number explained by the crusaders being more intent on conquering the region than the Lithuanians of the Highlands (Aukštaitija) were on defending it.

One more indication of how important the Nemunas region itself was for the Teutonic Order may be gathered from a comparison of the period of 1305–1409, for which Werner Paravicini counted 299 campaigns undertaken by the two branches of the Teutonic Order in Prussia and Livonia. If we take all the Nemunas raids (133) even from a somewhat longer period (1283–1410), it becomes clear that they constituted almost a third of all Lithuania-bound campaigns carried out by Teutonic Knights and their supporters. Teutonic troops raided Lithuanian lands most actively from the 1280s to the 1320s and in the second half of the fourteenth century, starting in 1360. In the late fourteenth century, there were only a few years when raids did not take place, namely in 1384–7, 1391, 1396, 1398, usually due to the winters being too mild.

The Teutonic Order launched its military campaigns either during winter or in the late summer and early autumn months. A considerably smaller number was carried out in springtime, thaws being extremely inconvenient for raiders. Nevertheless, daredevils existed then as they do now, and ambushes in the least expected circumstances did happen from time to time. Sometimes considerations of a strategic nature played a role, too. A case in point is a Teutonic raid to prevent the construction of Veliuona castle during the Easter holiday in April 1291. Unfortunately, the description of this expedition – like those of many others – does not tell us how the commander of Königsberg, Berthold Brühaven, and his native militia from Samland crossed the Nemunas so early in the spring. Could they have been transferred by boat to somewhere close to Ragnit castle and then marched east on foot or horseback? Or did they cross the river by some other means? A point in posing such a question is a suspicion that not only in summertime, but also under far harsher conditions, mounted troops could cross rivers of Lithuania by swimming or fording them. It happened that sometimes the waters of the Nemunas would run so shallow that one could easily cross it on foot. This was so in the summer of 1336 when the Lithuanians succeeded in preventing Teutonic troops from putting up a castle at Marienburg am Memel on the island of Romainiai, between Veliuona and Pieštvė (today the hillfort of Seredžius). Sometimes the Nemunas was flooding so much that would-be raiders could not cross it at all. This was so when the commander of Insterburg castle (Wystruć, Chernyakhovsk), Wigand von Baldersheim, and his men trekked through the wilderness in late April 1375, only to see the river too high to cross. The depth of winter, of course, offered good chances to cross the Nemunas on the ice. There were exceptions to this general rule exemplified by those Teutonic warriors who fatally broke through thin ice, the danger coming from unseen currents or sudden thaws. Four Knights so perished during the first Teutonic raid against the castle of Bisenė in 1283. On other occasions, the Teutonic troops experienced hardships they compared to those of the Israelites crossing the Red Sea. Peter of Dusburg was fond of telling about how the Nemunas ice rose up and down like a wave without breaking under the weight of troops in full military gear.

When the Nemunas was free from ice, Teutonic commanders had several options to choose among. The main crossing point was at Ragnit. Originally built as an earth-and-timber castle, it was primarily a base for scouting operations to warn against Lithuanian raiders and to guide the Prussian militiamen who made many unsupported raids into the Lowlands; it also served as a port of call for troops from Prussia on their way there. Since overland raiders into the region had to cross many swamps and dense forests – described in a late account as the *Wegeberichte* – using the river allowed for swifter movement. Ship crews would bring raiders to one point and then, after the raid was over, pick them up at another. These ships could also transport every kind of military materiel and victuals. However, shipping on the Nemunas has been explored far less satisfactorily than for the Vistula or the Oder.

There was a whole array of river ship types used on the Vistula, some of which were used on the Nemunas too. For instance, at the turn of the fifteenth century the commanders of Memel (Klaipėda) had at their disposal *Nassuten, Schuten, Deimeschiffe, Prahme, Körbchen, Fähren, Räuber* and others, but the Teutonic chronicles are not as specific as charter evidence about the types of ship used – general indications like *naves* and *schiffe*, are not helpful. The most frequently used river ship, or rather large boat, was *Nassute* – a small flat-bottomed vessel equipped with a square-rigged sail, with a rudder and oars, used mainly to carry personnel, often high-ranking officers, and their belongings. Larger ships were employed when it was necessary to transport building materials, siege engines and increased numbers of troops (mainly, though perhaps not exclusively, foot soldiers). Bigger vessels might have been similar in appearance to the so-called *Wittinen*, known from a somewhat later period than that covered in this book. The largest of them may have been up to 53 m. in length and 5–8 m. in beam (172 × 16–26 ft.); their carrying capacity might amount to 250 tons. They were too big and too cumbersome for use on the Neris, the largest tributary of the Nemunas, where Kaunas was built at its mouth. Even on the Nemunas somewhat smaller types of transport ships must have been used in the thirteenth and fourteenth centuries, as in April 1313, when Grandmaster Karl of Trier pulled together a fleet (*multitudo navium*) to construct the castle of Christmemel on the right bank of the Nemunas. There were enough ships to form a pontoon bridge across the river. The same year saw one more Teutonic fleet on the Nemunas, that belonging to the commander of Ragnit, Werner von Orseln, who had ordered the construction of a large warship equipped with protective bulwarks and destined to spearhead the expedition to capture the castle of Veliuona. The monster ship (an adaptation of a seagoing cog?) was difficult to handle, and it was nearly lost when a strong wind pushed it so close to the bank that its crew found themselves within range of the garrison's archers. This time the crew somehow managed to escape. The very appearance of the ship caused grave concern 'to the king of Lithuania and all of Lithuania along with him'. Consequently, he sent some 100 Lithuanian boats (each carrying six warriors) to deal with this vessel. This was an epic battle. It showed the Lithuanian riverine fleet at its strongest – 100 boats. When did it come into being?

An attempt to answer this question is predicated on the belief that a group of ships or boats does not necessarily amount to a fleet. An organisation for the maintenance and operation of vessels is indispensable for a fleet however primitive it might appear in comparison to some ancient or modern navies. There was a slightly earlier time in Lithuania when there was no organised naval force, as was clear from an exploratory expedition undertaken by the commander of Ragnit, Ernecke, in 1290 – he commanded a ship that sailed unopposed up the Nemunas. When the Lithuanian military learned of this, they had no other means but a ruse to stop and capture his vessel. A Lithuanian warrior named Nodamas, fluent in Polish, donned female garb and sat still on the bank waiting for the Teutonic vessel to pass by. Finally, at the right moment he began crying at the Teutonic vessel imploring them to save a miserable Christian soul from infidel captivity and liberate her from the snares of the devil. Once the crew headed ashore, the man and his comrades sprang into action. The fate of the vessel and its crew was sealed.

The Teutonic warriors, having learnt a lesson the hard way, did not make such blunders ever again. A more robust force was raised for amphibious attack in May 1295, the Teutonic troops going through the forest on horseback to emerge by the Nemunas in the environs of Grodno. There they stepped into boats and sailed downstream. They did not yet know the geography well, so they stumbled on a Lithuanian village unexpectedly. Somewhat later they met Lithuanian boats gathered to prevent their escape, and the first Teutonic–Lithuanian naval battle ensued (*bellum navale*). Although suffering casualties, they managed to break through and sail on to the castle of Veliuona. There the elements of nature seemed to conspire against them, the water becoming so shallow that they could go no farther downstream. In no time they were attacked by more onrushing Lithuanians. The Teutonic warriors who escaped with life and limb learned that rash actions have consequences.

However casual the 1295 naval battle might look, its shows that by then the Lithuanians had an organised force of boats already in place, something that was not true only five years earlier. Such a Lithuanian river fleet was made possible due to the resourcefulness of the grand ducal state. Because of the lack of well-documented evidence, it is hard to pinpoint which of the Lithuanian dukes may take credit for this. In all likelihood, it was great duke Butvydas (sole ruler 1292–5), father of the better-known grand dukes Vytenis (1295–1315) and Gediminas (1316–41). But Vytenis may have had his hand in this development, too, being an active warlord prior to ascending the grand ducal throne. In any case that was a group effort that changed the security situation of the Teutonic Order in the Nemunas region. One more incident of the same year points in the same direction. Just before the day of John the Baptist (June 24), the Lithuanians stealthily descended on the river island in which up till then the garrison of the Ragnit used to keep their horses and cattle. These animals became easy prey to the raiders and the Teutonic Knights never again kept livestock on the island.

The following twenty-five years saw Lithuanian boats being used more frequently than in the middle and second half of the fourteenth century. Lithuanian ships were used sporadically to bring troops down-stream, as likely was the case when Grand Duke Vytenis launched a swift attack on the castle of Christmemel in September 1315. As far as one can judge, the larger Lithuanian vessels could carry up to twenty men each. The Samland *Vogt* hijacked two such vessels in the upper reaches of the Nemunas in 1376, where they should have been at a safe distance from the Knights. This highlights questions about how the Teutonic Order managed to neutralise Lithuanian naval power. Did the Knights pull together larger numbers of boats provided with stronger protective equipment and more numerous crossbows to outshoot their Lithuanian opponents? We are still in the dark as to how this happened. From events on the ground, it becomes clear that after approximately two decades of sustaining their river fleet, the Lithuanian grand dukes largely abandoned it. This reversal may be dated tentatively to the time of Gediminas. During his reign and later it is difficult to recognise clear-cut instances in which the Lithuanians embarked on amphibious attacks down the Nemunas or sailed to meet Teutonic vessels coming upstream. Sustained casualties and cost-and-benefit calculations may have made a difference in the Lithuanian military mind. You could descend swiftly by boat but retreating upstream while laden with booty was quite another thing. In this case the flow of the Nemunas worked to the disadvantage of the Lithuanians. The war effort, after all, had to pay for itself. On the other hand, it is apparent that bringing military hardware up and down the river was a smaller challenge for the Teutonic Order. The best example may be provided by the epic siege of Kaunas in 1362 when the Teutonic Order launched a professionally executed military campaign. Their vessels, laden with troops and siege equipment, made their way upstream from Ragnit, covering some 130 km. (80 miles) in only three days. Even if some allowance be made for such imponderables as favourable wind and water deep enough to cover the sandbars and rocks, it was undoubtedly a feat in logistics.

Nothing on a similar scale was ever accomplished on the Lithuanian side. By that time the Teutonic dominance on the water was almost as secure as prior to 1295.

The Lithuanians for their part were and remained primarily forest fighters. Yet sporadically they could take themselves to the water. The rivers and streams offered highways that were too enticing to ignore altogether. An instructive case in point is supplied by the chronicler Hermann von Wartberge. In his *Chronicon Livoniae* he tells that in 1373 Lithuanian warriors performed a raid by using boats made of bark. Even though this raid was not a success, this expedition on kayaks may be viewed as a major improvisation meant to outwit the garrisons of Teutonic frontier castles (Daugavpils in this case). One-way travel by boat was safer than putting oneself in harm's way.

Concluding Remarks

The Nemunas was a military frontier zone for the period from 1283 to the battle of Tannenberg in 1410, some 127 years later. After that date no major or prolonged confrontation took place along the banks of the Nemunas. From the late Middle Ages on, the Nemunas represented a mental and geographical boundary militarily separating and sometimes peacefully connecting the Teutonic Order and Lithuania. The river served as a corridor for the parties to reach one another. The length of this corridor, in essence, extended from the mouth of the Nemunas to Kaunas, the space where the confrontation was felt most acutely. After prolonged hostilities the story ended up where it had begun. In contrast, the course of the river between Kaunas and Grodno was very difficult and the lands on both sides of the Nemunas were sparsely populated. Consequently, although the Teutonic Order began to raid this region in the early fourteenth century, it was able to start coming in force only in the 1370s, when the grand dukes had become more interested in expanding their domains to the east and the south and had domestic complications to deal with. This made the castle at Grodno of paramount importance to Lithuanian rulers, but it could not stop the Teutonic Knights from devastating Ruthenian lands via the Narew or from the upper reaches of the Nemunas. This pattern demonstrates that the defence system of the Grand Duchy of Lithuania along the Nemunas was based rather on individual strongpoints controlling some patches of territory, not on a continuous defence line. The attempt on the part of the Lithuanians to keep garrisons on rotation in the border castles along (at least) the Nemunas was a militarily sound idea that proved too difficult to keep going for more than a decade or so in the early fourteenth century. The Nemunas as a given geographical feature created an impression of a boundary. However, it was more like a corridor with many doors behind which any sort of danger could be expected.

Darius Baronas
(Lithuanian Institute of History)

Chapter Five

Poland and Lithuania, 1323–1343

Gediminas and the Papal Legations

As soon as the embassy to Vilnius reported that Gediminas's wishes were not clear, the grandmaster told the pope that the supreme duke had no intention of becoming a Christian, but that the military order would not hinder him if he sincerely wanted to convert. The Order's spokesmen emphasised Gediminas's insulting remarks and his attacks on Christian lands that featured burning, killing and kidnapping, with friars among the victims. It did not help – in February 1324 John XXII ruled that the Teutonic Knights were guilty of hindering Franciscan missionaries, oppressing converts, mishandling clergy, burning churches and ignoring justice. Then he warned that any repetition of these acts would result in excommunication!

Immediately afterwards, the pope wrote to Gediminas that he was ready to welcome him into the true faith, and that he would send legates to negotiate the details of conversion, including the establishment of peaceful relations with neighbouring Christian rulers and the end of the crusade. Implied in the establishment of relations was the recognition of Gediminas as *king*. The mission was led by the bishop of Alet and the abbot of Puy – two Frenchmen, one a Benedictine, the other a prominent Dominican scholar. They were accompanied by Archbishop Friedrich of Riga, who would be alert to any efforts by his enemies to influence them improperly.

The officers of the Teutonic Order took the threat of excommunication seriously. John XXII was ambitious, capable, stubborn and vengeful. The Lithuanian mission was an opportunity for him to raise his name into the ranks of the great popes and to give his office the prestige of leading Christendom to newer and greater achievements.

Ladislas's Conversion Efforts

Under these circumstances, it seemed a good moment for the Teutonic Knights to settle territorial questions with King Ladislas. In an unpublicised meeting in Kujavian Brest the grandmaster's spokesmen offered to pay 10,000 marks for the Polish claims to West Prussia. Ladislas was not in a strong position – his lands having suffered three years of famine, he was undoubtedly in need of money – but he still rejected the offer. Ladislas was developing a policy that later became a national goal: recovery not only of West Prussia, but also of Culm and perhaps the rest of Prussia as well.

The king could count on support from Charles Robert of Hungary, who in 1320 had married Ladislas's younger daughter Elizabeth (1300–81). Once this guaranteed co-operation in Galicia, Ladislas sought a similar alliance with Gediminas. The fifteenth-century chronicler Długosz carefully assessed the king's options – Ladislas could not defend Masovia, and he could not safely invade Lithuania. Therefore, in 1325 he began negotiations for the betrothal of his young son, Casimir (Kazimierz, 1310–70), to Gediminas's youthful daughter, Aldona (1309–39), hoping that this would lead to an alliance and perhaps even to permission to preach the gospel in Lithuania.

Meanwhile, the papal mission failed utterly. When the delegation returned to Riga, it brought along a prominent Lithuanian who denied that Gediminas had written to Avignon in 1323. As a chronicler reported, 'The king had sworn by the power of his gods that he did not wish to assume another practice than that in which his ancestors had died.'

Nevertheless, the Order's opponents did not give up. In April 1325 the archbishop of Riga excommunicated the knights in Livonia, and papal legates threatened an interdiction of church services if the Teutonic Order did not contribute 380 florins to their expenses. However, none of these actions were confirmed by the pope, who thereafter tended to ignore the archbishop's complaints. On the other hand, when John XXII sent a new legate to the east, he issued an order to the grandmaster to pay Peter's Pence – an indication that the land was under papal protection – and he stressed the fact that while the citizens in Culm had never paid the tax, West Prussians had. This seemed to say that if the grandmaster would submit to the extortion, he had little to worry about, but if he refused to pay, then the pope would acknowledge Polish claims to Pomerellia.

The Teutonic Order revived the war against Gediminas without waiting for the truce to expire. Most attacks were from Livonia, while the knights in Prussia set up a line of defence based on new castles in the wilderness and alliances with the dukes of Masovia and the bishop of Płock. Although the new castles – Gerdauen and Barten in 1325, Lauenburg in 1326, and Rastenburg in 1329 – were barely in advance of the old defensive line along the Alle River, they shielded Ermland from the devastating raids.

The value of the Masovian alliances varied over time. To ensure fairness in the division of lands, each of the three Piast dukes held some well-settled lands west of the Vistula and some wilderness territories to the east. Siemowit II (1282–1335) inherited the centre of the extensive duchy, the lands where Warsaw would later be founded, but since he never married, he became less relevant in the inheritance disputes that inevitably arose.

Trojden (1284–1341) was the most active of the brothers. Thanks to his marriage to a daughter of the last prince of the Romanovich dynasty of Galicia–Volhynia, he was able to place one son, Bolesław-Jerzy II (1305/10–40), on the throne there; then he married him to a daughter of Gediminas, who happily took part of Volhynia as his price, and lastly the son won over the nobles and clergy by converting to Orthodoxy. His other sons were Siemowit III (c. 1316–81) and Casimir I (c. 1330–55).

The third Masovian duke was Wenceslaus ('Vanko', 1313–36), the off-spring of their father's second marriage and named for his grandfather, who had been king of Poland at the time. He ruled Płock and Dobrzyń in the north, directly between the grandmaster and the king; he married Danila (Elizabeth, 1302–64), a daughter of Gediminas. His only surviving son was Bolesław III of Płock (1322/30–51).

This made for a complicated picture – at one time Masovian dukes were allies of the Teutonic Knights against the Lithuanians, at another allies of the pagans, but they were always worried about Ladislas, whose open ambition was to re-unite the Polish lands. This made them allies of Louis of Brandenburg (1315–61), who was particularly important because his father was the Holy Roman emperor-elect, Louis IV, and had named him the successor of the last Ascanian margraves; he was now fighting Ladislas for influence in Silesia. When Louis signed an alliance with the Teutonic Knights, he threatened the king on an even wider front, but Ladislas made a powerful response in October 1325. When he brought Gediminas's daughter, Aldona, to Cracow and married her to his son, Casimir part of the treaty was the release of 20,000 enslaved Poles; part was an alliance against the Teutonic Order and Brandenburg.

All high-status marriages were political – as Stephen C. Rowell demonstrated in 'Pious princesses or the daughters of Belial: Pagan Lithuanian dynastic diplomacy 1279–1423', but none more so than this one. Unexpectedly, it resulted in a genuine love match. (This marriage was central to the Polish television drama series of 2018, *Korona królów* – 'The Crown of the Kings' – and her name is today a favourite for Polish and Lithuanian patriots)

How Ladislas became King of Poland

Paul Knoll wrote in *The Rise of the Polish Monarchy* that both centripetal and centrifugal forces existed in the Polish state, and that dynastic hopes were not always the same as national dreams. This was true in every kingdom of the era, of course, but Poles could see once powerful neighbouring states collapsing. This made it even more necessary to support the one man who might hold the kingdom together.

In the spring of 1326 Ladislas took on his German and Masovian opponents, invading Brandenburg accompanied by David of Grodno. A chronicler expressed the crusaders' outrage at the devastation of churches, the desecration of the host, the murder of priests, the burning of convents, and the torture of prisoners of both sexes. He claimed that those scenes horrified even the Poles who had accompanied the pagans and that they killed all the men they encountered, as well as those children too young to make the journey to Lithuania, and the aged, then led away an estimated 6,000 captives.

The Teutonic Knights used these stories – translated into Middle High German by Jeroschin, in his *Kronike von Pruzinlant* – to inflame popular feeling against the pagans and their Polish allies. A rumour circulated that David of Grodno had been murdered by a Polish knight during the retreat to revenge the atrocities. This cannot be verified, but David does disappear from the chronicles. That made many wonder if the Polish alliance with Lithuania had suffered a fatal blow as well.

It had not, of course. The next year Lithuanians crossed Poland and attacked Saxony. This assisted Ladislas's efforts to dominate Silesia and hit at a crusader ally. The next two years saw furious fighting as the Teutonic Knights crossed into Kujavia and Masovia, while the Poles invaded Culm.

Ladislas had hired mercenaries, then persuaded King Charles Robert to send 8,000 Hungarian warriors. Lastly, he had arranged to join forces with Gediminas in Culm. This plan failed when Gediminas withdrew after his scouts were unable to locate the Polish forces. When both sides thought a pitched battle too risky and a stalemate too expensive, they signed a peace agreement and went home, only to resume the conflict later in Silesia.

Conflicts Great and Small

The history of the Holy Roman Empire can be seen as a series of conflicts between emperor and pope for supremacy in general and for control of the German church. The quarrel was marked by harsh words and empty threats, for neither party had the power to harm the other significantly. In 1326, after the pope laid an interdict over Germany, suspending all church services, Grandmaster Werner summoned representatives to a general chapter in Marienburg to discuss the matter. The decision was to support Louis IV – which the chronicler Jeroschin thought was right and just, because he could not understand why the pope would not crown a duly elected emperor.

At that same meeting the delegates made changes to the statutes. The principal innovation was to revise the worship service, but later generations remembered best a subsequent forgery that gave the German master authority to remove an incompetent grandmaster – the Orseln Statutes.

At approximately the same time, Ladislas's supposed vassals in Silesia were declaring themselves independent of Polish sovereignty and acknowledging King John of Bohemia as their rightful ruler. This was to have profound implications for the future.

King John was an inveterate traveller and campaigner who was so active that contemporaries said, 'nothing without King John'. In his early thirties he had left the government of Bohemia to his vassals so that he could concentrate on foreign adventures. One reason was that he could not get along with his Czech nobles, another that he disliked his wife, yet another was his desire for fame. He yearned to lead a crusade to the Holy Land, but since it was impossible to raise a Christian army that could challenge the Turks, he accepted Samogitia as a substitute. In the winter of 1328/29 John went to Prussia, accompanied by the French troubadour Guillaume de Machaut (1300–77), one of the most accomplished poets and musicians of his age, who wrote of John's exploits, praising his patron as having no interest in wealth and the things wealth could buy, but would happily sup on rye bread and soup, so long as he could pursue honour. To support this expedition, Grandmaster Werner reportedly called up 350 Teutonic Knights and 18,000 foot soldiers. (These figures are probably extravagant, although the chroniclers of the Order were usually reliable when their own forces were mentioned.) That made the army so large that the participants expected they could deal the Samogitians a fatal blow. All remembered the exploits of Ottokar II of Bohemia (1233–78), who had overawed resistance in Sambia by the sheer size of his army, and the fact that Königsberg had been named for Ottokar was a goad to John's ambition.

The crusaders marched across frozen swamps and rivers to an inland castle, where they persuaded the garrison to ask for terms. This provoked a dispute among the crusaders. When Werner argued for resettling the garrison in Prussia, he compared the pagans to wolves who would soon take off for the woods and resume their evil ways. The chivalrous king from Bohemia, perhaps influenced by the exiled archbishop of Riga, insisted that the pagans be given a courteous and honourable baptism, after which they be allowed to remain in possession of the castle. Priests had barely baptised 6,000 men, women and children, when news arrived that King Ladislas had invaded Culm on the very day that the crusaders had marched into the wilderness.

The messenger had ridden five days to report that Culm was being burned from end to end, and there were insufficient forces to drive the Poles away. Werner and John abandoned their plans for conquering the rest of Samogitia and returned to Culm, arriving too late. While they watched smoke rise from burned villages, the newly baptised Samogitians rebelled.

John and Werner agreed that it was impossible to invade Samogitia again until the threat to Culm was eliminated. Also, there was the question of honour, which was easily as important as the strategic situation: they had to have revenge for Ladislas's violation of the truce. Considering Wenceslaus of Płock a vile traitor for having joined the invaders, they signed an alliance against him, then crossed into Kujavia and Masovia. John asserted his claims to the Polish throne by right of inheritance and marriage, a fact which became important when John's queen surrendered her hereditary claims to West Prussia to the grandmaster.

By the time a truce ended the fighting, Werner and John had occupied the northern portions of Masovia and Kujavia, and they had ravaged much of the rest – looting and burning one district after another. After Wenceslaus of Płock had surrendered and become John's vassal, the Teutonic Knights occupied Dobrzyń, the province that protected the approach to Culm. A year later John sold the rest of the conquered area to Werner for 168,000 Prague *Groschen*.

Papal Intervention

John XXII had continued his efforts to collect Peter's Pence in Prussia, calling on the archbishops of Mainz, Trier and Cologne to use their influence on the members of the Teutonic Order in Germany and their friends; in addition, he sent a new envoy and repeatedly renewed the interdict. All was in vain until 1330, when he agreed to forgive all past debts if Culm and West Prussia would pay their taxes in the future. The provincial assembly, not the grandmaster, ratified the agreement.

That did not end the matter as far as the pope was concerned. He ordered the grandmaster and his officers to come to Avignon to explain their behaviour, warning that if they failed to do so, their privileges would be suspended, the excommunication would be confirmed, and their trial would be held *in absentia*. They did not attend.

John XXII had even less success in persuading the grandmaster to attack Louis IV and his son, Louis of Brandenburg. His one success was in a legate arranging truces between the Teutonic Order and Poland. What made it work was that both sides needed a pause in hostilities. Additional truces were arranged in 1330, 1332, and 1334, but there was no peace treaty – the parties were so far apart that only the passing of the principal figures could end the crisis. The truces brought a suspension of hostilities, but nothing more.

Meanwhile, in 1330 the war in Livonia had come to an end. The long siege of Riga had resulted in the desperate councilmen asking for terms of surrender, expecting a harsh punishment. To their surprise, they were offered such mild terms that an agreement was easily reached. All that the Livonian master required was that a stretch of the wall be torn down and thrown into the moat. One woman in Riga said that the Livonian master had to be a huge person not to be able to come in a door like other people but needed such a wide opening.

This permitted the knights in Livonia to join in the crusade, striking from castles on the upper Daugava River, and from Semigallia and Kurland. These were as close to the Lithuanian heartland as were the knights in Prussia, and from Dünaburg they could raid regions to the rear of the Lithuanian capital inaccessible from Prussia. Within a short time, they became an important reinforcement to the crusade.

War between the Teutonic Order and King Ladislas

In Ladislas's mind the situation in Masovia was intolerable. Urged on by Wenceslaus of Płock to recapture Dobrzyń, he turned to his allies in Lithuania and Hungary. Gediminas agreed to meet Ladislas's army in September 1330. Ladislas then sought to make good his shortage of experienced knights by sending Prince Casimir to Charles Robert of Hungary, hoping he could exploit his sister's influence – Queen Elizabeth was a religious fanatic who made life difficult for everyone, but Charles Robert hoped to undergird his shaky royal authority with a connection to a potential saint, as his family had done in Naples.

When Casimir arrived with Hungarian reinforcements, the way was open to retake the lost territories in the north. However, he was preceded by stories of a great scandal. The prince had enjoyed the informal but impressive courtly life at the gigantic Visegrád complex overlooking the Danube – an upper castle on the high hill, a lower castle on the river, and an expansive palace. There, with his sister's approval and aid, the blond prince had begun an affair with one of the royal ladies-in-waiting, Clara of Zać. Had Casimir been an eligible bachelor or had the affair been more discreet, the story might have had a romantic ending; or, if Długosz is to be believed, it was a simple rape that Queen Elizabeth had dismissed as a trifling matter. However, the girl thought otherwise. When the Croatian father stormed into the royal family's private outdoor picnic, swinging his sword, he wounded Charles Robert, cut four fingers off the queen's right hand, and was barely stopped from killing the young princes, Andreas and Louis. Royal vengeance was swift: the assailant's body was quartered, and the parts displayed throughout the countryside, his son was dragged to death behind a horse and the corpse given to dogs, Clara was deprived of her nose, cheeks and fingers, and her elder sister and her husband were beheaded; more distant Zać relatives were exiled from the kingdom. Even so, Casimir was urged to leave the country quickly, lest revenge be taken on him.

Werner of Orseln's Assassination

A short time later the grandmaster met his death at the hands of an assassin, in circumstances that provide insights into the process of justice among the Teutonic Knights. The assassin, a knight from Memel, had been reprimanded for threatening the commander with a knife. He had come to Marienburg in hope of obtaining a pardon, but Werner had simply ordered him back to his post. The knight left the audience room disappointed: light punishment was a year of isolation from his fellow knights, wearing dishonourable clothing, and subsisting on bread and water three days of the week; his would have been a heavy punishment, probably including both imprisonment and irons. Lurking in the corridor until Werner was leading the procession out of the church after Vespers, he stepped out and dealt the grandmaster two deadly wounds. Apparently having made no plans for escape, the assassin was promptly captured by a notary.

The four bishops in Prussia made the announcement of the crime, presumably thereby guaranteeing that there was no cover-up of a conspiracy by disgruntled knights. The officers who formed the court ruled that the accused was insane and not responsible for his actions, but they were unsure about the punishment they should inflict. The statutes provided the death penalty only for the crimes of apostasy, cowardice, and sodomy, but not for murder. Murder by a fellow knight had never been considered. Consequently, they wrote to the papacy for guidance. When the answer arrived, they followed the wisdom of the pope: life imprisonment.

Luther of Braunschweig

The next grandmaster, Luther of Braunschweig-Lüneburg (*c.* 1275–1335), was destined for a clerical life to avoid dividing the family property into irrelevance. When his father had left the duchy to two elder brothers, Luther had chosen the austerity of the Teutonic Knights instead of the comparative luxury of life as a bishop,

From his base at Christburg, 1314–31, Luther opened vast areas of swampy and forest land on the frontier to settlement, recruiting knights and peasants from his family lands. He founded the towns of Gilgenburg (Dąbrówno) and Osterode (Ostróda), bringing in Cistercian monks to drain the marshes. He also gave land to Polish-speaking knights from Culm who would bring in farmers and artisans from their own estates. He oversaw the construction of numerous churches in the villages, and he took such a personal interest in the cathedral at Königsberg that was begun about 1330 that it was no surprise that he chose to be buried there rather than in Marienburg.

Luther was also a gifted poet who used his patronage to encourage religious and historical compositions relating to the Teutonic Knights. While most of his own works have been lost, his 'Life of Saint Barbara', has been preserved because of the close connection of this saint with the Order's conquest of Prussia, and because Luther's own grandfather had been on crusade in 1242 when the knights captured the reliquary containing Barbara's head and enshrined it in Culm.

Luther linked poetry with successful wars in Poland and Samogitia. Consequently, a special lustre attached itself to his gracious and noble personality, a lustre that was enhanced by his exalted birth. Four years sufficed to make his memory bright a century later, when grandmasters were neither especially gifted nor much admired.

Determined to press the war against Ladislas, Luther announced that he would suspend military operations in the east until he had struck the king such blows as would eliminate him as a threat. He depended upon John of Bohemia tying down Ladislas in Silesia, where both kings claimed lordship. Knowing this, Luther could send his forces into the neighbouring Polish duchies without worrying that they would encounter the royal army, because Ladislas had to guard against Cracow falling to a quick Czech strike.

To assure success in this operation, Luther hired mercenaries from Germany and Bohemia, accepted the services of rebel Polish nobles, and prepared to conduct warfare on the scale of a great prince. As operations commenced in July 1331, English crusaders hastened to join the expedition. For them one fight was as good as another, and there would be more booty in Poland than in Samogitia.

The order's 500 mercenary knights were not well discipled. Wherever they went, reports of rape accompanied the usual lists of burnings, murders and kidnappings. The worst aspects of the conduct of war in Samogitia combined with mercenary habits in general to wreak havoc throughout northern Masovia and Kujavia. The use of mercenaries disguised as crusaders was a propaganda disaster for the Teutonic Knights and was skilfully exploited by the Poles at later papal hearings.

Of course, Lithuanian pagans fighting for a Roman Catholic king was a scandal, too, and they did more damage to Polish settlements near their camps than they did to Prussia – but the pope paid no attention to the grandmaster's complaints. In any case, Ladislas felt that he had little choice. Without Hungarian and Lithuanian assistance, his forces were overmatched.

Ladislas, now feeling the effects of age and poor health, put Casimir in command. The prince did not offer serious resistance to the Teutonic Knights' rampage across the kingdom's northern domains; in fact, he was almost captured at one point while in command of a small blocking force, but he managed to escape into a dense forest. Still, the 'Cross bearer' forces passed through without achieving much of military significance. The king did not concern himself with the destruction of his subjects' homes, churches and mills, and the mistreatment of commoners. In a war based on plundering, atrocities were common. What was important was that no castles were lost – Casimir had defended them well.

The Battle of Płowce, 1331

Like all his contemporaries, Luther of Braunschweig understood that the destruction of property was the only effective means of warfare against an obstinate enemy who took refuge in strong castles – without food or workers, no castle would hold out long – and so his mercenaries, auxiliaries and knights saw war as a licence to terrorise and impoverish the king's taxpayers. He had not captured cities or castles because, with the Polish army hovering nearby, it was too dangerous to start a siege until he had joined with the Bohemian army.

Luther had sent Dietrich of Altenburg to the proposed rendezvous at Kalisz in September, but the marshal had not been able to locate the Bohemian army. This was not unusual. Communications being poor, one party was often unexpectedly delayed or could not come at all. John, as a matter of fact, had just returned from his expedition to Italy and was unable to reach the rendezvous on time. Dietrich, seeing the Polish army beginning to come together from all directions – a result of a royal amnesty to rebels – and not knowing that John was not far away, began a slow retreat northward, plundering along the way. He thus separated himself ever farther from the Bohemian king, who himself turned about when he heard that the Order's army was retreating.

Dietrich was followed by Ladislas and Casimir with '40,000' men (a conventional number meaning 'a great many'). Ladislas, according to Długosz, was relying on sheer will to overcome his rapidly declining physical powers. Although his levy outnumbered Dietrich's host, he resisted offering battle because his force was less well armed. However, when the marshal divided his fighters into three parties (presumably to make for swifter marching along separate roads), the king swept down on the weakest division. Dietrich was at Płowce, about 65 km. (40 miles) due south of Thorn. There was no chance that he could have pushed on to safety and, in any case, he would have considered that dishonourable.

Despite the disparity of numbers, Dietrich aligned his men under five banners and placed his supposed Polish allies in the rear.

The king likewise formed his army in five units. The battle was cruelly contested, unusually so in an era when major encounters were rare and brief, and, according to the chronicler Długosz, lasted from sunrise until three in the afternoon. When the combat was over, Ladislas had captured fifty-six brothers and held them prisoner in a trench. When the king learned who they were, he seems to have realised that the other two armies were on their way. In any case, he ordered the captive knights stripped and slain.

When the commander of Culm arrived that afternoon and drove the exhausted Polish knights from the field, he captured 600 prisoners. He found Marshal Altenburg chained to a wagon, suffering from a terrible cut on his face that reached right to his mouth. Released, the marshal rode over to the area where the naked, dead knights lay piled high; trembling, he climbed down from his horse, wept, and gave orders to slaughter everyone they had captured. Although he pressed the pursuit hard, Ladislas and Casimir escaped. The king and his son had fought well and bravely, and they understood that it would be foolhardy to continue the fight with broken and exhausted units. Possession of the battlefield was not as important as the victory they had already won.

The king's fatal illness began in March 1332. Soon it was obvious that he would not last long. Seventy-three was old in those days, three years beyond the Biblical three score and ten. He died surrounded by his nobles and clergymen.

Casimir, advised in the matter by Charles Robert of Hungary, opted for a swift coronation. This preempted competing claims on the crown by John of Bohemia and the few surviving Piast dukes, but most of all, it undermined rebel hopes. After the clergy and vassals swore their allegiance, Poland was for the first time in living memory united under strong royal leadership.

Peace Talks at Visegrád

With Ladislas no longer a factor, Casimir was willing to open peace talks, agreeing with the grandmaster to ask Charles Robert of Hungary and John of Bohemia to arbitrate their differences, the former being favourable to Polish interests, the latter to Prussian. It was at a meeting in the late summer of 1335, in the high castle at Trenčín (Trentschin) in Slovakia, that Casimir first displayed those diplomatic talents whereby he later earned the title 'the Great'. It was, according to Paul Knoll, a glittering occasion, with impressive retinues brought by the three kings and the papal nuncio; soon the conference was moved to Visegrád, where there were 350 rooms available. Huge amounts of food were consumed, washed down with 180 barrels of the finest Hungarian wines each day. Lavish presents were exchanged.

There Casimir began to earn the praise of the chronicler Długosz, who wrote that because of his efforts Poland would become a land filled with buildings made of stone and brick. The days of wood and thatch were past.

The three kings – Charles Robert, John, and Casimir – enjoyed one of the most famous conferences of the Middle Ages. The castle complex high on a bluff overlooking the Danube, was considered the finest summer residence in East Central Europe. Magnificent spectacles mixed with hard negotiating over Silesia and offsetting claims on one another's thrones. When a delegation of Teutonic Knights arrived in November, they shifted the focus of their talks to the north. Since Luther of Braunschweig had died in April 1335 on a journey to dedicate the new cathedral in Königsberg, the Order's delegation was sent by his successor, Dietrich of Altenburg.

Neither side gave up much in the negotiations. At first the Teutonic Knights demanded that Casimir renounce his claims to West Prussia, then they made concessions beyond what their instructions permitted.

The mediators were unimaginative, proposing a return to the *status quo ante bellum*. By this formula (plus a gift of 400,000 Prague *Groschen*), King John abandoned his claims to the Polish throne, thus invalidating his grants to the Teutonic Knights; he nevertheless defended the military order's right to the lands for which they had paid him significant amounts of money. Casimir, who wanted peace in the north so that he could concentrate on other frontiers, offered one significant two-edged concession: he offered West Prussia as a gift from the Polish crown, implying that the territory was still his to give away. This was at least a step towards an agreement, though the Order's diplomats were wary of seeming to agree that Poland had ever had sovereignty over the land. The two parties were ready to stop hostilities, but the talks went no further than the grandmaster's offer to return Kujavia and Casimir's promise to obtain his subjects' renunciation of West Prussia. This was an empty gesture because it was unlikely that they would agree.

The young Polish king did not hurry home but accompanied King John to Prague. He was impressed by the magnificent Czech capital and the obvious wealth of its ruler. This visit further cemented the alliance between the two monarchs.

Still, Casimir remained untried, mocked by his enemies as the 'king of Cracow' – an insult that implied the true royal capital was in Silesia, and that he controlled only a distant corner of the kingdom. His father had left him a state close to bankruptcy, exhausted by continual wars, and an economy strangled by his enemies to the north and west – there was little trade directly over the Carpathian Mountains, and to his east Tatars still dominated Galicia. Knowing that he needed allies to drive the Tatars back, he sought peace with the grandmaster, good relations with the Bohemian king, and somehow to placate the Piast dukes in Silesia and Masovia; in addition, he had to deal with Benedict XII, who had denounced the Visegrád agreements – the pope may not have been a powerful figure, but he was still strong enough to cause trouble.

Although crusaders returning from Prussia in March 1337 were entertained by Casimir in Włocławek (giving King John another opportunity to propose an end to the wars), it was not until after 1340, when King John set out on new adventures, that serious peace talks began.

Poland Moves East

The political compromise that had made Bolesław-Jerzy duke of Galicia–Volhynia was crumbling by 1338, when the duke either met Casimir and Charles Robert in Visegrád or sent an ambassador. There was a new

Tatar threat, Khan Uzbeg having recently swept in from the steppe. The frontier was difficult to defend because there was no natural barrier, but also because the local nobles had long survived by bending to the winds of war – loyalty was an ideal, but not always practical. The warriors were often cruel, but they had a reputation for fighting well.

The chronicles of Ruthenia had always praised the glittering helms of its warriors and the courage of its leaders. But continual wars had worn down the farmers and herders, and the proud walls of declining cities were kept in repair only by requiring the lower classes to labour on them. Impalement was a traditional punishment in Wallachia to the south; it was common in Ruthenia, too.

Bolesław-Jerzy was in an impossible situation. After no Rus'ian prince offered to assist him, he had called on Ladislas, but two years after Polish forces had occupied Lviv, the king died. Bolesław-Jerzy changed allegiances repeatedly, even reaching out to the Teutonic Knights for a trade agreement that could help make Lviv a centre of commerce again, with Prussian merchants coming through Masovia and Volhynia to Galicia to obtain products from southern Rus'. But his nobles were unhappy that he had sought Western help. At the same time Roman Catholics were pressuring him to abandon Orthodoxy. Ultimately, he approached the Polish and Hungarian kings, made minor concessions to their Roman Catholic clergy, and hoped for the best. It was insufficient. In April 1340 he was poisoned, and several prominent Roman Catholics slain. Ten days later Casimir led his knights into Galicia.

Although traditional Polish accounts describe this as a victory march, Paul Knoll shows that the reality was more complicated. The speed by which the king moved down the Vistula River, then probably across the high ground between river valleys to Lviv suggests that he had been prepared to move; he was immediately joined there by Charles Robert, who must also have readied his forces for the intervention. They quickly captured the castle dominating the city, looted the royal treasury, then withdrew, leaving such government as existed in the hands of local allies.

A month later Casimir was back with a larger army. Although he claimed to have conquered all the cities of the region, he was hardly there long enough to have done more than reach an agreement with the nobles, who recognised him as their legitimate ruler on the somewhat shaky grounds of inheritance and the more convincing one of being on the spot with a large army. Of the plausible alternatives, only petitioning the Tatar khan to select a ruler had any chance of success, and nobody wanted that. In any case, when Tatars swept into Little Poland, Sandomir, and Galicia at the end of the year, Casimir was able to follow them to Lublin, where he interrupted their siege and routed them.

This left Gediminas as the principal rival, and he was well positioned to hold his recent gains. After studying the situation, Casimir and Charles Robert decided that it was not yet practical to annex Galicia. Instead, they appointed a local noble as governor, and when they discovered that he was not the person they wanted, Casimir petitioned Benedict XII to release him from the oath he had sworn to the nobles; the pope complied in mid-1341.

Paul Knoll calls this a turning point in Polish history – although Casimir did not lead another army into Galicia for another eight years, in the future Poles would look to the east, not the west, to fulfil their national destiny; the reverse was true for Galicia and Volhynia, which henceforth looked to Rome, not to Rus'.

Samogitian Operations

Meanwhile, the war in Samogitia had continued at an intense but unspectacular level. The pagans, facing invasions by the Order's knights in Livonia from Memel, Goldingen, Mitau, Riga and Dünaburg, and the knights from Prussia coming up the Nemunas, seemed close to defeat, but they never gave up. This was a bitter war, with no quarter asked or given.

In February 1336 Louis of Brandenburg brought a large crusading force from his own lands and probably more from his father's Bavarian domains. Other crusaders included counts of Namur, a count of Hennenberg and many Austrian and French knights, all transported on 200 ships to Pilėnai, an earth and wood fort historians cannot identify. They expected their siege would be short and the 4,000 refugees and all the herds and personal possessions inside the fort would soon be theirs. That was not to be.

When the garrison saw that the crusaders were too numerous to be prevented from storming the ramparts, they lit a huge fire and began to throw all their possessions into it. Next, they strangled their wives and children and threw the corpses onto the bonfire. The Christians' reaction to this was at first disbelief. Then, enraged at being robbed of their rightful booty, they recklessly charged the walls, heedless of the need to break greater holes in them first. The Christians prevailed by their superior numbers but not without heavy losses. The pagan chief, a heroic figure named Margiris, smashed many heads before he saw that his own capture was imminent. At the last moment he fled down into a cellar where he had hidden his wife. Swinging his sword, he cut her into pieces and then thrust the weapon into his own belly. The crusaders were only able to take a few prisoners to hold for ransom or make into serfs.

This influx of 'pilgrims' allowed for annual expeditions into Samogitia, but not raids deep into Lithuania. Lightly armed Prussians and Teutonic Knights were equipped for warfare in the forests and could move quickly on the way home, but that was not true of heavily armed Western knights who were accustomed to travelling with a large baggage train. So the strategy changed to capturing the Lithuanian fortresses on the Nemunas or building ones that would serve as bases for year-round attacks. Grandmaster Dietrich began construction of a castle at Georgenburg (Jurbarkas) on an island west of Veliouna, hoping to prepare the way for a greater expedition the next year. Unable to complete it as quickly as hoped, he burned the half-finished fort and retreated. In the winter of 1336/37 King John appeared at the head of crusaders from Bohemia, Silesia, Bavaria, the Palatinate, Thuringia, the Rhineland, Holland, and even Burgundy; prominent among these crusaders was the Bavarian duke, Heinrich XIV of Witttelsbach (1304–39), King John's son-in-law. Assembling in Königsberg, this army joined the knights and their hosts and militias from Nattangia and Sambia, ready to march upstream on the ice. That was impossible, it turned out, because the weather was extraordinarily warm. Instead, boats were used to transport the army. After taking two forts near Veliouna, they built an earth and log castle opposite the ruins of Christmemel and named it Bayernburg (Beierburg) in honour of Duke Heinrich. Bayernburg, with its garrison of 40 knights, 40 archers, 100 infantry and Prussian militia, was to be a base for raids and a waystation for larger expeditions headed for central Lithuania.

Gediminas, believing that this new castle represented a dire threat to his heartland, was pleased to hear from a Samogitian spy that the castle was poorly built and could be taken easily; moreover, he reported that a second spy was ready to open the gates. This spy was detected and hanged, but Gediminas nevertheless besieged Bayernburg in June for twenty-two days, using battering rams and other siege machines. As he retreated with heavy losses, the garrison sallied out to bear off the catapults and mount them on their own walls. Długosz's note that the 'duke of Trakai' was killed by an archer has led historians to wonder if this meant Gediminas, but since the grand duke did not die until December, that might have been an unidentified son.

King John left the 1337 expedition because of an infected eye. This was becoming worse by the time he reached Wrocław (Breslau), so he allowed a doctor to treat him. This did not work out well. Enraged at the doctor's bungling, he had the man drowned in the Oder. In Prague he consulted an Arabian doctor, but without finding a cure. Soon the infection spread to the other eye, making him totally sightless. Blindness, however, did not dampen the king's chivalric ambitions. If anything, his disability enhanced his reputation. Nor did it affect his daily routine. Before he left Königsberg he borrowed 6,000 florins for expenses he would incur in negotiating with Casimir, a task that he worked at through the worst days of his illness.

Casimir was ready for peace. His beloved Lithuanian wife had died in May 1339 after a long illness, leaving him with two young daughters. Although Casimir had enjoyed numerous love affairs, these could not provide him a legitimate heir, and war would distract him from the difficult business of arranging a marriage that would advance his political interests. As it happened, Casimir was extremely unlucky in his quest. He had hoped to marry John's daughter, Margarete, but she died in Prague literally on the eve of the wedding. Casimir then hurried into an unwise alliance with the homely heiress, Adelheid of Hesse (1323–71). Her principal attraction was not her physical beauty, as was indicated within a few days when Casimir claimed that her father had failed to pay the dowry. He then sent her into internal exile, refusing to see her ever again. From that moment on, it was obvious that the king would have no legitimate son.

This led to an ever-closer alliance with Hungary, where Casimir's sister was queen. In 1355 he named her son Louis (Nagy Lajos, 1326–82) his heir, thereby ending uncertainty about the future should the king fall victim to disease, accident or assassination. Such a concern was not irrational – hunting was dangerous, illness was everywhere, and the men and women of this era were passionate, with pride quickly leading to violence, sometimes without consideration of the consequences; they were sensitive of slurs on their honour; cutthroats were cheap; and alcohol flowed freely. Rulers had good reason to surround themselves with impressive bodyguards and to hire a trusted food taster. But what Casimir really wanted was a guarantee of support in his wars with the Teutonic Order and Lithuania. He got that.

When Gediminas passed away in the winter of 1341/42, his lands were divided among seven heirs. This led to speculation that Lithuania would soon fall into civil wars. Since that could do fatal harm to efforts to ward off crusader offensives from Livonia, Prussia and Poland, many believed that the crusade would end soon, in a Roman Catholic victory.

More Papal Investigations

Previous inquiries into the multi-sided disputes of Poland, Bohemia, the Teutonic Order and various dukes, bishops and cities had ended in a stalemate – ecclesiastical sanctions had been imposed both on the grand-master and the king. These had little practical effect, however, because neither ruler permitted normal religious services to be interrupted.

When the papal legates held hearings in Warsaw in 1339, the Order's representatives argued that since Casimir was under excommunication for imprisoning a churchman, he had no legal standing; moreover, Casimir had broken his oath by allying himself with pagans and he had violated the promises he had made at Visegrád. In response the Poles brought forth a host of witnesses, 126 in all, their detailed and shocking complaints registered in the *Lites ac Res gestae inter Polonos Ordineque Cruciferorum*. With the Teutonic Knights refusing to respond to these accusations, lest that seem to confirm the legitimacy of the process, the papal emissaries lost patience with the grandmaster, awarding all the disputed lands to Poland, and ordering the grandmaster to pay the king 194,500 silver marks. Then they asked the grandmaster to pay their expenses of 1,600 marks.

Although Pope Benedict had summoned the grandmaster to Avignon to explain his conduct, he relented when Dietrich wrote that he was needed in the east to meet an imminent Tatar attack – an invasion that threatened recent Polish gains in Galicia–Volhynia. More importantly, the pope could see that the legates' decision would have destroyed the military order, a result he could not approve.

Unsure what to do, the pope urged the Teutonic Order to continue its efforts to protect Christendom and praised its 'defence of the house of Israel, religious enthusiasm, morals, strong enforcement of its rules, and its maintenance of the peace'. Thereafter, it was easy for the pope to make additional concessions. His interest was in reforming clerical orders, not in destroying them. He ordered a new commission to hold hearings and urged the parties to compromise.

Casimir had recently been in Prague, where he had spent the summer of 1341 confirming that he had much in common with John's talented son, Charles of Moravia (1316–78), who at that time was still bearing his grandfather's name, Wenceslaus – he would change his name at his coronation to honour the king of France, Charles IV. Casimir and Charles had next travelled together to Thorn in the hope of bringing about a permanent peace with the Teutonic Order. The initial talks had seemed promising. Then the aged grandmaster suddenly became ill, dying shortly after exchanging a few words with Charles.

Charles would become one of the most important monarchs of the Middle Ages. He was already acknowledged as a brilliant man. Thanks to having lived his early years at the French court, he was fluent in French; and he was a close friend of Pope Clement VI. He learned Latin from his tutors, German and Czech to speak with his nobles and clergymen, and Italian from time spent there to defend dynastic lands. For several years Charles had been governing Bohemia in his father's frequent absences, and he had visited Casimir in Cracow after the death of his Lithuanian wife, persuading the king that his sister Margarete – the recently widowed duchess of Bavaria – would be a suitable spouse. Charles and Casimir had so much in common that it was no surprise that they liked one another.

Nothing was done about a peace treaty with the Teutonic Order because the electoral process for a new grandmaster would take months. Unlike in hereditary monarchies (on those occasions when the crown was passed down peacefully), elections were unpredictable.

Equally unpredictable was the future of Eastern Europe. 1341–2 was filled with deaths of significant rulers – Gediminas of Lithuania, Ivan Kalita of Moscow, Trojden of Masovia, Khan Uzbeg, the Byzantine emperor; and with Altenburg, Ladislas, Archbishop Borisław and Pope Benedict removed from the scene earlier, new leaders could seek an end to the conflict over Pomerellia and Culm that no one could win.

Dietrich of Altenburg's legacy could long be seen in the Order's castles that he had rebuilt of red bricks, so that they were virtually impervious to any but the best conducted siege. His masterpiece was Marienburg, which is sometimes still called the largest castle in the world. He adorned it with the high main tower that provided watchmen a view deep into the flat landscape and over the rivers; he built the church of the Blessed Virgin Mary, with its famous 'Golden Gate' entry, and commissioned her gigantic mosaic figure on the outside wall that can be seen today, restored from the extensive WWII damage; also the chapel of St Anne, where many grandmasters would be buried, and the bridge across the Nogat River. There was a central heating system that modern trials have indicated kept the main rooms comfortable through the cold winters, and a *Dansker* (or toilet tower) that extended 210 feet beyond the walls with a covered arcade for the comfort of the servants who carried the night soil out for disposal in the river. Pluskowski and Turnbull provide detailed descriptions of the high castle, then the middle and lower castles; however, little is known about the adjoining town, which has been destroyed repeatedly over the centuries, other than that it had a broad street leading from the southern gate to the castle which must have made a favourable first impression on visitors. There were also gardens, a fishpond and stables.

The new castle at Danzig – which did not survive into modern times except for a wall along the river and one tower – was also a marvel. Its moat was eighty feet across, and its high walls looming over the town were appropriate for intimidating townsfolk who had never fully accommodated to being ruled by the military order.

Peace between the Order and King Casimir

Relatively little is known about the career of Ludolf König of Wattzau (1280/90–1347/8) before he was elected grandmaster in June 1342. A native of Lower Saxony (a rarity, because knights from the Low German language regions were generally assigned to Livonia), he had served as master of the robes and grand commander. His policy was to seek peace with Poland.

Casimir was ready to negotiate. His close relationship with Hungary had cooled, it seemed, with the death of Charles Robert in 1342. The new Hungarian monarch, Louis, was not anti-Polish, but he had more interest in revenging his brother's murder in Naples – an adventure he could afford thanks to Charles Robert's effective taxation system. Similarly, the once warm relationship with Charles of Moravia cooled. Charles needed money, but he never repaid his debts – everything was being consumed in his father's chivalrous ventures, and King John, though now blind, seemed more intent on grand gestures than ever. Moreover, Charles was taking the side of the pope against emperor-elect Louis IV, positioning himself for the future of German politics. Likewise, Casimir's once-close relationship with Lithuania turned sour after his invasion of Galicia. Even the papacy was less friendly. Benedict XII had lost enthusiasm for breaking the power of the Teutonic Knights, and his successor, Clement VI, was urging a common front against the pagans – while imposing an interdict on Casimir's kingdom (because of royal efforts to control the national church) and raising the see in Prague to an archbishopric, enhancing that prelate's importance.

All this persuaded Casimir that he would be wise to remove at least one of his enemies from the political chessboard. The easiest to persuade would be the grandmaster, whose primary interest was the crusade. International politics, hereditary claims and church affairs were comparatively unimportant for him, while arranging marriages was of no importance at all.

The king and the grandmaster each brought large parties to Kalisz for formal negotiations. The ensuing Peace of 1343 was based on three propositions: first, the dukes of Masovia and Kujavia (possible heirs of the king, should he die without producing a legitimate son) renounced all claims to West Prussia; second, Duke Bogusław of Pomerania promised to see that the peace treaty was upheld no matter who inherited the throne; and third, Casimir obtained from the cities and greater nobles of Poland oaths to maintain the peace and recognise the validity of the treaty. Ludolf König, in his turn, promised to surrender Masovia and Kujavia. Pomp and ceremony, described in detail by Paul Knoll, ended twenty years of war: two pavilions were put up for the rulers, who listened while the agreement was read to the audience, after which they exchanged documents. Casimir swore upon his crown and the grandmaster upon his cross. The two rulers then exchanged a kiss of peace, after which all the dignitaries present swore as well to uphold the peace. Soon Długosz could write, 'The pope finally lifted the interdict he had hung over Prussia.' Then he added a blistering condemnation of the king for selling Poland out so that he could live a life of pleasure.

The Peace of Kalisz ended hostilities between the two greatest Roman Christian powers in the north-east of Europe. Although the peace was not to last for ever, it remained unbroken for seventy-five years. There were no fundamental reasons for the parties to quarrel again, the Teutonic Knights wanted to move against the Lithuanians, while Casimir planned to advance against the Tatars. The lands lying between the two Christian powers, Masovia and Kujavia, remained in the possession of minor Piast princes (Siemowit II and Casimir, Bolesław of Płock, and, after 1343, Siemowit III of Wizna), who were more or less neutral. Not even Casimir's diplomatic stroke in marrying a daughter to Duke Bogusław V of Pomerania (1318–74), the eldest of the three brothers who shared the rule, changed the balance of power; it should have, since the treaty required the duke to support Casimir in any future war against the Teutonic Order, but the Peace of Kalisz negated its purpose.

The grandmaster gave up the effort to bring Ermland under his jurisdiction. He made timely concessions to bring the bishop over to his side, thus removing an important witness for the Polish case at the papal court.

Samogitia Again

The peace treaty signed, the grandmaster renewed the crusade, this time without interference from the Franciscans, because in 1340–1, about the time of Gediminas's death, two friars were martyred in Vilnius. Baronas suggests that they had transgressed the boundaries of respect and restraint the grand duke had imposed on the religious communities, thereby causing him to lose his famously volcanic temper.

From that time until 1387, few friars were in the Lithuanian capital – five more were martyred about 1369, but information is so fragmentary that historians are uncertain about the date (or even the decade) when this occurred. Almost unnoticed, the Teutonic Knights used the presence of the duke of Bavaria on crusade in 1337 to petition for an imperial grant of three small territories west of the Dubysa River. One of these was Raseiniai, which the petition called 'Ruce'. A few historians who read this as 'Rus'' immediately claimed that the Teutonic Knights had a plan to conquer European Russia! Cooler heads decided that it was unlikely that they had petitioned Louis IV for two tiny regions, Karschausen (Karšuva, just east of Ragnit) and the area around Bayernburg (which was to be the administrative seat of the region), and then, by the way, all of Russia.

A New Generation Takes Charge

Popes Clement VI (1342–52), Innocent IV (1352–62), and Urban V (1362–70) abandoned the constitutional arguments over the imperial election to concentrate on combatting nepotism and corruption. They had good intentions, but each learned that it was easier to identify a problem than to correct it.

Charles IV had become king of Bohemia when his father died in 1346 at the battle of Crécy – John the Blind had earned immortal fame for his determination to strike a blow in the French cause even after it was obvious that the battle was lost. Charles had been badly wounded, but survived. John's incredible life story, with this supposedly glorious end, made him a model of chivalry for the era that followed.

Few recognised that Crécy represented the moment when the armoured knight lost his supremacy over foot soldiers. It may have been the cost of German and Flemish mercenary knights that persuaded the English king to recruit commoners skilled at using the longbow, but soon those archers were the masters of the battlefields of the Hundred Years War.

Whenever a pause in the war in France allowed Western knights to resume crusading, they went to Prussia rather than to the minor naval actions in the eastern Mediterranean or the skirmishes in the Balkans. One attraction was to participate in elaborate feasts and hunts while simultaneously fighting the enemies of Christ and doing so at reasonable cost and in relative comfort. While it is an exaggeration to say that Prussia became the showplace of the bored chivalry of Europe, there is some truth to the statement. Certainly, that was the opinion of Jonathan Riley-Smith in *The Crusades, A Short History*:

> Were it not for their brutality and the very real hardships which were a part of them, one is tempted to write of *reysen* as packaged crusading for the European nobility, and their popularity demonstrated how attractive this package could be when wrapped in the trappings of chivalry.

Out of Sight, Out of Mind

Important events were unfolding in Rus', but so slowly that most contemporaries were hardly aware of them. As far as most informed people in Central Europe were concerned, the power struggles there were a jumble of gossip, speculation and solid reporting; many stories were a combination of travellers' tales, mythology and pious wishes. Only historians looking back across the centuries can see past the clutter of local politics to discern the rise of Moscow to dominance. The grand dukes of Moscow represented Tatar authority in the north, but many nobles, burghers and churchmen nevertheless saw in them the best hope for throwing off the Tatar Yoke.

The popes followed these events closely. Although Western churchmen were wont to believe that a mass conversion of pagans, Eastern Christians or Tatars was imminent, those farthest away from Rus', Lithuania and Tatary were the most credulous, while those nearer to those almost mythological lands were more practical-minded and realistic. When Gediminas extended his authority into Rus', it was clear that his chief competitor was the grand duke of Moscow. Not surprisingly, Gediminas employed marriages to arrange a military alliance with Moscow's rival, Tver'. But after Gediminas's death, it was not clear what would happen to his improvised realm.

Chapter Six

Lithuania Expands South and East

The Balts, peoples organised into tribes along the south-eastern and eastern shores of the Baltic Sea, were linguistically different from their Slavic and Finno-Ugrian neighbours. They had once possessed vast lands stretching from the Baltic Sea to as far east as the upper reaches of the Don and Oka Rivers but starting in the sixth century they were pushed north and west by a Slavic expansion that also pressed into modern Poland, the Czech lands and the Balkans. Only in the tenth and eleventh centuries did the Balts stop the Slavic expansion approximately where the current eastern borders of Latvia and Lithuania run and where the southern border of erstwhile East Prussia was. None of this was directed by a powerful leader, so at some places the Slavic push was feeble and at others Baltic resistance was stiff, but there was no coordinated tribal resistance any more than there was a Pan-Slavic will to dominate. Cooperation existed only at local levels where linguistic affinity and common interests were sufficient to persuade the tribes to join in concerted actions – the tribes had nobles, warriors, commoners and slaves, but they mistrusted every potential leader as too ambitious, and hence they limited the power of those they chose to lead their armies.

In addition, each tribe lived in near isolation amid great forests, each near a timber and earth fort where the people could flee when attacked by neighbours who wanted cattle, slaves and military glory – raids were a way for young men to acquire the means and prestige to acquire a farm and wives. Communication with neighbours was limited – the Baltic languages have been mutually unintelligible from an early date, the differences between Latvian and Lithuanian, the only surviving Baltic languages, were less pronounced a thousand years ago than today, but even then, they were much more distinct than modern Polish, Belarusian, Ukrainian and Russian. Thus, despite geographical proximity to each other, the Baltic tribes had no sense of belonging to a 'supranational' entity as the Slavs did. This was a happy arrangement in times of peace, but a disadvantage when making war.

The Balts did not even have a name for themselves other than those of the individual tribes until 1845, when the German philologist Georg

Nesselmann invented theirs. Thus, Latvians and Lithuanians must thank Germans for helping them to recognise in each other cousins, if not brothers and sisters.

If nowadays it is difficult to speak of Germanic or Slavic commonalities in the Early to the Late Middle Ages, it is even more so for the Balts. From at least the tenth century on, the Old Prussians attracted the interest of Polish dukes; whenever possible, the Prussian tribesmen retaliated in kind. Farther west and north, Scandinavians were present – perhaps much like the British experiences with other Vikings, except that they produced no local settlements like the Danelaw in England. The eastern Baltic region was simply too poor to warrant large military expeditions.

A more persistent pressure on the world of the Balts came from Swedish Scandinavians turned Rus in the process of expanding along the 'way from the Varangians to the Greeks' during the ninth to eleventh centuries. This north–south axis in the making of the Kyivan Rus' state captivated the imagination of medieval and modern people alike as it was immortalised on the pages of the *Tale of Bygone Years* (also known as *the Primary Chronicle*). However, as Alexander Nazarenko has demonstrated convincingly, the east–west axis representing a branching out of the Silk Road, with its inception in China and its endpoint at Regensburg in Bavaria, was also an important factor in the rise of Kyiv as a major hub of trade.

The new ruling elite of Scandinavian Rurikids and their followers had started from Novgorod in the late ninth century to embrace Kyiv for good by the mid-tenth century. According to a contemporary authority, the Byzantine Emperor Constantine VII Porphyrogenitus in his *De Administrando Imperio*, they had used the wintertime, when sailing down to Constantinople was impossible, to make their 'rounds' of collecting tribute from the Slavonic regions, then sailed down the Dnieper once the river was free from the ice. Such was the basic nature of the early state of Rus'. It exercised a strong gravitational pull along the rivers that faded away with distance from the well-trodden trade routes. This meant that it was not strong enough to dominate the tribes living on the territories of modern Lithuania, southern and western Latvia (Semigallia and Curonia), much less Old Prussia. Somehow, the Balts living in what could be called Eastern Lithuania managed to put a stop to the expansionist drive of the Rurikid tribute-gatherers, and they were relatively too far away to be controlled easily.

It is one of the many ironies in the history of Lithuania that its very name was first mentioned in connection with Rus'. This occurred in

1009 in an account of the last missionary effort of St Bruno of Querfurt. He was visiting a frontier region between Rus' and Lithuania ('*in confinio Rusciae et Lituae*'). Thus, the fates of Lithuania and Rus' have been intertwined from the very beginning and extend, for better or worse, down to the present day, even to chauvinistic Russian claims to see Ukraine as theirs.

Soon afterwards the principality of Polotsk emerged as a major Rurikid power, its prosperity coming from it straddling the Daugava River trade route to the north-east of Lithuania. The rulers, however, tended to be highly unco-operative with the rest of the Rurikid clan, preferring to focus their attention on local trade and tribute-gathering. The princes of Polotsk even remained relatively passive when German crusaders arrived in the Daugava region and expanded inland, until within three decades they had been pushed back to where, by and large, the Latvian–Belarusian and Latvian–Russian borders are today. Nevertheless, trade continued, only sporadically disturbed by war. Eventually, Polotsk was ruled by the descendants of Prince Vladimir the Great's son Iziaslav (*d.* 1001), which has prompted some historians to consider Polotsk the political unit that led to the emergence of Belarus as an independent state and people.

Farther south, in the tenth and eleventh centuries Rurikid princes strove to entrench themselves, by fits and starts, on the upper reaches of the Nemunas. The strongholds of Grodno and Novgorodok in modern western Belarus marked the westernmost expansion of Kyivan Rus'. No less a prince than Yaroslav the Wise (*r.* 1015–54) launched a military expedition into Lithuania in 1040, but since Ruthenian chronicles do not mention any tribute or conquest, this incursion seems to have had no long-term consequence. The last attempt to collect tribute from Lithuania was undertaken by Mstislav I Vladimirovich of Kyiv in 1132. That campaign was essentially a failure, and the next half a century showed a relative equilibrium between Ruthenians and Lithuanians. Societies on either side of the divide seem to have prospered each according to its relative economic strength and respective standards of what, for them, constituted the 'good life'. In this respect, the case of Novgorodok is especially revealing. Although this town was almost a non-entity in the grander scheme of Rus' politics, its archaeological goods reveal a high degree of prosperity. This can be explained largely by its proximity to the Lithuanian lands, where cross-frontier trade was common. Rough commodities from Lithuanian woodlands were exchanged for luxury goods brought from the interior of Rus' and from as far away as Byzantium.

In the long term the relative prosperity of Rus' lands honed the appetite of more daring elements within the Lithuanian society so that Rus' would become for Lithuanians what England was for the Vikings. In a sense, by creating their polity the Lithuanians were repeating the Viking experience in Rus' of three centuries earlier, even though on a smaller scale and with different outcomes. In contrast to Scandinavian Varangians, a considerable part of the Lithuanian elite did not adopt the culture and language of their Slavonic neighbours. Most importantly, although they did not create a replica of Kyivan Rus' in all its geographical extension and cultural riches, the very existence of the later Grand Duchy of Lithuania made a significant contribution to the emergence of Belarus and Ukraine as polities separate from the 'rude and barbarous kingdom' of Moscow, as sixteenth-century English voyagers called it.

The Ruthenian chronicles tell us that in the second half of the twelfth century Ruthenian princes employed Lithuanian mercenary troops in their civil wars. The first were the princes of Minsk and Polotsk, who must have regretted teaching the pagans how to profit from their military skills – a generation later, about 1183, Lithuanians were launching raids for booty without any consideration for Ruthenian politics. The first known incursion was directed against Pskov, a client of Novgorod, followed quickly by attacks on Rus' in general. The most intensive waves of raids were into northern Rus', where the rich and prosperous republic of Novgorod held sway across vast, nearly empty expanses. It is estimated that Novgorodian lands were visited by Lithuanian warbands more than twelve times between 1183 and 1234. This complicated Novgorod's efforts to stop the advances of the German and Danish crusaders in 1210–24 and again in 1233–34 into Latgale and Estonia. After the death of the last strong duke of Polotsk, Vladimir, in 1216, this principality became, essentially, a playground for the armies of Novgorod, Riga and Lithuania.

As Polotsk faded away as a military power, Lithuanians reached towards principalities further east, Tver' and Smolensk. However, they found it difficult to collect booty from Latvian and Estonian lands, as William Urban explained in 'The Organisation of the Defense of the Livonian Frontier', the crusader states (the Teutonic Knights in Livonia, the Bishop of Riga – Albert Suerbeer became the first archbishop in 1253 – the Bishop of Dorpat, and the Danish governor of Estonia) established a line of castles on the frontier that housed scouts who would look for signs of incursions; warnings would be sent to the inland communities for the women and children to hurry to local forts, while the trained militia units gathered at the border castles ready to pursue the raiders with their slow-moving herds of cattle and lines of prisoners. This was a strategy that only centralised states with taxing powers could carry out. The Samogitians could not emulate it.

It is a bit ironic, that no matter how tense and hostile relations between the German crusader states and the Lithuanian pagans were, there was sometimes tacit co-operation directed against a third party in Rus'. There were also instances of co-operation between German crusaders and Ruthenians – in 1236 when Swordbrothers and their allies from northern Germany and Pskov and Novgorod attacked Lithuania, only to have the hurriedly organised and unruly crusader force destroyed at the battle of Saule. This shattering defeat prompted the pope to integrate the remnants of the Swordbrothers into the Teutonic Order in 1237.

The Lithuanian penetration into Ruthenian lands farther south was made more difficult by the existence of a strong Galicia–Volhynian principality. The first (known) hit-and-run raid into Volhynia was in 1209 by Lithuanians and the neighbouring Yatvingians, after which military threats and tensions must have persisted at least to 1219, a significant year in Lithuanian history because it marked the first international treaty concluded by the Lithuanians – in this case with the ruling family of Galicia–Volhynia. The peace allowed the Lithuanians to send their warbands across the ice of the Baltic to the Estonian island of Saaremaa (Oesel) in the winter of 1219/20 and to make war on Polish dukes who were hostile to the rulers of Galicia–Volhynia. This is a familiar pattern of events. The details of the 1219 treaty also provide clues as to the clan organisation in the Lithuanian lands, from Samogitia in the west to the land of Deltuva in the east. It indicates that Lithuania was headed by five senior dukes and at least twenty-one lesser potentates. They were all warlords in their chiefdoms, and all must have been consulted to achieve a (relatively) binding agreement. Historians tend to call this pre-state political organisation a confederacy of the Lithuanian lands, and all that was missing to call it a state was the lack of an acknowledged ruler. The concentration of power at the local level was accompanied by an outburst of booty raids in all directions. Reflecting on devastations wrought in the land of Novgorod in 1225–6, the chronicler lamented that Rus' was targeted by more troops than ever seen since the very creation of the world. Little could the chronicler imagine that something incomparably larger was in the making in the faraway steppes of Mongolia.

The Mongol invasion of Rus' (1237–40) shook the regional geopolitical edifice to the core and spelled the end of the Kyivan Rus'.

This opened up unexpected possibilities for Lithuanians to carry out raids deep into the south. The change is graphically described by a papal diplomat and Franciscan missionary, John of Plano Carpini, who had travelled via Kyiv en route to Karakoram in distant Mongolia in 1245: 'Nevertheless we always travelled in deadly danger because of the Lithuanians who often carry out secret attacks as far as they are able over Russian territory, especially in the area through which we had to pass, and because most of the Russian men have been killed or captured by the Tatars they can hardly resist them.'

In that same decade Lithuania came to be dominated by one of the five senior dukes named in 1219. By dispatching his relatives to carve out for themselves whatever lands they could conquer in the region of Smolensk, Mindaugas hoped to remove the last obstacle to achieving unchallenged rule over Lithuanian lands. The whole plan misfired badly in early 1249 when, instead of taking out his equally ambitious relatives, Mindaugas saw himself beset on all sides, with some of the Lithuanian and Samogitian nobility rising against him as well. Among his enemies were the Bishop of Riga and the Landmaster of Livonia, and, most importantly, the formidable Daniil Romanovich, duke of Galicia, who came to the aid of Mindaugas's ousted nephew, Tautvilas, who was also his brother-in-law.

In 1250 Tautvilas accepted baptism from the ambitious Bishop of Riga, Nicholas, who hoped to replace the pagan ruler with a Christian one, thereby making himself the foremost political figure in Livonia. However, Mindaugas understood how to exploit the feuding factions among the Christians by persuading Andreas von Felben, the Land-master of Livonia, to collaborate instead of joining his enemies. When the Landmaster made it clear that unless Mindaugas accepted baptism, no co-operation could be forthcoming, a deal was quickly struck: Mindaugas received baptism in the Roman rite in 1251 and in 1253 was crowned King of Lithuania with a papal blessing and with a crown procured by the same Andreas von Felben. The Lithuanian and Teutonic co-operation was mutually beneficial for at least some time. As the civil war died down, so too did the involvement of Galicia–Volhynia. As their reward, the Teutonic Knights were granted the lands of the recalcitrant Samogitians (who in any case would not recognise any outside lord). The crusaders, however, had to conquer these lands on their own which proved a task beyond their capacity. That failure was sealed in the battle of Durbe (13 July 1260) in which the Samogitians defeated the combined forces of the Knights from Prussia and Livonia along with their Swedish allies and conscripted tribesmen.

While the Teutonic Knights were busy with the Samogitians, Mindaugas could focus on the east. When Tautvilas made peace with Mindaugas in 1254, he was installed in Polotsk, where the local dynasty of the Rurikid princes had so low a profile that it is difficult to tell who they were. Farther south Mindaugas annexed Grodno and installed his son Vaišvilkas as duke in Novgorodok. The quasi-hagiographical biography of Vaišvilkas depicts his reign of terror to underline the profound transformation once the bloodthirsty pagan prince accepted the light of the faith by becoming an ardent Orthodox believer. This was the beginning of a pattern that remained in force to the late fourteenth century: the Rurikid princes were replaced by Lithuanians; then these newcomers would become Christians to be more palatable to their new subjects. Most embraced Orthodoxy, but that was not a rule followed without exception. A point in case is Duke Algirdas, who in *c.*1318 married the heiress of Vitebsk, but remained pagan to his death. This probably reflected his ambition to become grand duke of Lithuania, as did happen from 1345 to 1377, because remaining pagan was essential to retaining the loyalty of the pagan warrior elite. Indeed, not only Algirdas did this, but his beloved son Jogaila remained pagan until baptised in Cracow in 1386, a requirement to his becoming King of Poland, as Ladislas II (better known as Jagiełło).

It is one of the saddest ironies in Lithuanian history that Mindaugas as Christian ruler was not a successful military leader. The Samogitian victories against the Teutonic Knights were suggesting that the pagan gods were more powerful than Christ, and they also weakened his support in eastern Lithuania, which was his power base. Moreover, in 1255, when King Mindaugas and his Ruthenian counterpart, King Daniil of Galicia, reached out jointly to Kyiv, that provoked the Tatars to retaliate. When the steppe horsemen came, they came in force and struck almost without warning. In the winter of 1258/59 the Tatars, led by warlord Burunday, devastated Lithuania so harshly that even the Teutonic Knights in Prussia felt insecure, and the pope could provide no help. This Mongol invasion doomed the king, who could not offset the cumulative effect of pagan military victories by Samogitians and Mongols alike. This made possible the emergence of contenders to royal power, with Treniota, Mindaugas's nephew, becoming the chief challenger. As Treniota and his warriors scored impressive victories and made themselves rich from booty taken in Livonia, Masovia and Prussia, Mindaugas's men wasted their strength and stamina in sieges during faraway expeditions. While they were away in a campaign against Briansk in 1263, Mindaugas and his two sons, one the heir to the throne, were slaughtered by Treniota's henchmen. With the royal family of Lithuania removed, the Roman Christian kingdom of Lithuania died as well. Subsequently, Lithuania fell into turmoil and fratricidal strife.

The state itself had to be reconstituted almost from scratch, the task falling eventually to a formidable pagan warrior named Traidenis who exercised grand-ducal power from 1268 until his death in 1282.

Lithuanian raiders stormed into Livonia in the north, into Galicia–Volhynia in the south, and into Polish lands as well. Traidenis also succeeded in integrating the Ruthenian lands closest to Lithuania: Novgorodok and Grodno. The latter commanded a strategically important position on the right bank of the Nemunas, a superb point of departure for expeditions into Poland and south-east Prussia. It also offered access to the Bug, an important trading route to Volhynia, and via the Vistula to the Polish lands and then to Prussia all the way to the Baltic. An attempt by Traidenis to occupy the town of Drogichin on the Bug in 1274 failed because the dukes of Galicia–Volhynia were still strong enough to dislodge the Lithuanian garrison there. Despite this setback, the direction in which Lithuanian power was projected is clear enough, and although temporarily frustrated, it was never abandoned. The dukes of Galicia–Volhynia had to call on Tatars for help in the winter of 1275/76, and again in the winter of 1277/78. The combined Tatar–Ruthenian efforts resulted in curtailing the Lithuanian expansion south of the Pripet marshes until the first decades of the fourteenth century.

Meanwhile, Lithuanians had found another outlet for their expansionist drive. This was at the headwaters of the Daugava River, where lay the quite prosperous but militarily weak principalities of Polotsk and Vitebsk. Grand duke Vytenis was a true Viking-style warrior who did not shun participating in hand-to-hand combat. However, he was also smart enough to conduct negotiations with the burghers of Riga, who were eager to hire reliable mercenaries against the overbearing Teutonic Knights in Livonia. The Lithuanian alliance was maintained until 1330 when at long last the Teutonic Knights managed to starve the city into surrender – the castle built to guarantee control over the burghers remains in good repair and today serves as the residence of the President of Latvia.

During the long spell of co-operation between the Rigans and Lithuania Vytenis integrated Polotsk into his realm; starting from about 1305, the pagans enjoyed new opportunities for trade with Christians, even penetrating further upstream in the direction of Vitebsk. The new situation is explained by a unique piece of evidence dating from

1286–1307, a document from the Rigan magistrates complaining to the authorities of Vitebsk that the latter failed to maintain conditions conducive to business as usual – some Orthodox monks had interfered with a German merchant attempting to buy slave girls from Lithuanian troops camping just outside the city of Vitebsk; the monks had hurried from their nearby monastery to beat the merchant badly. The duke of Vitebsk threw the merchant into prison, then confiscated his merchandise, thus adding injury to insult. On another occasion, when Rigan merchants on their way to Smolensk were robbed by Lithuanians, the duke of Vitebsk again did nothing about it.

Law and order were restored in *c.*1318 after Algirdas married the heiress of the last Ruthenian duke of Vitebsk. The circumstances of Vitebsk's integration into the Lithuanian realm are unusually well documented in comparison to other Ruthenian principalities that were similarly absorbed – Drutsk, Minsk, Pinsk and others. Judging by analogy, Lithuanian military pressure resulted in the erosion of local power that was eventually supplanted by a duke of Lithuanian origin.

The next ruler was Gediminas (*r.*1316–41), who in contrast to his brother Vytenis was blessed with a numerous progeny. He may be regarded as the true patriarch of the nation – the very name Gediminids became, like the Arpads, Piasts and Rurikids, a symbol of legitimacy. Under his rule the family business of expanding the Lithuanian empire – if we may use such a term – began to gather pace. Gediminas proceeded along the lines established by Vytenis, but he surpassed him in fame and glory. From early in his reign, Gediminas paid close attention to the lands of Galicia–Volhynia, in 1316 sending troops against Brest-Litovsk. When the rulers, dukes Andrei and Lev II (*r.*1309–23), rushed to make a treaty with the Teutonic Knights, Gediminas managed to persuade them to make a marriage alliance, probably with the daughter of Duke Andrei being given to Gediminas's brother Liubartas. By May 1323 both dukes were dead – the circumstances presenting historians with one of the darkest mysteries in the political history of that time. Most likely, but unproven, their demise came in battle with Tatars, whose increased threats to Poland were cited by King Ladislas as being a grave concern even to the pope. On the other hand, this new situation sparked a decades-long rivalry and strife between Poland and Lithuania over the region known also as Red Ruthenia. Meanwhile, other neighbouring powers, notably the kingdom of Hungary and the Golden Horde, involved themselves in this war, too. Hungary alternately favoured Polish claims and put forward its own, while the Tatars tended to support Lithuania, presumably in hope of containing the advances of both Poland and Hungary to the east.

A compromise was found when the throne of Galicia and Volhynia was offered to the Masovian duke Bolesław, who had in his veins Polish, Ruthenian and Lithuanian blood. Furthermore, Bolesław ingratiated himself with his new subjects by converting from Latin to Greek Christianity, thus becoming known to posterity as Bolesław-Jerzy (Yury II, r. 1324–40). For a while this compromise solution brought together Lithuanian and Polish rulers in an alliance against the Teutonic Knights. This was followed in 1325 by an agreement aimed at the Teutonic Knights' supporters, most especially John of Luxembourg, king of Bohemia, and Louis IV the Bavarian, Holy Roman emperor-elect. The next year saw a Lithuanian army of 1,200 men headed by a special friend of Gediminas, David, the captain of Grodno castle, wreak havoc across Brandenburg, doing their best to reciprocate what the Teutonic Knights were doing in Lithuania year in, year out. Since this was the first pagan incursion in two centuries, since the westernmost native Slavs had been finally subdued and subjected, painful memories lingered among the Germans in the Brandenburg march for decades to come.

This daring expedition could be mounted only with the co-operation of the Polish king, but it helped that Pope John XXII forced the Teutonic Knights to abide by the armistice with pagan Lithuanians in 1324–8 – thanks to Gediminas having disseminated far and wide the idea that he would accept the Christian faith. To this effect he wrote a series of famous letters in 1322–3 denouncing the Teutonic Knights and inviting prospective settlers to Lithuania by promising them the most favourable conditions. This had resuscitated high hopes in the Roman curia in Avignon regarding not only the possible conversion of numerous pagans, but of Ruthenian Orthodox believers in his realm. When Gediminas balked at accepting baptism himself, he did his best to convince the envoys of the papal legates that only the intrigues of the Teutonic Knights stood in his way. This worked. Thus, enjoying respite on the western front, Gediminas was able to move in the direction of Kyiv.

Alas, the Lithuanian drive eastward is shrouded in mystery even more opaque than that covering the first Lithuanian moves into Volhynia and Galicia. We know that when the papal envoys were in Vilnius in November 1324, envoys of the Golden Horde were also present. Although Gediminas made sure that the Western diplomats did not meet their Eastern counterparts, somehow they got wind that something was taking place parallel to their efforts to persuade Gediminas to convert to Roman Catholicism. Even if they failed to convince the pagan ruler of the benefits in store for him as a neophyte ruler, they registered the otherwise unknown case of Tatars taking pain to dispatch their embassy to a region that was peripheral to the world they lived in, at a time when relations with Persia were very tense. It was also a time when Lithuania was annexing the central lands of what is now Belarus (Minsk was within the confines of Lithuania by 1326) and projecting its power beyond the vast Pripet Marshes. A troublemaker like this could no longer be ignored. Nor could it be dealt with by military pressure alone. Previous attempts by the Tatar scourge to punish Lithuanians were not yielding the desired results after the second half of the thirteenth century. A Burunday-style expedition as of 1258–9 being no longer feasible, a balance of relative power of Lithuanian and Tatar interest had to be negotiated. After sabre rattling and some actual fighting, in 1331 a certain Theodor was acting as duke in Kyiv in unison with the Tatar *basqaq*. The Theodore in question was, in all probability, one of the brothers of Gediminas, known only by his Orthodox Christian name. Lithuanian outreach into the lands of present-day Ukraine, then subject to the Golden Horde, did not result in their liberation from the 'Tatar Yoke'. The Tatar–Lithuanian compromise was a solution beneficial to both parties, its main characteristic being that both Tatars and Lithuanians would enjoy a share in the goods extracted from the territory.

The Lithuanian expansion to the north-east along the Daugava did not stop with the acquisition of Vitebsk in 1318–20, but continued up the Daugava to its headwaters at Toropets, a dependency of Smolensk. When Gediminas annexed this about 1320, he opened the way to the headwaters of the Volga. By 1335 he had taken two small strongholds there, Osechen and Riasna. His activity was also felt in the region where Pskov, Novgorod, Tver', Smolensk and Moscow had vested interests. His control over the headwaters of the Daugava, Volga and Lovat' gave him leverage over the flow of trade and other economic activities in the cold lands of north-western Rus'. In 1322 Pskov would invite David of Grodno to serve as a mercenary captain against the threat of the Livonian Knights and the claims of superiority from Novgorod the Great. In 1333–5 Novgorod would follow Pskov's example by inviting Narimantas, another son of Gediminas, to push back Swedish and Muscovite intrusions on its zone of interest. In 1320 Gediminas gave his daughter, Maria, in marriage to Dmitry Mikhailovich, prince of Tver', thereby initiating the first of many matrimonial and politico-military alliances between the ruling families of Lithuania and Tver'. In 1339 Duke Ivan

Aleksandrovich of Smolensk (1313–59) acknowledged Gediminas as his 'elder brother', guaranteeing undisturbed trade relations with Riga and making the Lithuanian ruler an ally in his confrontations with Briansk. These instances show that Lithuanian expansion was far from being a conquest *tout court*. Although the use of military power was always an option, it was used sparingly, one of many weapons in the grand duke's political arsenal. Common interests against common enemies was the usual motivation, along with trade incentives, matrimonial liaisons and desires to expand the circle of friends and allies. Territorial expansion was accomplished by peaceful penetration rather than conquest. Where territorial gains were possible without too much cost and strain, force might be applied, but where that was not feasible, as in Pskov and Novgorod, other solutions would be found. The territorial expansion of Lithuania was to be achieved at minimal cost – and perhaps only after consultation with other important groups in Lithuanian society. This is especially evident, for example, in those frontier regions in which neither Lithuania, nor Novgorod were strong enough to elbow each other out. In such cases the powers would settle down to a regime of condominium, akin to that of Tatar–Lithuanian relations further south.

Before his death Gediminas divided his realm among his sons. The grand ducal throne in Vilnius went to Jaunutis (*r.* 1341–5), who was known as 'Youngish'. Unsurprisingly, Kęstutis (Kiejstut) of Trakai and Algirdas of Vitebsk soon dethroned him, the latter assuming leadership but working closely with Kęstutis.

The first years of Algirdas's rule (*r.* 1345–77) saw activity in every direction: Prussia, Livonia, north-eastern and south-western Rus, and Poland. Like their father, Kęstutis and, especially, Algirdas were blessed with numerous sons and daughters, all of whom had either to be provided with decent livelihoods or allied in marriage to foreign houses. Satisfying these needs was one of the driving forces for expanding the family enterprise called the Grand Duchy of Lithuania. It was an arduous task, especially after the Teutonic Knights inflicted a heavy defeat on the Lithuanian army at the Strėva River on 2 February 1348. This slackened the Lithuanian grip on the lands of south-western Rus', a situation that was soon exploited by Casimir III the Great of Poland.

It was probably because of this looming danger and uncertainty that Algirdas dispatched his brother Karijotas as envoy to Janibeg, Khan of the Golden Horde (*r.* 1342–57). All calculations as to the possible Lithuanian–Tatar collaboration to contain the Polish push to the east were turned upside down once Duke Simon of Moscow (Semën the Proud, *r.* 1341–53) complained to the khan that Algirdas was going to devastate Moscow. This convinced the khan to extradite the Lithuanian embassy to Moscow and hold Karijotas and his entourage as hostages.

Algirdas meanwhile was facing another problem in Galicia, where in 1349 Polish forces had taken Lviv, positioning themselves to advance on Volhynia. The claims of the Lithuanian side were most vigorously defended by Liubartas until 1357, when Galicia was recognised as Polish, and Volhynia as Lithuanian. In 1366–70, however, Casimir III was able to exploit disagreements between Kęstutis and the sons of Karijotas to annex most of Volhynia. Upon the king's death in 1370, two Lithuanian dukes, Kęstutis and Liubartas, recovered Volhynia for Lithuania for good.

The Karijotas brothers (Yury, Aleksandr, Boris, Constantine, Fëdor and Vasily) were more successful in establishing an independent realm in Podolia, a process in which they were helped by closely co-operating with Polish and Hungarian rulers. Hovering between the greater regional powers – Hungary, Poland, and Lithuania – they promoted internal colonisation and even contemplated, in the late 1370s, resuming the fight against the Tatars of the Golden Horde, the fight that had first opened for them the possibility of setting foot in this region.

Whenever the Lithuanian dukes did not have to fight in Volhynia, they turned to the north-east: the endpoint of Lithuania's expansion there proved to be Rzhev – a strategic location on the Volga that remained under Lithuanian rule from 1355/60–81 – until a dynastic squabble provided the Muscovites with the chance to reclaim it. After the duke of Smolensk, Sviatoslav Ivanovich (r. 1358–86), attempted to recover the recently lost stronghold of Belaia, Algirdas reacted by annexing Mstislavl' to his holdings in 1359 and by 1367 had enveloped the principality of Smolensk on three sides. As early as 1356 Algirdas instigated the revolt of a pro-Lithuanian party in Briansk and occupied the town. The swift expansion of their realm in the second half of the 1350s was so dizzying that in 1358 the Lithuanian dukes let the Western audience, eager to see them converted to Roman Christianity, know that they would like to see all of Rus' dependent on Lithuania ('*omnis Russia ad Letwinos deberet simpliciter pertinere*'). Even if the meaning of what 'All Rus'' signified back then is not clear-cut, this expression is a most straightforward declaration of empire-building intentions on the part of the Lithuanians, a project which has recently been made into an epic story by Zenonas Norkus, *An Unproclaimed Empire*.

Once a 'Time of Troubles' began for the Golden Horde after Khan Berdibeg was murdered in 1359, Algirdas saw an opportunity to move into the steppe world. This led to what historians in the East and West like to see as a watershed event in the 1362 battle of the Blue Waters, where it was long believed that a Lithuanian army inflicted a crushing defeat on Tatar forces, ending the era of condominium and thus contributing to liberating the lands of today's Ukraine from the Tatar Yoke. However, this historical mythmaking comes primarily from the wishful thinking of sixteenth-century Lithuanian chronicles. Contemporary sources, notably the *Rogozhskii chronicle*, tell only of the devastation caused by Lithuanian troops in the region of the Blue Waters River. Devastation is a far cry from a pitched battle of epic proportions. In any case, that meant nothing more than a slight modification of the status of Kyiv, where Lithuania became more assertive in 1365–70, when Vladimir, son of Algirdas, became duke – this time without the attendance of the Tatar *basqaq*. It seems that this 'silent conquest' must have been brokered with the Tatars, who continued to receive tribute from much of the Ukrainian lands as before.

These observations are indebted to Olena Rusina, who has argued quite convincingly that in general terms the Tatar–Lithuanian relations were far from always being confrontational and tended to be built on agreement and consensus. Such a pragmatic approach allowed Algirdas to extend, without much bloodshed, his power over a vast region from Chernigov, Briansk and Novgorod-Siverskii in the east, and to the eastern approaches of Podolia in the south.

Although a Tatar–Lithuanian accommodation was possible, an almost intractable pattern of hostile relations emerged between Lithuania and Moscow. This began in the time of Gediminas, where his intrusion into the lands of Novgorod caused concern for Duke Ivan Kalita of Moscow (*r.* 1325–40). Initial talks resulted in the marriage concluded between Kalita's son Simon and Aigustė, Gediminas's daughter, but the marriage did not prevent clashes between Lithuanian and Muscovite troops over Osechen and Riasna in 1335. Simon denounced his brother-in-law to Khan Janibeg, but he was open to talks and negotiations. This was instrumental in giving the Tver' princess Uliana in marriage to Algirdas in 1349.

As Moscow became more assertive towards the other principalities of north-eastern Rus', the more confrontational its relations with Lithuania became. Moscow had a major advantage over other principalities in the region because the khans of the Golden Horde had entrusted its rulers with tribute-gathering and thus had an interest in protecting them. The first cases of overt defiance to Tatar rule came only in the late 1370s, after Moscow had grown in strength and the Tatars were (almost) irreparably weakened by civil war. Another Muscovite advantage, both symbolic and political, was the fact that since 1326 the metropolitan of Kyiv and All Rus' resided in Moscow. The first instance of active collaboration between ecclesiastical authorities and the grand dukes of Moscow was that of Metropolitan Aleksii (r. 1354–78) and Dmitri Ivanovich (r. 1359–89), when the grand duke sought to supplant the principality of Tver' as the major power in north-eastern Rus', a project that the metropolitan supported.

This led Michael Aleksandrovich of Tver' to turn to his brother-in-law, Algirdas of Lithuania, for support. Out of this came the Lithuanian–Muscovite war of 1368–72. Even though Algirdas and his relatives and allies from among the Ruthenian princes laid siege to the *kremlin* of Moscow twice (in 1368 and 1370), he was unable to achieve a decisive victory. Finally, in 1375 the duke of Tver' acknowledged his subservient position vis-à-vis his Muscovite 'elder brother'. The stand-off between Lithuania and Moscow extended, with some fluctuations, until the peace treaty of 1449 when the Grand Duchy of Lithuania disowned its dreams of expanding into all of Rus'. Since the late fifteenth century Lithuania has found itself on the defensive against Moscow – in a sense, a stand-off that continues today.

The eastern expansion of Lithuania into the lands of Rus' was a phenomenal development of the fourteenth century. In a little more than a hundred years the territory of Lithuania increased tenfold: from around 70,000 to 700,000 square kilometres. This took place at the time of almost continual aggression from the Teutonic Order, so that the grand-ducal domain of ethnic Lithuanians remained circumscribed by the Neris, Nemunas and Merkys Rivers and was centred on Vilnius and Trakai. This central core of the Grand Duchy of Lithuania had a plethora of Rus'ian principalities attached to it, including today's Belarus, some of north-western Russia and a major part of today's Ukraine.

The vigorous dynasty of the Gediminids possessed a military machine accustomed to continuous warfare. The Lithuanian boyars (as the leading nobles were called) earned most of their income from military expeditions and from shares of tribute and tolls. However, such vast expanses could hardly have been governed had it not been for political fragmentation of the Ruthenian principalities and the decline of the power of the Golden Horde. By finding accommodations with the Ruthenians and Tatars, the Lithuanian dukes and their followers were able to insinuate themselves into positions of power and maintain their presence in lands that otherwise would have been too difficult to control by any of the harsh political methods then used by centralised governments.

A change in this general pattern came into evidence only when Lithuania became a Roman Christian country in 1387. After Jogaila left for Poland to rule there as king Ladislas II, he recognised his cousin Vytautas, son of Duke Kęstutis, as the *de facto* grand duke of Lithuania (*r.* 1392–1430). Vytautas was given free rein to re-establish and increase the grand-ducal power without, however, trying to challenge Jagiełło's title to the (nominally) supreme power over Lithuania. His first move was to remove the Orthodox sons of Algirdas from their thrones in Ruthenian principalities by replacing them with vicegerents stemming from the Lithuanian nobility. Having consolidated his power at home, Vytautas launched two military campaigns against the Tatars in the steppes north of the Black Sea in 1397 and 1398. After they ended in success, Lithuanian troops could rest on the littoral of the Black Sea in relative safety for the first time ever. Vytautas wanted to consolidate his gains there by erecting a castle of St John on the estuary of the Dnieper. The name of the castle and the support of the Teutonic Knights in the expedition of 1398 bear testimony to the fact that newly Christian Lithuanians were beginning to learn the usefulness of crusading ideology. Something very close to a real crusade was planned by Vytautas for the summer of 1399, when he had the support of the ousted khan Tokhtamysh (Toqtamïsh, *c.* 1342–1406) who was happy to renounce his rights to Lithuanian-held territories of Rus', thus bringing the era of condominium to a close. However, the international host, made up of Lithuanians, Ruthenians, Poles, Teutonic Knights and allied Tatars suffered a devastating defeat. Vytautas survived the carnage of the battle of Vorskla (12 August 1399) and learned the lesson well. Never again did he launch massive expeditions into the steppe against the Tatars – it was much easier and no less effective to play off pretenders against each other. The precarious presence of the Grand Duchy of Lithuania was maintained on the coast of the Black Sea to about 1475 when the Ottoman Turks and their subjects the Crimean Tatars finally pushed Lithuanian authority back north into what are now the central regions of Ukraine.

Vytautas also formally annexed Smolensk. Even though this principality had been within the Lithuanian sphere of interest since the time of Gediminas, it was never formally annexed until 1395. When the usual methods of gradual penetration and incremental influence did not work well, Vytautas captured Smolensk by deception and removed its duke. When Vytautas was weakened in the wake of the battle of Vorskla, the townspeople of Smolensk rose in revolt and recalled the ousted Duke Yury. That did not last – Vytautas retook Smolensk in 1404. But that was the end of the era of expansion – Lithuania's easternmost possession became Viazma, captured in 1403, a town some 200 km. west of Moscow.

Subsequent confrontations with Pskov and Moscow (1406–8) served as adjustments of respective spheres of influence and attempts at stabilising Lithuanian territorial gains, not as preparations of the ground for further expansion. After Smolensk, a demonstration of Lithuanian military power served to make the desired impression. This aspect of triumphal rulership is clearly evident as early as 1411 when, in the wake of the victory at the battle of Tannenberg, both Vytautas and Jagiełło progressed in full display of their power across the most significant Ruthenian towns of the Grand Duchy of Lithuania. Vytautas reached the pinnacle of his prestige and power late in his reign, when in 1425 he enjoyed the rights of guardianship over his grandson, the future grand duke Basil II of Moscow (r. 1425–62). In 1427 Vytautas and his army visited the Ruthenian principalities on the headwaters of the Oka River, where the princes showered him with gifts and gestures of submission. His superiority was even recognised by the distant duchy of Riazan'. In 1428 Vytautas took probably his largest bombard, drawn by teams of dozens of horses, through marshlands where bridges had to be made while on the march, to the town of Porkhov. Several shots were enough to make the Novgorodians rush to Vytautas to throw heaps of silver rubles and bundles of precious furs at his feet. The power of Grand Duke Vytautas to make foreign rulers come to him laden with precious gifts was recognised as the most impressive imperial trait of his rulership, or so said Bishop Gerasim of Smolensk (r. 1428–34), the sponsor of 'Praise of Vytautas'. Finally, by the end of his reign Vytautas could be said to have dominated a territory of close to one million square kilometres. He is the only ruler of Lithuania to have been decorated with the epithet 'Great'.

Lithuania without Ruthenian possessions would hardly have survived the push to the east of the Teutonic Order. Facing that difficult situation on their western doorstep, Lithuania's rulers eagerly plunged into the Ruthenian world in search of resources and power. In this they were highly successful, thanks not so much to the use of naked military force but rather thanks to their pragmatic approach and flexibility in their dealings with the Tatars and Ruthenians. The country expanded into the Orthodox East, but its rulers and native ruling elite threw in their lot with Western Christendom by receiving Roman Christianity in 1386–7. They went east without forgetting their interests to the west, a dramatic balancing of concerns that had effects that have lasted until today.

Darius Baronas
(Lithuanian Institute of History)

Chapter Seven

The Chivalric Crusade

Early Opportunities Wasted

The period later regarded by the Teutonic Order as its finest began in 1343 with three important events. The first was the Peace of Kalisz. The second was the great Estonian Insurrection, when oppressed Estonians massacred every German and Dane within reach. When the Livonian master intervened, using troops from his border castles, that opened the way for the third challenge – attacks from Pskov and Lithuania that threatened the Roman Catholic hold on the region.

Lithuania was no longer ruled by Gediminas. After his death in late 1341, six of his sons and a brother had divided his empire, then quarrelled. Jaunutis (c. 1300–66) took Vilnius and the other sons made alliances with Rus'ian neighbours. In 'Pious Princesses' Stephen C. Rowell tells us that this might have been the first time in Lithuanian history that a queen mother was the actual ruler. Little is known about her except that after her death in 1344, civil war broke out and Jaunutis fled to his brother-in-law in Moscow. There he was baptised into the Orthodox faith with the name of Ivan. In 1347 he made up with his brothers and was given a minor principality near Minsk to rule.

The feud rocked the empire, but the crisis passed when the third and fifth sons of Gediminas seized control. Algirdas took the title of supreme duke and governed Vilnius, Vitebsk and Minsk. He married successively two Rus'ian Orthodox princesses, but he reared his children as sceptics who could play the role of Christian for the benefit of devout subjects; although he constantly dangled the prospect of conversion before the eyes of clergymen in Rus' and the West, he discouraged missionaries from entering his realm. In 1347, when three came anyway, he tortured them to death as a warning to others – the three martyrs were canonised in 1364 through the influence of his wife, Uliana Alexandrovna of Tver' (c. 1325–92), and the Church of the Holy Trinity was built on the site of the martyrdom to hold their relics; the monastery soon became a centre of Orthodoxy in Lithuania. Otherwise, Algirdas scrupulously avoided offending his devout Rus'ian subjects.

Kęstutis (c. 1297–1382, prince of Trakai from c. 1337 on and grand duke of Lithuania in 1381–2) took the lands opposite the Teutonic Knights:

Samogitia, Trakai, Grodno and Brest-Litovsk; his marriage to Birutė, a beautiful Samogitian noblewoman who was rumoured to have been a pagan priestess, may have been important in securing pagan support during the struggle for power.

Algirdas and Kęstutis left their brothers the lesser, outlying territories that needed personal supervision. Although their trust in their brothers' loyalty was often betrayed, they still felt it was safer to endow family members with duchies rather than ambitious clan leaders. In the course of time, as some brothers rebelled and others died, Algirdas and Kęstutis redistributed their lands. They shared power in what was later called a diarchy (one state ruled by two men). Power was divided so that Algirdas looked east and Kęstutis west.

Although crusader attacks were eventually to outnumber those of the pagans, at first pagan attacks predominated. The number of raids by small parties cannot even be estimated, but those were generally confined to the settlements in or near the wilderness; moreover, they were risky affairs – border patrols pursued such bands aggressively.

The Estonian uprising of 1343–6 allowed Algirdas and Kęstutis to go on a rampage through Livonia. As military successes mounted, their authority grew steadily, internally over their *Witingen* and externally over subject peoples. Their neighbours referred to them as kings (though officially Roman Catholics denied them that Christian title) or called Algirdas Supreme Duke and Kęstutis Grand Duke. Rus'ian princes eagerly sought their sisters and daughters as wives; Western merchants requested permission to trade in their lands; and missionaries dreamed of their conversion. In issuing a coinage, Algirdas and Kęstutis were probably as concerned with demonstrating their authority to do so as much as meeting the needs of their people; even so, the Prague *Groschen* was the most popular coin because it could be used easily in international trade. In their Livonian policy, however, they were prisoners of the past – when Livonian rebels asked for their help, they scornfully demanded an unconditional subjection. The now haughty Lithuanian rulers – perhaps drunk on victories, but not on alcohol, since Algirdas drank no beer, wine or mead – saw Livonians only as slaves or a source of rich booty.

Grandmaster Ludolf König organised a great expedition for the winter of 1344/45, intending to smash the Lithuanians once and for all. Since there was a general peace in Eastern Europe at that moment, he was able to recruit as crusaders King John of Bohemia, his son, Charles of Moravia, and King Louis of Hungary, all of whom were eager to win prestige. Louis had prospects of becoming king of Poland, Holy Roman emperor, and king of Naples. To gain attention in Germany he had dedicated a great chapel in Aachen, in the cathedral built by Charles the Great, where every German king must be crowned; but he knew that his military reputation still suffered by comparison with the deeds of his Luxemburg rival. John of Bohemia had a reputation that could hardly be augmented, but that obliged him to perform ever greater and more daring feats lest his blindness encourage anyone to regard him as an antiquated relic. Charles of Moravia, more cautious and farsighted than his father had ever been, was himself not fully immune to the lure of chivalry and the crusading movement. Charles was an unimpressive young man, but he was ambitious to be elected Holy Roman emperor, and his prospects were enhanced considerably by his close personal friendship with the pope. At this point in his career, he was still enthusiastic and an idealist.

In the winter of 1344/45, French, Rhenish and Austrian crusaders gathered at Insterburg, where they were joined by King Louis and Charles of Moravia. Two days into the campaign rain began to fall. Soon the ice became too soft to hold the heavy warhorses. Rather than risk losing knights in freezing waters, the grandmaster ordered a retreat. The crusaders returned to Königsberg, where they waited, playing at dice and feasting, and praying for cold weather. As the days passed, they heard that the pagans had struck into Livonia while the crusading army there was occupied with Estonian rebels on the island of Oesel. In place of their own anticipated victory, they heard of nothing but defeats. The grandmaster eventually dismissed his guests politely, saying that it was too late in the winter to expect a return of weather sufficiently cold for campaigning and that they should use the remaining winter weather to return home before the roads turned to mud. We know much about this abortive campaign because Wilhelm of Holland's accountants left a detailed record, listing his expenses for horses, weapons, clothes, gifts, alms, minstrels, transport and many minor items. Also, the book provided an exact itinerary of his journey to Prussia via Jerusalem, Venice, Vienna and Wrocław. The chivalric nature of his expedition is clear and beyond doubt.

A vow of poverty and strict discipline prevented the knights of the Teutonic Order from making individual displays of chivalric excess, but they did what they could as a corporation to impress their guests – their castles, their feasts, their armour and their warhorses were of the finest quality; and the organisation of their complex army – scouts, infantry, light and heavy cavalry, the supply caravan and, when appropriate, ships, impressed the professionals who judged them.

Purchase of Estonia

In December 1345, with the grandmaster incapacitated by depression, a general chapter at Marienburg elected as his successor Heinrich Dusemer. About sixty-five years of age, born in Franconia, he was the most experienced warrior in Prussia. He had served at Ragnit, then as advocate of Sambia, and most recently as marshal; he had been in Livonia, seeking to ward off the Lithuanian attacks. He was also the foremost critic of Ludolf König's leadership.

Heinrich Dusemer's first coup was not military, as one might expect, but diplomatic. The Danish king, Waldemar IV (1320–75), had wanted to sell Estonia, which had been in turmoil since the peasant uprising. Waldemar could not afford to send an army there or even pay the Teutonic Knights for the assistance already rendered, much less cover future expenses – after his father's military disasters and the death of an older brother in battle against the dukes of Holstein, the kingdom had been mortgaged to German princes. He himself hardly even knew his own land, having grown up with his elder sister, the wife of emperor-elect Louis IV. Therefore, the best he could do for Estonia was to pluck his elder brother Otto out of prison and send him there to see what could be done – which turned out to be nothing. Whether his brother was feeble-minded from birth or the result of his long imprisonment, any kind of useful employment was far beyond Otto's limited abilities.

For all these reasons Waldemar was willing to sell the territory before it was attacked by his Swedish enemies. He had made this offer before, but Ludolf König had believed that the Order's knights in Livonia already had all the advantages of ownership, without any of the disadvantages entailed in its governance. The knights and gentry of Estonia had always assisted in regional defence and often joined in offensive operations, but they were notoriously difficult and independent vassals who would not be easy to rule. Now the situation was different – many of those knights had been slain in the uprising and the Danes could not restore order alone, much less ward off Lithuanian and Rus'ian raiders. Heinrich believed that it would be easier to defend the country if the Livonian master was allowed to rule directly rather than through discredited and almost powerless royal officials. Once the negotiators agreed on a price of 19,000 marks, Heinrich loaned the Livonian master 14,000 marks.

Waldemar sailed from Lübeck to Marienburg in August–September 1346. No chronicler described the ceremony, the presentation of the money from the Marienburg treasury, or the signing of the documents, but there must have been tolling bells and musical fanfares, because that was customary for welcoming crusaders. Then Waldemar's brother Otto was inducted into the Teutonic Order.

Apparently, Waldemar believed that Otto would be less of a threat as a Teutonic Knight than if he sat in prison another fifteen years. Moreover, it appears that the brother lacked any kind of talent – the Teutonic Order never gave him any significant administrative duties, and he eventually just disappeared from official notice.

Although Waldemar and Eric II of Saxe-Lauenburg had announced that they would crusade against the Lithuanians, they instead left for Jerusalem, where Eric II knighted the king as a member of the Order of the Holy Sepulchre. Pope Clement VI was not pleased, because he had not given the king permission to travel to the Holy Land. Waldemar ignored him.

Technically, Estonia remained under the grandmaster, not the Livonian master, but in practice it was easier to make the latter responsible for administration and defence.

Lithuanians on the Offensive

Heinrich Dusemer made only border raids on Samogitia. Since he had sent a significant part of his field army to Livonia and few crusaders were present to replace them, he barely had sufficient knights to garrison his castles and completely lacked the resources necessary for offensive operations. The knights and officers in Prussia were beginning to realise what a drain on their strength their northern possessions could be.

To make matters worse, Kęstutis and Algirdas had caught the fever of victory. Now they hotly pursued fame and booty through even greater exploits in Prussia. Heinrich never knew where those daring brothers would appear next. In early 1346 the dukes struck at Rastenburg, capturing the castle and burning it as they led the villagers away as prisoners. In response, Heinrich built a fortress at Johannisburg and hoped that its garrison could protect the frontier settlements better.

The Lithuanians struck Rus', too. The *Chronicle of Novgorod* reported tersely that Algirdas marched to Novgorod-Severskii (Novhorod-Siversky in Ukraine, not to be confused with the merchant city Novgorod the Great) with all his brothers, complaining that the local prince had called him a dog and that he was taking the province as recompense. When angry citizens murdered the hapless prince and called on Algirdas for peace, Algirdas named a new governor. This was a very confused period, with many decisions being made by the Tatar khan, who collected a heavy annual tax and punished those who were late or could not pay.

It seems that Lithuanian dukes ruled the principalities and often the cities as well for the rest of the century. Sometimes the governors were named by the supreme duke, sometimes exiles opposing his policies, and sometimes nominees from the Tatar khan, but because Algirdas dominated Pskov, Polotsk and Smolensk, and his wife was a princess from Tver', and his brothers ruled important towns in Rus', his ambitions came to the notice of the far-away Tatar khan. The khans' vassals in Rus' obediently protested that they were the proper rulers of that region – they represented the Rurik dynasty and were Rus'ian Orthodox, while the Lithuanians were obviously foreign upstarts. Algirdas attempted to counter this by establishing his own metropolitan in Kyiv.

The grandmaster was undoubtedly aware of these developments. Merchants who traded in Lithuania, Novgorod and Smolensk, or even farther afield, provided information to all sides in this war. And prisoners talked as well. But he probably saw Algirdas's eastward expansion as only a long-term threat. Short-term it meant that the crusaders had fewer Lithuanians to face in the Nemunas River valley.

Kęstutis was another matter – his base was in western Lithuania, and his obvious ambition was to expand his empire. He saw Poland as the weaker enemy and, potentially, the richer one; moreover, crusader attacks were on the periphery of his state, in Samogitia, whereas if Casimir established himself in Galicia and Volhynia, he would in time become a more dangerous enemy.

The grandmaster, anticipating another raid in early 1347, gathered French and English pilgrims and units from distant Culm and West Prussia in Königsberg, but when Kęstutis struck as expected, Heinrich's scouts were unable to locate his invading army. Kęstutis sped from one area to another, surprisingly going ever deeper into Prussia rather than retreating. This misled Heinrich, who had marched his forces to Insterburg in the hope of cutting off the retreat. However, from Rastenburg Kęstutis's forces went into Bartia, briefly besieged Gerdauen (Zheleznodorozhny), then turned south again through Ermland on the way home through the Lake District. The 'damned sons of the devil' wrought such destruction that the grandmaster later reorganised the depopulated Rastenburg district into a minor territory supervised by a lesser official.

Heinrich was sufficiently worried that he had his archivist copy thirteenth-century papal documents declaring the Teutonic Order freed from the tithe and absolving excommunicated warriors who participated in the crusade. He was willing to risk any censure to bring more knights to Prussia.

In the spring Kęstutis attacked Sambia and led away long lines of captives. Later he besieged Ragnit for three days, just long enough to lure the crusaders into believing that he intended to storm the fortress, and then he slipped off to raid Insterburg, after which he boldly advanced to Wehlau (Welawa, Znamensk), not far from Königsberg, capturing the castle and burning it. Not yet satisfied, he went south into the Alle River valley, destroying an entire convent of fourteen knights who came out to resist him, and going on to Gerdauen.

Obviously, the grandmaster's defensive strategy was not working. No sooner would Heinrich hear that Kęstutis was at one place than news would come that he had struck somewhere else. Every plan to anticipate Kęstutis failed. Only a counter-offensive seemed to offer any hope of success.

The Battle on the Strėva

The prospects for an offensive improved in 1347. First Emperor Louis IV died of a stroke while hunting a bear. This resulted in a two-year pause in the conflict between the pope and the imperial forces until the electors reluctantly agreed upon Charles of Bohemia; his coronation as German king in Aachen followed, then tense negotiations with the pope over the imperial crown – it was helpful that the emperor-elect and the pope were friends, but there was much more to the dispute than personalities. Second, a truce between France and England resulted in an extraordinarily large number of crusaders being able come to Prussia. Grandmaster Heinrich again called up units from Culm and West Prussia that were usually too far from Samogitia to be employed. The army that assembled in Marienburg for a January 1348 invasion was so large that contemporaries numbered it with their usual exaggeration at 40,000 men.

At first the weather looked promising, but then a thaw set in. In mid-January there was cold, clear weather that promised easy travel, but when a snowstorm hit, the grandmaster and most of the militia stopped at Insterburg. Only the small armies led by Marshal Siegfried Dahenfeld and Grand Commander Winrich of Kniprode proceeded into central Lithuania. The ferocity of the foreign crusaders was as remarkable as their staying seven days deep in enemy territory. Their boasts of killing everyone they met may have been braggadocio typical of the Hundred Years War, but they may have reasoned that what's good enough for Frenchmen was good enough for pagans.

Indeed, they enjoyed themselves too much, for large numbers of the best warriors that Lithuania could raise were soon in pursuit. Leading the army was Kęstutis (or perhaps Narimantas, the second eldest of the brothers, who had just returned from visiting the Great Khan). Kęstutis had heard of the crusader force gathering at Insterburg and had summoned thousands of men from as far away as Polotsk, Vitebsk and Smolensk; Manvydas, the eldest brother of the dynasty, also brought his men from Kernavė. When Kęstutis learned that the grandmaster had stayed back to guard the frontier, he realised that he was now facing a smaller army than expected. Pursuing the crusaders down the valley, he pinned them against the Strėva (Strebe) River that flows into the Nemunas. There he had them trapped.

The water level is usually not high at this time of year, but the crusader position was still difficult. If the marshal attempted to slip his men across the half-frozen river, he could do so only a few knights at a time. Dahenfeld and Winrich knew that Kęstutis would be watching, and once major units were across, he would annihilate those still waiting. Thus, retreat would be successful only for the leading units – and their Order's prestige would never recover. Waiting seemed impractical – the crusaders had only the supplies they had collected during their incursion. Pitched combat against such heavy odds seemed little better. There was a good chance that Dahenfeld and Winrich could lose their entire force. Still, of the three choices, offering battle seemed the best, or at least the only honourable one.

The Lithuanians were in a similar situation in that they did not even have the grain and cattle stolen from the local population, and they had a larger army to feed. Much as they would have liked to put off battle, they knew that they could not keep a hungry coalition army together for long. Also, the intense cold of January weather was burning off calories, and there was little time to make a secure camp that would provide some shelter.

The marshal and grand commander had many of the same concerns, but with less room to manoeuvre. Therefore, they put their forces into a line of battle and waited for an attack. Experience gathered in the Hundred Years War suggested that there were considerable advantages to standing on the defensive, then counter-attacking once the enemy horsemen had been repulsed – a charge into the backs of retreating cavalry would drive most of them into a wild flight, allowing the victors to destroy units that chose to stand and fight. The problem was how to persuade Kęstutis to attack. Dahenfeld and Winrich certainly worried less about the disparity in numbers than in maintaining battlefield discipline – if some knights became overly enthusiastic, they could charge prematurely, reversing the advantage of a counter-attack and leaving the line in disarray, or, if thinking themselves the victors, they raced ahead until their horses were exhausted, then fell into a trap themselves.

But Kęstutis had his problems, too. He could not wait the invaders out, nor could he expect them to attack – they could stand in their ranks longer than he could contain his multi-national army. In any case, his men were best at the ferocious charge that overwhelmed foes. So Kęstutis ordered his men forward.

While his Rus'ian troops showered the crusader lines with arrows, Kęstutis sent his best horsemen directly against the main body of knights, throwing their spears. They wounded many crusaders and their horses, then forced them back towards the river. Missiles slew the commander of Danzig, the episcopal advocate of Sambia, and about fifty others gathered around the battle flag. As the Lithuanians pressed forward, the lines merged, then disappeared. The combat of the main units became a mêlée. The other Lithuanian and crusader units faced each other, watching warily, and waited. Finally, as this combat reached a critical point, the crusader leaders sent their heavy cavalry forward, drove back the horsemen facing them, and then turned onto Kęstutis's flanks, precipitating a general flight.

It had been a hard-fought battle, with heavy losses on both sides – Prussian chroniclers claimed that the crusaders had slain 10,000–18,000 of their foes and had perhaps only lost sixty men. Those were unlikely figures, but it was clearly a lopsided victory. Still, it had not been easily won. The crusaders were persuaded that they had survived only because of the intervention of the Virgin, whose image had been borne on the main battle flag. Grandmaster Winrich von Kniprode subsequently established a Cistercian monastery in Königsberg and a Franciscan friary in Wehlau to commemorate the battle.

The victors praised God, then proceeded over the ice a few at a time and hurried home. They had won an unexpected victory over the greatest army they had yet faced and had slain two of Kęstutis's brothers, Narimantas and Manvydas. With them died the family's hard-won reputation for invincibility. The dukes had lost many of their best men, and many of the wounded must have perished later. Even the uninjured warriors probably suffered from lack of shelter and food on their way home. Moreover, since the pagans had entered battle only after receiving favourable omens, some must have been discouraged by the inaccuracy of their shamans' forecasts; similarly, Orthodox saints were seen to be ineffective this far from home. The dukes must have been concerned that their prestige would be shaken among Rus'ian subjects who relied on them for protection against enemies more dangerous than the Teutonic Knights.

Kęstutis put up little resistance to subsequent crusader raids into Samogitia, and he was unable to help the garrison at Welun when the crusaders attacked later in the year. When Welun fell, he lost the most important link in his defensive system along the Nemunas River. Although he rebuilt the castle after the crusaders returned to Prussia, Kęstutis was unable to replace the stalwart tribesmen who had defended their homes so desperately. The crusaders baptised the 1,500 prisoners and resettled them in Prussia.

Still, luck had not completely deserted the Lithuanian princes. Grand-master Heinrich Dusemer, having become ill, could not give the strong leadership needed to profit from the victory. In late 1351 he summoned a general chapter to take his resignation, then died somewhat over a year later. The eulogies were favourable but terse. He was a good leader, but he lacked the personality and luck of his successor. The chronicler Wigand had barely finished writing about Heinrich before launching into lavish praise of Winrich of Kniprode.

The Plague, Pilgrimages, and Pogroms

The plague arrived in Prussia during the Easter celebrations of 1349. The death toll in the cities was 'beyond computation'. In Sambia so many Prussians died that it was necessary to cremate the bodies (a practice Christians avoided because of its pagan overtones). Many knights, commanders and native warriors were struck down. Potential crusaders were fearful of crossing plague districts or were blocked by quarantines designed to prevent spread of the disease.

As elsewhere, the plague produced bizarre behaviour: bands of flagellants went through the countryside, stopping in cities and villages for ritual whippings, hoping to remind onlookers of their danger and to invoke God's pity. Some spent their last healthy hours in riot and pleasure, yet others blamed the Jews. The pogroms in Germany were so terrible that tens of thousands of Jews fled into Poland – joining communities founded by refugees who had escaped the massacres committed during the First Crusade – and a handful, some converts to Christianity, went to Prussia, where they had been formerly unknown. Most Jews were allowed to live quietly, but at least one was burned on Gotland on charges of poisoning wells in Prussia and Kurland, and Długosz noted that the Jews were blamed for poisoning the air; the chronicler also condemned the dissolute life of King Casimir, who later took a Jewish mistress – a disgraceful and dishonourable act in his eyes.

Some Christians, consulting astrologers, believed that the plague was the result of a convergence of Saturn and Mars. Others saw it as the fulfilment of prophecies. Yet others believed it was a punishment for their sins. During the holy year 1350 pious folks made the long pilgrimage from Prussia to Rome, seeking help at the apostles' graves. Many more went to Aachen, the closest major pilgrimage centre.

Prussians were, in fact, already enthusiastic pilgrims, bringing home badges as mementos, badges archeologists have found in the ruins of their homes. There were local saints and festivals aplenty, but for long journeys they formed groups – there was safety in numbers.

Most likely the plague hit the young and old hardest, and the rich the least – such was the pattern in Western Europe – so that its full impact would not be felt until the next generation. Still, so many potential crusaders, so many Prussian warriors and so many Teutonic Knights died in these recurring disasters that the Teutonic Knights had to rely on smaller, more efficient armies than before. They hired mercenaries and bought modern weapons. They pressed their surviving subjects to make up the shortfall in labour services and taxes.

The Lithuanians were seemingly spared. Their rural isolation might have meant fewer black rats, fewer opportunities for the fleas to spread the contagion. However, this impression of rural immunity may be incorrect. Their Rus'ian subjects suffered pandemics in 1352–3 and 1360, and the plague became endemic in Rus' thereafter; the frequent references to 'waste lands' seem to indicate the impact was greater in the Rus'ian countryside than we know.

Serfdom had always existed, but while the labour shortage led to less serfdom in the West, in Central and Eastern Europe rulers responded by preventing peasants from changing manors or moving to the cities. That policy protected the *Witingen*, the monasteries and landowners, but it consigned the region to long-term backwardness. The Tatars apparently suffered huge losses, too, thus eroding the khan's power just as it was being challenged by Lithuania and Poland.

New leadership appeared, usually younger and more ambitious men. In Lithuania younger men replaced those fallen at Strėva, perhaps even marrying their widows. The same was true for the Teutonic Knights, without the wedding celebrations.

Grandmaster Winrich and Chivalry

Winrich of Kniprode's election to be grandmaster on 6 January 1352, at a comparatively young age, was recognition that the Order had a genius among its ranks. Winrich possessed a gift for command: a genial combination of self-confidence, easy manners, quickness of thought, and hardness of determination. No one who met him went away unimpressed; he was a prince in every way except for distinguished ancestry. He fitted the age of chivalry so well that none of his successors could equal him.

Of Rhenish ancestry – his mother's family had provided several knights to the Teutonic Order – he first appeared in Prussian records at the age of twenty-five; four years later he was commander of the Danzig convent, one of the most important posts in the country; thence he moved quickly to become marshal and grand commander. Thus, at a comparatively early age he had held several important military posts, and in the extensive reordering of offices following the death of Ludolf König, he alone was not replaced. In his five years under Heinrich Dusemer, he learned the skills of government by experience and observation.

As a symbolic act that well defined the role of chivalry in his administration, Winrich required the Order's secular vassals to give him an oath of allegiance. Through this feudal ceremony he sought to bring those warriors into the system of chivalric values. While some knights were, legally speaking, little more than rich peasants, he treated them as nobility and made them judges and tax collectors. Moreover, following examples in Germany, France and England, Winrich held numerous meetings with the assemblies, a practice that his successors formalised for the making of laws and the discussion of policies.

He issued new regulations concerning convent life, then followed up with unannounced inspections. These 'visitations' were nothing new, but the thoroughness and regularity were. He often moved officers around so that they would not become too closely identified with one region, because that could easily lead to complacency and corruption.

Later generations were to describe Winrich's reign with nostalgic exaggeration, as did *Die Ältere Hochmeisterchronik* [*Earliest Chronicle of the Grandmasters*]:

> Master Winrich was a worthy man in his appearance and bearing . . . During his reign the Order in Prussia had many noble and wise brothers, so that wisdom, counsel, manners, courage, honour, riches and handsome brothers flourished; and in that era there was no convent in which one could not find one or two brothers who could be compared to the master

in wisdom and honesty. The visitors of that time said that they had not seen in any land so many men outstanding for maturity and wisdom as in the Order in Prussia. Therefore, many nobles, knights, and squires in Christendom desired to see the Order and came with arms to Prussia.

Among the 'guests' were members of the Order of the Tiercelet, knights from Poitou,who permitted members who had taken the Cross to Prussia to gild the talons of their falcon emblem. Some guests came by sea, others across Poland or Pomerania. Security, convenience, and cost determined the route each took to Prussia.

Such visitors were entertained royally in Marienburg and Königsberg and other Prussian towns along the way. (Surprisingly, the Order's convents in the Holy Roman Empire do not seem to have offered crusaders accommodation or entertainment.). At each halt pro-crusade propaganda (in the most positive sense of that word) was laid on as thickly as the gravy, as often as the beer tankards were lifted, and was surely included in the frequent prayers. Constant references were made to the Maccabees, those Jewish patriots who against all odds had defeated the armies of the Seleucid Empire and re-established the Temple in Jerusalem. This became the ultimate argument in favour of holy war. Tying this to the cult of Lady Mary, the warriors of the Apocalypse, and St George was a stroke of genius. It was relatively easy to make a connection to the cult of chivalry, something that the crusades to the Holy Land had not emphasised as much as the religious nature of the enterprise.

By the mid-1300s, when the Hundred Years War was giving knightly champions great opportunities to win fame, chivalry had become immensely popular. Winrich of Kniprode not only personified the concepts of chivalry, but he understood how to use them to attract a new class of recruits to his crusade. Still, his efforts to exploit this phenomenon might have been less successful if he had not received a crusading pledge from one of Europe's most noble princes.

Crusader Difficulties in Reaching Prussia

Henry of Derby (*c.* 1310–61) was a cousin of King Edward III. A brilliant warrior with vast experience in the early part of the Hundred Years War, his journey began with all the publicity and pomp that fashionable society of that era expected. He arrived in Stettin (Szczecin) in January 1352 with a force of 400 men, then, while visiting his relative, Barnim of Pomerania, he issued a formal declaration of hostility against Casimir of Poland.

The great castle at Marienburg (Malbork in Polish) was the headquarters of the Teutonic Order from the early fourteenth to the mid-fifteenth century and was later a Polish possession. It is seen here when the author visited for a historical conference in 2010, with much restoration work complete. The 2010 event was part of a commemoration of the 1410 battle known by Germans, Poles, and Lithuanians under different names: Tannenberg/ Grunwald/Žalgiris.

Marienburg is often considered the largest castle in the world. It was never captured but came into Polish hands in 1457, when mercenaries surrendered it after the grandmaster was unable to pay them. The Nogat River flowed close to the walls, but not so close that armed men could spring from vessels' yardarms onto the parapets. The luxurious grandmaster's palace stands to the left.

Siegfried of Feuchtwangen was grandmaster during the tumultuous years 1303–11. He approved of the intervention in the disputes in Pomerellia (West Prussia) that led to the Teutonic Knights occupying the region. He also moved the seat of the grandmaster from Venice to Marienburg.

Entrance of Grandmaster Siegfried of Feuchtwangen to Marienburg Castle in 1309, by Carl Wilhelm Kolbe the Younger (1825). Of course, it would not have looked like this because the castle had not been expanded yet. But it does convey the colour and excitement of a feudal ceremony, with the festive costumes, flags, trumpets, and accompanying clergy.

John of Bohemia (1296–1346), in a sculpture in St Vitus Cathedral in Prague. John was among the most interesting rulers of the Middle Ages. To escape frustrating disputes with the Czech nobility and clergy, he devoted his life to chivalric adventures. At the age of forty he lost his eyesight while on crusade in Lithuania, the infection perhaps starting with snow blindness. He died at the Battle of Crécy, fighting on the French side despite his disability.

Gediminas of Lithuania in the *Sapieha Genealogy* of 1709. Gediminas (*c.* 1275–1341) began the process of expanding into Rus'. He divided his empire among his sons, hoping that civil war would not destroy what he had built.

Queen Jadwiga by Marcello Bocciacelli (1768–71). She became a romantic figure in the nineteenth century, when Polish fortunes were so low that the future national anthem proclaimed 'Poland is not yet lost!'

Jogaila (1352/62–1434) brought about the final conversion of Lithuania to Latin Christianity. After his marriage to the Polish queen, Jadwiga, he took the name Władysław II (Jagiełło). In 1410 his Polish and Lithuanian forces won the battle of Tannenberg, ending the era of greatness for the Teutonic Knights and beginning that of Poland. He is depicted here in a fifteenth-century triptych in Wawel Cathedral, Kraków.

Right: The castle in Königsberg, in a photo from 1894–1900. Although much enlarged by later rulers, one can see why visiting crusaders were impressed. Almost all crusaders gathered here before starting their campaigns into Samogitia. Known as Królewiec in Polish, and Karaliaučius in Lithuanian, the name meant 'the King's Mountain' and was given to honour King Ottokar II of Bohemia (1233–78), who brought his army there on crusade in 1254–5. Settled largely by German-speaking immigrants, it was the largest city in East Prussia for centuries. In 1945 everything changed – it was heavily damaged in fighting, then the Germans were expelled and replaced by Soviet citizens, and it was renamed Kaliningrad. The remains of the castle were destroyed by 1974.

Left: The cathedral in Königsberg. Several prominent crusaders had their coats-of-arms painted on the walls, and some who died during the campaigns were buried here. The eastern shores of the Baltic Sea have few sources of stone suitable for building, but the clay is excellent for making bricks. As a result, most buildings, like this High Gothic cathedral, are made from local bricks.

Vilnius Upper Castle. The late 13th century saw the first wooden castle built on the hilltop. The earliest masonry may have appeared there in the reign of Algirdas (1345–77). What we see today are for the most part the remains of the castle constructed by Vytautas in the early 1400s. This castle, along with the Lower Castle nearby was the strongest point of defence in Lithuania. It resisted crusader attempts to capture it in 1377, 1383, 1390, and 1394.

A strong wooden castle was erected at Veliuona in 1291. The Teutonic Knights immediately attacked it but failed. After that Veliuona withstood numerous sieges until it was taken for the first time in 1348.

The modern Kartupėnai hillfort was once the site of Bisenė castle – the first stronghold that was attacked and burned down in 1283 by the Knights once they emerged on the lower reaches of the River Nemunas. It was rebuilt and withstood several sieges but in 1316 it was burned for good, once the Teutonic troops spotted that it was derelict. It had become too exposed to make it worthwhile for the Lithuanian rulers to maintain whatever the cost.

The crusaders reached the castle at Medvėgalis for the first time in 1316 but could not take it. When reinforced by the large army of John of Bohemia and by crusaders from Germany and England in February 1329, Werner of Orseln took the castle, but only after stubborn resistance. Werner wanted to put all the captives to death, but King John's counsel prevailed, so they were set free after being baptised.

Trakai Island Castle dates from the early 15th century and is intimately bound up with the name of the grand duke of Lithuania, Vytautas. Back then it was the most modern castle in Lithuania and was built in the French style.

Kamianets-Podilskyi was captured by Casimir III in 1352. Afterward it was a major Polish stronghold in what is today Ukraine. Its fortifications, like all others in the region, were modified later to reflect major changes in military technology.

Martyrdom of St Adalbert. Adalbert (956–97) was the most prominent Czech martyr in the heroic era of Christian missions to East Central Europe. As Bishop of Prague, he felt it his duty to preach to the pagans in Prussia. The bronze doors (c. 1175) of the cathedral in Gniezno show the moment of martyrdom.

Prussian idols were usually made of wood and mostly destroyed by Christians; this survivor was made of stone. Too little information about pagan deities and practices remains to inform us what such figures represented. Later Christians were eager to identify Baltic paganism as similar to Germanic and Scandinavian mythology and even tempted to see parallels to Classical mythology.

Winrich of Kniprode (1310–82), seen here in a statue in Marienburg (Malbork), was grandmaster from 1351 to his death, years in which his military order was the dominant power on the shores of the eastern Baltic Sea. Contemporaries saw in him the highest ideals of chivalry and the crusading spirit.

Marienburg had fallen into disrepair before World War II and was then heavily damaged, as shown. Because it had been the largest brick castle in the world, it had literally collapsed into a pile of masonry. Since many Polish cities had also been devastated, there was no money for repairs. However, when reconstruction began in 1962, the work proceeded swiftly and the castle soon became a popular tourist destination.

As this woodcut of the castle and town from 1696 shows, the modern reconstruction is less gothic than its earlier form. This is a reminder that castles, like people, change as they age, and that we must rely on imagination to see them as they were.

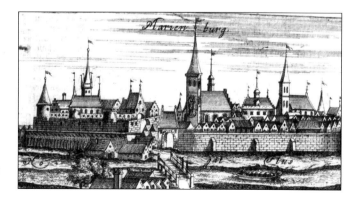

Ragnit was the most important of the castles along the eastern border of Prussia that served both to defend the interior against Lithuanian raids and for attacks into Samogitia and Lithuania. However, the ruins we see today are those of the square fortress built between 1397 and 1409, not the castle that crusaders would have seen. Destroyed in WWII, it is now in the Kaliningrad region of Russia and is called Neman (the Russian name for the Nemunas/Memel River).

Ragnit and its castle, an engraving taken from Christophorus Hartknoch, *Alt- und Neues Preussen* (1684).

Seal of Ladislas I (1260–1333, r. 1320–33). Known to contemporaries as Władysław I Łokietek, the 'Elbow-high' or 'the Short', this seal shows the importance of propaganda. Then, as now, because tallness was considered an attribute of leadership, his short stature allowed his enemies to mock him until he became king in 1320. In the few years left to him, before he died in 1333, he unified Poland, making possible the successes of his son, Casimir the Great.

Karl of Trier, 16th Grandmaster (1311–24). Karl reigned in a troubled era. After Karl's efforts to introduce reforms met strong resistance, he had to oppose complaints against his order. After arguing his case before the pope in Avignon, his health collapsed.

Werner of Orseln was the 17th Grandmaster of the Teutonic Order. He governed from 1324 until his murder in 1330. A later forgery called the Orseln Statute gave the German master authority to remove an incompetent grandmaster.

Luther of Braunschweig, 18th Grandmaster (1331–5). He was the youngest son of a powerful regional lord and could have lived a long and comfortable existence, but he chose the rigours of a military order. His reign was noted for a flourishing of the arts.

Dietrich of Altenburg, 19th Grandmaster, took office in 1335, the year when King Casimir agreed to renounce claims on West Prussia in exchange for provinces in Silesia held by Dietrich.

Ludolf König, 20th Grandmaster, succumbed to depression after his 1345 campaign against Lithuania failed. He resigned and when he recovered he never held high office again.

Heinrich Dusemer, 21st Grandmaster. His campaigns against the Lithuanian pagans were so successful that it appeared that he would conquer the entire country. Then the Black Death hit.

King Władysław I Łokietek breaks negotiations with the Teutonic Knights at Brześć Kujawski, a painting by Jan Matejko 1879 in the National Museum, Warsaw. The king was noted for his violent outbursts of temper, especially when dealing with the Teutonic Order from a position of weakness.

Algirdas (*c.*1296–1377), here pictured in Alexander Guagnini's bestseller *Sarmatiae Europeae descriptio* (1578), ruled a Lithuanian empire that included Kyiv, Chernigov and Briansk. He kept his brothers and nephews in check, expanded the empire to the east, and fended off attacks led by the Teutonic Knights.

Vytautas the Great (1350–1430) had a tumultuous career, first feuding with his cousin Jogaila, then reconciling. After the conversion of Lithuania to Roman Catholic Christianity, he expanded his realm beyond Smolensk and to the shores of the Black Sea. In 1410 he joined Jogaila (Jagiełło) to defeat the Teutonic Knights at Tannenberg.

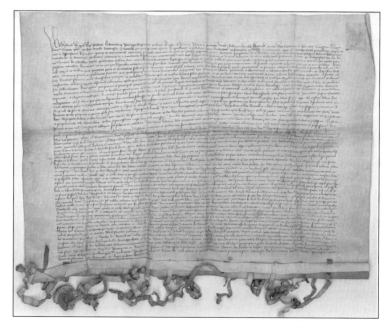

The Peace of Thorn (Toruń) ended the War of 1409–11 between the Teutonic Knights and Poland–Lithuania. It was the beginning of the military order's long slide into obscurity.

Konrad Zöllner, 23rd Grandmaster. Konrad I rejected the 1387 conversion of Lithuania to Christianity as fake.

Konrad of Wallenrode, 24th Grandmaster. Konrad II's violent temper led to quarrels within the order and to his own death by apoplexy in 1393.

Konrad of Jungingen, 25th Grandmaster. Konrad III oversaw his order's greatest successes, notably by occupying Samogitia in 1400.

Map of Samogitia from 1659. It shows how the terrain was criss-crossed by numerous rivers that hindered both attack and defence. The River Nemunas was navigable, but only as far up as Kaunas, in the very centre of today's Lithuania.

Lithuanian swords of the thirteenth century,
from the Vytautas the Great War Museum in Kaunas.

That a crusader against Lithuanian pagans should challenge the unquestionably Christian king of Poland may seem strange, but this was a strange time. Winrich, having failed to persuade Casimir to agree with his views concerning the boundary between Prussia and Masovia, had asked Henry to aid him. The English duke agreed. War against the mighty king of Poland was certainly a greater exploit than chasing pagans through forests. Soon afterwards, however, the grandmaster signed a truce with Casimir; and since Henry had kept his forces in a position to attack Poland, he could not reach Königsberg before the winter expedition set out. Therefore, he led his men west, reaching Cologne in April.

There Henry's adventures multiplied. He quarrelled with Otto (1320–98), the new duke of Braunschweig-Grubenhagen and a person who would later be important in France, Italy and the Mediterranean. Organising a formal duel was very complex in that era because each had to obtain the permission of his lord. Furthermore, each wanted to attract as much attention to himself as possible by making difficulties concerning both the place and date of the encounter. In short, the publicity was more important than the fight. Presumed enemies often feuded verbally for years, each demanding that the other stand up and fight like a man, while avoiding combat with skilfully contrived excuses. Eventually, the duel was scheduled to take place that December in Paris. At the last moment, however, it was delayed by King John of France, who did not want to see either lord killed or maimed. Henry of Derby then set off hurriedly for Prussia, hoping to join the next winter expedition.

When Henry reached Cologne, he heard a report that the king of France and the duke of Braunschweig had sent men to capture him. When he hurried on into Westphalia, a notoriously lawless region, he ran into a band of robber knights – apparently a free company that had just been released from service in the Hundred Years War – who stole 3,000 gold pieces. Henry, being unable to proceed without money, returned home with a story of having been kidnapped and held for ransom, a much more honourable fate than having been robbed at sword point. Given the times, it was a highly plausible tale.

Henry's adventure was not unique. In 1388 the duke of Guelders was attacked in Stolp (Słupsk) by robbers who used a ruse to gain his companions' confidence, then took all their horses, weapons, gold and silver plate, and held them all for ransom. When the grandmaster set out to rescue him, the kidnappers' leader informed the duke that he expected him to appear as his captive wherever he directed, but that it would not be prudent for anyone who had offended the grandmaster to wait around until he arrived. The duke accompanied his rescuers to Königsberg, but soon became despondent that he was violating his word. He sent home to Guelders for ransom money and had it delivered to Stolp along with a promise that there would be no effort to revenge the insult.

The episode demonstrated why it was so important to control the lands east of Brandenburg – Stolp, Butow and Neumark. Stolp was a sparsely populated province of Eastern Pomerania between the Neumark and West Prussia that had formerly been held by the duke of Pomerellia, then the margraves of Brandenburg, then passed around in the frequent divisions of Pomerania. That robber barons ignored their titular lord was common in Silesia, northern Poland, and even Germany.

It was a problem that Winrich could not resolve. In any case, he had more pressing issues to deal with. The winter expeditions in the years after 1352 achieved little; in 1353, bad weather prevented the count of Nuremberg, the count of Mark, and the count of Ottingen from campaigning. Viscount Aimery of Narbonne's expedition did not even reach Prussia, having been stopped by the count of Braunschweig (who may have been on the watch for more crusaders). The southern French knights had caused a fire at an inn, and they had departed without paying the damages. The duke intercepted the party in Lüneburg and demanded that they compensate their host 400 florins. They wrote home, but by the time the money arrived, it was too late to reach Prussia before the expedition began.

For a while thereafter few large groups of crusaders came to Prussia, being temporarily homebound by the renewal of war in France, the annual ravages of plague, and economic problems caused by war and disease. The grandmaster and his officers were sufficiently worried about the plague that they obtained papal decrees allowing them to take last rites when they fell ill. Meanwhile, the crusading movement languished. Winrich waited in vain for an army led by a well-known prince. This kept him on the defensive through 1353 and 1354 while Kęstutis raided Ermland, then quickly fled away. The arrival of small groups, such as Robert Beaufort's Englishmen in 1356, was insufficient for a major offensive.

Efforts to Obtain Imperial Aid

The failure of the Bohemians to resume crusading in Prussia was disappointing, but Charles IV had other plans. Like all emperors-elect, he wanted to be crowned by the pope, a goal he partially achieved in 1355 when a cardinal authorised by the pope performed the ceremony.

Immediately after this he left Rome, abandoning ambitions to exercise imperial rights in Italy. The next year he persuaded the Imperial diet to revise the election process in ways that reduced the pope's ability to interfere; this was famously known as the Golden Bull from the large imperial seal affixed to it. Henceforth, there were to be seven electors – three archbishops and four secular princes – who would meet with the emperor annually to discuss important matters. Although Charles initially believed that God had selected him to restore peace and stability in the Empire and the Church, sour experience taught him not to hope for too much. He learned that the careful management of resources worked better than radical changes or wars. He was not interested in expensive undertakings that would not advance Bohemian interests.

This was most obvious in his attitude towards the Teutonic Order's difficulties with Poland. Casimir was a co-operative ally, and Charles saw no reason to anger him. For the first time in many decades the grandmaster could not depend upon imperial support beyond vague promises of future aid. Charles used the Teutonic Knights to further his domestic and foreign policy, but he did not reward them significantly. A sallow-cheeked, round-shouldered, superstitious monarch, he knew how to use patriotism, bribery, and flattery to achieve his goals.

Winrich adapted his policies appropriately. To attract the attention of an emperor who understood nothing but power, he would become a semi-secular ruler and prove that he was the equal of the king of Poland and most of the German dukes who came on crusade. He strove to win the friendship and neutrality of the emperor, particularly through the German master of 1330–61, Wolfram of Nellenburg, but he placed more emphasis on winning respect than on obtaining active assistance.

King Casimir Moves East

Winrich was a hard and determined demi-monarch who understood *Realpolitik*. This willingness to put rational interests above ideals determined his relationship with Casimir, who was concentrating on expanding his Polish kingdom south-eastwards into Galicia and thence around the Pripet Marshes into Volhynia. The king intended to supplant the Tatars and Lithuanians in those turbulent regions and make it impossible for those dangerous enemies to invade his kingdom. He had first marched east in 1340 to support Duke Bolesław-Jerzy, but by the time he arrived the childless duke was already dead from poisoning.

Although Siemowit III and Casimir of Masovia had the best claims to succeed their brother, Casimir III being only a cousin, the king had declared Galicia his because Bolesław-Jerzy had been his vassal. This feudal innovation was new to Galicia, but over time the king overcame the nobles' opposition by promising to enlarge their lordships. Occupying territories, however, was child's play compared to holding them.

The Lithuanians had strong claims on Volhynia. Kęstutis was Bolesław's brother-in-law and his younger brother Liubartas (*c.* 1310–83), had married a daughter of the last duke from the Rurik dynasty. Liubartas had been able to defend the territory around Lutsk from the Tatar invasion of 1323, a feat that had made him many friends among the Orthodox nobles. Then he had built the large fortification known as Liubart's Castle that loomed over the Styr River, enclosing his palace, the cathedral, and the bishop's palace. To counter Liubartas, the Polish king needed an ally. Only the Teutonic Knights were able to aid him.

Casimir had made peace in 1343 partly to obtain this alliance. At first this only slowed the deterioration of his position in Galicia, but within five years his forethought paid off handsomely. After the battle on the Strėva weakened the Lithuanians, he was ready to annex Galicia. That region had been so worn down by repeated invasions that local resistance would be minimal.

In 1349 Casimir confirmed his friendship with Heinrich Dusemer by resolving several potential sources of trouble. At this point the relationship between Prussia and Poland was so friendly that it seemed the conflicts of the past had been forgotten. Their alliance against common enemies outweighed any remaining disagreements.

Casimir made a lightning sweep through Galicia that September, marching from Lviv to Vladimir, then sending part of his army to besiege Lutsk while he led the rest down the Bug to Brest-Litovsk. He captured every place he had besieged except Lutsk, moving his frontier 240 km. (150 miles) eastward. This touched off an intense conflict with Liubartas.

When a Lithuanian army invaded in May 1350. Casimir hurried from Cracow, drove the intruders north, and there, joined by the Masovian dukes, inflicted a defeat on Liubartas at the Bzura River. It was a different story in August, after Liubartas received reinforcements that allowed him to recapture all the towns in Galicia except Lviv, which fell later. As the chronicler Jan z Czarnkowa described it, although God gave the Poles victory in every battle, the Lithuanians had sacked Vladimir and Lviv, and many castles, villages and settlements as well. Casimir, seeing that the Lithuanians would not offer open battle, but only dash into his lands and hurry away, made a settlement with the

Lithuanian dukes, giving them Vladimir in return for peace. This was apparently no more than a truce, but it saved the king from maintaining an expensive occupation force there.

The chronicler Długosz was pessimistic, noting that every strategy the king pursued ended in failure. Partly, this was because he could get no help from Hungary after King Louis left for Naples to avenge the murder of his brother. Casimir constructed new brick fortifications at strategic locations, but his real problem, as he and contemporaries saw it, was that God was angry at his murder of a churchman in Cracow who had dared criticise his relationship with his Jewish mistress. Casimir appealed to Pope Innocent VI for absolution, and within two years managed to work out an arrangement. This was an expensive compromise.

Hopes for a peaceful conversion of the Lithuanians had been high, but now priority had to be given to the Tatars, who were rumoured to be planning an attack. Casimir wrote to Avignon, describing his desperate situation so effectively that the money-starved pope awarded him Peter's Pence from Poland for the next four years. Then Casimir persuaded Louis of Hungary to hurry back from his Italian expedition.

Casimir had not exaggerated his troubles. Although the Tatars never appeared, 1351 was a difficult year. The Lithuanians not only held most of Volhynia, but also Galicia, including the strategic commercial centre of Lviv. Moreover, they were helped by Poles who guided them through the swamps and forests in return for generous payments. This did not always work as anticipated. Once Polish guides marked a difficult ford with tall rods, then returned to the Lithuanians to explain how to find the crossing. In the meantime, fishermen saw the rods and, guessing the purpose, moved them to deep water. The Lithuanian commanders led their raiders to the spot, only to lose hundreds of heavily armoured men to drowning. They immediately beheaded their guides.

Soon afterwards, according to Długosz, Henning Schindekopf, the commander of Ragnit, pursued a Lithuanian raiding force so closely that it fled into a swamp, where 500 drowned, together, it was believed, with one of Kęstutis's nephews. But the Lithuanian defeats in Prussia were only part of a difficult period. They faced even greater challenges from Poland.

The situation seemed to change when Casimir's forces retook Lviv and captured Liubartas. Warfare and politics being personal, not national affairs, this should have ended the war. Indeed, the Galician nobles and the wavering Masovian dukes swore allegiance to Casimir. However, soon after the king returned to Cracow in triumph, he fell ill. That paralysed Polish policy: Casimir's presence at the scene of combat was every bit as important to the Polish cause as Liubartas's was to the Lithuanians.

This situation left authority in the hands of Louis of Hungary, who came over the Carpathians with an army in the summer of 1351. Taking command of the Polish and Masovian forces, he invaded Volhynia in what seems to have been a determined effort to smash Lithuanian power there once and for all. The campaign was going well until Kęstutis daringly came into Louis's camp alone and announced that he was ready to become a Roman Christian if the Poles and Hungarians would assist him against the Tatars.

Louis was impressed. He agreed to discuss the matter further with Kęstutis and broke off his offensive. He even promised that, for his part, he would ask the papacy to crown Kęstutis king. Then he freed Liubartas from close confinement. That was what Kęstutis was really seeking. The entire episode was a deception which no chivalric monarch from Central Europe would likely have been prepared to condone. The elaborate ceremony in which Kęstutis sacrificed a red bull seemed convincing proof that the pagan ruler had sworn a significant and binding oath to his gods: Kęstutis had first cut two veins so that he could observe the flow of blood, then, pronouncing the omens favourable, he hewed the bull's head off with an axe. Louis knew too little of pagan customs and relied too much on promises – he was not even aware that the ritual shouts were in White Russian, thus invalidating a ceremony that had to be conducted in Lithuanian.

They signed a treaty, then set out for the Bug River, which they would follow towards Cracow. One night soon afterwards the Lithuanian brothers escaped, violating their word of honour and making Louis appear a fool. Suddenly a Lithuanian host appeared, slaying Bolesław of Płock. Louis retreated hurriedly, but before he reached safety, it was clear that he had lost everything Casimir had won.

Casimir led the joint armies the next year, 1352, but did little better than Louis had done. The Hungarian king was wounded in a failed effort to capture a fortress, then both monarchs had to retreat when a Tatar army swept in. It was a moment of great significance to both kingdoms, because when Casimir fell deathly ill in Lublin, he turned over the management of both armies to Louis. It being necessary to explain his decision to the Polish nobles and clergy, Casimir extracted oaths from them to recognise the Hungarian king as their monarch, while requiring Louis to give oaths respecting Polish traditions.

Desperate for money, Casimir rid himself of the expenses incurred in defending Dobrzyń, which had reverted to him on Bolesław's death, by mortgaging the region to the grandmaster for 40,000 florins. Furthermore, since the trade routes to the Black Sea were closed, Casimir promised to do what he could to drive the Tatars away and to protect German merchants in Galicia and Volhynia.

In 1353 Algirdas and Kęstutis made a multi-pronged attack on Poland from south to north. Liubartas led the first army, capturing Halich and, according to Długosz, killing the women and children, 'as is the Lithuanian habit'. The second army, led by the three dukes, ravaged Prussia without resistance and carried away 500 captives. Casimir built a brick fortress at Płock, but he was otherwise as incapable of protecting the frontier settlements as were his allies in Prussia and Hungary.

Dobrzyń

The interests of the Teutonic Knights and the Polish kingdom coincided to a remarkable degree. Both were fighting Lithuanians whose trickery and resourcefulness were now legendary, but Poland, having the longer frontiers, had suffered the more severe raids. Masovia and Sandomir were being attacked despite the Piast dynasty's repeated marriages to Lithuanian princesses. However, in 1351 the friendship of the grandmaster and the king was tested.

The issue was the Masovian–Prussian border. The lands in question were deserted stretches of forest where both the military order and the dukes kept garrisons in isolated castles such as Michelau and Wizna to watch for pagan incursions. No one had marked the frontier accurately, and the claims overlapped, but that was of no consequence as long as the dukes needed the grandmaster as a potential supporter against the pretensions of the king and as a military ally against their Lithuanian relatives.

However, when two Masovian dynasties became extinct (Płock in 1351, Wizna in 1353), Casimir III laid claim to their lands. The king had the law on his side, and he reminded his subjects of the agreement with Charles IV, which effectively traded John of Bohemia's feudal rights in Masovia for Casimir's claims to southern Silesia. Winrich was not pleased to find a powerful king on his southern border because the Masovian dukes had never threatened Prussia seriously even when they were not friendly. Casimir, on the other hand, was a potential danger even under the best of conditions.

Winrich did not act rashly or prematurely in this matter. He first made broad hints that something should be done to guarantee him a fair settlement, then he tried diplomacy. Nothing helped. Casimir had a royal flair for ignoring important business. He had an eye for pretty ladies and a passion for the hunt, and he only pressed for decisions when holding the advantage. He understood that not all promises had to be kept. For example, he still used the title 'duke of Pomerellia' that he had agreed in the Treaty of Kalisz to abandon, and there was a real possibility that Casimir might produce a legitimate son.

Casimir's love life was stormy and complicated. Casimir had been trying to end his marriage to Adelheid of Hesse, but the neglected wife had defended herself by calling on the pope. Even so, it seemed likely that Casimir would prevail (although no one expected him to enter a bigamous secret marriage and then send Adelheid home to her father, as happened only a year later). As often occurs, when one scandal becomes public, previously hidden ones come to light. For years Casimir had kept a Jewish mistress named Esther and allowed their daughters to retain the mother's religion. When the vicar of the Cracow church criticised this relationship, he was found drowned in the Vistula River. The king was excommunicated for a short period; and when the mistress died, a riot broke out at her burial and one of her sons was lynched.

Casimir's marital difficulties show that medieval marriages were not purely matters of state. Moreover, they indicated that the Avignon papacy was not so weak or corrupt as is often imagined. In expecting to obtain a annulment easily, Casimir made a serious mistake – his alternately bullying and cajoling of the pope disturbed his relationship with the Church for the following decade. In addition, these actions gave observers grounds to question his integrity and good judgement. Winrich, believing that Casimir would not honour his promises to him any better than he did those made to his women, decided to resolve the Masovian issue himself. In 1355 Winrich apparently agreed to a truce with Kęstutis that permitted merchants from Thorn to travel to Volhynia. Then he seized Dobrzyń, which was lightly defended because Casimir was in Galicia, fighting the Lithuanians and Tatars.

This attack was a violation of everything the Teutonic Order professed to represent. If a military order had any reason for existence, it was to further the crusading effort against the pagans of Lithuania, the Tatars and the Orthodox Rus'ians. Casimir had been accompanied by an army of crusaders from Brandenburg led by his son-in-law, Louis of Wittelsbach, and was stunned by the invasion. Casimir should not have been so surprised – when he informed the grandmaster of his plans, he had demanded his aid, on pain of losing the right to trade across Poland and Ruthenia – a privilege that Winrich's subjects valued highly. It had apparently not occurred to him how insulting this was. (Those with longer memories must have reflected ruefully or with a smile, remembering how Casimir's father had interrupted Prussian expeditions into Samogitia, but they would have wisely held their tongues. Wise men avoided the royal wrath whenever possible, a practice that deprived the monarch of useful advice.) Winrich, seemingly angered by the pretension of sovereignty over Prussia implied by the king summoning him to perform military service, caught Casimir completely by surprise.

The king broke off his campaign and returned home, furious. He became even more angry when rumours came that Winrich had made an alliance with the Lithuanians. That charge proved false, but there was no denying that the grandmaster had interrupted Casimir's crusade and set back the goal of defeating and converting the Lithuanians. Since Casimir had already told the pope that the pagans were ready to accept Christianity, the grandmaster's actions fitted what was now a traditional narrative – that the military order impeded the conversion of the pagans. Winrich, however, would not be distracted. His Order's safety came first; crusades to the east came second.

The logic was more complex, of course. If there was no Prussian base, there could be no effective crusade. The goal was conversion, not conquest. Similarly, when the pope had demanded a truce so that his legates could investigate letters supposedly from Gediminas suggesting that he was ready to become a convert, the Teutonic Knights had agreed – reluctantly agreed, of course, because they suspected that, as proved to be the case, Gediminas had never authored or authorised them. The present truce might represent a similar situation. Still, if conversion were possible without conquest, good; if only conquest could bring about conversion, so be it.

The Teutonic Knights never had the resources to occupy all of Lithuania. Samogitia, yes, but medieval Lithuania was a vast, multi-cultural state, more populous and more able to defend itself. The officers and knights of the military order were ambitious, arrogant, proud, and even cruel; they rarely conceded an advantage or ceded a territory without exacting some payment. But they had no reputation for foolishness. Imposing Catholicism on all of Rus'? Casimir's charges were hardly better. In short, Kęstutis was the only plausible convert in sight, and most likely Winrich would have taken seriously any hint that he was willing to convert. Seriously, but not naively.

Another reason to agree to a truce was the renewal of significant fighting in France. Whenever the Hundred Years War resumed, there could be no armies from France and England until the two kings and their taxpayers were exhausted.

From the correspondence with the papacy only, one might not notice how important Casimir's connection with Louis of Hungary was. A less astute ruler than Winrich might believe that Casimir's continued use of the title 'duke of Pomerellia' was only for self-glorification and not a serious threat, but Winrich knew that Casimir had made Louis take an oath to recover the lost territories. He understood the Hungarian king's ambitions – once Louis came to rule Poland as well as Hungary, with excellent prospects of acquiring yet additional lands in the Balkans, in Galicia, and in Italy, he would be more dangerous than Casimir. Consequently, Winrich felt the need to resolve the border questions now; and Dobrzyń was an excellent lever – it had been in the Order's possession before; it could easily be made into another West Prussia. The real issue was power, security and sovereignty, but that was not likely to impress the pope. Border disputes were much easier to explain.

Pope Innocent listened carefully to Casimir's complaints and wrote to Winrich, admonishing him for his failure to aid the Polish crusade. When Winrich failed to respond with sufficient humility, the pope wrote again. Innocent was not in the weak position of his predecessor, who had embarked on an unnecessary quarrel with Emperor Louis IV, thereby alienating even his best friends in Germany. Innocent had his former pupil, Charles IV of Bohemia, as emperor and friend; and he was temporarily relieved of worries that free companies would sack Avignon. He believed he had leverage that could be used to assure obedience to papal orders.

Relations with Emperor and Pope

The pope, though close to Charles IV, apparently did not understand that the Teutonic Knights embodied German patriotism, with possessions throughout the Holy Roman Empire. The German convents had even sent knights to accompany Charles IV to Rome for his coronation. This was important because so few of his vassals had volunteered for that dangerous expedition. Winrich, feeling sure of imperial gratitude, did not yield to the pope.

Winrich's diplomats were too sophisticated to refuse papal demands brusquely or to embarrass the emperor. Their replies never lacked a polite tone or humility, but neither did they ever concede essential points. The procurator-general, Winrich's representative at the papal court, always had an excuse for delay, such as pleading that the grandmaster's conflicting responsibilities prevented him from acting – when the pope gave orders, he had to consult the emperor; when the emperor gave orders, he had to obtain the pope's permission. He knew how to complicate discussions, how to play one enemy against another, and how to suggest that the Teutonic Knights were acting in the service of Christendom, while the Polish king was interfering with long-established Church policies. He accused Casimir of having allied himself with the Lithuanians and of having threatened to make an alliance with the Tatars – and both charges were probably true. Interpreting Polish foreign policy for the pope, he could confuse the issues and justify his own plans. He also had many friends at the curia now, friends won by money or favours, former crusaders, family members and personal contacts of important officers. Using these, he was able to frustrate Casimir's demands for justice.

The negotiations at the curia give us one interesting insight concerning the native Prussians. The bishop of Ermland had brought a delegation to plead the case of the Teutonic Knights. According to later legend, Innocent VI was very impressed by a handsome young boy who addressed him through an interpreter. Upon inquiry, he learned that the boy was a native Prussian who did not speak German, so that even the bishop could not converse with him directly. The pope, remarking that such talented boys should be trained for the priesthood, ordered the bishop to establish a school for Prussian youths. The bishop did so, then began treating his native subjects better, granting them fiefs and plots of land in the new settlements along the frontier in such numbers that they came to make up a large percentage of the rural population there.

A Pause in Crusader Operations

Because Winrich had to station forces in West Prussia, he was less able to ward off Lithuanian attacks, as in 1356, when Kęstutis raided Ermland. Thanks to archeological excavations on a nearby town burned in 1354, we know much more about such small frontier towns than we knew from the chronicles. (The findings of the joint German, Polish, and Lithuanian team have been described vividly in 'Burning Alt-Wartenburg'). Wartenburg had a market hall, a church, a pub-bathhouse, and about two dozen half-timbered houses. Earthen fortifications other than the gate were little more than a ditch with a low dirt wall topped by a palisade; there was a lake close by. The fort – not yet located – was probably on a nearby hill. Kęstutis apparently made no effort to take prisoners – experience had taught Kęstutis that captives moved too slowly to get out of the country before pursuers arrived, so he killed them all.

These experiences made more galling Casimir's allegations that the grandmaster had joined the pagans, selling weapons, building roads and sending warriors to assist them. But what was really upsetting was that the accusation referred to Mindaugas, the Christian king of a hundred years earlier. In any case, commerce had a logic of its own. No matter how unscrupulous the diplomats were, merchants were usually able to make some arrangements for continuing commercial activities that benefitted all parties. Merchants had always thought of themselves as neutrals, because their wares – cloth, iron and other metals going east, furs and luxury items coming west – were highly valued by all sides. When Casimir placed a heavy toll on Prussian goods travelling through his kingdom – probably up the Vistula to smaller streams that led into Galicia – the grandmaster's secret treaty with the Lithuanian dukes allowed Prussian merchants to bypass Poland, reaching the Black Sea through Belarus. In addition, there were numerous agreements to permit mutual hunting rights in the border wildernesses. (No one should have to worry about ambushes while hunting.)

There was yet one more reason why few attacks were made on Samogitia in these years: England and France were once again locked in combat. The Hundred Years War was entering a critical phase. France was not yet in disorder, but not far off was a dangerous period of peasant risings, demands for a meeting of the Estates General, and swarms of ruffian bands and unemployed mercenaries ravaging the undefended countryside.

Silesia was in disorder, too, according to Długosz. The discovery of gold there was not unusual, since copper and gold deposits were being constantly discovered around Złotoryja (Goldberg, or gold mountain) in lower Silesia, but the local lords fought over the 140 marks being mined each week, and the one who eventually secured most of the income spent it lavishly for eight years, going bankrupt when the vein ran out.

Prussian chroniclers recorded little in these years. Ragnit burned twice in late 1355, small fires having got out of control. The loss of equipment, supplies and horses was significant, but each time Winrich brought armies to rebuild the fortress. In May 1356, while inspecting construction at an unnamed castle, perhaps Ragnit, he fell from scaffolding and broke his right leg.

Significant numbers of crusaders came only in the winter of 1357/58. The capture of King John of France at Poitiers had meant that the war could not be resumed until he was ransomed; though technically a prisoner, the king was housed comfortably in England and entertained, as they say, royally.

The campaign, however, was a failure. After the marshal established a base near Welun and sent units to plunder neighbouring districts, Samogitians overran the camp, killing the 150 guards, stealing clothing and tents, and burning the supplies that they could not move. The angry crusaders marched home empty-handed, murdering and burning along the way. War along the Nemunas had always been brutal, but these crimes were the habits of the Hundred Years War – no mercy for anyone.

This expedition was followed by a two-year truce while the pope and the emperor sought to obtain the peaceful conversion of the Lithuanians. This benefitted Poland, too. By 1356, according to Długosz, Casimir was enjoying peace and prosperity. Most important, by offering lower taxes and more freedom, he was attracting many German immigrants – farmers, knights and burghers who became loyal subjects. However, by protecting the peasants, Casimir alienated his nobles. (There was, apparently, no policy that could please everyone.) The chronicler's only complaint was the dissolute royal lifestyle – the king's many concubines, his bigamous marriage, and, worst of all, the king's unusually liberal policies towards Jews. However, Casimir was willing to flout convention, conventional ideas and the expectations of his nobles and his clergy. He was, after all, a king. And being a king surely excused one from the more conventional expectations of any age.

More Efforts at Conversion

The close co-operation of pope and emperor in 1358 made it impossible for Winrich not to assist papal and imperial commissioners who were on their way to Vilnius. Although the pope and the emperor had not been approached directly by the Lithuanian dukes, they had heard rumours the year before. Whatever the source of the most recent information (which remains obscure), Charles IV wrote to Algirdas and Kęstutis in April 1358, inviting them to become Roman Catholics. To impress them with his seriousness, he fixed a golden seal on the document which can be seen today in Cracow.

The Lithuanian dukes quickly sent their brother Karijotas (*d. c.* 1365), the duke of Novgorodok, across Poland to Nuremberg. (Some historians think it was Algirdas himself.) Now about fifty years of age, Karijotas was an experienced negotiator. In July Karijotas spoke to Charles IV, saying that Algirdas and Kęstutis were ready to accept baptism under certain conditions, and that the emperor should send a distinguished embassy to negotiate on his behalf. The emperor subsequently sent the archbishop of Prague, a Silesian duke, Bolesław, and two Bavarian nobles. The party reached Königsberg in late October, visited the Lithuanian court, and returned in December. Charles IV was waiting in Wrocław with the German master, hoping to celebrate Christmas by baptising the dukes of Lithuania.

The mission was a failure. The Lithuanians demanded extensive territorial concessions: all of Prussia east of the Alle River, all of Kurland, and all of Livonia south of the Daugava. Then that the Teutonic Knights move to the frontier of Rus', to defend them from the Tatars, although they would not have any independent territory there to feed themselves, because the land would belong to the Lithuanians. And they said, 'If you can accomplish those conditions, we will submit to the emperor.'

As Stephen C. Rowell remarked in *Lithuania Ascending*, the dukes could purchase many of the advantages of Christianity with money or warriors rather than their souls. But in asking the Teutonic Knights to surrender so much territory (and it was not clear whether the rest of their possessions could be retained) and then to send the knights to almost certain death on the steppe or southern Bug, they had gone too far. Their promises had always changed with the political winds, but this offer was insulting, and members of the delegation supposedly reported that pagans had spoken derisively and insulted them, ridiculing their efforts. The derisive answers gave new life to the crusade; and when the next generation of dukes did undergo baptism, the Teutonic Knights cited the experience of 1358 as reason to question their sincerity.

Casimir III used the truce talks to negotiate for the marriage of his fifteen-year-old grandson, Casimir of Pomerania-Stettin (Kazimierz IV, 1351–77), to Algirdas's ten-year-old daughter, Kenna. Pope Innocent VI aided this by granting a special dispensation to disregard their close blood relationship. In 1360, when the wedding took place, the king was still hopeful that he would have a legitimate son himself. In 1356, while visiting Prague, he had met at court Krystyna Rokiczana, the widow of a wealthy merchant. When their secret marriage became public, Adelheid of Hesse packed her belongings and returned home. Unfortunately, this marriage did not last either – Krystyna suffered from a skin disease and the loss of her hair. In 1365 Casimir would marry a fourth time, to Hedwig of Sagan. They would have three daughters, most importantly Anna, whose daughter, Anne of Celje, would become queen of Poland upon her marriage in 1402.

The peace talks of 1358–9 had permitted Casimir III to consider southwards expansion into Wallachia and Moldavia, where tumult suggested that he could make that region his before the Turks or Hungarians or Tatars did. However, the Polish army was ambushed.

All those not slain were taken prisoner; none escaped. Casimir paid a heavy ransom for the captives, among whom was Jan of Oleśnicki, who would walk with a limp for the rest of his life from a broken shin. Jan would later be important in the Christianisation of Lithuania, and his son, Zbigniew, would dominate the Polish church in the next century.

Chapter Eight

The Era of International Prestige

Changing Concepts of Chivalry

The Teutonic Knights now had the financial resources to live like lords at the very moment that chivalry was entering an era of extravagance and luxury beyond previous imagination. This was fortunate for them: though the grandmaster was no longer able to entice kings to Prussia, he was able to entertain lesser, but still important, nobles from Germany, France, England and other nations.

The strategy of putting less stress on monkish values and more on chivalric ones had begun with Luther of Braunschweig, then thrived under Ludolf König's successor, Heinrich Dusemer. However, it was Winrich of Kniprode who brought all the strands of chivalry together. Consequently, it was his era – 1351–82 – that became the spiritual and moral apex of this crusade.

His was an era of triumph, of public acclaim and international popularity that compared favourably with competing crusades: the Holy Land had been lost, the Turks were moving into the Balkans, the Spanish effort to retake lands lost long ago to Muslims was slowed by the Hundred Years War, and the last crusader states in the eastern Mediterranean were in danger. It was important for Christendom that there be at least one successful crusade, because holy war was an expression of a cult of chivalry which gave meaning to fourteenth-century noble society. Chivalry and crusading were not essential to good government or a prosperous economy, but they were important to nobles whose role in government, in economic life, and even in warfare was declining.

Chivalry was expensive and impractical, but that was one of its attractions: while most mercenaries were unwilling to serve as unpaid volunteers and minor nobles could not afford lavish gestures, knights were augmenting their incomes by mercenary service, burghers needed money for investments, and churchmen were no longer comfortable with what the Church had become. Yet all these groups were attracted to a code that emphasised generosity, service, honour, good manners, and gracious living. Everyone, in short, believed that society needed ideals, albeit unrealistic ones. Even the critics of chivalry agreed that it was necessary to defend Christendom against its enemies, and they understood that Western Christianity was better defended through victories rather than by defeats. The crusade identified with Prussia was popular because it offered both chivalry and victory, and for the many who were genuinely religious, the Church offered substantial spiritual rewards.

The religious traits of chivalry were not superficial – compassion, fidelity and justice were essential to it. In addition, there were erotic aspects – women swooned over daring men who wore colourful clothing and spent money lavishly. However, as Huizinga noted in *The Waning of the Middle Ages*, sentimentality elided quickly into self-mockery. Elaborate forms of poetry and pageantry could disguise the self-deception, and everyone was willingly drawn in.

The numbers of crusaders at this time never equalled those of earlier centuries, but they were by no means a rare sight on the roads of Europe. It was no surprise for Chaucer's audience to read in the prologue to *The Canterbury Tales* the following lines:

> A knight ther was, and that a worthy man
> that from the time he first began
> to riden out, he loved chevalrie,
>
> . . .
>
> Ful often time he hadde the bord bigonne
> above alle nations in Pruce.
> In Lettowe hadde he reysed and in Ruce
> no cristen man so often of his degree.

The *bord* or Table of Honour was well-known in England (as was to be expected in the homeland of King Arthur), and while the greatest lords of chivalry were invited to sit there, the place of honour was not given to the most highly born, but for courage in battle. Englishmen saw this as a religious pilgrimage on behalf of the Virgin Mary and St George. These were a special sort of pilgrim, for they did not walk barefoot, practising poverty and humility, and praying. These new pilgrims were the epitome of display and pageant. While there were spiritual benefits that would offset mortal sins, veterans came to share the feasts and hunts, and young squires hoped to be dubbed as knights by a famous warrior, perhaps by a king or a duke.

As Richard Barber put it in *The Knight and Chivalry*, 'It was a chivalric festival without compare, the ultimate accolade for prowess awarded by the acclaim of those expert in all things knightly.' The list of those selected for this honour in 1385 included only simple knights, with the great lords seated further down the hall. Each knight was given a shoulder patch with the words 'Honour Conquers All' in golden letters. Each announcement that a Table Round would be celebrated was soon answered by letters from prominent lords that they would be coming to Prussia; this, of course, served to attract yet more volunteers – it was the opportunity of a lifetime to see such a collection of chivalric heroes and to earn spiritual benefits at the same time. Although the institution lasted only a few decades, Barber concluded, 'This was perhaps the ultimate manifestation of chivalry in real life, the nearest to the ideal of the Arthurian round table that was ever achieved.'

Chivalry in Prussian Literature

By 1345 there was already an outpouring of literary creativity in Prussia, with knights and priests composing religious and historical works of moderately high quality and significant local importance. Encouraged by two grandmasters, Luther of Braunschweig and Dietrich of Altenburg, who were both authors themselves, Prussian writers produced lives of saints, translations of selected books of the Bible, and histories of the northern crusades. Composing in their native Middle High German dialects, the authors were more noted for the ambition of their poetry than for their success, but that was a shortcoming to be expected among men untrained in formal rhetoric, whose strength came more from passion and effort than from refined reflection. Although one can belittle the poetic achievement, it is more fitting to be astonished that there was any literature at all. How much easier it would have been to be satisfied with the chivalric and spiritual creations of the homeland. Yet the fact remains that the Teutonic Order did not do so. It created a literature for its own needs.

Had the grandmasters not promoted the writing of history, the volume that the reader now holds would be very slim. The chroniclers of Poland and Scandinavia had other stories to tell, and the native Prussians and the Lithuanians wrote nothing. Peter of Dusburg was a priest of the Order who wrote in Latin, perhaps continuing in 1324 an earlier text now lost. Not many years elapsed after the completion of his *Chronicon Terre Prussie* in 1326, until there was a demand for a translation into German. This resulted in the lively *Kronike of Pruzinlant* by Nicholaus of Jeroschin, who added more information of his own and aimed his poem at a lay readership (presumably prospective crusaders), using simple words 'that even a child can understand'. From Dusburg and Jeroschin we learn much about the native peoples, about politics, and about the Teutonic Knights themselves. However, these works may have been read mostly by knights who lived far away, because more copies survived in German convents than in Prussia.

The flowering of literary composition was brief. It had sprouted in the late thirteenth century, come to full flower before the middle of the next century, faded quickly, and died after the fateful events of 1410, when the united armies of Poland and Lithuania annihilated the grand-master's field army at Tannenberg. Lists of the books kept in various convents and personal libraries suggest that the decline can be attributed to the authors having met the limited needs of the military order and not to an end of interest in literature. Few libraries in 1394 were large. The Marienburg collection of forty-one books in Latin and twelve in German was a respectable library for northern Europe.

Although the stories in Dusburg's and Jeroschin's chronicles may have been more important in distant convents where the warfare had to be enjoyed vicariously, there were also books of the Old Testament and Apocrypha (Judith, Esther, Ezra, Nehemiah, Job, Maccabees, and the histories of the kings and prophets). One could say without too much exaggeration that the medieval world generally found the Old Testament more appealing than the New Testament, and nowhere was this truer than with the Teutonic Order. Moses, Solomon, and David were men that knights could understand. The book of Judges had rules like those they followed every day. They easily grasped the essential elements of combat between the Lord's chosen people and their multitude of enemies. Understandably, they saw a close parallel between themselves and the Maccabees, both fighting valiantly for the Lord against overwhelming odds – and triumphing!

The knights were less concerned with the New Testament. They were interested in Christ's message principally as it related to miracles, the Crucifixion, and the Last Judgement. Knights could easily imagine themselves at Armageddon. Appropriately, a prose version of the Apocalypse was among the first translations produced. Legends of the saints, especially martyrs for the faith, were popular. Order priests also celebrated a local anchorite, Dorothea of Montau (*d.* 1394 in Marien-werder, canonised 1976) and recorded her miracles for the edification of posterity.

Education was the province of the bishops and canons. Priests obtained a master's degree in theology to qualify for advancement, literature was studied as a guide to grammar (then abandoned as quickly as possible). Even so, hundreds of ambitious young men from Prussia and Livonia went to study abroad, most going to Italy, where the universities were the best and most famous. Bologna attracted the largest number, although in the second half of the fourteenth century many went to German universities.

The Teutonic Knights considered founding a university of their own in Culm, and in 1386 obtained papal permission to do so; however, they failed to act on it. The most that can be said is that Prussia had its own backwater Scholastic Renaissance in the fifteenth century, impressive in its aspirations and accomplishments, but also very limited.

Lady Mary

Completely lacking was the love poetry so common in the courts where the knights had spent their youth. That this could be suppressed so completely tells much about the austerity of their religious practices.

The significance of the devotion to Lady Mary and a small group of other female saints (Barbara, Dorothea) is difficult to assess fully, but doubtlessly it was partly a sublimation of sexual drives into religious experience. The struggle to remain chaste was an unceasing one, a process that was aided by constant physical activity in the hunt and training for battle, simple food, a closely regulated daily life, attendance at church services day and night, fasts, watches, and the encouragement of a personal piety connected with saintly figures. The veneration of Lady Mary was also the logical culmination of conventional romantic poetry, a poetry that exalted the virtues of women beyond what any mortal could live up to. This idealisation was easily transferred to the ultimate mother image, the Mother of God. Lastly, there was the purely religious significance of her intervening to protect and save suffering mankind. The warriors of the Teutonic Order felt themselves to be suffering voluntarily on her behalf both in the austerity of their daily life and in their possible death on the battlefield.

In 1389 one Western author of crusader propaganda, Philippe de Mézières (1327–1405), wrote a description of the holy wars in the Baltic, using the device of a dream in which Divine Providence guided him throughout the world in the company of Queen Truth and the court ladies Justice, Peace and Mercy. As chivalrous literature it has some merit of its own, but its source of inspiration was France, not Prussia. In the hope of bringing about peace with England by involving both monarchs in crusading ventures, his poem only indirectly reflected the knightly values of the Teutonic Order. No matter how many French and English crusaders came to Marienburg and Königsberg, they could not put aside the habit of regarding the real crusade as the effort to retake Jerusalem.

Chivalry never lost its popularity. Jean II le Meingre, best known as 'Boucicaut' (*c.* 1366–1421), was marshal of France, crusader to Prussia and Spain, warrior against the Turks, and hero of the Hundred Years War. Indefatigable traveller and defender of chivalry and courtesy, his ardour for the memorable gesture led him to rash attacks that more cautious commanders would have avoided – most memorably in 1396, when it led to the almost total destruction of the crusading army at Nicopolis. In *The Waning of the Middle Ages* Johan Huizinga comments that 'One might have supposed him cured of all chivalrous delusions after the catastrophe . . . yet he remained devoted to them.'

Poets, Troubadours, and Musicians

The Teutonic Knights liked secular literary works, especially histories and Bible stories filled with battles, acts of valour, humorous incidents, and short reflections on God's justice and man's limited capacity to understand why He awarded victory at one time and at another time defeat. Stories of warfare across the Samogitian frontier were detailed and explicit, offering lessons applicable to future combat.

The order's patronage of poets was generous. *The Treasurer's Book at Marienburg* (1399–1409) recorded numerous payments to jongleurs and fools, singers and orators, musicians and entertainers. Not only were the grandmasters patrons of the arts, but they needed performers to entertain crusaders. However, an assumption that the *Treasurer's Book* accurately reflects court life sixty and seventy years earlier is probably a wishful anachronism. More likely the grandmasters of the 1330s and 1340s relied on visitors to provide entertainment, something they were often willing to do.

It is not easy to evaluate the quality of the music. Numerous poems mention music, song and dances for the visitors, but we do not know what was played or sung; moreover, women were not present at any entertainment provided by the military order, despite a popular account by a much later historian who described Winrich of Kniprode leading a lady into the ballroom. Dancing was offered by the secular nobles and burghers in the cities where the crusaders stayed overnight on their journey to Königsberg, and by Bishop Heinrich III of Ermland (Henryk, bishop 1373–1401) until he took his office more seriously. Heralds, fools and servants were eager to please, certainly eager for a tip. Crusaders from famous courts brought their musicians and singers to increase their own prestige while passing long evenings of the northern winter in banquets and feasts. Guillaume de Machaut, the foremost composer of the era, was there.

The Teutonic Knights had drummers, buglers and pipers who played on every campaign. No intrusion into the wilderness was made without brass music and rolling drums; but that was military music, not professional entertainment. Lastly, there was music for prayers and masses. Choirs accompanied mass in the major convents, where Order priests provided free schooling for boys on the condition that they sing in religious services.

The Teutonic Order combined this piety with a love of political intrigue, a delight in war, an enthusiasm for the hunt, and an enjoyment of good food and entertainment. That was an expression of the complexity of their minds, not their simplicity. If at various times one aspect of this complexity stands out among the documentary evidence, that must be accepted with caution, because whim and luck have determined what was written down and what has survived. At the same time, a love of worldly display was becoming increasingly obvious. This evidenced itself less in the literature than in the architecture. The Teutonic Knights impressed their contemporaries more by their achievements in building than in any other way.

Castles and Chivalry

Castles constructed before 1320 were designed for war; they were often simple square log and earth forts, with thick walls and high, stout towers. After that date, however, once the danger of serious pagan attacks passed, these were rebuilt and enlarged. They became convents as well as forts, comfortable and convenient, suitable for guests as well as for the garrison. Impressive brick structures around a central courtyard contained a dormitory, a chapel, a chapter room, a dining room, and often a small recreation area on an upper floor; the private rooms of the commander were generally located there as well. On the ground floor were work areas: a brewery, bakery, offices, equipment storage and repair, and the powder magazine. In the basements were storage areas, the kitchen, and the central heating plant.

After 1350 the men who designed the castles (apparently clerics who had studied architecture) gave even greater emphasis to comfort and elegance. They had towers rising to a height of 55 m. (180 ft.), decorated capitals, carved archways, gothic windows, and toilet and bathing facilities. This was not practical for the purposes of defending a fortified position against attack, but the mock-military adornment made a great impression on subjects and visitors, and probably reinforced the self-confidence of the knights and half-brothers. These architectural details underscored the commitment to holy war.

The showplace of Prussia was Marienburg. Karl of Trier had begun an expansion of the existing small rectangular castle about 1320 because the simple chapel, refectory and dormitory were insufficient for the number of visitors who expected lodging there. His architects followed recent French designs, and later grandmasters copied ideas from Avignon, where the popes were building a palace that was the wonder of the age. Karl's plan for Marienburg emphasised a central court surrounded by multi-storey red brick buildings. This High Castle, as it was called, was 52 m. (170 ft.) square, with machicolated walls and gothic windows and doorways. The north gate was a monumental 14 m. (45 ft.) high, very suitable for ceremonial entrances, but still practically unassailable. Around the courtyard was a two-storey walkway, covered for protection from the weather and decorated with columns and gothic openings for a harmonious aesthetic effect. The buildings were four storeys high, topped with tile roofs, and so spaced that it seemed that building was piled atop building, each going further into the sky. In fact, everywhere in the castle, inside and out, there was a successful effort to create the impression of monumentality: wall after wall, building after building, each topping the structures in front, all done in a dark red brick which gave a unity to the composition.

The low basement with broad arches contained large rooms for supplies, workshops, cells for a few prisoners, an iron-lined treasury vault, and the kitchen and furnace. Public offices were on the ground floor to be easily accessible for visitors.

The convent was upstairs, the north wing of which contained the large Mary Chapel and the chapter room. The chapel was entered through the highly decorated Golden Door (which was finished only in the fifteenth century). To provide light for the large gothic windows, the chapel jutted beyond the square outline of the castle. Some 38 m. long, 10 m. wide, and 14 m. high (126 × 33 × 46 ft.), the chapel was covered with a new form of arch: eight ribs stretched down from the boss to the corbels mounted half-way up the walls; this created a complicated and pleasing star pattern on the ceiling. Below the chapel of St Mary was the Chapel of St Anne, where many grandmasters were buried.

In the chapter room, where important business was discussed, there was another striking innovation in arching based on three narrow central pillars. The ribs formed a series of triangles, giving an air of spaciousness and ease. Its pleasing proportions (2 : 2.5) aided in setting a mood suitable for harmonious business and memorable receptions.

The architects enlarged the dormitories in the east and south wings, built day rooms, and constructed walkways to the toilets beyond the walls. The priests' tower soared high above the battlements, giving a magnificent view of the surrounding countryside and the rivers.

Winrich of Kniprode began the Middle Castle, a much larger but lower structure with a huge courtyard. As a visitor entered through the main gate, he saw the great refectory on the left, with a large kitchen, hospital and rooms for guests. Straight ahead was the main gate of the High Castle. On the right, along the river front, he saw the palace of the grandmaster, a five-storey residence that was one of the most remarkable palatial homes of the Middle Ages. The gothic decoration on the towers, built outward in successive rows of brick, with strong vertical lines in the windows and a peaked roof, caught every visitor's attention immediately. The interior, with its fantastic vaulting, lived up to the promise of the exterior. The large rooms had the feel of grace and comfort. The air of simplicity created by the plain brick and the austerity of the furnishings stood in stark contrast to the lavishness of the gothic detail around the windows and doors; and the intricacy of the ribbing was in great contrast to the puritan restraint found elsewhere.

The Middle Castle was no sooner completed than a Lower Castle was started. This addition was necessary to bring all the outbuildings inside the defensive system. Although the High and Middle Castles were intended to be defended separately, the whole formed a unit that was stronger than the sum of its parts. The town, which lay to the south, had its own walls and towers, and the entire castle was protected by the river and extensive moats. The three castles covered forty-five acres. The visitor approaching by water faced powerful walls extending to the narrow beach and set back just far enough that ships could not approach close enough for men to spring from the masts onto the walls. There was no true harbour, but there was a strongly fortified water-gate at the landing place. Visitors coming by land passed through successive lines of defences, each more heavily guarded.

The very size and complexity of this fortress was useful for psychological warfare: the effect on visiting crusaders and diplomats was notable. The effectiveness of the whole fortification proved itself in 1410, when a few thousand defenders repulsed far larger numbers of Polish and Lithuanian besiegers.

Marienburg was also designed for comfort. There were at least five separate bathhouses for the eighty knights, the grandmaster, the hospital, the servants and visitors. In each were hot rooms, steam rooms, and bathing tubs; and there were skilled attendants who knew how to bleed painlessly and to apply the hot towels considered essential to curing the colds so common in the wet northern climate. There were also nineteen wells lined with stone, and numerous toilet facilities. The central heating produced a room temperature of 20 °C (68 °F) in a modern test; the servants were probably able to do even better in the fourteenth century. There were covered walkways between all buildings so that no one needed to go out in the rain or stand guard in discomfort.

Königsberg was also enlarged and beautified. As the residence of the marshal, it would be the assembly point for armies planning to march up the Nemunas. Ultimately, it would be the home of the secular dukes of Prussia, a fitting residence for important regional princes.

While the emphasis on monumentality was found across Europe, in Prussia only Marienburg was exceptionally large, but the marshal in Königsberg was able to entertain the annual influx of crusaders from across Europe. The beauty of a castle was becoming as important as its military function, and its comfort as important as its beauty.

As builder of many of these fortresses, Winrich of Kniprode became famous far beyond the frontiers of the Holy Roman Empire. His successors improved upon the decoration and comfort, adding innovations as quickly as they heard of them.

Chivalry and the Decorative Arts

The decorations of the palace, the chapels, and the cathedrals were not slavish copies of Italian and French models, but rather adaptations suitable to the climate and local building materials. The lack of good local stone, for example, presented challenges to the sculptors who were to ornament the altars, walls and doorways. The methods chosen were diverse: some artists applied stucco, others terracotta; a few imported limestone blocks from Gotland; and some used linden wood. The climate was not kind to art – few statues and paintings have survived the centuries in good condition; damp attacked the wood and frescos relentlessly, and mould grew prolifically. Only stucco and terracotta have resisted the wet and cold well, but mosaics provided interesting wall and floor decorations. Although puritan restraint discouraged portraying animals, plants or objects, the tile floors were both aesthetically satisfying and easy to clean.

In the cathedrals and abbeys there was a strong emphasis on wall painting not found in the convents of the knights. This may seem surprising, since three of the four bishoprics were staffed by priests of the Order, who presumably shared the same artistic tastes as the designers of the convent chapels. However, there was an important difference. In the cathedrals there was a strong influence of Italy, Avignon and Bohemia, which the bishops and individual canons visited more frequently than did the knights and priests in the convents. They were apparently greatly impressed by what they saw, especially during the reign of Charles IV, when Italian artists were active in Bohemia. They wanted high-quality reproductions of Bohemian triptychs and frescos, altars and reliquaries. They imitated as best they could Charles's jewelled chapel at Karlštejn, with its motifs of King Arthur. They patronised artists from Cologne and other German cities, as well. The *Marienburg Account Book* informs us that Grandmaster Ulrich of Jungingen spent significant sums on sculptures, paintings and illuminated manuscripts. Unfortunately, only a few of the artworks of that time have survived, but if we dare extrapolate from those which did, we conclude that the medieval holdings of the Prussian convents and churches must have been impressive. However, the quality was not always high – as an artist warned those who viewed his portrayal of a knight on the wall of a small church near Königsberg, 'Cursed be he who criticises this painting!'

Painting was less important and therefore less innovative than architecture for several reasons. First, the officers of the Teutonic Order were less interested in religious art than were their bishops. The knights were members of a military organisation whose members had little training in the appreciation of fine art and less time to study it. Secondly, the Order was relatively puritan in its attitude towards decoration. Poverty was the first vow taken by the members, a pledge shared by the Franciscans and Dominicans, the two most popular religious orders in Prussia. The Cistercians, the most important order in northern Poland, relied heavily upon whitewash to give a mood of simplicity and austerity to their churches. Lastly, visiting crusaders, neighbouring princes and enemy chieftains were more impressed by monumental castles than delicate paintings or graceful statuary.

The emphasis on the military arts might have been even stronger had the rules of the Order permitted tournaments. Jousting was expensive and distracting, and it could not be justified as training for warfare. Nor would it enhance the reputation of the Order should its best knights fall before the lances of French, English or, God forbid, Polish warriors!

Coinage an Expression of Chivalry

The art of the mint master improved greatly during the reign of Winrich of Kniprode. Although the Teutonic Order had pursued a careful monetary policy for over a century, this had been confined to assuring that the various civic mints produced a uniform currency. Many foreign pennies circulated in the cities, and only slowly did the Order produce large quantities of its own *bracteats* (thin silver pennies impressed so strongly on one side as to carry the pattern onto the reverse). Although we cannot determine the age or provenance of the majority of the *bracteats*, we know that mints existed in Culm, Thorn, Elbing and other cities.

Presumably those *bracteats* showing the Order's cross on a shield reflected a deliberate effort to publicise the crusade. That seems to be part of Winrich of Kniprode's currency reform which introduced the *Schilling* about 1350, worth twelve pence.

The *Schilling* displayed the grandmaster's cross and his name on the face, with a crusader's cross on the reverse. It was a beautiful coin, a propaganda triumph for the Order, and a visible reminder of the wealth of the state. There was a larger coin, the *Halbschoter*, was based on the popular *Groschen* and was worth sixteen pence, and a smaller one, the *Vierchen*, was worth four.

The grandmasters did not put their personal coats of arms on their coins, as the Livonian masters did. That seems to have been a concession to tradition, to avoid personal ostentation and sinful pride, and perhaps to emphasise the motto on the reverse, that each coin was money of the Teutonic Order in Prussia and, therefore, could be relied upon.

The Model Chivalric Knight: Grandmaster Winrich

Winrich of Kniprode lived at the right time. Chroniclers such as Froissart honoured individual heroes such as the Black Prince, Bertrand du Guesclin, John Chandos, and others who fought heroically in the Hundred Years War. Perhaps contemporaries honoured those knights because there were so few heroes left. New tactics being introduced in France made it difficult to live long enough to become famous: archers and gunners were shooting down potential champions at long distance. Italian towns and princes were hiring mercenaries to fight their wars, and many noble knights became no better than military merchants peddling their services.

There was no hope of recovering the Holy Sepulchre, but Christians could still strike a blow against enemies of the Cross. The Spanish crusade had the advantage of being easily reached and there was the pilgrimage shrine at Santiago de Compostela. But the Moorish hit-and-run tactics were uncongenial. The tragic fate of the Scots who fulfilled a vow by taking the heart of their late king Robert the Bruce on crusade in Spain in 1330 was well known – advancing steadily against the Moors, the Scots were abandoned by their allies, surrounded and killed by a sea of light cavalry (though the heart was eventually taken home). This was a weighty argument in favour of campaigning in Prussia.

The Teutonic Knights were fortunate in that Prussia was growing wealthier. Policies to encourage immigration and trade were now paying handsomely in taxes and cheap produce. As a result, Winrich of Kniprode was able to build great castles, fill banquet halls with furniture and food, and offer visitors an opportunity to meet great men from all parts of Europe, even dukes and heirs to crowns. A young knight could return home with exciting stories of men and deeds to enliven long winter evenings for decades to come. If the forays into Samogitia were manhunts, they were hunts for armed men of exceptional skill and tenacity, men whom it was an honour to fight and defeat. Lastly, Winrich conferred a means of serving God by defending Christians against barbaric foes who threatened Germans, Poles and native converts with death and slavery.

The reality was more brutal. Długosz described the wars as incredibly hard-fought, with few scruples about methods on either side. As daily life for the Order's own knights became less monastic and more secular, grandmasters issued injunctions against modish dress, against long hair, and against riding around the countryside just to hunt or to frequent inns. Private property and money were banned, but individual knights acquired fur coats, pointed hats, and buckled shoes; some even decorated their scabbards and painted their shields as they had been accustomed to doing before they took a vow of poverty. The inability to maintain the outward appearance of a monastic calling reflected class traditions that encouraged them to feel that they *were* better than their subjects. Some behaved arrogantly towards city councils and secular knights (slighting their contributions to the crusade, imposing new taxes, and quarrelling over the extent of their self-government); this slowly exhausted their moral capital and left behind a reputation for haughtiness and ambition. Among the noble families whose sons joined the Order, however, these very characteristics were proof of their superiority and worth. What their subjects thought, and what bourgeois historians of an unimaginable democratic future might write were of little importance. Courage, prowess and honour were all that really mattered.

The always provocative Norman Davies wrote in *God's Playground*:

Modern Poles . . . may be forgiven for imagining that the Teutonic Order provided the shock troops of a national German enemy. But the Order was the manifestation of something more universal. Its armies, though predominantly German in complexion, were swelled by professional recruits from all over Europe, and by the seasonal ranks of 'guests' who had ever less interest in converting pagans. The military order was the incarnation of the most un-Christian elements of the Christian world and it was enjoying immense worldly success.

The International Crusade

Prussia could be reached by either land or sea, and it lay at sufficient distance from the turmoil of the Hundred Years War, the vicissitudes of the Holy Roman Empire, the advance of the Turks, and the troubles of the papacy that Western politics seldom disturbed it. It was an island of peace with a war on its eastern frontier that it was winning. The crusade was so successful, in fact, that in 1358 Holy Roman Emperor Charles IV would propose using some of the Order's resources to fight the Turks on the Danube. This became a serious suggestion, however, only between 1414 and 1418, and an actuality only between 1426 and 1434 and then later in the sixteenth and seventeenth centuries.

This was no longer just a German crusade, as it had been after the mid-thirteenth century when armies of Polish knights ceased to participate. Chaucer's English Knight came, as did an Orsini duke from Naples, and French princes. Although the King of Poland abstained, Poles from Silesia and Masovia came, as did Bohemians, some Hungarians and a few Scots.

Knights made life-long friends on the crusade. Froissart tells a story about the capture of Caen by the English in 1346, when the constable of France and other notables were afraid that they would be slaughtered by Welsh and Irish foot soldiers. No mercy was being given. Seeing Sir Thomas of Holland (later Earl of Kent and one of the first knights given the Order of the Garter), whom they knew from having served together in Prussia and Spain, they called to him for protection.

Each expedition into the Samogitian forests and swamps was an opportunity for squires to 'win their spurs' (to become knights) honourably and cheaply, and for rich nobles to earn respect by lavish hospitality and displays of courage. The Austrian poet Peter Suchenwirt described the great expedition of Albrecht of Austria to seek knighthood in 1377 – the poem remains one of the best pieces of medieval literature, with its exhortation to knights to serve 'God, Honour, and Chivalry'. He concluded his long narrative with this exhortation:

One counsel I give to noble folk: He who will become a good knight, let him make as companion Lady Honour and St George. 'Better knight than squire!' Let him bear that word in his heart, with will and with good deeds; so shall he defy slander, and his name shall be spoken with honour.

Many squires took that admonition to heart. So did experienced campaigners. Several knights came back for a second, third and fourth crusade. Friedrich of Kreisbach, the hunting master of the Austrian duke, participated three times, once travelling through Poland and Masovia to Prussia, then to Livonia, and on to Belarus and Sweden and Norway. He also visited the Holy Land three times, France, Italy, Spain, England, Scotland, Egypt, Byzantium, Cyprus, Majorca and the Balkans. One poet said:

> One knight goes to Prussia, another to France and another to Flanders, yet another to Hungary, some to Swabia and to Apulia, and even some to Greece. That's so that we all have enough room, not crowding one another.

There were many gallant feats. In 1355–6 Johann of Traun (Jan or Hans, *d.* 1378), an Austrian knight, 'charged out ahead of the army at the heathens, taking the lives of seven and capturing five, he and his comrades, then returning without loss'. Later he selected twenty-six of the best knights, attacked the Lithuanians and slew another thirty-two. As the raid came to an end, he transferred over to the Livonian army and fought against Belarusians, slaying a duke with his own hand, and capturing another. Not surprisingly, he was selected for the honour of bearing the St George banner. He had fought on the English side at Crécy and would do so again in 1356 at Poitiers; his chivalric career was extraordinary even in an era filled with extraordinary men.

What opportunities for adventure! If East Central Europe seems strange and exotic to Westerners even today, the knights who went on crusade there thought so as well.

But these were not gentle tourists, however much we may think of this as a 'grand tour' or a graduation party for a military finishing school. In 1345 the count of Nuremberg was knighted on crusade with the kings of Bohemia and Hungary. This famous occasion was celebrated by Peter Suchenwirt: 'One saw many guests, numberless, from distant lands, attacking Lithuania. They made many orphans, left without father and mother.' They achieved this at relatively low cost – in their own casualties, that is. The expedition itself was expensive and had its hardships and dangers (disease, accidents and arrows). As Werner Paravicini reminds us, without merchants extending credit, there would have been no crusade. But few noble crusaders died in Samogitia. No more, as best we can tell, than the average of any military campaign that did not culminate in a major battle (and since the weaker forces usually avoided a direct confrontation, there were more sieges than battles). The greatest danger was disease, but that was a problem even for those who stayed safely at home.

Volunteers from the lower nobility and wealthy burghers who were trained at arms were being augmented by mercenaries, men who would serve for longer periods. This would provide the grandmasters with new challenges. How could they recruit volunteers, when the lure of well-paid employment was drawing them away, often into the armies of the Hundred Years War?

Chapter Nine

Desperate Combats

It is widely believed that a pope had to declare each crusading expedition. That is only partly true. The popes would have liked to control the crusades – for all sorts of reasons, good and bad – but in fact it was impractical to do so. They had other problems to deal with, they were far from the battlefield, they died, they became incapacitated, and they became distracted. Pope Urban V was even besieged in Avignon by free companies – organised but unemployed mercenaries from the Hundred Years War who demanded ransoms, food, horses, cattle and lodging from everyone. Urban V tried to persuade his besiegers to fight against the Turks, but they understood that he really wanted to get them killed, or at least out of the country, so they refused.

The Teutonic Knights did not want to wait for papal approval of each campaign. That would be time-consuming and rob them of all flexibility; moreover, they could imagine a pope demanding some financial or political reward in exchange. Fortunately for them, Urban V was more interested in reuniting the churches, and his successors would have their own priorities.

King Casimir shared the fear of too much papal interference, so he routinely ignored inconvenient papal instructions.

As a result of these factors, and inertia, direction of the 'perpetual' crusades on the periphery of western Christendom remained decentralised. Almost everyone understood that this was the only effective way to operate.

Preparations for an Offensive

From 1359 the marshal was a capable Thuringian, Henning Schindekopf, whose entire career had been spent on the Nemunas River frontier. He must have rejoiced over the grandmaster's decision to establish footholds on the right bank of the Nemunas, rather than make intrusive raids, then retreat. In 1360 Winrich built Neuhausen (the new castle, Guryevsk) across the Nemunas from Tilsit, where the Nemunas divided into several branches, while Henning supervised the building of Windenburg (Ventė) on a peninsula at the mouth of the Minija River. This guaranteed safe passage from the sea to the Nemunas.

In the summer they built two additional castles to protect the route to Livonia over the sand spit which separated the Baltic from the Curonian Lagoon. But priority went to establishing more bases on the Nemunas. When crusaders led by Otto II of Hesse (called 'the bowman' after a romantic tale) was intercepted by pagans near Welun, his crusaders charged, shouting *'Hessenland!'* They inflicted such a defeat that Welun rarely figured again in the chronicles.

Winrich and Henning pressed their advantage in the winter, employing prominent crusaders from the Mosel–Nassau region, then a Thomas Spencer – apparently not related to the English family that became famous in the following century – came in the summer of 1361 and was still there when a stroke of luck came the crusaders' way.

According to the confusing, fragmentary account of Wigand of Marburg, crusaders led by Duke Albrecht V of Saxe-Lauenburg (c. 1335–70) had raided the Narew River valley. On Palm Sunday, as the duke was returning to Prussia, his escort of Teutonic Knights heard that Algirdas and Kęstutis were on their way into Galindia through the Masurian Lake district. The hurrying Christians caught the pagan armies pillaging. First, they dealt with the most organised force – probably the men left to guard the plunder – killing 130 while losing only 14. Then they set out against the raiders scattered across the countryside. Algirdas had fled at the first sign of danger, thereby easily outrunning the exhausted crusader mounts.

Kęstutis might have been killed in the fighting had he not identified himself to his captor; but his very act of surrender ended all hope of escaping in the confusion. Wigand of Marburg reported that the Teutonic Knights led him in triumph to Marienburg, then put him into the prison, watched by two knights during the day but by none at night. Thus, in mid-November, with the aid of a Lithuanian convert who worked in the castle, Kęstutis escaped from his basement cell – a rather more comfortable prison than it sounds – by slipping a loose stone out of the wall. He stole a white cloak with the black cross and then walked through the castle, unrecognised by anyone – every knight wore a beard, as did most Lithuanian warriors. After the gates were opened, he saw a horse saddled for the grandmaster, mounted and rode quietly out the gate. Soon the 65-year-old duke let his horse run free while he hid for several days in a swamp near Elbing. While his pursuers were searching the roads leading towards Lithuania, Kęstutis went south on foot, moving only at night, to Masovia, where his sister was the dowager duchess of Płock. His clever escape did nothing to hurt his already impressive reputation among the crusaders.

While this was an exciting tale, scholars have found it confusing. First, only contradictory fragments of the chronicle survive. Moreover, aspects of the story defy logic: did nobody note that he was not in his cell? Were Lithuanians waiting for him outside? After reading all the versions of what this well-informed chronicler said, we come away uncertain about what had happened. Długosz, who is among the best chroniclers of the era, says that there were two captures and two escapes! The second was perhaps associated with a 1362 campaign, but that is not clear. It may be that, given the ease with which the crusaders were winning battles in Lithuania, the Teutonic Knights may not have considered his capture that important. Or perhaps, as Baronas has argued, the Teutonic Knights needed a pagan enemy to justify their crusade, and therefore merely released him to return home and serve their propaganda purposes as a dangerous enemy of the faith. This, of course, requires historians to believe that the portrayal of the Teutonic Knights drawn by its enemies was accurate, a view made popular by novelists such as Henryk Sienkiewicz, whose *Krzyżacy* (*The Crossbearers*, 1900) was important in keeping the flame of Polish patriotism burning when the tsars were trying to stamp it out.

Documents from this time confirm that the officers of the Order were very confident of victory. They were issuing grants of land that detailed the obligations of the new vassals: requirements to deliver quantities of rye, wheat and wax, in addition to a tax and the obligation to perform military service. The conditions were not light, as one might expect if the recipients were reluctant to move into newly opened lands. However, by summer the officers' attention was drawn to Kęstutis again because his attacks were becoming bolder and more menacing.

In the years that followed tales about Kęstutis reached mythic proportions, and more stories of his exploits circulated in Lithuania and Poland. For example, a sixteenth-century tale recounted how he had fallen in love with Birutė, a beautiful Samogitian priestess, who refused his suit. The episode climaxed with his kidnapping her, taking her to his castle at Old Trakai, and marrying her amid great celebration. They had, evidence suggests, six sons and three daughters, but historians still quarrel over the identity of some of the sons.

Four times Kęstutis suggested that he was ready to become a Christian; and he encouraged Western churchmen to worry about Orthodox competition. Paganism had lost its vitality – so that opposition would be minimal – but it was not yet so weak that he could ignore it. There were still *Witingen* and common folk who believed in its power, but even they had been so affected by Christian ideas and practices that their resistance to crusaders was based more on dislike of foreign domination than loyalty to a religion so vague that the crusaders had never captured a shaman or found a pagan temple. Another reason was that their Orthodox subjects were willing to tolerate rule by pagans but would never accept a Roman Catholic. The unbridgeable gap was the pope – not as an individual, but as a symbol of Western claims to supremacy. Everything else was superficial – East and West alike believed in saints, miracles and visions, faith healers and magicians, and holy men and women who knew the secrets of nature. Everyone was superstitious. If one Christian read the Bible in Latin, another in Greek, that was a problem that could be overcome. Even priestly celibacy was often observed as a formality in the West, and it had only been required since the late eleventh century – discussion of possible compromises had indicated that it would be possible to allow the Orthodox priests to retain their wives. But there was too much history. This allowed Kęstutis to explain that he would have to be paid handsomely for kneeling at a baptismal font.

In March 1362, during Lent, the grand commander and the marshal gathered warriors from all parts of East Prussia, added crusaders from Germany, England and Italy – with a count of Blois as the banner-carrier – and rode from Königsberg to Ragnit. Although several days would have been required to load the vessels, once aboard, the crusaders could rest for the two or three days it took to sail or row upstream to Kaunas, then disembark.

The grandmaster followed along later, presumably when the boats returned for the rest of the army. The *Litauischen Wegeberichte* shows that there was no direct road to Kaunas – everything in between was wood and swamp. It would have taken three weeks for heavily armoured horsemen to slog their way east, only to arrive exhausted.

Kaunas was situated on a peninsula where the Neris flowed into the Nemunas. It was strongly fortified with a powerful wall, towers, bastions and keep, with wooden houses for the garrison of 3,500 men commanded by Kęstutis's eldest son, Vaidotas (1330–*c.* 1401). The sudden appearance of the fleet must have stunned the defenders because the Lithuanian dukes had not received word soon enough to be ready to attack the first crusaders ashore, and once there were walls across the peninsula – one to guard the crusaders against a sortie, another to prevent any relief force from reaching Kaunas, with a ditch filled with water from the rivers – there was little they could do. Part of the Christian army remained on an island with the fleet, with a bridge across the Neris, while the rest constructed catapults and a gigantic tower. After ten days the besiegers attacked the extensive fortifications, hammering away at the wall with a gigantic ram.

The Polish scholar Krzysztof Kwiatkowski wrote a detailed account of the siege in the *Zeitschrift für Ostmitteleuropa* in 2008, enhancing the many details provided by the chronicler Wigand of Marburg. The defenders were well-equipped, and there were many archers among them; in addition, they sallied out at night in efforts to destroy the siege machines. Meanwhile, Kęstutis and Algirdas approached the crusader lines, but withdrew after one combat with the grandmaster's forces. All that they could do was to besiege the besiegers. While the crusaders could be supplied from the ships, the dukes must have found it difficult to feed their large army. Camped on a high hill nearby, they watched with dismay as the siege progressed.

Sven Ekdahl's numerous publications tell us much about warfare in this era. The siege tower dominated the ramparts, allowing archers to rain deadly missile fire down on the defenders; once infantry filled the dry moat, the ram moved to the wall, undermining it until it crashed into a pile of rubble. When the buildings began to burn, the crusaders charged into the breach, slaying almost 600 men before they had to retreat from the conflagration. Perhaps 2,400 of the garrison died in the inferno, but there were some prisoners: Kęstutis's son, Vaidotas, 36 *Witingen* and 500 commoners. The crusaders' losses had been about 200. Laughing, they sang in German, 'We can all be happy, the heathens are all in hell.'

Because this three-week siege included Easter week, Kwiatkowski suggests that this might be the moment when '*Christ ist erstanden*' ('Christ is risen') became the battle hymn of the Teutonic Order. One chronicler recounted how on Good Friday Kęstutis called out to the grandmaster, 'If I'd been in the castle, you wouldn't have captured it so easily! With all your crusaders, you'd never have taken it from me!' The grandmaster retorted, 'Why'd you leave it then, when you saw us coming?'

Kęstutis answered, 'My army didn't have a leader, I had to be with it.'

'Well, come occupy it now. We'll let you in!'

'How could I do that? The whole field is filled with ditches and fortifications.'

Winrich almost laughed, apparently, 'If you want to come down, we'll flatten it all out for you.'

The grandmaster consulted his engineers, who advised him that the castle could not be repaired before the army had to leave. Not daring to leave a garrison in the ruins, the grandmaster decided to burn what remained of the castle and to return to Prussia. First, however, the bishop of Sambia celebrated Easter. When the victory banquet was concluded, the crusaders destroyed the bridge over the Neris to prevent a pursuit, then filed aboard their vessels and slipped away downstream.

Kwiatkowski suggests that the vivid description and dialogue were for a dramatic reading to large audiences. It would certainly have entertained crusaders and potential volunteers from the Holy Roman Empire and might even have been used as the text of a play, like the one staged in Livonia a century and a half earlier to teach Biblical history to converts.

The Lithuanian dukes hurried to build a new castle, one more strongly fortified, but less vulnerable to naval attack, lest the Christians advance unchallenged up the Neris into the Lithuanian highlands. For several years to come the two sides would contest vital pieces of real estate around Kaunas, but there were no major encounters, because bad harvests and epidemics prevented Winrich from assembling another large army. This was ironic because the political situation had suddenly become favourable for attacks on Lithuania. Not because Lithuania was weak, but because it had grown comparatively strong in the east while the Tatars were distracted by a sanguinary civil war.

Lithuanian advances into Rus'

Algirdas's greatest claim to fame was that in 1362/3 he defeated a Tatar army in the Battle of Blue Waters, a claim that has likely been exaggerated by Lithuanian and Ukrainian nationalists. According to this tradition, he began his campaign by riding south from Volhynia into thinly populated Podolia, then made his way down the Southern Bug River to where it flowed into the Black Sea. The Tatar army that came to meet him was smaller than usual because many khans had joined in the feud between the Crimean khan and the ruler of New Sarai.

Tradition says that it was a hard-fought battle, with the Lithuanians apparently fighting on foot. The details are sketchy and come only from a chronicle dating from the late sixteenth century that describes the Tatars' cavalry attack, with the customary hail of arrows, then the slow advance of Lithuanians armed with swords and spears immobilising the Tatar forces until the four sons of Algirdas's late brother Karijotas could arrive in the Tatar rear with men from Navahrudak.

This victory apparently encouraged two of Karijotas's sons to demand Volhynia and Galicia as payment for their services. When Algirdas refused, they fled to Cracow to plead for Casimir's assistance. Meanwhile, Algirdas rode south to let his horse wade in the Black Sea before returning home. It made no sense to try to hold the region, but he had routed the Tatars from much of the western steppe. Since it was years before order was restored in the Golden Horde, Algirdas was able to place a son in Kyiv. The achievement was more symbolic than important, because the Mongol and Tatar depredations had reduced the number of peasants and herders to a point that the ancient capital had declined to a minor town.

This led to Algirdas's long and desperate struggle with young Dmitri of Moscow (1350–89) for hegemony over Rus', a struggle that would occupy the supreme duke's attentions so fully that he could seldom send help to Kęstutis in his wars against Poland and the Teutonic Knights. Algirdas had some successes, thanks to his alliance with the prince of Tver', his brother-in-law, and Suzdal, and distractions for the new Tatar khan. Algirdas loosened Dmitri's grip on the minor principalities of central and eastern Rus' sufficiently to appoint brothers, sons, and nephews to rule various cities there. In 1368 and 1370 he advanced right to the new stone wall of the Kremlin and once he threw his spear into the main gate so forcefully that it stuck. However, in the end he failed to establish his dynasty as firmly in the east as he had done earlier in the south.

Algirdas failed in his ambitions partly because the Rus'ian people – who jealously guarded their rights – tolerated the rule of Lithuanians as a necessary evil but were uncomfortable with their paganism or the sincerity of anyone who converted so easily to the Orthodox Church. Whenever an opportunity appeared to be governed by a member of their traditional ruling dynasty, they would acclaim him. This required Algirdas to be constantly on the alert for rebellion.

A second, closely related problem was the challenge of the Golden Horde, the popular name for the Turkish tribes which had replaced the Mongols in Turkestan and on the steppes in 1363. The khans practised a balance of power in Rus', which typically meant supporting the weakest party in every dispute, thus undermining whichever duke seemed most likely to become independent; however, no fewer than fourteen khans ruled between 1360 and 1380, making it impossible to have a consistent policy.

Although the Tatars were still potentially as dangerous as the Mongols had ever been, their distant master – Timur (Tamberlane, 1336–1405) – was invading Persia, India and the Ottoman Empire. His policy in the north was to pit one ruler against another, with quarrelling local khans holding the balance, and collecting taxes from everyone.

Historians have held very diverse views about the Russian–Tatar relationship, some saying that Moscow was the heir of the Tatar state, others that the Tatars had no influence on Russia. Charles Halperin took the middle ground, pointing out administrative and political borrowings, necessary copying of military equipment and tactics, but refusing to go so far as the proverb, 'Scratch a Russian, find a Tatar.'

Marking Time

Fortunately for Kęstutis, Winrich's army poised little danger to the Lithuanian highlands, which were guarded better by the plague than by fortresses. The pandemic wave of the early 1360s had struck Rus' (and perhaps Lithuania, too) as horribly as it had Prussia earlier. So many peasants died or sickened that work in the fields was interrupted and famine resulted. Consequently, even had Winrich been able to raise a large army, he might well have hesitated to lead it into an infected district.

The grandmaster had less reason to fear the plague in Samogitia, where his small armies were reinforced by knights from England, Bavaria and other nations. Most of the fighting was in the Nemunas valley, where he could put his superior naval power to good use. Only occasionally did crusaders make their way by land up the Neris valley towards Vilnius. Most military operations were raids intended to wear down border communities.

The knights in Livonia were becoming an important factor in the war now. From the great fortress at Dünaburg, at the southernmost bend of the Daugava, raiders could reach into the central highlands. Moreover, Livonian armies could strike into Samogitia from Goldingen, Mitau, and several smaller castles. Two decades earlier Lithuanians and Samogitians could range freely over the Livonian frontier, even striking deep into the heart of the country. Now the circumstances had changed – the Order in Livonia was leading coalitions of knights, episcopal vassals, secular knights from Estonia and native militias. Livonia even had its own chivalric hero, Robin of Eltz. His exploits, which go far back before he served as Livonian Master, 1385–9, are described in Urban, *The Livonian Crusade*.

As the pestilence shifted from central Europe to the east, fortune began to favour Grandmaster Winrich again. He followed developments as best he could through merchants who visited Novgorod, Pskov, Polotsk, Brest-Litovsk and Lviv, and from prisoners. Although he probably did not understand fully what was transpiring, he knew that Kęstutis would not be able to call on his brother for reinforcements.

In January 1364 Winrich met the Livonian master in Samogitia and transferred some visiting crusaders to his command, after which both armies withdrew slowly, devastating every district they passed through. Winrich made extensive preparations for a surprise attack on a religious gathering, then, after collecting his best men from Ragnit, Sambia and Culm, he hurried to the gathering place before the shamans could be warned. When he got close to the gathering, he ordered the main force to make camp and sent the commander of Ragnit to capture the shamans.

The supposed holy men escaped into a swamp, having received warning at the last moment, but the commander did not give up. Despite the warnings of his scouts, who feared they could be trapped by local militiamen, he rode several kilometres farther until he came to a fort where a captive holy man said the fugitives would be hiding. He attacked. Only after he had killed or captured everyone there, did he retreat. Winrich had worried about the raiders' failure to return on time, but the anxiety caused him to rejoice greatly when they reappeared. There is no record of what happened to the captives. No shaman was ever exhibited to the public.

In the summer of 1365 Kęstutis's son Butautas appeared in Insterburg with several of his *Witingen*. Welcomed joyfully by the commander, Butautas was conducted to Königsberg and baptised as Heinrich, with bishops and English crusaders in attendance. His defection, however, had been caused less by Winrich's victories than by internal Lithuanian politics. Apparently dissatisfied with his small lordship along the Bug River, he had tried to overthrow Algirdas (presumably with secret aid from the Teutonic Knights). Failing, he fled for his life. Winrich was unable to make immediate use of Butautas beyond having him guide English crusaders to Vilnius via Kernavė. A year later he sent him to Charles IV, who gave him estates in Bohemia, a residence in the palace, and took him on imperial business. However, nothing came of plans to use him in the conversion of his homeland. Butautas died in 1380, a curiosity of eastern politics.

Shortly before Butautas's death a person some believed to be his son, Vaidutis, arrived in Prague. This prominent, but unidentified Lithuanian entered the Church and, after studying at Paris, became a canon in Cracow, then Sandomir, and was later rector of the university in Cracow. One of his twelve *Witingen*, Thomas Surville, became Winrich's translator and was later trusted with diplomatic missions and the command of small armies.

Another strange person appeared in Prague in 1364 – King Peter of Cyprus (1328–69), who had just made a successful invasion of Cilicia, the nearest part of Asia Minor to his island kingdom. He was on a European tour to recruit crusaders, starting in Avignon, then proceeding through France and Germany to Bohemia. The imperial reception was a glittering affair, but it was eclipsed by the twenty-one-day feast at the Congress of Cracow, when Casimir III hosted a gathering of notables to celebrate the visit. Among the guests were Emperor Charles IV, Louis of Hungary, Waldemar IV of Denmark, Siemowit III of Masovia, Bolko II the Small of Świdnica (the last surviving son of King Ladislas), and his son, Ladislas of Opole (Władysław Opolczyk, 1332–1401, the count palatine of Hungary), Archduke Rudolf IV of Austria (1339–65), Bogisław of Pomerania and his son Casimir IV (the king's grandson), and two sons of the late Holy Roman emperor Louis IV of Bavaria who currently shared the governance of Brandenburg – Otto V (1340/2–79) and Louis VI (1329–65). It was a brilliant occasion, one of the highlights of the age of chivalry.

King Peter's jousting skills were lavishly praised by the poet Guillaume de Marchaut, but the meeting had less lasting importance than two other events that took place in Cracow that year: first, the founding of a university to teach sacred and Roman law, achieved after difficult negotiations with the pope; second, the marriage of Casimir's granddaughter, Elizabeth of Pomerania (1347–93) to the Holy Roman emperor, Charles IV. This resolved the crisis that Charles had provoked by a thoughtless slur on the reputation of the queen mother of Hungary. The bride's children, especially Sigismund (1368–1437), would become major political figures in the next century.

King Peter subsequently visited Denmark and England, then he led a naval force to Alexandria in Egypt – an event that historians often count as the last crusade – but after taking the city, he could not persuade the knights to push on to Cairo. In 1366 he attacked Lebanon. All this was short-term adventurism, expensive and without significant results. Worse, his wife took lovers during his long absences, and his determination to seek revenge brought on his assassination.

Among the visitors to Prussia was Philippe de Mézières, a well-born soldier-of-fortune, writer, diplomat, and teller of tales who was hoping to bring new life to the crusades. Mézières's interests were mainly in Byzantium and the kingdom of Cyprus, which he felt were being neglected by the dispersal of crusader energies and the lack of discipline among the nobility; his proposed solution was a new military order that would incorporate all the existing orders under its leadership – a plan not likely to have been welcomed by Winrich. Late in life, in 1389, the Frenchman wrote the *Songe du Vieil Pèlerin*, an allegorical poem combining his own experiences, stories he had heard, and political philosophy. Through the romance of travel and strange sights Mézières hoped to persuade the still youthful Charles VI of France (1368–1422) to end the schism in the Church, bring an end to the Hundred Years War, and lead a crusade to liberate Jerusalem. In the travel journal he kept while accompanying King Peter, he described the passage by ship through the Danish Sound, the herring catch in the Baltic, characteristics of native Prussians, his impressions of Gotland and Königsberg, and his meeting with the 'heavenly lady' in Marienburg.

Numerous scholars associate Mézières's stories with his visit to Marienburg, where he heard tales about the marvellous cremation ceremonies for Lithuanian kings. He reported that a large funeral pyre would be constructed, with the royal corpse mounted on a living warhorse, then surrounded by pine logs. At this point the king's best friend would be invited to mount the pyre, to die beside his lord. Once, he was told, a captured Teutonic Knight who had become very close to the king was invited to serve as the 'best friend'. The knight, however, pointed out that he had only one eye and was therefore not a proper sacrifice. The chronicler Wigand noted that when Algirdas was cremated, eighteen expensive warhorses were sacrificed to accompany him into the other world.

Mézières was by no means the only traveller with wide experience. It seemed that all Western Europe was on the move. Sometimes this was early tourism, but more likely the motives were as mixed as those of the pilgrims in *The Canterbury Tales*. For inhabitants of Prussia the most popular pilgrimages were to Rome, Santiago de Compostela and Aachen, and to pray at the grave of Dorothea of Montau, just south of Marienburg.

Winrich's Golden Years

The war intensified when Winrich led his best men against Kęstutis's half-completed forts on the Nemunas – Welun and Pisten. A former herald called Wigand wrote that the attackers rushed forward, then after reaching the walls, threw fire inside. While troops from Elbing kept the garrison busy by assaulting one corner – always a weak place in a log fort – the fire grew and grew until the Lithuanian commander shouted to Marshal Henning that he was ready to surrender. Unhappily, the men taking the prisoner to the camp murdered him. The remaining Lithuanians begged to be allowed to surrender, but only a handful who dug under the walls managed to escape in the confusion. About a hundred perished in the flames, fighting to the last. Not long afterwards, when Kęstutis learned from captured fishermen that his two forts were taken, he would not believe it.

It is not necessary to describe all such encounters. However, it is important to note that the crusaders and Lithuanians were becoming more appreciative of one another and more alike. Kęstutis was a prince, unfortunately (in Christian eyes), a pagan one, but still a prince. For his part, Kęstutis curtailed the burning of captives. Kęstutis's fighters were now well-armed and wise in the ways of war. If his Samogitians were slow to adopt Western European noble practices and farming techniques, this was not true elsewhere in Kęstutis's domains. It would be incorrect to believe that Kęstutis and his Lithuanian *Witingen* were Westernised, but they shared the ultra-masculine sense of rough humour.

One example from the year 1366 was when Henning Schindekopf went from Ragnit with a small party of officers to meet Kęstutis near Insterburg. His scouts were approaching the Lithuanian party when they saw a large aurochs and could not resist attacking it with a spear, then pursed it towards the Lithuanians. When Kęstutis saw this, he warned his *Witingen* that the scouts were armed. Fearing a trap, he and his men armed themselves and hurried away until they came to a small castle belonging to the Teutonic Knights. When the lookouts saw the Lithuanians coming, the knights were barely able to hurry from their meal in time to raise the drawbridge. Kęstutis then stole the brothers' horses and took fifty men prisoner. When they returned to meet the marshal, Kęstutis and his men were sitting on the Order's horses, which caused the commander to say that he had not expected such treatment. Kęstutis replied that was the way things were done in these times.

In the spring of 1366, the archbishop of Riga came to Danzig to make peace with the Order's knights in Livonia, bringing a welcome end to the dispute over regional hegemony. It was, furthermore, an acknowledgement of the grandmaster's leadership in northern ecclesiastical matters.

Everything Winrich touched seemed to turn to gold in these years. Even what we would now call a bank robbery in 1364 enhanced his reputation. It could have been a major embarrassment. How could someone break into the vault in Marienburg castle and carry away its treasure without the grandmaster appearing negligent? However, when Winrich's officials learned that several men staying in Marienburg had left town suspiciously, they searched their residence and found part of the loot buried in the basement. The owner of the house confessed, providing information that connected the robbers to Goslar, where they were arrested. The story spread throughout the Empire, enhancing both the Order's reputation for wealth and the long arm of its law.

'Ihis was the moment for Winrich to invite King Casimir to Prussia for a frank discussion of the problems which still troubled their relationship.

Casimir was now stronger than ever. According to Długosz, in 1365 he had summoned Ladislas the White (*c.* 1327–88) of Kujavia to answer charges of having abused his vassals' rights. In Cracow, the flaxen-haired Piast, already despondent over the death of his wife, surrendered his lands to the king for 1,000 florins so that he could travel to Jerusalem. The pilgrimage never happened, though Ladislas kept his vow not to remarry, thereby condemning his Piast dynasty line to extinction. After a visit to the court of Charles IV, Ladislas went to Prussia for the 1366 winter crusade, carefully avoiding any castles that once belonged to him. However, before he ever saw a pagan warrior, he abruptly returned to Bohemia, then went to Avignon, where he briefly became a Cistercian monk. Disgusted with the strict practices of the White Monks, he transferred to the Benedictines. While he lived most his last fourteen years with the Black Monks at royal expense, from time to time he emerged from the monastery to claim his former lands and the royal crown. Ladislas was an extraordinary man in extraordinary times. Had he controlled his emotions and worked towards achievable goals, he might have been Casimir's successor.

In the autumn of 1366 Casimir made a state visit to Marienburg, at which time Winrich literally 'opened the cellars' to provide for him and his following. The grandmaster gave him a complete tour of Marienburg castle, taking him into the most secret areas and into the storehouses, to demonstrate how well prepared his military order was to withstand any challenge. Casimir was reportedly impressed, having been told by his informants that the castle was practically out of provisions. Obviously, this was not so. For three days they feasted and conversed. Although differences of opinion still existed after Casimir went home, the two leaders had agreed to a formula for peace that lasted reasonably well until 1409.

Casimir needed peace because it was still not clear who would become king after him. It would take two years to obtain papal blessing for another marriage, and for that he had to send Polish knights to fight for the pope in Italy. Although his new wife bore him children, all were daughters. His two daughters by Aldona had died, leaving one grandson, Casimir of Stettin – if his marriages had produced a son, the king might have named him his heir, ignoring his promises to Louis of Hungary. (The younger Casimir died in 1377, fighting Ladislas the White.) In the meanwhile, everyone knew that even if the king had a son soon, there would be a long and troubled regency.

Polish ambitions to annex Galicia and Volhynia made the Hungarian alliance more popular. While little is known about the summer campaign of 1366, its results can be seen in two treaties with the Lithuanian leaders that assured Polish possession of some borderlands, created a process for adjudicating disputes, and obtained a Lithuanian promise to come to Casimir's aid in any war – a commitment that was swiftly amended to their remaining neutral, because it was awkward for a Christian king to make an alliance with pagans. In any case, Casimir's authority in these eastern regions rested on his personal relationship with the local lords, not their incorporation into the Polish kingdom. That would come later.

Casimir seems to have hoped that closer contacts with Lithuania would facilitate the process of Westernisation and conversion. But the idea of opening additional trade routes between his kingdom and Lithuania was not new. In 1360 he had ordered a castle built at Rajgród in the Masovian territory of Wizna, which the Peace of Kalisz had given to the care of the Teutonic Knights. Marshal Henning had demanded that the construction stop, saying the castle was being built at the request of Kęstutis. More likely, the castle was designed to prevent Prussian merchants from reaching the Southern Bug River valley, and thence the Black Sea, thereby increasing competition with Polish merchants' access. This would have been a blow to Prussian economic interests, but hardly a reason the grandmaster would have cared to explain to the pope. The Polish commander denied that Kęstutis had even been there, admitting only that a son had been, and he asked the marshal not to attack until he could contact the king for orders.

The negotiations were very friendly in tone, but neither side was ready to yield. When the marshal ordered the agreement about the boundary read aloud by a notary from Marienburg, the Polish official refused to listen to it. Obviously frustrated, the marshal emphasised his desire to have Poles as friends, not as enemies, but he could not sit outside the castle and wait for a messenger to go to Casimir and return; on the other hand, it was obvious that he had sufficient men to take the place. That was a powerful argument. When the Poles left, the marshal destroyed the half-finished castle.

Winrich understood well the importance of commerce for his Order's wealth and influence. Taxes from prosperous cities allowed him to buy equipment and luxuries, hire mercenaries and artisans, and pay the expenses of diplomacy. From the earliest days the policy of his Order had been to give the cities self-government except in the realm of foreign policy and to protect their ability to trade abroad. The usual complaint of merchants concerned foreign rulers taxing their wares or shutting them out of important markets. Winrich used his influence to assure Prussian merchants of fair treatment in England and Flanders, even threatening to retaliate on Western merchants by denying them access to Prussian and Livonian ports.

Six Prussian cities (Culm, Thorn, Elbing, Braunsberg, Königsberg and Danzig) were members of the loosely organised Hanseatic League, thereby assuring themselves of the right to trade practically everywhere in northern Europe. This involved more than the right to use the harbour facilities: the Hanseatic League provided hostels, warehouses, and religious services. Also, the united cities demanded that all merchants receive fair and equal treatment. Moreover, their near monopoly on international trade shut out competition, stabilised prices, and, through an extension of credit, made possible a significant expansion of commerce. Membership in the Hanseatic League stemmed from the fact that Prussian cities had been settled partly by immigrants from Hanseatic towns. Parents, brothers and business partners saw to it that they enjoyed Hanseatic rights from the very beginning, and succeeding generations continued these ties to Germany, especially to Lübeck. The Hanseatic cities wanted Prussian grain, animals, amber, lumber, beer and furs; and they appreciated the safety, the dependable justice and the low taxes of Prussia. They earned rich fees from crusaders who travelled to Prussia and Livonia by sea and who purchased gear and supplies in Hanseatic centres. Much of this trade was possible only if the Danish straits were open, but since the kings of Denmark had always hated to see vessels sail almost right under their noses without paying a toll, Winrich had to side with the Hanseatic League during the desperate nine-year struggle with Waldemar IV of Denmark that began in 1361.

Waldemar had not intended to become involved in this war – he was ruthless, cruel and vindictive, but he was not foolish. He was only twenty when he ascended the throne of the bankrupt kingdom, so his enemies underestimated what he could do. He recovered some territories, then taxed them heavily; in addition, he had the 19,000 marks the grandmaster paid for Estonia – this allowed him to travel to Jerusalem, becoming the first of several northern rulers to become a Knight of the Holy Sepulchre. On his return he made war on Holstein, thus ending a controversy over which dynasty should rule there (but creating a problem that was resolved only in 1864); in 1349 he invaded Brandenburg. After this he employed a powerful mercenary army to attack the king of Sweden (with whom Denmark was almost always at war, or on the brink of war), over the provinces which today make up southern Sweden.

In 1360 Waldemar seized control of the entrance to the Baltic Sea, hoping to dominate the rich fishing grounds and the sea lanes. The next year he landed his army on Gotland. After annihilating the Visby city militia in battle, he tore a gap in the city walls, then demanded a huge ransom. The citizens surprisingly managed to pay the ransom, but Visby never recovered.

While Waldemar was engaged in destroying Swedish trade, Hanseatic merchants began to wonder what his next move would be. The Hanseatic League believed in a balance of power in the Baltic, so that its navy could be decisive in tipping the scales at a minimum cost. (Direct military hegemony would be too expensive and would require a stronger central government than most cities wanted.) Because the league members feared any strong ruler, they viewed Waldemar's expansive policies as a threat to their livelihoods and independence.

Grandmaster Winrich agreed with the Hanseatic analysis of the situation. At first, he only promised diplomatic support, because he realised the absurdity of committing his land army to a naval war. But later he saw that unless he intervened more directly, he would expose Prussia and Livonia to attack by sea. To build ships and man them, Winrich would have to suspend the crusade. Then, once he had achieved victory, what would he do next? Knowing that there was no future for the Order on the seas, Winrich reluctantly declared that the Teutonic Order would remain neutral in any war between the Hanseatic League and Denmark.

Winrich told the league that he sympathised with their cause, but as a crusading leader he could not declare war on a Christian king, and as a loyal subject of Emperor Charles IV, he could not fight a very close imperial ally. The most he could do was to permit the Prussian and Livonian cities to send military aid to Lübeck. As time passed and the league suffered defeats, his support became more open. He aided diplomatic efforts to exclude Danish and Norwegian shipping from the Low Countries and encouraged German cities to join the Cologne Confederation that shared many of the Hanseatic League's concerns.

Meanwhile, Waldemar IV's ambitions had grown. In 1360 he even entertained the idea of re-establishing Danish rule in England – despite the passage of centuries since any Danish king had set foot there – and thereby knock England out of the Hundred Years War. This wild scheme ended when the French failed to pay him the promised subsidy. Such was Waldemar's reputation, however, that no one doubted his readiness to act rashly, or his brutality, as in his senseless destruction of Visby.

In the end the Hanseatic cities under Lübeck leadership defeated Waldemar. As a reward for the Prussian contribution to the victory, the 1370 Treaty of Stralsund gave those cities trading privileges in Scandinavia that led to a modest but welcome growth in commercial prosperity.

Control of Pomerania

In the late 1360s Casimir III attempted to extend his authority over Pomerania, a region then disturbed by the war between Waldemar IV and his many enemies. Casimir's plan was perhaps only dynastic in intent, but Winrich viewed any threat to the land route between the Holy Roman Empire and Prussia as more dangerous than one to the sea route. Therefore, he encouraged Charles IV to intervene, a move supported by the electors and princes of the Holy Roman Empire, who always opposed any German territory passing under foreign control. The emperor adroitly arranged marriages, concluded alliances, and in some cases, when properties were for sale, outbid the Polish king. But he was not always successful.

In 1368 Casimir sought to acquire small but strategically important castles in Lower Silesia that drove a wedge between Brandenburg and West Prussia, threatening communication lines between Germany and Prussia. Two years before, when the Hospitallers had indicated a desire to sell their estates at Schoeneck (Skarszewy), Winrich had sent negotiators to represent his interest. The Hospitallers had been at Schoeneck for a long time, since perhaps as early as 1198, and had gathered their once-scattered parcels into a territory of seven castles, one town, and twenty-three villages. Although they had not participated militarily in the crusade against the pagans, being sheltered from attacks in the thirteenth century by the small intervening territory owned by the Spanish Order of Calatrava and later by the Teutonic Order, they had always remained on excellent terms with the grandmasters. They had improved their lands by draining swamps, establishing markets, and bringing in settlers. In short, the local convent was not unhappy with its situation. However, their order needed money for the emperor's journey to Italy, and a general chapter had decided to sell these northern holdings if a good price could be obtained. Winrich alone had the ready cash. In June 1370 he bought Schoeneck for 10,265 marks.

Winrich's unease about Polish ambitions faded only with Casimir's unexpected death in 1370. His successor, Louis of Hungary, was busy fighting Turks and Tatars. He had no interest in a distracting conflict with the grandmaster.

The Battle of Rudau

Winrich of Kniprode's luck reached its high point in 1370 at the Battle of Rudau. The very rarity of pitched battles accounts for much of the fame of that contest. Winrich's name explains the rest.

In retrospect the battle seems to have been the result of Kęstutis's pride and perhaps of disappointment that he could not match Algirdas's victories in Rus'. The grandmaster had invited the confrontation by building a fortress on an island near Kaunas on the Nevėžis River. This was a post that could be easily re-supplied by ship, but most importantly, sallies by the garrison might discourage Kęstutis from rebuilding Kaunas, as he had done three times in seven years. When Winrich arrived at Inselburg in mid-April 1369 he found Lithuanians once again at work on Kaunas. He crossed the river, drove the workmen away, and then used their materials to build a castle of his own on an island so close to the shore that horses could easily wade across.

Ignoring Kęstutis's recommendation to build the castle elsewhere, far, far away, he finished the work in five weeks, left behind a garrison of twenty knights and eighty soldiers with supplies for a year, and took his Prussian workmen home. Gotteswerder (God's Island), as Winrich named the castle, was expected to be able to repel any pagan attack, but just to be sure, he sent his men out to burn local crops, steal cattle and destroy woods that might provide lumber for siege machines and fuel for a conflagration.

Winrich must have assumed that the water obstacle would hinder any Lithuanian attack during the summer, when the vessels of the Order ruled the Nemunas, except where the shallow ford could be easily crossed. In winter ice would make all sides of the castle vulnerable, but surely the annual winter campaign would disrupt any siege. The strategic position of the fortress was unsurpassed and Lithuanian leaders understood that it would be necessary to remove this menace to their lands and people.

Kęstutis needed three months to gather his forces, then, in the late summer, when the water level was lowest, he attacked. Employing eighteen throwing machines to weaken the earthen walls, he moved a tower to the moat, halting briefly until the ditch was filled, then advancing it to the wall. After five weeks of day and night combat,

Kęstutis's men breached the final defences, leaving the garrison no alternative to honourable surrender other than a futile death.

The crusaders were obviously surprised at how well the Lithuanians had mastered siege technology. Kęstutis had never brought together so many men for such a long time, fed them, provided them with siege materials, and guided them through the intricate process of breaching well-defended walls. Kęstutis immediately repaired the damaged defences, added new wooden forts to guard the ford, and put his own garrison in the castle. Then he dismissed his men and returned to Trakai.

Seven weeks later Marshal Henning opened the wearisome negotiations for ransom of the prisoners, meeting Kęstutis personally. Although each expressed a willingness to sign a peace treaty, neither the marshal nor the duke was willing to give up claims to Samogitia; each stood on his pride and dignity, returning insult for insult in the courteous manner of that era. Eventually Henning gave up and took home the few enfeebled knights he was able to ransom, experiencing a difficult journey because of the inclement weather. When he arrived in Ragnit, he took command of an army sent by Winrich. In mid-November, after a short halt in Bayernburg for supplies, he reached Gotteswerder. His attack came as a complete surprise because the Lithuanians had assumed the weather was too wet and cold for the movement of armies.

Henning's men took the outlying forts without fighting, then brought up siege machines. Soon the earthworks, supported only by the damaged wooden frames, were crumbling; in five days he repeated what the Lithuanians had needed as many weeks to accomplish. Kęstutis hurried to the scene, but he did not have enough men to risk a pitched battle; all he could do was to threaten the rear of the army, to hinder a general assault, and to prevent small units from scavenging for supplies.

The chroniclers gave conflicting accounts of the siege, but it seems likely that the crusaders first captured the walls, taking many prisoners, then built a fire around the keep. At that point Kęstutis asked that the lives of his men be spared. The marshal refused even to answer Kęstutis's herald but watched as 109 Lithuanian warriors perished in the inferno. As soon as Henning could make a list of the survivors, he sent it to Kęstutis and arranged for an exchange of prisoners.

According to a sixteenth-century chronicler, Kęstutis said to the marshal on meeting him face to face, 'When winter comes next year, I will make a raid into Prussia and pay the grandmaster a visit.' The marshal replied, 'Kęstutis would be welcome and will be received as befits such a worthy guest.' Another chronicler, the more contemporary Wigand of Marburg, reported this same conversation, but with a rather blunter response: the Order's knights would come out to meet him and smash in his head!

All winter they armed for the confrontation. Kęstutis raised a force of Samogitians and Algirdas brought perhaps an equal number of Rus'ians, so that the total Lithuanian force numbered 2,000 or 3,000, a large army for the time. When Marshal Henning learned of the preparations, he sent a reconnaissance force from Ragnit. Learning that the warriors had departed Samogitia, Henning knew that an attack was coming, but he did not know where. All he could recommend to Winrich was to call up the units from West Prussia. The grandmaster did this reluctantly, knowing that the attack was just as likely to fall on Livonia or Rus'. While Winrich could remember times when units had been summoned to the frontier, only to wait in vain for an opportunity to fight, he sensed that this was different. He ordered distant convents to send their best men, perhaps a thousand in number, to Königsberg; and took up residence there himself.

On 17 February 1370, Algirdas and Kęstutis passed through the Samogitian wilderness, crossed over a frozen arm of the lower Nemunas onto the ice-covered Curonian Lagoon, and into central Sambia. At one point their army was sighted by scouts from Ragnit, but they lost its path, perhaps because of snowfall.

The dukes' original plan had been to enter Sambia on the first day of Lent, when the defenders would still be intoxicated from the last pre-Lenten celebration; but the shamans who observed the flights of birds for omens had insisted on an immediate departure. Even so, there was no resistance worth mentioning. Kęstutis and Algirdas, perhaps themselves surprised by their success in evading detection, held a council of war to decide how to exploit the opportunity, then sent raiders out to burn and pillage. Kęstutis wanted to ravage Sambia so thoroughly that the Teutonic Knights would not be able to draw workmen and warriors from the region for many years to come.

As soon as news of the raid reached Winrich, he called together his council. He had about 2,000 men in Königsberg, including units from Ermland and Pomesania and several cities. He summoned the Sambia militias but did not wait for them to come; in any case, many would be defending their families in log and earth refuges. Winrich and his officers agreed to move quickly, to cut off the Lithuanian line of retreat, then force them to do battle.

As the grandmaster crossed a hill near Quedau, just north of Königsberg, he could see the smoke and flames from burning villages. When he was closer, he sent out twenty men to take a prisoner and make him tell what he knew. When he learned that Kęstutis and Algirdas were waiting in battle formation, he led the army forward.

Although the details of the battle are so meagre that even the exact site of the combat is unknown, the chronicles say that it began about midday in an open field near the village of Rudau (Melnikovo). The opening skirmishes were followed by a general engagement of equal numbers of cavalry. The decisive moment came when the knights from Culm charged. These 120 horsemen had either been held in reserve or had only just arrived at the battlefield. One chronicler wrote that Kęstutis was so shocked at seeing the wavy red and white banner that he fled immediately.

Kęstutis, and probably most of his men, understood that it was not the quantity of troops on the field that mattered, but the quality. Those from Culm were the best; some spoke Low German, others Polish, but all were well equipped and well trained. Prudence counselled retreat. His own forces escaped largely intact, because the Teutonic Knights concentrated on Algirdas's men, who were waiting on a wooded hill. The fighting there was so desperate that two of the Order's commanders fell, but by evening Algirdas was in flight, too.

It is an axiom of war that the worst casualties occur during a rout, and so it was now. Hot pursuit by the knights caught many who were on foot; some horsemen escaped for the moment by applying their spurs to their exhausted mounts. Those who were too tired or too proud to flee found themselves alone against growing numbers of Germans and Prussians. Pursuers fell, too. Marshal Henning was following at breakneck speed when he was struck in the face by a spear and killed. Nightfall must have confused the situation, but even the best mounted invaders had to evade patrols in an unfamiliar land, then cross the ice and wilderness without supplies.

At the end of the combat the Teutonic Knights were missing 26 brethren and 100 other fighting men, a number that usually came only from total defeats. The Lithuanians, however, left behind perhaps a thousand dead and numerous captives who were later imprisoned in scattered castles.

That was the last major Lithuanian threat against Prussia. Surprisingly, Kęstutis ceased to harass the crusader castles on the Nemunas, while Algirdas was able to organise expeditions against Volhynia and Moscow.

Winrich commemorated the victory by founding an Augustinian convent in Ermland. It was appropriately the site of a legendary contest between Christians and pagans in the early missionary days – when the native Prussians had defied a missionary to cut down a holy oak, the axe sprang back at the first stroke, but prayer and persistence lent him strength that dismayed the pagans. The missionary built a chapel of the wood and installed the holy axe (*Heiligenbeil*) as the principal relic.

Troubles in Masovia

The Lithuanian dukes were able to make up their losses at Rudau because King Casimir died in a hunting accident in late 1370. Casimir had been only sixty and was in good health despite being overweight – the product of overeating at rowdy banquets and drinking excessively. He still had all his curly hair and his full beard. In short, he was happier than he had been for years, filled with hope that his wife would yet produce a son, and was working towards a revision of the succession law so that, if that dream failed to materialise, his grandson, Casimir of Stettin, could inherit the throne. Of course, everything was already in place for Louis of Hungary to become king and Kaźko – as the young Pomeranian prince was known – was politically unproven.

The king had worked diligently to equip his grandson with every-thing he would need to take revenge upon the Teutonic Knights for their long-ago seizure of Pomerellia; most importantly, during the change in dynasties possessing Brandenburg, he was able to secure small territories that formed a narrow salient stretching north from Greater Poland to Pomerania. He had prepared the way for this even before the death of Louis of Brandenburg in 1365 had upset all political calculations, then he had accepted the fealty of minor Pomeranian vassals whose lands completed a potential barrier for all German crusaders hoping to reach Prussia by land. There was no way the grandmaster could undo this without war.

As Paul Knoll reminds us, the historian of these years can usually do little more than pick up scraps of information here and there, then try to make them into a coherent narrative; but for Casimir's last days there is a wealth of information. When the king was returning to Cracow from Silesia he was invited to a hunt; this was so delightful that he extended his stay for another wild ride through the forest that ended with his horse stumbling. When the king was pulled from beneath his horse, everyone could see that his leg was badly injured. Immediately a high fever set in.

When Casimir recovered enough to travel, his party set out for Sandomir. There he decided to take a bath – against the advice of his doctor. Another onset of fever followed. A few days later the king again disregarded his physician's warning. This time he became so ill after bathing that he had to be carried in a litter to a Cistercian monastery 15 km. (10 miles) away. After eight days Casimir rallied enough to proceed towards Płock. On the journey a second physician recommended that he drink some mead. His primary physician objected but was overruled. The king became so ill that the party started towards Cracow, a journey of seven weeks. When it became clear that he had only hours to live, Casimir dictated a carefully worded will, leaving estates to his two illegitimate sons, granting jewels and silver to his infant daughters and wife, and providing large gifts to churches so that prayers might be offered eternally for his soul.

When word of his death went out, his enemies hurried to take advantage of the succession crisis: Siemowit of Masovia seized Płock, Brandenburg took a border castle, and the Lithuanians crossed the frontier at numerous places. Only the arrival of Casimir's sister, Elizabeth, with Hungarian troops, put some backbone into the Polish forces. Nevertheless, her son, Louis, hesitated to join her, not being sure how to govern two very different states with different needs. But at last delegations of Polish nobility and clergy, suitably encouraged by gifts and promises, persuaded him that he would be welcomed as their monarch.

Norman Davies dourly summarised Poland's history to this point as an unimaginative copy of Western efforts to create a state out of 'a remote and backward people'. But the foundations had been laid for the flowering of a nation that would dominate Eastern Europe for 400 years.

The Angevin Dynasty comes to Poland

Winrich of Kniprode must have been relieved. Just as the Polish (or Polish–Danish) encirclement of Prussia was becoming complete, Casimir's policies were abandoned. As for bathing, the grandmaster would have recommended a sauna over a bath – every castle of the Teutonic Order had at least one sauna, and the knights used them. Bloodletting, too, because it often seemed to reduce fevers.

The political fever would likely diminish, too, now that bloodletting seemed likely to be avoided. There was a strong likelihood that the new king, Louis, would have very different interests than those which had driven Casimir. Hungary had long been more efficiently administered, thanks to its association with Naples and France (the dynasty's name, 'Angevin' derived from this connection). Louis was also much less distracted by women and entertainment. (Perhaps he was inhibited by his mother's piety. Once he had sent her to be regent of Poland in his place, his wife became pregnant for the first time in their seventeen-year marriage, and two more daughters appeared in the following two years.) But most of all he had little time to devote to Polish affairs: he did not want to be distracted by Poland's politics. The situation in the Balkans was critical: the Turks were pressing north, threatening the Serbian kingdom that barred the way into the lands of Louis's Bosnian wife. He had work to do there.

Critical to the success of Louis's many policies was the Hungarian palatine, Ladislas of Opole, a minor Piast prince who had gone to seek his fortune in Hungary, then advanced from office to office, until finally the king appointed him as regent in Poland when Queen Elizabeth gave up the post. Ladislas was a descendant of kings, but what Piast prince was not? More important, his Silesian inheritance lay at a strategic point on the Moravian border, enabling him to play Polish, Czech and Hungarian rulers against one another. Louis had recognised Ladislas's great diplomatic and military gifts, was appreciative of his marriages with first a daughter of the prince of Wallachia, then in 1369 with a daughter of Siemowit III of Masovia – from whom he got five daughters but no heir. Louis was also pleased with Ladislas's military campaigns in Bulgaria and Serbia, then with his successful negotiations in 1370 with the Polish magnates and bishops that secured him the crown. Although the terms of that agreement were the beginning of a process by which royal authority was traded away for short-term benefits, Louis cared little – he was principally interested in having peace on that frontier and, by appointing Ladislas to manage affairs, he was sure to have that.

Louis first stationed Ladislas in Volhynia, then later generously bestowed on him authority over other territories threatened by pagan armies – governor of Galicia–Volhynia, count palatine of Poland in 1378, and finally duke of Dobrzyń and Kujavia. These included potentially rich lands, so that with luck, he might someday come to rule a fiefdom that extended across the eastern borderlands. It was up to Ladislas to find some way to make those almost empty lands pay, but that was a task he took up willingly. Defending borders was his specialty, and the Lithuanians daunted him less than did the Tatars or Turks.

Other than this – and one subsequent visit to Poland – Louis neglected his northern kingdom. This was especially true regarding Masovia, because Siemowit III had agreed to be a vassal of Casimir only for the king's lifetime. Casimir, in fact, had worked so hard to draw Siemowit away from his alliance with the Teutonic Order that he had promised to give him Płock and several other small regions in his will; he also donated a reliquary of St Sigismund to the cathedral at Płock.

Siemowit refused to co-operate. Instead, he behaved as a completely sovereign ruler, causing Ladislas of Opole to treat him as a rebel. He made reforms that would, in due course, turn his poorly populated land into the future centre of Poland, but in 1373 he showed that he was still a man of his time – he divided his lands between his sons, an almost universal tradition in Central Europe that often made substantial states into unimportant ones. Janusz I (*c.* 1347–1429) and Siemowit IV (1353–1429) received the lands around Warsaw, guaranteeing them control of the central Vistula River valley. As often happens with brothers, they drifted apart. When Janusz married Danutė, one of Kęstutis's daughters, that soured his relationship with the Teutonic Knights and caused him to seek a close alliance with King Louis. In contrast, when Siemowit IV came of age, he made it very clear that he considered himself the lawful heir of King Casimir and led him to want an alliance with the Teutonic Order.

The matter became terribly complicated. Siemowit III's prospects had seemed good, but eventually he lost out to Ladislas of Opole's Hungarian forces. Even so, he refused to acknowledge Louis as his feudal lord. A man of fiery emotion, Siemowit took swift action when he learned that his second wife was widely suspected of having become pregnant by a lover: he tortured the ladies-in-waiting into providing testimony, had the presumed boyfriend tied to horses and torn to pieces, then threw his wife into prison until she delivered her child, after which he had her strangled. He gave the boy to a peasant family to rear. It was a fairy-tale story in real life.

As it happened, after a few years passed, the child's aunt Margareta, duchess of Pomerania, adopted him. A few years later, when the child, Henryk (*c.* 1368–92), was ten or twelve, Siemowit III would be encouraged by Janusz and Siemowit IV to admit that Henryk resembled him strongly, especially in his extraordinary strength. The duke acknowledged him as his son but was still unwilling to make him legitimate (and thereby deserving a share of the lands), so he arranged for him to enter the Church. In 1392, when Henryk became bishop-elect of Płock, that would have great consequences for the crusade.

Meanwhile, Poland once again seemed on the verge of disintegration. Louis was a strong king in Hungary, where he possessed such vast lands and such a reputation for gallantry and generosity that he would eventually be called Louis the Great. Poland, however, was a distraction.

He concentrated on defending his southern frontier from anarchy and the Turks and relied on Ladislas of Opole to protect his interests in Poland.

The Masovian lands Ladislas acquired as dowry gave him good reasons to seek peace with the Teutonic Order. Otherwise, he could not assist the king in Galicia and the Balkans. Winrich was pleased with Ladislas's friendly attitude because it allowed him to make war in Lithuania without fear of attack on Culm and West Prussia. He would have preferred an active ally in Masovia, but had to be satisfied that Ladislas was in constant conflict with Lithuanian princes who were eager to expand their domains into Rus', and that he was distracted by the turmoil in Wallachia and the Balkans.

Advances and Retreats

Unable to rely on Polish assistance, Winrich looked to the Livonian master for help. In 1371 and 1372, Livonian and Prussian armies invaded Samogitia simultaneously, once approaching within 20 km. (12 miles) of one another without meeting. Those raids reached deep into the last pagan sanctuary, and Lithuanians were no longer able to strike effectively into Livonia. In addition, more Samogitian *Witingen* were crossing into Prussia, accepting Christianity in return for new fiefs. However, no matter how many invasions the crusaders directed at Samogitia, Kęstutis and Algirdas were retaliating in the nearby Lake District, which was too thinly settled to support defensive forces.

Progress in the war was hard to measure, but certainly the chronicler's remark that, 'Master Kniprode sought out places in the wilderness in which he could build castles to protect the fatherland,' tells us that he was not looking to invade the enemy heartland. In time the establishment of watch posts in the Galindian wilderness would give more protection to Prussia and Masovia, but they could not serve as bases for the kinds of blows that would yield a total victory.

The contest continued until 1377 without significant gains by either side. The struggle was bitter, conducted by enemies who, despite their mutual hatred, respected each other. Like most conflicts of this era, this was a war of attrition, conducted mainly against the peasants and herders who provided the sinews of war. Both sides avoided pitched battles deep in the enemy countryside, since even a victorious army would find retreat difficult, burdened as it would be with wounded men and exhausted animals. Peasants found it necessary to take refuge during dangerous seasons and to expect losses in men, herds and crops.

At the prompting of Siemowit III, Pope Gregory XI wrote to the Lithuanian dukes in 1373 to urge the blessings of peace that contrasted with the horrors of war (if they would only accept baptism), without even getting a reply. That suggests that Kęstutis and Algirdas believed that they were slowly gaining the upper hand. In 1376 the marriage alliance with Janusz of Masovia allowed them to strike into Poland, ravaging Sandomir and coming close to re-occupying Galicia and Volhynia. When Louis tried to drive them back, they fended him off.

The Christians' best hope appeared to lie in traditional policies that would draw the Lithuanians closer to the West – that is, to resume the exchange of brides. The example of Casimir marrying Aldona was on everyone's mind. And nobody forgot that this would remove the Teutonic Knights from the equation – as celibate friars in a religious order, they had no need of wives and had no daughters to offer.

There was a fleeting moment when peace might have been arranged. This was right after Algirdas's death, when Kęstutis hosted a delegation of Teutonic Knights at Trakai. However, though the prince was willing to dine with his guests and talk in generalities, he would not release captured knights. The talks fell through. Efforts to involve the emperor failed as well. Charles IV had just built a castle and residence at Tangermünde in Brandenburg, an impressive palace with towers and gates that still remind modern visitors of Prague. Bishop Heinrich of Ermland visited him there in May and June 1377. In vain. The emperor sent a valuable reliquary of St Catherine to a friend in the Order, but no aid.

Time was on the side of Kęstutis in the sense that Lithuania was evolving into a more complex state. Western construction methods can still be seen in the ruins of Lithuanian castles and other structures, and the swift adoption of cannon further emphasised the importance of the rulers' ability to raise large sums of money and to order individual warriors into military specialties that were far removed from the freeman's ancient infantry traditions. Tactics mirrored the more effective methods of the Westerners, especially the organisation of cavalry units which were divided into 'banners'. Lastly, the Lithuanians were adopting the inner and outer trappings of their feudal opponents – the rulers had marshals and other court officials; the *Witingen* looked and acted ever more like knights.

Time, however, was not on the side of the Lithuanians in one important sense: their dukes could not live for ever, and the role of the individual was vital in the success of a medieval state. Kęstutis was ageing and his current strategy was not likely to end in victory.

This caused Algirdas's son, Jogaila, to plot quietly for a change of strategy.

In 1381, with both the crusaders and Samogitians exhausted, Winrich sent Marshal Gottfried of Linden to meet secretly with Jogaila near Vilnius, the journey through the wilderness disguised as a hunting holiday. Jogaila – later famous under his Polish name, Jagiełło – was still an obscure prince, so obscure that historians can only guess at his birthdate, some time between 1352 and 1362. In three days of talks they hammered out a truce.

Meanwhile, the Livonian master came to a similar arrangement with Duke Andrew of Polotsk, Algirdas's eldest son. Experienced in battle and diplomacy and handicapped only by the physical deformity that caused his enemies to mock him as 'the hunchback', Andrew would become Jogaila's greatest rival. Everyone could see that the elderly supreme duke would not live much longer.

Winrich was more interested in his marshal's talks with Jogaila, who professed himself so eager to end the war that he might convert to Roman Christianity. Winrich also reached out to Kęstutis and his favourite son, Vytautas (Witold, *c.* 1350–1430), dining with them, feasting in the open, seated on valuable carpets, then signing a truce that exempted their lands from attack. To the public it appeared that this war, like the contemporaneous Hundred Years War, was coming to an end. Neither side seemed to have the strength or will to continue fighting. Not so. Though no one knew it, this truce represented not the end of the conflict, but the end of the stalemate in the crusade against Lithuanian paganism.

Chapter Ten

Alliances with the Lithuanian Dukes

Changing Circumstances

Circumstances had favoured Winrich in the early 1370s – peace with Poland, valuable assistance from the Order's knights in Livonia, political stability in Germany – but Lithuania was simply too strong to defeat. That seemed likely to change, however, when the death of Algirdas undermined the unity of the Lithuanian empire, opening the way for the now aged grandmaster to lead his crusaders towards the fulfilment of their dreams.

Kęstutis and Algirdas had shared responsibilities in a manner paralleling contemporary practices in Germany and Poland, brothers sharing inheritances, but eventually founding separate dynasties. Algirdas had married two Rus'ian princesses, but his paganism and support of West-leaning Orthodox churchmen caused some Orthodox subjects to yearn for a return to days when the ancient dynasty of Rurik ruled, rather than an outsider speaking a strange language and whose mercenaries practised an even stranger pagan religion. It seemed that Algirdas's children appreciated this because most of them learned Rus'ian and became converts to Orthodoxy.

Kęstutis had chosen to live at Old Trakai, a fortress on a hilltop about 8 km. (5 miles) from Lake Galvė, and later at another on a nearby peninsula that was in due course rebuilt by his son into a residence that, restored from the ruins of time, is today a popular tourist attraction. Old Trakai was perhaps the first brick castle in the region, perfectly sited for conducting war against the Teutonic Order, the Masovian dukes, and the Polish king. On those rare occasions that he received accurate advance warning of crusader invasions, he could call on Algirdas's Lithuanian and Rus'ian warriors, but in recent years Kęstutis had often made his headquarters in Samogitia, the homeland of his wife, where he could more closely monitor crusader activities. To ensure that his most gifted son, Vytautas, could someday take over this responsibility, he had him learn German in addition to the other regional tongues. He also increased his influence in Masovia after Janusz and Siemowit IV succeeded their father in 1381.

The Lithuanian empire was filled with paradoxes. The largest state in Europe, it was sparsely populated, culturally diverse, and open to attack from all sides. Nevertheless, thanks to the genius of its leaders, it had remained remarkably stable; moreover, its leaders had been successful in war against a wide variety of armies, each distinctively equipped and employing vastly different strategies and tactics. Once the guiding hand of Algirdas was removed, however, this stability ebbed away. And it was Algirdas who was to blame: like his father, he had disposed of his portion of the vast empire like a private inheritance, dispersing it among many sons. A younger son, Jogaila, stood out. He was quiet, and introspective, so much the opposite of a burly military chief that his opponents always underestimated him. When Andrew of Polotsk, his elder half-brother, challenged his right to be supreme duke, Jogaila drove him into exile; when Andrew sought aid from Moscow and Livonia, Jogaila forestalled him by making his own alliances with the rulers of those lands.

Kęstutis stood by Algirdas's arrangements loyally and allowed Jogaila to have the title of supreme duke, but he was not willing to accept the subordinate position that the title implied. Kęstutis believed that his experience and seniority gave him the right to do more than offer advice and counsel. He expected Jogaila to share authority, even to defer to him.

Jogaila's Pride and Ambition

Jogaila was not willing to share, much less to defer. The second son by Algirdas's second wife, Uliana of Tver', he inherited his mother's strong personality and her lust for power. Her mother had come from Volhynia to marry the prince of Tver', then when he was murdered by the Tatars, she had fled to Moscow. Thus, when Algirdas had sought an alliance with Simeon of Moscow in 1350, it was agreed that he would wed Uliana and Liubartas would marry Simeon's niece. Such an important alliance required approval from the Golden Horde, which was not easy. Then that arrangement fell apart – Simeon and his sons died of the plague, he was succeeded by a brother, then by that brother's young son, Dmitri (1353–89).

Although the sons of Algirdas's first marriage were extremely jealous of their new stepmother, by producing numerous sons and daughters – scholars disagree on the number – she had great influence on her husband. She was devoted to the Orthodox church, but when Algirdas insisted that the children be reared as pagans, she obeyed.

Jogaila apparently lived with his mother until he began to follow his father on his travels around Lithuania and Rus'. Algirdas taught him obstinacy, patience, caution, and a dislike of alcohol in any form, and probably to bathe and shave daily. In 1377, when his father died, Jogaila may have been as young as seventeen (though he could have been as old as twenty-seven), but he possessed an unconventional wisdom that included disguising his plans until it was too late for rivals to counter them.

Jogaila was a good commander, but few recognised that because he rarely led his men in the wild charges his *Witingen* loved; instead, he directed combats from the rear. Never using force where guile or negotiations offered some hope of success, he made the avoidance of combat through tardiness into a high art. This preserved his troops, made his allies bear the brunt of the fighting, and saved him from the accusations of cowardice that staying at home would have provoked. But it prevented him from winning the respect and devotion of the young hotheads who provided much of the manpower for any army, but especially medieval armies.

Jogaila was a cunning diplomat, better so than most rivals, not only because he could read their minds so well, but because he could combine plausible arguments and moral pliability better than they. He was, on the one hand, almost completely free of those scruples, prejudices and sentiments that handicapped others in the pursuit of their ambitions; on the other hand, he was not obviously corrupt. He was superstitious, but no more than many contemporaries. His only weakness was his hatred of those who stood in his way, and even that was subject to a remarkable self-control. The Teutonic Knights stood foremost on his list of enemies, but Jogaila disciplined himself when necessary to make them into friends and allies. He could turn instantly on his closest friends and relatives, even on Vytautas, who loved and trusted him completely. Jogaila knew how to say what his audience wanted to hear, and he was willing to pose as Rus'ian, Lithuanian, or, later, Pole, whatever was to his advantage. He was not eloquent, so no one objected when he declined to make long and florid speeches; by remaining quiet and listening he avoided situations when he might let slip more than he wished to say. He disliked the hilarity and laughter of drinking parties, preferring the solitude of the deepest forests. But he did not hesitate to act when necessary, and he could be ruthless. However, he avoided excessive cruelty, and he rewarded proven supporters generously. This inspired many subjects to take pride in his accomplishments, even when they mistrusted him.

Jogaila's complex nature made him a controversial figure – a traitor to some Lithuanians, a national hero to most Poles, and practically the anti-Christ to the Teutonic Knights. The controversy that began early in his career continues today among modern historians. Joseph Končius had nothing good to say about him: 'Much of Jogaila's time was spent in hunting, fishing, and banqueting; his lack of native ability in the duties of his exalted office was aggravated by a carelessness which made him little better than a pawn of his associates.' In contrast, Karol Górski described a much different Jagiełło – calm, taciturn, capable, and superior to his more active, unreflective rivals; he became a great king of Poland. To complete the confusion, Pawel Jasienica argued that Jagiełło remained a Lithuanian at heart and was a disaster for Poland.

It was Vytautas, Kęstutis's favourite son – whose pride, passion, and daring contrasted so strongly with Jogaila's reserved, disciplined nature – to whom the Lithuanians gave their love. But he was slow to learn his father's political skills. Kęstutis had been notorious for his contradictory and ever-changing nature. No one ever knew quite what his intentions were, and even the Teutonic Knights, despite all their experience, were unable to match him in diplomacy. When a crusader army was in the heart of his lands in February 1377, Kęstutis offered to talk peace. The crusaders interrupted their attacks, not realising how badly the duke needed a respite at that moment. Later, when they learned that Kęstutis had no interest in conversion but was only buying time until Algirdas's heirs could sort out their troubles and come to his aid, they concluded that they had been tricked again. They vowed to be more careful in the future. However, when they allied with Jogaila against Kęstutis, they do not seem to have sensed that however good Kęstutis was in deception, he was surpassed by his nephew, Jogaila.

The Crusader Alliance with Jogaila

In the early autumn of 1379 Jogaila sent his brother Skirgaila (Skirgiełło, c. 1353–97) to negotiate secretly a more permanent arrangement with the Teutonic Knights. Jogaila's purported intent was to deprive Andrew of Livonian support, but when hostilities resumed after a short interlude, the crusader attacks concentrated suspiciously on Samogitia, not against Jogaila's lands around Vilnius.

Skirgaila was an inspired choice for such diplomatic service. Utterly unscrupulous, he could lie to anyone's face and make himself believed. Ambitious, courageous, multi-lingual, Skirgaila charmed drinking companions, famous monarchs, and discerning churchmen alike. The Westerners understood that he was devious, deceitful and dangerous, but they also believed that he was a person they could work with. If there was anyone who could turn his back on Lithuanian traditions,

Rus'ian boyars and clergy, and generations of promises, Skirgaila was their man.

This understanding permitted the knights in Prussia and Livonia to be more daring in their raids than before. They were confident that Jogaila's relief army would arrive in Samogitia too late to threaten them, and that Jogaila would not attack Prussia while their forces were attacking Kęstutis. It was fortunate that foreign crusaders were coming in larger numbers, allowing them to strike farther up the Nemunas than they had in recent years, reaching as far as Brest-Litovsk; meanwhile, the knights in Livonia attacked castles protecting northern Lithuania. In 1377–8 Winrich of Kniprode welcomed various worthy lords including Albert III of Austria (1349–95), who brought with him 1,500 horsemen on his five-month adventure.

This was not Skirgaila's only contact with the crusaders. In 1379, before going to visit King Louis in Hungary and possibly the pope and the emperor – with Charles IV having just died, this would have been Wenceslaus IV (1361–1419) – he came to Prussia with thirty followers and obtained the crusaders' promise not to attack Jogaila's territories. In return, he promised that Jogaila would not help Kęstutis resist crusader incursions.

That arrangement was replaced by a truce signed in Trakai by the grandmaster's representatives and by both Kęstutis and Jogaila, then it was quickly modified by new agreements between the grandmaster and Kęstutis and Jogaila separately to protect their own lands. Then, in May 1380 Jogaila signed a secret treaty of mutual aid with Winrich, the Treaty of Dovydiškės – the original document with the seals still survives.

This treaty allowed Jogaila to act more forcefully in Rus', where the grand duke of Moscow, Dmitri, had made himself the leader of the anti-Tatar forces. Against all expectations – in 1377 a Russian army had lost a battle on the Pyana because the army and its commander were too intoxicated to fight (as the name of the river suggests – *pyana* means 'drunken') – in 1378 Dmitri had defeated a Crimean Tatar army led by Mamay (1335–80), one of the few clan leaders not descended from Genghis Khan. Now he was expecting Mamay to bring an even larger army north. But rather than wait for Mamay to strike, he collected his forces in the summer of 1380 and marched south to the Don River, challenging him right on the steppe. Among his allies was Andrew of Polotsk. That was enough to make Jogaila promise to join the Tatar forces.

The two armies clashed in September on a field called Kulikovo, not far from the Don. Jogaila was still on the march when the battle began

– and historians are not certain whether he was late on purpose or not, because on the one hand he wanted his half-brother dead and on the other he wanted the Tatar power broken. The battle opened with Dmitri selecting a champion, Mamay selecting an opponent, thereby potentially avoiding the carnage of pitched combat. When the two warriors killed one another on the first charge, however, the armies could not be restrained. In the next few hours 200,000 men were reputedly slain – surely the total was far less, but still a great many. The grand duke of Moscow was honoured for his victory by being known henceforth as Dmitri Donskoy.

Russian historians have long debated the significance of this battle, even disputing whether the basic facts are accurate. There were several accounts written immediately after the battle, but they were more literary and legendary than historical. Tokhtamysh seems to have taken advantage of Mamay's defeat to approach Timur for support; he also quickly dispatched Mamay and reunited the fragments of the Golden Horde. In 1382 he marched on Moscow and obtained its surrender. As part of the subsequent peace treaty, Dmitri sent his son, Basil (Vasily, 1371–1425) to the khan as a hostage. As it happened, Tokhtamysh being unable to discipline his Tatar sub-khans sufficiently to exploit the victory, Dmitri came back to become the leading prince in northern Russia.

The battle of Kulikovo seems to have had no influence on the contest between Jogaila and Andrew. With Kęstutis having the power to determine the winner, Jogaila's best hope for prevailing seemed to rest in his childhood friendship with Vytautas, Kęstutis's favourite son.

Although Winrich had his secret alliance with Jogaila, he continued negotiations with Kęstutis. For face-to-face talks the grandmaster and his representatives relied on Thomas Surville, their Lithuanian-born translator and advisor. Although Winrich tried to keep the arrangements with Jogaila secret, there were too many people involved, and too many others wondered why Jogaila lacked enthusiasm for fighting crusaders. As rumours concerning possible treason circulated through Samogitia. Kęstutis heard them and worried, but his young son, Vytautas, reassured him that his friend Jogaila could be trusted.

The fundamental disagreement between the two was over whether to continue the advance eastward into Rus' and onto the steppe or to defend the Lithuanian heartland against the Teutonic Knights. Jogaila argued for occupying more of Rus', which would have meant war with Dmitri. Twice his father had almost captured Moscow, and now there was the new fortress that Dmitri had built – the Kremlin, a huge limestone wall which could give shelter to all the citizens. (The brick walls came later.) Not even the Tatars had been able to capture it. That was a reason for avoiding this war.

Kęstutis insisted on fighting in the west – and Kęstutis was the head of the family even though Jogaila held the title of supreme duke. This contributed to Jogaila seeing the removal of his uncle as the necessary first step to the creation of a great empire in the east. If that meant co-operation with the Teutonic Knights, so be it.

Vytautas, meanwhile, was participating in his father's exploits and observing carefully. Under Kęstutis's guidance he was gaining a reputation for valour in war, but even at the age of twenty-nine, he had not developed an instinct for guile. Meanwhile, Jogaila strengthened his position for an eventual seizure of power.

Jogaila's chief advisor was the governor of Vilnius, Hans (Hanul) of Riga. Hans had probably begun his career as a German merchant. Settling in Vilnius, he impressed Jogaila sufficiently that he made him his interpreter and secretary. On occasions Hans represented the supreme duke at diplomatic meetings, and under his influence, Jogaila opened Lithuania to Polish and Prussian merchants as well as Livonians. His wife later supervised the ladies at the Polish court.

Next to Hans, Jogaila relied on his own brothers, especially Skirgaila and Kaributas (Koribyt, *c.* 1350–after 1404). In 1379 Jogaila sent Skirgaila on the previously mentioned mysterious journey to the west. Records indicate that he went through Prussia to Masovia on the pretence of attending a wedding, then vanished and did not reappear in Lithuania for months. Such a conspiracy could not be kept quiet forever.

In 1381 the counts of Mark and Cleves came to Prussia, achieving such success that Kęstutis was persuaded that he could not rely on his nephew for assistance. As time passed more people began to gossip, to speculate, and to complain, thereby forcing Kęstutis to act. In the summer of 1381, he arrested his nephew and took the title of supreme duke for himself; lesser enemies he hanged. Kęstutis then made a mistake – believing Jogaila's repentant apologies, he forgave him. He even gave his nephew a small territory in the east which Jogaila used as a base for plotting revenge. How could Kęstutis not sense that Jogaila would never be satisfied with that?

This time, however, Jogaila was more careful. He was the person-ification of subservience until Kęstutis marched away to deal with Kaributas, who ruled the region between central Lithuania, Moscow, and the steppe. Kęstutis took with him a vast number of his most trusted warriors to besiege the castle at Navahrudak – a strong wood fortification atop a steep mound, an impressive structure that had already withstood attacks by crusaders and Tatars – and made Vytautas responsible for governing Vilnius in his absence. However, when Vytautas went to Trakai, the centre of the family's power, he entrusted Vilnius to Hanul. That was Jogaila's opportunity. He hurried to Vilnius, took control of his ancestral seat, and sent for the Teutonic Knights. As Jogaila marched against Trakai with his army, Marshal Cuno of Hattenstein hurried east as quickly as he could. The critical moment was at hand, and the fate of the crusade hung in the balance.

When Kęstutis returned – it was only 150 km. (95 miles) from Navahrudak to Vilnius – he realised that the highland Lithuanians had rallied to Jogaila. Hurrying across rebel lands to Samogitia, he raised a large force of lowlanders who could be trusted to be loyal, then marched towards Trakai, hoping to arrive before Jogaila could capture Vytautas. Jogaila, for his part, had not been idle. Well aware of the need for swift results, he had ordered his men to storm the fortress. The attack had failed. Perhaps it had been attempted too soon. However, Jogaila did not dare abandon the siege lest his men consider it an admission of defeat. Knowing that Kęstutis was on the way, he was at first deeply disconcerted when news came that an army was approaching from the west. If Kęstutis had returned already, the game was over. Then, seeing the Christian banners, he spread the word that the Teutonic Knights had come to save him. Soon his pagan and Orthodox warriors were cheering in jubilation that the crusaders had arrived!

Not long afterwards, when Kęstutis saw the situation, he hesitated, not knowing whether to fight or to retreat. Either decision had its dangers, but delay was worse. It was clear that he was an old man, abandoned by his friends, and that no one was coming to his rescue. While Kęstutis negotiated, an army led by the Livonian master came up in his rear, cutting of all hope of retreat. Although Kęstutis could perhaps have abandoned his army and escaped, he chose to negotiate with Jogaila. However, as he had left his bodyguard behind, he was seized and loaded with chains; Vytautas was imprisoned as well.

If Kęstutis hoped for lenient treatment, he was disappointed. Jogaila sent him to the brick fortress at Kreva, in modern Belarus. Five days later Skirgaila 'found' him dead in his cell. Jogaila said that Kęstutis had committed suicide, but few believed this. This became a central point for later propagandists, as did the accusations that Jogaila subsequently drowned Kęstutis's wife, then murdered some of her relatives. This would become a political liability in the long run, so much so that he later went to great lengths to deny it. But there was no doubt that it strengthened his position in Samogitia at the time, and when Skirgaila told the Samogitians that there was no alternative to accepting Jogaila as their lord, they grudgingly agreed.

Surprisingly, perhaps, Jogaila put Vytautas into a comfortable prison. He could easily have arranged his death, but mercy to relatives was customary in the Gediminid dynasty, and the *Witingen* frowned on dukes killing family members. Vytautas's death would have been one murder too many.

Kęstutis's cremation in Vilnius was an impressive pagan ceremony. Skirgaila prepared the pyre carefully, sacrificing horses, clothing, weapons and even hunting dogs for the future enjoyment of the supreme duke. It was the last big performance of the native religion, a great anachronism. Surely many recognised the hypocrisy of Jogaila's gesture.

Jogaila rewarded the Teutonic Order for its help with a four-year military alliance, a promise to be baptised as a Roman Christian, and possession of western Samogitia. He brought the Livonian master and his officers to Vilnius to witness his formal resumption of the title, supreme duke.

Winrich's Passing

Winrich of Kniprode lived to hear of the victory, but he died before the treaties could be ratified in October 1382. Because the Prussian officers were at a general chapter to elect Winrich's successor, it was the Livonian master who represented the Teutonic Order in Vilnius when Jogaila signed the treaties.

The chronicler Wigand wrote, 'Magister Wynricus Knyprode died eight days before the kalends of July at the third hour of the day of Saint John the Baptist, confessed, contrite and in full command of his senses, with the last rites, having been grandmaster in Prussia thirty-one years.' He went on to say that Winrich had maintained the Order's religious standards, ruled justly over knights and vassals, governed burghers and peasants well, and protected the widows and orphans. Furthermore, he had devastated far and wide the lands of the Lithuanians, built castles to warn of attacks. There was peace inside his Order and his lands.

The general chapter meeting in Marienburg found it difficult to select a new grandmaster. Most of the surviving officers of the council were too aged to assume the burdens of that office, and Marshal Hattenstein had just died. Misled perhaps by the brilliance of his reign and the chivalric reputation his order had earned, at the end Winrich had fallen victim to cronyism, a fault common to men those hold power too long. By trusting only experience and proven ability, he had guaranteed competent performance during his lifetime, but by not nurturing younger knights he had served his successor poorly. The only officer in the prime of life was the master of the robes, Konrad Zöllner of Rothenstein (1325–90). This accounts for the controversial election of a grandmaster with little experience in diplomacy and warfare.

Any change in high office is accompanied by some uncertainty, and it was true now. Konrad Zöllner had no time to organise his new government and to master its peculiarities before events began to press him. His most important duty, as he saw it, was to meet with Jogaila personally, but no sooner had he arranged for a meeting than Sigismund of Brandenburg, the fourteen-year-old son of the late emperor Charles IV, arrived in Prussia and as margrave of Brandenburg demanded a personal interview. King Louis had just died, and although many wished to see the union of Poland and Hungary continued, there were too many notable people in each country who disliked the power that this would give the sovereign. Sigismund, who was betrothed to the king's eldest surviving daughter, had learned Hungarian at Louis's court and had recently been sent by his half-brother, King Wenceslaus of Bohemia (1361–1419), to learn Polish in Cracow. Clearly, he expected to rule in one, if not both kingdoms. The grandmaster agreed to meet Sigismund and sent the grand commander, Rudiger of Elner, and Marshal Konrad of Wallenrode (*c.* 1330–93), to Jogaila. Nothing of importance came from the meeting between the grandmaster and the brash young man – who assumed that he would soon be wearing the Polish crown. It was otherwise with the conference with Jogaila.

Jogaila Cedes Samogitia

The meeting on the Dubysa River – which flowed into the Nemunas near Welun – was highly successful from the crusaders' point of view. On the last day of October in 1382, after six days of negotiations between the marshal and Jogaila and Skirgaila, they agreed that Jogaila would make Lithuania Roman Catholic within four years. Also, and more plausibly, he would surrender Samogitia west of the Dubysa River. Of course, Jogaila did not actually give up anything belonging to him, because most Samogitians remained loyal to Kęstutis's memory and to his son, Vytautas. Though he retained the provinces which lay closest to the Highlands, he abandoned the rest of Samogitia to the Teutonic Knights. Now they had to conquer it.

When Jogaila promised not to make any war without the grandmaster's permission, it was an impractical arrangement that implied a vassal-lord relationship. All the concessions, with Jogaila's brothers signing the document, too, must have raised the grandmaster's suspicions, because he immediately pressed for another meeting on the Dubysa to affix the official seals on the treaty. However, that issue was soon overshadowed by a more important one. The commissioners had hardly returned to Prussia before Vytautas escaped from prison.

Jogaila had permitted Vytautas's wife, Anne, to visit him in prison to assure herself that he had not been harmed. It was the least Jogaila could do for a boyhood friend and the daughter of the ruler of Smolensk. He never suspected that Anne (or a lady-in-waiting) would exchange clothes with her small, beardless husband and wait quietly in the cell, pretending to be him as long as possible, while Vytautas made his way out the castle and fled directly west across the wilderness and down the Narew River, apparently hoping to take refuge with his sister Danutė in Masovia. However, her husband, Janusz, feared that giving him refuge would anger Jogaila, so he sent him on to his brother, Siemowit IV.

Siemowit seems to have persuaded Vytautas that he should travel on to Prussia, but only after another baptism, one that allowed him to present himself as Konrad – an ancient and respected Masovian name, but also that of the grandmaster! This seems to have had two reasons, the first of which was that Siemowit hoped to become the next king of Poland. King Louis had died in September 1382 after suffering a lingering illness – some speculate that it was leprosy – and being distracted by events in Naples and Wallachia. While Louis had made the Polish nobles and clergy recognise his daughter Mary as the legitimate heir, there were difficulties over the details. Few Poles trusted Mary's fiancé, who was behaving like the spoiled teenager he was. This meant that Siemowit, as the senior member of the widespread Piast dynasty, might yet be called to ascend the throne. If he could boast of having contributed to the conversion of the Lithuanians, his chances of selection would be improved.

From Masovia Vytautas wrote to the grandmaster that he and his brother Tautvilas were willing to become Christians, but he wanted to speak with him personally about it. This was a difficult case. If Konrad Zöllner allowed Vytautas to come to Prussia, Jogaila might cancel the recent treaty; however, Vytautas might be able to convert the Samogitians peacefully. When the grandmaster received Vytautas at Insterburg, he asked him why he had not come forth when he had possessed vast lands and castles. Vytautas answered that his former love for Jogaila had turned to hatred. He promised to become a Roman Christian, to give hostages, and to guarantee the conversion of his people.

Jogaila gallantly allowed Anne to leave Lithuania and join her husband. Soon many other relatives and supporters came to share Vytautas's fortunes and to escape Jogaila's wrath.

The End of the Polish–Hungarian Joint Monarchy

Nobody was particularly surprised when the Polish–Hungarian union ended with the death of Louis the Great. The common interests of the two peoples – at least as far as the nobility and clergy were concerned – were too different. Poles were concerned about challenges from Germans, Lithuanians and Tatars; Hungarians were preoccupied with the Turks and the Venetians, and hardly at all interested in Tatars and Germans. They retained some common interests, one celebrated by a later piece of folk wisdom cited in Davies's *God's Playground*:

> Węgier, Polak – dwa bratanki
> Tak do szabli jak do szklanki.

> Pole and Hungarian– Two brothers,
> Whether with sword or with tankard in hand.

Had there been a foreign challenge to unite the nations, as there had been in 1370, necessity might have kept them together. But Louis seemed to have brought the Lithuanian danger under control – the invasion of 1376 was the last great incursion. However, Louis's measures to prevent another attack were unpopular because he had appointed too many Hungarians to high offices. If Louis had been granted a son, dynastic loyalties might have sufficed, but there was only Casimir's grandson, who had died five years earlier fighting in Brandenburg. Louis had only two young daughters, and power would be exercised by whomever they married. In 1382 it appeared that the elder, Mary (1371–95), would marry Sigismund of Luxemburg, while Jadwiga (Hedwig, 1373–99) would wed a young Habsburg prince without a powerful territorial base. Both prospective bridegrooms were princes in Germany and the Poles had come to see Germans as the national enemy.

Three years before his death Louis had called a great assembly of nobles and churchmen to announce that the crowns would go to his daughter, Mary. At the time Masovia was still ruled by Siemowit III, who did not object, but his death in 1381 gave his younger son, Siemowit IV, a power base from which he could challenge the king's will. He argued that the Polish kingdom should remain in Piast hands while continuing Angevin practices that the nobles and clergy admired. Siemowit IV rallied support in Kujavia and Great Poland, where many believed that the nobles and clergy of Little Poland had become too important. As if to confirm that analysis, many powerful clan chiefs and clergymen in Little Poland resented the arrogance of their counterparts to the north.

Meanwhile, the queen mother realised that the teenaged Sigismund had alienated almost everyone in Poland. He could be charming when he wished, especially to women, who responded so enthusiastically to his efforts at seduction that he found the conquests almost boring. He spoke Polish, Hungarian, German, Italian and Latin, but beyond highly quotable witticisms he was rarely able to persuade listeners that he had anything to say. He was a gifted athlete, but untested as a military leader. His greatest attribute was that there seemed to be no alternative to taking him as king.

For the Poles that was not enough. Louis had kept the Polish throne by enriching and empowering the nobility, and once the nobles had tasted power, they were not about to surrender it to a foreigner. Certainly not to Sigismund, whose arrogance was beyond enduring. The sticking point was that Sigismund refused to promise that he would live in Poland. He could have lied boldly, but he would not. Perhaps it was pride, perhaps a realisation that the Hungarians would not understand having a king living so far from their threatened frontiers to the south.

The solution was to divide the kingdoms. The problem was that, even if Sigismund could suppress Polish resistance, it was unlikely that Jadwiga could overcome the Hungarian desire to have a mature male who could deal with the challenges from Turks, Venetians, and rebel lords. There was a strong faction endorsing Charles III of Naples – who two years later actually managed to establish himself in Hungary long enough to be crowned, only to be murdered by Queen Elizabeth's followers. Early in 1383 a compromise was reached: the Hungarians would take Mary (and Sigismund), while the Poles took Jadwiga, but without the awkward Habsburg bridegroom. It helped that both girls were too young to object strongly.

In January 1383 Siemowit came to Cracow with plans to force Jadwiga to marry him, counting on employing the 7,000 *Gulden* the grand-master had given him in pawn for the strategic castle at Wizna to bribe the nobles. However, the nobles closed Wawel Castle and sent word to Jadwiga to wait in Hungary until it was safe to come north. This caused Siemowit to withdraw to Great Poland where a terrible civil war had already begun. When clans began slaughtering each other over ancient feuds that only needed an excuse to break into violence, Sigismund and Ladislas of Opole intervened with German, Hungarian, Czech and Polish troops, ravaging widely across the northern provinces. Siemowit abandoned his claim, but Great Poland never recovered its ancient importance in the kingdom.

War with Jogaila

The grandmaster meanwhile moved cautiously. He upheld most agreements with Jogaila to the letter, but he insisted on having a free hand in western Samogitia, including the right to name whomever he wanted as governor. Then, almost like a direct challenge to Jogaila, he sent Vytautas there, equipped with weapons, clothing and horses. If Jogaila did not object, the Teutonic Knights would have Vytautas as a vassal prince to rule Samogitia on their behalf; if Jogaila turned against them, they could support Vytautas in a bid to overthrow him. Konrad Zöllner thought that he had divided the Lithuanians and weakened them.

This did not work. Konrad's ruse deceived nobody, except perhaps himself. The Teutonic Knights had been making 'secret' alliances that far too many people were aware of. Such a policy could not be successful for ever. If pride goeth before a fall, the Teutonic Knights were overdue. The grandmaster lacked the experience to evaluate foreign princes. Perhaps he had laboured so long in Winrich's shadow that the blinding light of responsibility made it impossible to see that Jogaila was more subtle and duplicitous than he expected.

Jogaila's response was quick and clever – he attacked Janusz and Siemowit IV in Masovia, thus undermining their ability to fight in Silesia. The grandmaster was careful not to intervene, since that would give Jogaila an excuse to invalidate all treaties with the Teutonic Order, but Jogaila revealed his intentions when he warned the grandmaster that sending Vytautas to Samogitia was nurturing a viper in his bosom.

Another meeting on the Dubysa was scheduled for May 1383, but it was delayed because plague was ravaging Prussia, sweeping away some of the Order's highest officers. When Jogaila said he would meet only in July, the grandmaster left to visit the stricken districts. Two months later, when the grandmaster sailed up the Nemunas, he took the bishops of Ermland and Pomesania with him, intending to baptise Jogaila. Shallow water forced their vessels to stop at Christmemel, where Skirgaila met them and explained that Jogaila was waiting 25 km., (14 miles) inland. Marshal Konrad of Wallenrode borrowed a horse and rode to Jogaila, hoping to persuade him to come to some castle on the river for a personal meeting. Jogaila explained that his vassals forbade him to go where crusaders would be able to arrest him – he had already established the precedent for that – but the grandmaster could come to him. Konrad Zöllner, certainly remembering Jogaila's promises to

Kęstutis, chose not to risk becoming Jogaila's captive – he replied that he lacked the horses to go to Jogaila's camp in proper style.

At this point all pretence of courtesy ceased. Konrad Zöllner gave Jogaila fourteen days' notice to resume peace talks, and failing that, to prepare for war. Then he summoned Vytautas's Samogitians and the Prussian militia. When Vytautas arrived at his father's former capital at Trakai in mid-September, he found the people eager to surrender to him. The grandmaster left Johann Rabe (advocate of the bishop of Pomesania) with sufficient men to defend the place, then marched on Vilnius. There the crusader army met stiff resistance. After desperate fighting on the watergate bridge, the grandmaster retreated. He had been in Lithuania eleven days.

Jogaila struck back at Trakai, beginning a siege that the grandmaster could not break – Konrad's men were tired, and the native troops had completed their required service. In November, after resisting for six weeks, Johann Rabe realised that no help was coming. The fact that he was allowed to surrender on honourable terms and ride home at the head of his men, suggests that he could have repelled every attempt at storming the walls and that Jogaila's army wanted to go home as well.

Vytautas was baptised a second time in Tapiau (Gvardeysk), a stone castle in eastern Sambia. He was given the Christian name of Wigand, and many of his retainers were baptised with him. Vytautas confirmed Jogaila's treaties, then promised to give the crusaders the remainder of Samogitia and become a vassal of the Teutonic Knights. In return, the grandmaster gave him a castle on the Nemunas as a base from which to govern his territories. This arrangement was apparently successful, because many *Witingen* swore allegiance to the grandmaster in February 1384. No missionaries were sent to Samogitia, however. That and all other internal affairs were left to Vytautas, who argued that he could not risk offending his pagan subjects by baptising them midway through a war against Jogaila.

Meanwhile, the attacks on Samogitia continued. When a future hero of the Order, Marquard (Markward) of Salzbach (c. 1360–1410) took 150 men on a night raid into Lithuania, they captured a pagan who told them that 400 Lithuanians were camped nearby. Marquard attacked at dawn, killing or capturing most of the enemy, and taking all their horses. It was the start of a heroic, almost unbelievable, career.

In May 1384 the grandmaster began building a large castle near Kaunas. Workmen hauled timbers to the island, dug trenches and built earthworks. The knights and mounted warriors raided nearby villages until Jogaila and Skirgaila appeared and routed one of the smaller parties. Konrad Zöllner thereafter kept his warriors nearby to protect the workmen. When construction was complete, he named the castle Marienwerder am Memel (Saint Mary's Island on the Nemunas – there already being a Marienwerder between Marienburg and Culm) and returned to Prussia.

Vytautas was taking a great risk by co-operating with the crusaders, but his options were limited. His only living child was his daughter, Sophia. The story that he had sons who were murdered by a grand-master must be dismissed as a myth – such a crime would have been brought to the popes' attention repeatedly. The rumour can be blamed on the lack of contemporary Lithuanian sources and good records, and the convoluted and confusing family tree (in which some members have a pagan name, a baptismal name and sometimes a second baptismal name – all further complicated by the different conventions of spelling). Those stories have been dismissed by modern historians, but they illustrate how old and how deep the hatred of the Teutonic Knights was. The reality was that although Vytautas did not have a male successor, neither did Jogaila. Lithuanians who yearned for a predictable future had to be frustrated; therefore, while it was clear that many preferred the exciting and emotional Vytautas over the cool and calculating Jogaila, the survival instincts of the rest favoured the supreme duke. Most seem to have based their support for either candidate on their past allegiances. In Samogitia this favoured Vytautas.

Konrad Zöllner had every reason to be pleased. Vytautas was reconquering his ancestral lands more easily than expected. The combination of Samogitian patriotism and crusader arms seemed invincible. In the summer of 1384 Vytautas and the crusaders broke in on a forest ceremony and captured thirty-six leading pagans. This alliance, unimaginable before, eliminated many pagan opponents quickly and undermined the prestige of those who remained at large. Not a single holy wood remained that the crusaders had not used as a campsite. Everything was going so well that the grandmaster could not imagine that Vytautas might be unhappy or that he would abandon an alliance which was so profitable. His calculation was fundamentally wrong. Vytautas believed that he had been responsible for the victories, and now that he had established himself safely in Samogitia and was winning support in the Highlands, he saw the Teutonic alliance as more hindrance than help; certainly, the alliance was not popular in the Orthodox regions that Vytautas wanted to win over. Nor did Vytautas want to spend his life as anyone's vassal – his subjects could not have tolerated that. As a result, Konrad Zöllner overestimated Vytautas's hatred of his cousin. When Jogaila sent Vytautas word that he could have his ancestral lands back, Vytautas was prepared to listen.

Jogaila and Vytautas Reconciled

Jogaila must have told Vytautas that he was willing to give up western Lithuania, because he needed peace at home so that he could marry Jadwiga of Poland, the younger daughter of the late Louis the Great. Not only was he willing to return Kęstutis's lands, but he would add Volhynia to them. Vytautas could not resist the offer.

This may have saved paganism in Samogitia at the last minute, but the episode hurried the acceptance of Roman Christianity in the rest of Lithuania, because Jogaila was already negotiating the conversion of his people. Had he not won Vytautas over, his subsequent conversion to Christianity might had led to a war between Poland and Prussia in which Lithuanian interests vanished almost completely – Poland had long been torn apart by civil war, as was now Lithuania; moreover, his many Rus'ian subjects might have turned to Moscow. Jogaila was too astute to leave such questions to chance.

Vytautas was somehow able to keep his arrangement with Jogaila secret until the summer of 1384, an amazing feat considering how sharply Lithuanian loyalty was divided. Moreover, he planned a general uprising in Samogitia, starting with three castles along the Nemunas where the garrisons contained more Samogitians than Germans. It would be just a matter of choosing the right moment to join Jogaila.

On 9 July 1384, Vytautas appeared at Georgenburg and told the commander that Jogaila was on the way and to send to Ragnit for help. The commander did so, fearful that his small garrison would be unable to hold out without reinforcements. The commander then foolishly invited Vytautas to bring his 400 men into the castle; they quickly overpowered the defenders and seized control. (This incident may have occurred at Bayernburg, which was also burned in 1384 and later rebuilt on the site of Georgenburg, with the result that the two were often confused.)

Vytautas sent another small castle up in flames, then tried to ambush the relief force from Ragnit, but the knights heard what was planned and were on their guard. Word had spread, so that when Vytautas reached Marienwerder a/M, he found the garrison had also been warned. That castle dominated the mouth of the Dubysa River and had been the crusader base for recent attacks on Samogitia and central Lithuania. In urging Jogaila to help him capture it, Vytautas reminded him they could invest the castle for a month before any relief army would be able to make its way up the river. It was essential that the castle be taken.

The garrison in Marienwerder a/M had not worried about Vytautas, because he lacked siege machinery. It was a different matter when lookouts from nearby forts signalled that the combined forces of Jogaila and Skirgaila were approaching.

Jogaila's men first sought to capture the castle by assault. There was desperate fighting that evening, as Lithuanians tried to climb the walls on ladders. Next Jogaila turned to siege tactics, setting up catapults and building a bridge across the Nemunas for better access to wood and food. Meanwhile, the chief engineer in the castle was having difficulties with his catapult. After only two shots, it 'broke like an egg'. A few days later, after he had repaired it, his missiles caused numerous casualties among the besiegers. Hurling stones and shooting arrows at each other, the two forces marked time for four weeks.

On 16 October the grandmaster's relief army arrived on the bank of the river opposite Marienwerder am Memel. When the marshal sent the commander of Ragnit to observe how the garrison was doing, he learned that many of the men were injured or exhausted. Even as they looked across the river, they saw a stone decapitate the castle's commander.

The relief forces were frustrated completely. The Lithuanians held all the strategic points around the castle and prevented the crusaders from going in or coming out. Konrad Zöllner did not have sufficient supplies to besiege the besiegers, and, therefore, after a brief display of energy, he ordered a retreat and left the garrison to its own devices.

Jogaila attacked the waterfront wall. His engineers constructed platforms for catapults and archers on the river, but these attacks, too, were unsuccessful. During the following weeks it appeared that the garrison might well hold out until another relief force arrived. However, in December a Lithuanian warrior slipped up to the wall and spoke to the vice-commander. Saying that he had a wife and children in Ragnit, he offered to deliver a message there. The vice-commander wrote that the grandmaster should hurry his relief force faster than its expected January arrival, since the castle could hold out only another two weeks. The letter was taken straight to Jogaila. When the supreme duke learned how weak the garrison was, he ordered an assault.

The Lithuanians filled the moat with wood and pitch, then started a huge fire. As the flames rose, Jogaila called on the vice-commander to surrender. He promised to treat the captives well, and he gave him his handshake as a guarantee of good faith. Jogaila kept his word in principle – his men murdered only a few knights, and he had only one decapitated. He took the other 55 knights (and perhaps 600 men) into captivity.

Meanwhile, an otherwise insignificant combat took place in the wilderness. On this occasion a unit from Culm which had been making raids from Ragnit had been on the march all night. On reaching a good campsite, its commander had the horses sent to pasture and his men were beginning to prepare breakfast when Vytautas struck. That was how Marquard of Salzbach was captured. Somehow, he and Vytautas soon became fast friends. Marquard remained in honourable captivity as the duke's companion and advisor for six years. When Marquard returned to Prussia, his fluent Lithuanian and intimate knowledge of Lithuania and its people was invaluable.

With so many of the Nemunas fortresses now in his hands, Jogaila was willing to talk peace. He had sent Skirgaila to Poland with an offer to convert all the Lithuanians to Roman Christianity if the heiress of Poland would marry him, but he knew he would have a better chance of winning her hand if he could come to some agreement with the grandmaster regarding his conversion. Nevertheless, although Konrad Zöllner appeared as agreed at the Dubysa River in May 1385, Jogaila did not come.

In August 1385 Rhenish knights came in sufficient numbers to allow the grandmaster to attack, but leave the militia at home with the harvest. The invasion started off with a great parade – the crusaders first, following the banner of St George, then (presumably) the secular knights and militia following the banner of the Blessed Virgin, and lastly the Teutonic Knights behind the grandmaster's banner. They loaded onto vessels to make their way up the Nemunas, presumably hauling the vessels when the winds and rowing were insufficient. As they reached the Neris, near Kaunas, they disembarked and moved inland. When they reached the first ford, however, they discovered that the Lithuanians had built a stout palisade and were prepared to defend it. Losses were high on both sides as the crusaders fought their way past the barrier. Among those drowned at this time was a prominent noble, Wilhelm II of Katzenellenbogen.

The crusaders marched inland to Vilnius, then went beyond, where they spent almost three weeks ravaging a countryside that had been long spared. Meanwhile, Skirgaila and Vytautas assembled large forces at the fords to block all routes out of the country. When Konrad saw the defensive works at the fords on the Neris, he sent his contingent of Teutonic Knights to find a way past the barriers. He had only a few of his own knights, but he would not trust such an important task to strangers, whose reactions to danger were unpredictable. Under the cover of missiles, his knights charged into the river and routed the defenders. Four Teutonic Knights and three other knights drowned, but the way was clear. That day, 19 September, was thereafter celebrated as a day of deliverance.

What is unclear, given the nature of the sources, is whether there were two battles at a ford or only one. That is a problem typical of everything we know about these years. We know much about the many small incursions of this period – where they were made, when, and by whom, thanks to the *Wegeberichte* – but not how they fit into the larger picture.

Although the 1385 campaign had been a success, it had also pointed out the difficulty of operating without a base on the frontier. Having failed to make headway in Samogitia, where Vytautas was presumably concentrating his men, the grandmaster shifted his attention to the region between Vilnius and Grodno. Presumably, this meant crossing the Lake District.

After the capture of Marienwerder a/M, Jogaila no longer needed Vytautas's co-operation. Although he had promised Vytautas his father's lands, he now withheld those around Trakai. These he gave to Skirgaila, who technically became duke of Samogitia as well but exercised little authority there. This left Vytautas with little more than a few territories along the Bug and Narew Rivers, bounded by Prussia, Masovia and Volhynia. The only castle of any importance was Grodno. Thus, Vytautas found himself a marcher lord, subordinate to and dependent upon Jogaila, doing the dirty work of defending the country without hope of profit or advancement. Moreover, Jogaila kept him nearby where he could keep an eye on him.

When Liubartas died in 1383, the lordship of Volhynia became vacant. Vytautas underwent baptism in the Orthodox Church, so that he would be acceptable to the nobles there, but that plan failed when Jogaila gave Volhynia to Skirgaila.

Jogaila Marries the Queen of Poland

In August 1385, a Polish delegation representing Jadwiga appeared at the castle at Kreva. In a document sealed by Jogaila, Skirgaila, Kaributas and Vytautas, Jogaila agreed to be baptised whenever the Polish princess wished and promised that all the Lithuanian pagans would become Roman Christians as well, a promise which could sway Jadwiga, whose religious devotion was stronger than her attachment to Wilhelm of Habsburg, the playmate who had pursued her right to Cracow.

The nobles of Poland may have been more interested in the promise to 'restore the lands stolen' in recent decades and to end the struggle over Galicia–Volhynia. Likewise, there were many in the Lithuanian empire who wanted Jogaila to marry Sophia, the daughter of Dmitri of Moscow, because that would reduce the likelihood of war in Rus'. Because of this internal resistance, Jogaila was taking a risk in reaching out to the Poles – who were being warned that he was not a man known for keeping his word.

Darius Baronas and Stephen C. Rowell have argued that this was not much of a risk, because Western Christian ideas and practices had already permeated Lithuanian society. Intermarriage, increasing trade, and political contacts had brought the two worlds together. The greater risk would have been to accept Orthodoxy, with the implied superiority of Moscow and the Tatar khans.

The final decision rested with the young woman who had thought she would have no crown, then the crown of Hungary, where she had been residing with her mother, and was now queen (*rex*) of Poland. Some Poles had raised the question of her virginity, since she seems to have gone through an improvised marriage ceremony with Wilhelm of Austria, who was still hoping to appeal to her passions to overcome all the practical obstacles to their union. When Jadwiga came to Poland in October 1384, she was pursued by a variety of suitors, and Siemowit IV seems even to have attempted to kidnap her. Wilhelm of Habsburg had rushed to Cracow and somehow obtained access to her quarters by night, a scandal that persuaded her advisors to hurry the negotiations with Jogaila. This prompted contemporary chroniclers to insist that at this time she was still only eleven or twelve years old (a conceit that her admirers continued to believe until very recently despite evidence suggesting that she was fourteen). No marriage could have been consummated if she were only twelve, but fourteen would not have been uncommon; more importantly, the younger age would have rendered invalid a private marriage, if any such had taken place.

In any case, events rendered the discussion moot. Jadwiga had been persuaded that she could not marry Wilhelm and remain ruler of Poland, and since she was eager to please her spiritual advisors by assisting in the conversion of countless pagans, she agreed to marry an older man with whom she had nothing in common, not even a language for simple conversation. Even so, if was only after Wilhelm was banned from the kingdom in August 1385, causing him to flee in such haste that he left behind the treasure he had brought for bribes, that her advisors knew they had won.

Then and later there were heated discussions as to whether her marriage to Wilhelm had been consummated, and there were also rumours that she had taken lovers. Such stories may have been obstacles to having her declared a saint later. Certainly, nineteenth-century novelists were wrong in portraying her as a willowy young woman, because those who opened her tomb later reported that she was tall and well-built.

By January 1386, all remaining opposition to Jadwiga's marriage to Jogaila had vanished. Masovia resisted, but that ended when Jogaila promised Siemowit IV Ruthenian lands previously belonging to his uncle, Bolesław – and wed him to his sister Alexandra (the couple were eventually blessed with thirteen children who lived to maturity). Events then moved swiftly, for no one wanted the pope or emperor to raise objections. Once Jadwiga was persuaded that her potential groom was not deformed or fat – one story was that she sent a knight to investigate, and after Jogaila invited him to the sauna, he made a favourable report. (It turned out that the future king was a bit of a dandy, wearing fine clothes, taking great care for his personal hygiene, and even bathing daily. He might even have been as young as twenty-four.) As for Jogaila, he was mainly concerned that she would make him king, but he was reportedly struck by her beauty and modesty when they met.

In Cracow Jogaila was given some days of instruction in the practices of Roman Catholicism, then baptised and married to Jadwiga. On 4 March 1386, he was crowned Ladislas II, a significant name for Poles who wished to recover Danzig from the Teutonic Order, but also a reminder that Ladislas of Opole was still a power to be reckoned with. Vytautas was rebaptised as Alexander, thereby washing away all previous holy waters. It was a momentous occasion, such that the citizens of Poland took the great wind that blew down giant trees and church towers as an omen of sweeping changes to come.

That Jogaila should be willing to undergo baptism was no surprise. It was well known that he was ambitious. The opportunity to become king of Poland was no small matter, even considering that Jadwiga was the hereditary ruler and that she had the final voice in all decisions. That his brothers should agree to be baptised and given new names was also nothing unusual, either. Lithuanians were now accustomed to ruling over and living among Christians and many had married foreign spouses. But it was still not a step taken lightly. When Catholicism became his religion, Jogaila surely knew it would put Lithuania within the sphere of Western culture and Western ideas (and Western cannons); and it might well divide his country in two, the western Roman Catholic half looking towards Poland, the eastern Russian Orthodox half looking towards Moscow. Jogaila, however, was not overly concerned. He must have calculated the situation carefully –

that was his behaviour throughout his life – and concluded that he could not hold out forever against the growing strength of the Roman Catholic states to his west. That is, Poland had become a formidable power under King Casimir, and Polish control over Galicia had increased under King Louis; meanwhile, the Teutonic Knights had been squeezing Samogitia from the north and west; and gains in the east would not compensate for the loss of the Lithuanian homeland – Rus'ians would eventually want to govern themselves, just as Orthodox True-Believers already expected their pagan governors to convert. Jogaila had to make a choice, East or West. If he chose Poland, with luck he might be able to hold on to Lithuania, too, but if he chose Rus', he might lose everything, with Vytautas becoming king of Lithuania.

The Polish choice of Jogaila also had, in retrospect, the logic of a foregone conclusion. The nobles wanted to end the union with Hungary. They blamed inept Hungarian governors (specifically Ladislas of Opole) for recent setbacks in the eastern territories; they were angered by Hungarian ambitions to annex Moldavia; and they feared that Sigismund, the husband of Jadwiga's sister, Mary, would use the resources of Brandenburg, Bohemia, and Hungary against them. They also wanted help against the Tatars and peace with Lithuania. Most of all, they were outraged by the thought of any German becoming their king (and especially Sigismund – to meet him was to mistrust him, most particularly around their wives and daughters). The churchmen wanted to convert the pagans. Practicality and piety went hand in hand. Jogaila was the only suitor who could fulfil all the national goals. He could learn Polish later.

Jogaila had the valuable support of Ladislas of Opole, who was then consolidating his power in Upper Silesia, Masovia and Dobrzyń. In 1382 he had won considerable backing among the clergy in Little Poland by founding a Pauline monastery of Our Lady in Częstochowa and two years later placing the ancient, venerated icon of the Black Madonna there, probably brought from the Pauline monastery in Hungary. The icon was widely venerated across the Orthodox world, especially in the areas of Rus' where Ladislas had spent years as a Polish and Hungarian governor.

Ladislas probably did not stand as the royal consort's godfather, and the friendly relations did not last. Jogaila took upon himself the command of the forces in Galicia, Volhynia and Moldavia, while the queen pursued a policy of peace with the grandmaster that made Ladislas's presence in Masovia and Kujavia superfluous. Soon Ladislas was in revolt, trying to hold on to his Silesian possessions. His only ally of importance was the grandmaster, but even he was reluctant to go to war for an unpopular Hungarian upstart.

At first, little changed – power remained in the hands of prominent nobles and clergy. Despite the young queen's dislike of court life and preference for quiet religiosity, she learned Polish quickly and proved surprisingly adept at politics; most importantly, she was firmly against any unnecessary war. Despite romantic legends of the nineteenth century, she does not seem to have missed her husband's company. Meanwhile, Poles ceased to call him Jogaila. Formally, he was Ladislas, but more commonly Jagiełło – the name he is remembered by today.

The Impact on the Crusade

If Poles, Lithuanians and the pope had hoped that the conversion of the Lithuanian ruler would bring immediate sweeping changes to the region, they were disappointed. It was unclear to outsiders whether the *Witingen* would accept the supreme duke's actions; some Lithuanians must have wondered if they could trust Vytautas, who had recently been their enemy, while others must have wondered whether he would soon change sides again. The reaction of the Orthodox towns and Lithuanian governors there to Jagiełło's conversion was yet unknown. Since it would have been unwise for the crusaders to lay down their weapons, they continued their fight against the Samogitians who were unwilling to abandon their ancient faith.

The question of Lithuanian loyalty was resolved during Jagiełło's procession through the Grand Duchy, introducing his followers to Siemowit IV and his new wife – Jagiełło's sister – to confirm for all parties what was being done. Documents show that Jadwiga was not with him, the testimony of Długosz notwithstanding. There were baptisms of the nobles (as *Witingen* would be called henceforth) and a few churches erected in the major castles. No protests from angered pagans were mentioned, but until there were Lithuanian-speaking priests available, the message of Christ could not be carried into the countryside. Still, there was no rush. Too much change, too fast, always causes a reaction; and the men who led the Church now perhaps remembered past disappointments; in any case, they were realistic about what could be done. By and large, they left the peasantry alone. There was little to be gained by persecuting them, and little by little paganism faded away.

Meanwhile, Jagiełło was learning that marrying the *rex* was not the same as being king. For many years he was to be little more than the consort of Jadwiga, who despite her youth was a strong political figure. She often ignored her husband's advice and worked against his plans, but she had the backing of her most powerful nobles and churchmen; moreover, her piety made her immensely popular. Therefore, Jagiełło left to deal with the disordered affairs south of Podolia between the Carpathian Mountains and the Black Sea.

This had no immediate effect on the Teutonic Order, but Konrad Zöllner was nevertheless worried and angry about the turn of events. Although he had received an invitation to the wedding, he did not attend. The Poles had suddenly stolen his Order's special field of activity and compromised its reason for existence. He refused to believe that Jagiełło's conversion was real; and he spread warnings about Jagiełło's perfidious nature to the farthest courts of Europe, to the papacy and to the emperor. Nor was he alone in talking about the king's notoriously superstitious nature. Moreover, there was some truth to one of his arguments: Vytautas, not Jagiełło or Skirgaila, had influence in Samogitia; and Vytautas was a multiple apostate. Therefore, even if Jagiełło were a convert (and one should doubt his sincerity), that was not as important an issue as the conversion of Samogitia. As far as the grandmaster was concerned, the crusade had to continue. He did not interrupt the military expeditions.

This antagonistic relationship could perhaps have been resolved if there had been effective leadership in the Holy Roman Empire or the Church. However, the emperor was the incapable Wenceslaus IV, the king of Bohemia, whose unpredictable behaviour was blamed on alcohol, and the papacy was contested by two antagonistic and irreconcilable parties, one in Avignon and the other in Rome.

The Great Schism

A succession of popes had ruled from Avignon from almost the start of the fourteenth century but the return of the papacy to Rome was no surprise. Every pope had talked about it. The Order's procurator-general had followed Pope Urban V into Italy in 1376 and purchased a large residence in Rome near St Peter's, only a few hundred metres from the old church and the papal residence. But his dream of remaining there in comfort vanished abruptly when the pope returned to Avignon. In 1377 the experience was about to repeat itself when Gregory XI died suddenly on the eve of his departure from Rome. This occasioned the unfortunate election that led to the Great Schism, with a mob threatening to lynch the cardinals unless they elected an Italian pope. They did so, but the aged cleric who became Urban VI quickly proved so irascible that the French cardinals withdrew to Avignon, declared the election invalid, then selected a pope of their own. European opinion divided as to which was legitimate. The grandmasters of the Teutonic Order, like most Germans, recognised the Roman pope, but remained in close contact with the Avignon pontiff.

The political morality of the Roman court was observed by contemporaries with a shudder of distaste and disgust. The pope was a poor example to the Teutonic Order, which already was much too cynical and practised too much *Realpolitik* for its own good. The procurator-general, however, saw opportunities to be had from corruption. He wrote that the Order must make friends at the court, listing a number who must be given gifts, because 'unfortunately, in the curia it is known that whoever has and gives, keeps and gains'.

Using these means, the procurator-general overcame the protest by the archbishop of Riga that had moved a reluctant pope to send yet another legate to investigate charges against the Livonian master. The procurator-general not only obtained a reversal of the legate's actions, but he persuaded the pope to name as the next archbishop of Riga a man who promised to incorporate the entire diocese into the Order's Livonian branch. Such an action would end once and for all the problems with the archbishop.

The procurator-general then took up the comparatively easy task of casting doubt on exaggerated Polish claims of having converted all the Lithuanians to the Roman Catholic faith.

Conversion of the Lithuanian Highlands

When Jagiełło returned from his coronation in Cracow, he brought Franciscan friars to Vilnius. At the dedication of the brick cathedral of St Stanislaus near the confluence of the Neris and Vilnia Rivers, Jagiełło took it upon himself to teach the crowd the essentials of the faith, especially how to recite the 'Pater Noster' and the 'Credo'. His Lithuanian subjects obeyed his orders to accept Roman Christianity, but he had too few priests to baptise everyone immediately, much less teach them the doctrines of Christianity. Few friars spoke Lithuanian, and there were so few translators that it was difficult to provide religious instruction. Moreover, the few priests were in cities and castles where the small communities of Christian merchants and artisans already lived, so the daily life of most people was not immediately affected.

Conversion did not mean that the Lithuanians adopted Polish or German forms of worship. Wise missionaries (and these prevailed at this moment) understood it was not necessary to abolish traditions and ceremonies that were not hostile to Christian doctrine. They knew that Christianity spread quickest when it incorporated local customs, artistic traditions and sacred sites into its ceremonies. Conversion should be a process of amalgamation rather than of forcing new believers to abandon old habits and practices for new ones. The unfortunate result was that converts celebrating ancient pagan holidays might persuade observers to conclude that they had not changed their practices at all but were merely hypocrites and apostates. This probably confused some converts, too.

The Teutonic Knights did not understand this mixture of practices and did not want to understand it. They preferred to believe that this conversion was another hoax. Accordingly, whenever they captured a Polish knight in Lithuania, they executed him for aiding apostasy and paganism.

Darius Baronas reminds us that paganism was more a collection of folk practices than a religion. It had no hierarchy, few cult sites, and was thoroughly penetrated by Christian ideas. That is why there was no significant resistance to Jagiełło's orders. There were 'trouble-makers' who were concerned about abandoning important traditional practices, but these were offset by boyars who feared losing their property if they did not conform. When Jerome of Prague visited Lithuania – most scholars believe Samogitia – in 1395–8 or 1401–4, he encountered women who appeared to have already been baptised but were vocal in complaining that they did not know where to look for God. This is as simply explained by the lack of priests as by the region being still thoroughly pagan. Healers and magicians could be as easily found in Germany and Poland as among the pagans of Lithuania.

Jagiełło proved to be extraordinarily devout: he placed his Orthodox mother, Uliana, in a nunnery, and surrounded himself with clerics; in 1410 he would delay the start of the battle of Tannenberg by ordering mass after mass to be sung, until finally Vytautas lost patience and launched the attack. Vytautas's wife, Anne, became renowned for her piety and in 1400 made a pilgrimage to see the relics in Prussia – several pieces of the True Cross, the head of St Barbara, and the relics of Dorothea of Montau; she visited sites associated with St Anne (and it is assumed that the early church in Vilnius was named to flatter her). Paganism never had much chance of a revival, in fact. Pope Urban VI named a Polish friar as bishop of Vilnius. By the time that bishop died in 1398, he had created a well-organised diocese with seven parishes. However, most of rural Lithuania remained almost untouched, and Samogitia did not get a bishop until 1417.

For several years the priests in Lithuania were predominately Poles appointed by the archbishop of Gniezno. Once priests who spoke native

Lithuanian entered the mission, the process of conversion went more swiftly. Unfortunately, the university Prague was already experiencing those quarrels between Czechs and Germans that were the first stages of the Hussite movement. It was years before many suitable priests were in Lithuania, and there was little money for their support.

Since most Lithuanians lived in the countryside, this first phase of Christianisation affected them but little. Friars and priests eventually found a way to make an impression on them and their forest cults by affixing crucifixes to holy trees and erecting small chapels, thus associating the new religion with the old one whenever a pagan worshipper went to the holy grove with flowers or food for the gods or deceased relatives. This innovation was so popular that it spread to Prussia. As a result, in 1426 the bishop of Sambia forbade anyone to erect a cross in a graveyard, lest it become a platform for depositing gifts to the spirit world.

The Growth of Towns in Lithuania

In time Vilnius came to resemble a small Western city in its churches, holiday celebrations and displays of personal piety. There was a German quarter to the south of the castle, with the merchants' church of St Nicholas, and a Rus'ian quarter to the east. Since rivers ran along the north and west sides of the town, there was little room for expansion in those directions, and no suburbs existed there.

There were two or three parts to the castle complex, each of which could be defended separately. The Upper Castle stood on a steep hill at the north-eastern side of town, the Lower Castle slightly below and west of it. The former was to provide a refuge in case of attack, the latter the royal residence. Only the Upper Castle was of stone and brick in the most advanced gothic design, with four-storey towers and walls 3 m. (10 ft.) thick and impressive crenellations. There were artificial moats strengthening the natural defences provided by the surrounding rivers and hills.

In dress, manners, military tactics and equipment, the Lithuanians were sufficiently Westernised to be seen as a civilised people. Inwardly not even the nobles had yet adopted patterns of thought common among their Western counterparts, but they were often chivalrous. The chroniclers of the Teutonic Order, especially the herald Wigand of Marburg, recognised that openly. But, he said, one could not trust their word. That is, they did not lie in the same way that Westerners did. Contemporary French nobles, for example, could be paroled by their captors because they would return to captivity voluntarily if their ransom could not be paid. Kęstutis and Algirdas would never have done such a thing, nor Jagiełło or Vytautas, despite their recent baptisms.

The Lithuanian dukes had converted to Roman Catholicism for the same reason they had earlier adopted Orthodox beliefs – profit. Vytautas wanted his duchy back; Jagiełło wanted to become king of Poland. Each remained Roman Catholic because it was politically useful to do so. Polish churchmen had Jadwiga's ear, and Jagiełło was beholden to her for his crown. Christianity and commerce provided hard currency, luxury items, weapons and prestige.

The Introduction of Cannon

One major advantage the Lithuanians saw in the union with Poland was access to cannon. Without question the recent successes of crusader expeditions can be laid to their technological and organisational superiority. (It is the combination which is important: it is too easy to think that technology alone can resolve all problems.) They had large vessels for transporting supplies, catapults and cannon, but they also had accountants, engineers and cannon masters. Jagiełło and Vytautas wanted to offset those advantages.

The Teutonic Order had introduced cannon into Prussia in the second half of the fourteenth century. They appear in the chronicles for 1362 and in the inventories in 1374. Winrich of Kniprode placed cannon first in Liepe, on the Vistula facing Poland, then in Ragnit. By 1392 the Order had cannon in twenty castles. Although they took few gunpowder weapons into the field at first (a gun, perhaps a small calibre gun firing a lead ball, was mentioned at the siege of Kaunas in 1362, but the chronicler implied it was not particularly useful), by the 1380s they commonly employed mobile cannons – not yet mounted on gun carriages, but easily moved by wagon or on a sled. Although the knights liked heavy calibre siege guns (which had to be transported by ship), they had a variety of weapons: light cannon, using stone shot 15–25 cm. (6–10 in.) in diameter, which could be employed in battle; heavy cannon, with shot 25–50 cm. in diameter, for use in sieges; and a giant gun firing shot 50–75 cm (20–30 in.) in diameter for crushing defensive works.

Recent research by Grzegorz Żabiński shows that all cannon made in Marienburg by the Teutonic Knights' bellmakers were cast from brass or bronze, cast iron being too brittle to withstand the shock of firing. This made those weapons very expensive.

Grandmasters acquired most of these weapons from Germany and France. The cost was high and their effectiveness uncertain. Wet weather and shaking during transport could make the powder unusable, and the terrain might be unsuitable to train the weapons properly, because elevating and lowering the barrel was a difficult and slow process. Nevertheless, gunpowder artillery was so effective under proper conditions that every grandmaster procured cannons despite the expense, the difficulty of transportation, and the likelihood that they could not be used when needed most. Cannon resolved the most critical problem in sieges: to break down defensive walls before the besiegers' supplies became exhausted. With the introduction of siege guns the initiative once again lay with the offence rather than the defence. No longer could Lithuanians and Samogitians stay comfortably within their fortifications, hoping that the crusaders would have to retreat without attempting a serious assault. Cannon, together with weapons brought by crusaders, such as the English longbow, tipped the balance temporarily in favour of the Teutonic Knights.

Jagiełło sought to offset this advantage by using the contacts of Cracow merchants with Italy, Austria, Bohemia and Germany, to acquire the best weapons available. Jagiełło's difficulty lay in getting the cannon to the Nemunas River valley. The Teutonic Knights at Wizna blocked ships from coming up the Narew towards Grodno, the route he would have preferred to use.

Weapons and Mercenaries

The Teutonic Knights had an initial superiority in crossbows, but it was no monopoly – the Lithuanians adopted them quickly. This move from relying largely on swords and spears (which perhaps stands in contrast to more conservative noble practices in the West) was a natural one in Prussia, where the knights had always relied heavily on missile weapons. Much of the fighting was in the forest, where a horseman with a cocked crossbow was instantly ready to face ambushers. Moreover, in defending a fortification, a crossbow could be fired by anybody, even by women and youths. While we have been led by the fame of the bowmen of Sherwood Forest and Crécy to believe in the superiority of the longbow, archers elsewhere found a shorter bow more effective, overwhelming enemies with showers of arrows.

Crossbows were kept in every one of the Order's castles, and as many as 12,000 crossbow bolts were stored in the armouries. There were three different types of crossbows. The older varieties, in which the bowstring was drawn into the cocked position by a *Wippe* was being replaced by a weapon with a footrest that allowed the archer to use the strength of his lower body to draw the bowstring. This was probably the type carried on horseback. The newest innovation employing a windlass was rare, perhaps because that method of cocking was so slow.

Other Western weapons were modified for local conditions. While knights often carried heavy cavalry lances, in the forests they preferred lighter Lithuanian spears. The wide variety of helms included the native conical helmet, which perhaps had an oriental origin. With a movable visor it later became well-known throughout Europe as a *Pickelhaube*. The most common shield was the small *scutum prutenicum* adapted from the native light cavalry.

In time the Teutonic Knights no longer needed native *Witingen* as mounted infantry and scouts, but employed Lithuanians for those tasks – after all, those horsemen knew Samogitia well. A greater use of heavy armour – replacing chain hauberks – can be observed, not just among the Order's own knights, but among the secular vassals, who after 1380 were required to obtain plate armour and warhorses. Since native and immigrant knights alike found this very expensive, the grandmasters promised to reimburse them for losses of mounts or equipment. When grandmasters suspected their vassals of taking advantage of this provision; they responded by seeking ways to convert the personal service of knights into cash payments that could be used to hire mercenaries; they required *Witingen* to choose between remaining with the militia as baggage carriers and labourers on fortifications or immersing themselves more completely in Western technology and culture. Those who chose the latter eventually became knights, but lost their close connection to ancient tribal roots.

The failure of the secular knights to appear for muster properly equipped is a common theme in the Order's correspondence. The basic unit was the *Spieß*, which consisted of a horseman (with 'complete armour head to foot'), a crossbowman (with chain armour, iron helmet, and crossbow) and a youth; all were mounted, preferably with a fourth horse available. The horses were listed carefully by type, colour, and size. The warhorse was usually a gelding. Records are, unfortunately, rare. It is clear, however, that properly equipped mercenaries were increasingly preferred over poorly outfitted vassals, were more likely to be good fighters, and did not object to long periods of service. This naturally led to complaints by the secular knights and gentry that they were no longer appreciated.

Mercenaries tended to be young men trained in arms, willing to fight whenever and wherever, and unburdened by worries about families at home. They were much like the knights in the Order, only without the religious calling and the distractions of administration, and, because they could be easily replaced, they never grew old.

Relations with the Prussian Estates

The grandmasters had to deal with the same difficulties as rulers in the Holy Roman Empire and elsewhere, in that the cost of modern weapons could be met only by increased taxation, and the burghers who paid the taxes were unhappy about it. In 1388 the Prussian assembly protested the high tolls and tariffs; in 1391 they complained that officials were refusing to grant export licenses for grain, so that only administrators of the Teutonic Knights were able to take advantage of high prices abroad. Indeed, the merchants' past exploitation of foreign market fluctuations had occasionally left local consumers hungry, but public complaints increased now that the managers of the Order's grain supplies sought to increase their share of the export market.

Despite these complaints about interference in commercial activities, the grandmasters were still able to persuade assemblies to raise taxes for the support of the border castles, to restrict trade in horses and weapons, and to assist the foreign policy. In return the grandmasters were expected to act on complaints that their officers were too haughty and insulting, which was difficult to do, because that was what nobles did instinctively. By doing too little to respond to popular complaints, the Teutonic Knights would eventually lose the support of the citizenry – the rich were offended, while the poor lacked political power.

Secular knights began organising, too. The knights of Culm were already beginning to think as a class in the first steps towards the creation of the so-called Lizard League as the legitimate organisation to speak for them – the 'Lizard' was a dragon, a universally popular symbol. The knights were as eager to profit from the rising prices of grain as they were concerned by the decline in the available labour force caused by the plague. They objected to the Order's policies regarding native farmers, the regulation of trade and taxation. More fundamentally, the knights and gentry wanted to have a voice in government such as was exercised by nobles in Germany, France and England, and especially by their relatives in Poland. They felt that secular knights, not clerical knights, should rule; and since many knights in Culm were of Polish descent, the Teutonic Knights were concerned lest they look to Poland for support.

There was little danger of that yet, especially after Jagiełło became king. They were familiar with the experience of Ladislas of Opole, once the most powerful man in the kingdom, whom he stripped of estates and offices, humiliating him. Even more notorious was the case of Siemowit IV, when he asked for the Volhynian lands which had been promised him. According to a Polish chronicler, the king asked to see the letters, then when the king had them, he passed them over to his vice-chancellor, who, in the presence of the assembled court, cut them up with a knife.

Siemowit protested, citing his past and present services (and probably the dowry of his wife, Jagiełło's sister, Alexandra), whereupon the king awarded him two small territories south of Masovia. In return Jagiełło extracted a formal acknowledgement that Siemowit was his vassal, thereby renewing feudal ties that had lapsed since 1370. This was not the bargain that Siemowit had envisioned when he first began dealing with Jagiełło. The whole notorious transaction stood as a warning to those who lightly put their faith in either Jagiełło's word or his written promises. As Kęstutis, Vytautas, and many others could testify, betrayal was a characteristic of Jagiello's statesmanship.

This puts Prussian complaints into perspective. In addition to the traditional mistrust of Lithuanian promises, the Prussian burghers and knights were not hostile to the grandmaster. They were accustomed to speaking their minds, and they were completely medieval in the self-righteous hyperbole used when complaining. When a grandmaster called his subjects together to discuss a specific problem, he usually found that they shared his concerns.

Chapter Eleven

The Conquest of Samogitia

Samogitian Isolation

It was only a matter of time now, almost everyone could see, before Samogitians would succumb to the Roman Church. Although Vytautas's rebellion might seem to have put the Teutonic Knights back where they were at the beginning of the century, raiding Samogitia from its periphery, with little prospect of dealing paganism there a fatal blow, the situation was neither so simple, nor so hopeless. The Samogitians had been worn down by the decades of unrelenting warfare, and their strongest forts had been laid ruin. Moreover, they were now politically isolated: in refusing to accept Christianity, they had made it impossible for Polish clerics to speak on their behalf; by refusing even to recognise Jagiełło's right to appoint Skirgaila as their governor, they had offended those lords. Jagiełło and Skirgaila considered the Samogitians dangerous rebels who would support Vytautas if there was another struggle for power. Consequently, from their point of view, it would be better if Samogitia were occupied (temporarily) by the crusaders. Vytautas, for his part, dared not speak out against the supreme duke. Even giving secret encouragement to the rebels could be a fatal mistake. Consequently, the Samogitians stood alone against the grandmaster's offensive.

Still, it was no secret that all was not well in Lithuania. Jagiełło had given Skirgaila lands which he had promised to Vytautas, presumably to prevent Vytautas from developing a personal following among subjects who had once been loyal to Kęstutis. Then agreeing to marry his sister Alexandra to Siemowit IV of Masovia won favour with a family that had long been allied with Kęstutis. Vytautas was unhappy about this, but he kept his temper and his tongue, for that was the only way he could remain alive. Observers noticed that Jagiełło hardly let Vytautas out of sight, and Jagiełło's betrayal of his promises spoke for themselves. Everyone knew that Jagiełło could not casually murder Vytautas because Vytautas would certainly be avenged, but if Vytautas made trouble, Jagiełło would eliminate him, whatever the consequences.

For a short time after Jagiełło's baptism Konrad Zöllner had worried that the pope would suspend the crusade. However, Western churchmen were so preoccupied with the Schism that they could give little attention to Lithuania, and those few who expressed interest were persuaded by the Teutonic Knights to continue the crusade. First, the Order's representative at the curia was reminding them that Jagiełło's word of honour depended on what was to his advantage, and that Vytautas was no better. Jagiełło still held fifty-five Teutonic Knights in captivity. If he were serious about becoming a Roman Christian, he should free those champions of the Cross. Secondly, the claims of conversion were not accurate. There were no missionaries in Samogitia yet, nor any likelihood of any going there soon. Samogitians would fight even sincere efforts by Jagiełło to convert them, because they understood that accepting Christianity meant adopting its entire social and political philosophy, including a more rigid hierarchy of classes. They could put off the day of reckoning only because the Lithuanian dukes were too busy elsewhere to concern themselves with them. The nominal ruler, Skirgaila, was defending his Rus'ian possessions against his half-brother, Andrew, and even after he captured Andrew in 1387, he had other problems in the east. Since Jagiełło was in Poland and Vytautas in Grodno, neither could substitute for Skirgaila. Lastly, the Teutonic Knights were ready and eager to bring the crusade to a successful conclusion. With prospects for victory over the pagans so promising, they argued, it would be foolish to disrupt the military operations.

Crusader Preparations

Konrad Zöllner did not hurry into a premature offensive. Instead, he sent word that a great army would assemble in the winter of 1386/87. Among the principal guests were Count Wilhelm of Holland, the counts of Namur, Schwarzenberg, Hohenstein and the Mark. Probably present also was the famous French knight, Boucicaut. Nevertheless, the campaign was a failure. Marshal Konrad of Wallenrode (c. 1330–93, a future grandmaster) had taken a large scouting party from Memel into the upper Windau (Venta) River valley – perhaps with the intention of opening a secure route to Livonia – and apparently reported that the weather was too warm for heavy cavalry. The visiting knights celebrated the holidays, grumbled at the waste of time and money, and went home.

Truce talks continued through the next year and a half. The discussions were sufficiently promising that Konrad Zöllner summoned the Livonian master to Thorn to give his advice. The Polish delegation was led by the archbishop of Gniezno and was joined later by Jagiełło, the two Masovian dukes, and a vast contingent of nobles. However, the talks ended without the grandmaster and the king meeting personally.

Jagiełło was angry that the grandmaster had not acknowledged his baptism or his new title; moreover, Konrad Zöllner had addressed him in his letters with the informal *Du*, a form of address that implied equality. Jagiełło considered this a deliberate insult. For his part, the grandmaster wanted the prisoners released, and he demanded that the king ratify the treaties which gave Samogitia to the Teutonic Knights. Jagiełło would not bend, nor would Konrad Zöllner.

The talks resumed in March 1389, the parties meeting on an island in the Vistula. When the Poles spoke of the conversion of the Lithuanians and the missionary work already in progress, the Teutonic Knights displayed eight papal bulls from the thirteenth century that confirmed their rights to Samogitia. At that one of the Poles exclaimed, 'Now we see that it is for the Lithuanian lands that you are fighting and not for the Christian faith!'

The Teutonic Knights, however, had proof that the Samogitians were far from Christianised. Only a month before, the Samogitians had destroyed a force led by the advocate of Sambia and had sacrificed the commander of Memel, burning him alive on his horse. Moreover, the Teutonic Knights were aware that Polish soldiers were helping the Lithuanians. In the autumn of 1388 Marshal Engelhard Rabe of Wildstein and Grand Commander Konrad of Wallenrode opened a new route from the Nemunas into central Lithuania to attack Skirgaila's castle west of Vilnius, but they were driven away by cannon fire. Most likely the cannon had been brought from Poland, though some may have been captured in the Order's castles in the last revolt.

If the Teutonic Knights were to conquer Samogitia, they had to hurry, while those pagans still hated Jagiełło, and before Polish military aid cancelled their technological advantage.

Vytautas's Frustration

Vytautas's unhappiness was no secret. Although in July 1388 he had captured Wizna for Siemowit IV of Masovia – opening the Narew River for Polish arms and merchants – he had subsequently quarrelled with Skirgaila so dreadfully that Jagiełło decided to keep an even closer watch on him. Crusaders saw him at the king's side during the autumn campaign and at the truce talks in November, but Jagiełło did not allow him to speak. In early 1389, when Skirgaila learned of a plot to seize Vilnius in Vytautas's name, Vytautas denied involvement and did not protest when the conspirators were executed. It made Jagiełło nervous that Vilnius, once so loyal to him, was now a centre of unrest. Lithuanian nobles were obviously looking to Vytautas to defend their interests, not to him. They were less than enthusiastic about Jagiełło's entourage of Polish nobles and clergy.

Jagiełło faced a dilemma. To satisfy the Poles, he had to take steps towards a rapid Christianisation of Lithuania. To satisfy his former countrymen, he had to move slowly and circumspectly. This was closely interwoven into his relationship with Vytautas, who was the person-ification of Lithuanian traditions. Uppermost in his mind at this moment was Vytautas's loyalty. He could not accuse Vytautas of treason without solid proof, and yet he respected Skirgaila's opinion that their cousin could not be trusted. Skirgaila, of course, was in an even more intractable dilemma: he could not impose Roman Catholicism on his Kyivan subjects, but if he tolerated Orthodoxy, he would antagonise those Polish churchmen who were Jagiełło's chief supporters. Skirgaila thought the problem could be resolved best by eliminating Vytautas. The benefits of an assassination were worth risking civil war. Jagiełło disagreed.

Jagiełło was a superb diplomat. He never took an unnecessary risk. In this case, he feared Skirgaila's impetuosity and drunken rages as much as Vytautas's potential revenge. When he summoned both parties to meet in Lublin in May 1389, he hoped that he could persuade them to act reasonably. Vytautas made oral concessions and gave the kiss of peace, but soon the hard-drinking, violent Skirgaila sent word 'to beware of him, just as he would be on guard against him'.

Jagiełło could not help Skirgaila in the south. Too many Lithuanians and Rus'ians resented the presence of Polish Catholics. Similarly, in the north, there were many who feared Polish domination almost as much as they did German aggression. Meanwhile, Skirgaila's formerly happy relationship with the Order's knights in Livonia and the grandmaster had deteriorated. Jagiełło could not intervene, because Jadwiga, on the advice of her clergy and nobles, was determined to remain at peace with the grandmaster. In short, Jagiełło was less the master of events than their prisoner.

Jagiełło even had frequent quarrels with his wife – stirred up, the chronicler Długosz said, by flatterers and conspirators, especially her chancellor. Without much question, she disliked what she was hearing about her newly acquired state, as she would have seen Lithuania. The disturbances could only hurt the process of conversion that lay so close to her heart. Jagiełło also heard rumours that the queen had lovers. The rumours were dispelled when twelve of her knights announced they would challenge to a duel anyone who accused her. No one took up the gauntlet – certainly not the chancellor, who was a cleric and therefore unlikely to be experienced with weapons – and the special tribunal called to judge the matter ruled her innocent.

The whole scandal was implausible. The queen's vice, which contemporaries took for saintliness, was religiosity. She disliked ceremony and celebrations, ate little, prayed much, and was so averse to sex that her advisors warned her repeatedly that the kingdom needed an heir. She complied as much as she could, but her husband's long absences on campaigns made her courtiers and clergy worry about another succession crisis.

As for Jagiełło, he made few demands on his wife and had no mistresses. He never drank alcohol and, knowing little Polish, avoided idle conversation; even when speaking Lithuanian, he was taciturn.

Difficulties en route to Prussia

The Teutonic Knights found it difficult to guarantee the safety of the overland route to Prussia. This was especially true for Stolp, a small but vital territory in Pomerania bordering West Prussia. Once Jagiełło again closed Polish roads to crusaders, the best road for travellers to Prussia was through Brandenburg and Stolp. Jagiełło was hoping to block off that route, too.

There were two parties in Stolp, just as there were two dukes. One supported the Teutonic Knights, the other the king. If the dukes co-operated with Jagiełło, they might inherit Masovia, to which they had a distant but legitimate claim. However, Jagiełło was known for forgetting promises. If they worked with the Teutonic Knights, they might get Dobrzyń, and have an ally who would help defend it against Jagiełło. In the end, Konrad Zöllner was willing to pay cash for several strategically placed estates, whereas King Jagiełło had no ready money. The dukes and their nobles also received thousands of *Gulden* for a promise to serve in the grandmaster's army should a war with Poland come about.

Into this situation came the young duke of Geldern, Wilhelm (1364–1402), a warrior praised even by Froissart for his daring. He had taken the Cross twice before, in 1383 and 1386, but had not fulfilled his vows. In 1388 he made a third vow during battle, promising to go to Prussia if he survived. Then, at the head of 300 knights screaming 'Geldern!' he routed his enemies and captured seventeen banners. That December he set out for Prussia. Jagiełło, who wanted to demonstrate that the roads were not safe even for the most prominent crusaders, persuaded Count Eckhart of Walde and more than forty local knights to kidnap the duke in Cammin, a small episcopal territory in Pomerania. The kidnappers killed two knights from Geldern and took their prisoner to Falkenburg in the Neumark.

When Konrad Zöllner sent a request to Stolp asking the dukes to rescue Wilhelm, he learned that one was in Denmark and the other did not want to get involved. Unwilling to let the matter wait, the grandmaster cancelled the winter expedition and sent the army against Falkenburg, which he captured after a three-day siege. Complications set in when Wilhelm of Geldern said that he had given his word of honour to remain a prisoner, and the flight of the count of Walde to Poland made no difference to him; an honourable knight, he would remain in Falkenburg until released from his oath.

The grandmaster requested imperial aid, but Wenceslaus refused. Neither were the dukes of Stolp co-operative. Letters went back and forth. Months passed. In April the grandmaster sent another army to Falkenburg, took the castle again, and had Duke Wilhelm brought in chains into Prussia, so that he could personally try to persuade him to change his mind. The duke could not complain that his honour was stained by any suspicion that he had co-operated, but he was so obstinate that the grandmaster sent him back to Falkenburg and continued negotiations.

At length Konrad found an elegant solution to his dilemma. Long ago the pope had made the bishop of Pomesania responsible for protecting crusaders travelling through the region The bishop, once reminded of this long-forgotten authority, warned the kidnappers that in seizing a crusader they had violated the rights of the Church and that, unless they released their prisoner immediately, he would excommunicate them. The count then absolved the duke of Geldern of his oath, the Teutonic Knights freed their hostages, and on 15 August 1389, the duke proceeded to Prussia to fulfil his vow. (He came on crusade to Prussia three more times in the next decade.) Although the Pomeranian dukes and their nobles were temporarily mollified by cash payments, there were more incidents in 1393 and 1394, after which a new treaty allowed crusaders free passage through Pomerania.

Vytautas's Alliance

In 1389 Vytautas sent a message to Konrad Zöllner with two liberated captives, the count of Rheineck and Marquard of Salzbach. They told the grandmaster that Vytautas wanted revenge on Skirgaila so much that he would fulfil all his earlier promises if the crusaders would support him. The grandmaster sent Marquard back to negotiate a secret alliance, and he gave orders to drive a hard bargain: first, that Vytautas cede Samogitia, secondly that he give numerous hostages, and lastly that he promise to convert the Lithuanians to Roman Christianity. Not being able to haggle, Vytautas sent relatives as hostages; one was the husband of his wife's sister, Ivan Olshansky (Alšėniškis, *d.* 1402), a noted warrior and governor of Kyiv, then later his own wife and daughter. In January 1390 the grandmaster signed a treaty at Lyck (Licke), deep in the Lake District forest. There Vytautas renewed all the promises he had made previously and requested refuge in Prussia.

Immediately after the ceremony the grandmaster distributed the hostages among the various castles in Prussia in order to minimise the danger of an uprising, while Vytautas set off for Grodno with a huge Prussian army. The marshal had gone ahead with crusaders from Franconia, Cleves and the Saar, and when the reinforcement arrived, he took the castle easily. Presumably, Vytautas's supporters were numerous there, but that was not so in Vilnius, where the crusaders went next. There they found that Jagiełło's brother, Kaributas, had driven out those suspected of favouring Vytautas and put the city in a state of readiness. Not having siege engines, the crusaders withdrew towards Kaunas, ravaging central Lithuania as they went. They found the castle in Kaunas in ashes, burned by its garrison before they fled.

In view of this, Konrad Zöllner refused to grant Jagiełło the truce requested by minor papal officials who visited him on their way home from Vilnius. The grandmaster explained that his military order had been created for the defence of Christendom, and that its mission was not yet completed. He argued that a truce would merely provide the enemies of the Church with opportunities to rest and rearm. The Lithuanians, moreover, were refusing to meet even the most basic pre-conditions for a truce – releasing their prisoners and fulfilling the terms of past treaties.

The next crusader invasion, assisted by Vytautas's supporters, suc-ceeded in taking numerous castles in distant Ruthenia, a move that threatened to isolate Vilnius and the Lithuanian highlands from the kingdom of Poland. Therefore, Jagiełło concentrated on retaking those fortresses, most of which he captured easily. In early March Jagiełło brought a Polish army to assist Skirgaila in his siege of Grodno. Although Marshal Engelhard and Duke Vytautas tried in vain to interrupt the attacks, they could not cross the river to get at the besiegers; their effort to build a bridge of boats failed when Skirgaila cut down trees and floated them down the swift current to break the chain. After six weeks the fortress fell. Thus, Vytautas lost his most important foothold in Lithuania. Momentarily it appeared that the grandmaster's gamble had failed.

In signing the Treaty of Lyck, then in sending a delegation of Samogitians to promise their allegiance to the grandmaster, Vytautas had taken a great risk. By changing sides so often, he had alienated many Lithuanian warriors who had once loved him unquestioningly. Now having to make concessions, Vytautas promised to consult his supporters on frequent occasions (later he called them together in meetings that became known as the Council of Lords) and promised to allow them to countersign important treaties and affix their seals to documents; and he swore that he would not discuss important matters without some of them present.

Although Vytautas acknowledged the rights of his nobles to a voice in the government, he was ruthless with those who threatened his position as grand duke. He was a hard man now, ambitious, and arrogant when he chose to be; at other times he could be generous, conciliatory, even chivalrous. In promising the boyars what they wanted and assuring the Teutonic Knights that they would possess Samogitia, he made seemingly contradictory policies into complementary ones. Most Samogitians understood their situation and bowed to his demands. In May 1390 thirty prominent *Witingen* appeared in Königsberg to conclude a treaty with the grandmaster on behalf of themselves and 'King' Vytautas. This was a visible sign that the Samogitians were ready to fight for their grand duke, even though they had to join the hated crusaders and become their subjects.

Meanwhile, the grandmaster spread word throughout Europe that the late summer campaign of 1390 would be unusually important. Foremost among the many crusaders who responded was the 23-year-old son of John of Gaunt, Henry of Lancaster (1367–1413), who was called Bolingbroke from his place of birth. His English archers, famous for their exploits in the Hundred Years War, reckoned themselves invincible, and few doubted them. For his part, Henry was unusual in the Plantagenet dynasty in that English was his mother tongue, not French.

According to Stephen Turnbull, he had been recruited by Boucicaut at a tournament in Calais that March. Announcing that he would fight against the 'Saracens', he probably planned to join a French expedition against the Barbary Pirates in North Africa, an ambitious venture led by the unsteady duke of Bourbon, but he could not obtain the necessary safe-conducts to travel overland to Genoa. Bolingbroke was fortunate, perhaps, in not being able to join the 5,000 French knights and soldiers who suffered terribly from heat, disease and attacks by overwhelming numbers of enemies before Bourbon finally signed a meaningless treaty and sailed home.

Henry might have remembered that his grandfather (for whom he had been named) had gone on crusade to Prussia in 1352. As for the 'Saracens', he might have meant the Tatars who occasionally fought in the Lithuanian armies – people were as lazy in their understanding of far-away places then as they are today.

English Crusaders at Vilnius

The crusading adventure of Bolingbroke is one of the best documented stories of this era, thanks to the exhaustingly detailed financial accounts kept by his English bookkeepers. Accountants noted down every half-penny expended, from the purchase of supplies to gambling debts, from repair of weapons to pittances given to the poor. Consequently, we know with what care this battle-hardened young man prepared his voyage from the island kingdom to Danzig, how his officers bought warhorses, riding horses, pack animals, hay, straw, horseshoes, saddles, girths, bridles, cloth for new liveries, blue banners, and winter clothing; how a new silk and gold tapestry from Cyprus was hung by the table, and the Lancaster coat-of-arms was painted on the door of various hostels where the duke lodged, and what gifts were purchased for his hosts.

Bolingbroke's two ships landed near Danzig in August 1390. Learning that an expedition was about to march, he hurriedly sent his men for supplies, rented thirteen wagons to carry equipment, and pressed on overland to Königsberg. When he arrived at the grandmaster's residence, he found Konrad Zöllner on his deathbed. Henry rested his 80 bowmen a few days while his servants purchased chickens, cattle, 48 large casks of beer, 300 casks of wine, and other supplies. He provided his 300 men with the equivalent of eight bottles of beer for each day of the campaign.

Marshal Engelhard Rabe of Wildstein – whose career is almost totally unknown before he was raised to high office in 1387 – invited Bolingbroke to sail with him to Insterberg, then travel together by land to the rendezvous of the Prussian and Livonian armies at Old Kaunas. At the ceremonial feast that opened the campaign Marshal Rabe presented the prince with a horse and two Prussian attendants, and the Livonian master gave Bolingbroke handsome animals for a future feast. The marshal and Bolingbroke became fast friends.

Another prominent crusader was Boucicaut, who had originally planned to join the crusade to North Africa organised by Louis of Bourbon. When the king forbade him to serve a rival, Boucicaut came to Prussia for a second time, bringing with him knights who were spoiling for a fight, any kind of fight. War for war's sake. Many knights were supported by the duke of Burgundy, a champion of chivalry.

While crusaders began a siege of Georgenburg on 25 August, news came that Konrad Zöllner had died. Being told that a truce was to begin on 30 September, the marshal summoned his officers and the important crusaders to a council. Under other circumstances the marshal and commanders would have hastened to Marienburg for the election of a new grandmaster, but Rabe knew that he was unlikely to have such a large army under his command again soon, and the crusaders did not want to return home without having achieved something. Someone, perhaps Vytautas, suggested that Jagiełło and Skirgaila would not expect the crusaders to continue their campaign under the circumstances, and therefore an attack on Vilnius would catch them by surprise. When others agreed, Marshal Rabe abandoned the attack on Georgenburg and marched north through the Samogitian province of Raseiniai.

Skirgaila was not caught completely by surprise. He had already brought Rus'ian troops west, so that he was able to block the way across the Neris. The English crusaders may be excused if the similarity of the German pronunciation of Raseiniai (Russe) and Rus' (Ruce) and the nationality of their enemy led them to believe they were fighting Rus'ians in Rus' rather than facing Rus'ians in Samogitia. It should be no surprise that Chaucer had his fictional knight serve with crusaders in 'Ruce'.

Skirgaila had blocked the main river crossings, but when scouts reported that he had ignored fords further north, Marshal Rabe moved quickly, letting the ships precede him and leaving the bulk of the army to follow. He took the finest knights through the wilderness towards Kaunas, then crossed a ford and struck Skirgaila by surprise. It was a complete success in every way except for Skirgaila escaping. Rabe did capture three dukes and eleven nobles, whom he sent back to Prussia. Then when he met the ships, he replenished his supplies and, with a week left in August, resumed the march towards Vilnius.

When the crusaders reached the old capital at Kernavė, they found that it had been burned. By the time they arrived at Vilnius, Vytautas's supporters had already made one failed assault on the castle complex. According to later testimony by the Teutonic Knights at the Council of Constance, they had sent wagonloads of meat to the castle gate, each wagon having armed men hidden in it; however, a German spy betrayed the ruse.

This time, with a huge army ready to attack him, Skirgaila made no attempt to defend the suburbs. Some of the inhabitants, in fact, processed from St Anne's to show that they were Christians. The advancing Westerners, nevertheless, attacked the unarmed congregation, killing one Franciscan and sending the rest fleeing into the castle. Then they burned the suburbs.

The crusaders concentrated on the wooden fort, the Twisted Castle. Being near the principal depot of foreign traders, it was filled with merchants and their goods. Once this isolated height had not been considered vital, but since the introduction of artillery it was the key to Vilnius. Since it was garrisoned by picked troops from Poland and Rus', the combat there was desperate. Vytautas's brother, Tautvilas, fell in the fighting. At length, after cannons and stone throwers had weakened the wall, an Englishman waving the Lancastrian banner led the crusaders though the breach to slaughter about a thousand warriors and refugees; the defenders, seeing that the place was lost, set the castle ablaze. This caused the crusaders to retreat, but it also made it impossible for the last defenders to flee. Jagiełło's brother, Karigaila, emerged from the flames and was immediately captured and beheaded. The triumphant crusaders may have stuck the trophy on a long spear and waved it at the garrison in the high castle. The king held that act against the 'crossbearers' to the end of his life, though the crusaders denied having done it, saying that Karigaila had perished in the fighting and that they had not even found his body until five days later.

Długosz added that Polish warriors had saved the situation – when the Lithuanians and Rus'ians abandoned the flaming fortress, they stepped in, replacing gaps in the walls with a curtain of skins that absorbed the crusader missiles, then sacrificing their own bodies to hold the position.

The defence did not collapse as the crusaders hoped. Although the French and English now had good positions for bombarding the main castle and had ample foodstuffs (thanks to Vytautas and his native followers), they were short of time and gunpowder. Długosz wrote that a prominent Rus'ian lord, Narimantas – presumably from Pinsk and descended from Gediminas – was taken prisoner and hung by his heels in front of the cannon until killed by the arrows fired at the gunners.

None of the crusaders were eager to mount an assault on walls defended by cannon, and there were too few English bowmen to drive the defenders from the parapets by rapid arrow fire alone. A hurried effort to undermine the walls came to nothing when the weather turned bad. Then the Prussian militia began to complain that their period of service had expired. Moreover, the truce was about to take effect. Realising that victory was beyond his grasp, the marshal was satisfied with proving that a crusader army could remain in hostile country for five weeks and almost capture the foremost fortress in the land. His armies broke camp and marched home without trouble. The last part of the journey was made in comfort aboard ships.

Bolingbroke rented a house in Königsberg for the winter. His reason for remaining there was never given, but since he did not participate in the winter expeditions, it can be assumed that he discussed long-standing commercial disputes that were hampering trade between England and Prussia. Also, the naming of a successor to Konrad Zöllner took far longer than expected because of disagreements among the electors. We know that while Bolingbroke waited, his officers made purchases of furs and winter clothing, quantities of beef, chicken, pork, and the usual massive amounts of beer. He lived in royal style, nibbling on pastries and sweets, using many candles, listening to his minstrels, attending mass, and entertaining; he hunted with falcons, needed a large fire on one outing, and was given three bear cubs by a native woodsman; he celebrated the news that a son had been born and passed the holidays in a festive manner. In February he went overland to Danzig and opened negotiations with King Jagiełło for the ransom of two men captured at Vilnius (we do not know if he was successful). In April, after apparently completing his business with the new grandmaster, Konrad of Wallenrode (c. 1330–93), he took ship from Danzig, laden with gifts and captured Lithuanians. Two presents were notable: a table engraved with a map of Prussia (a Christmas present from the bishop of Sambia) and falcons from the grandmaster. His accountants reckoned the cost of his crusade at 2,000 pounds sterling or 3,000 marks. Of this expense, he paid only a quarter, his father, John of Gaunt, covering the rest.

Vytautas made further incursions into Lithuania, but Jagiełło's appearance with reinforcements and supplies stabilised the situation – Długosz says that without Polish grain, the Lithuanians would have starved. He was probably correct – Vytautas and the crusaders were roaming the countryside, burning villages and fields, even making another assault on Vilnius, capturing Polish knights who would languish in prison for seven years. They surrounded Kaunas with three forts, one of which repulsed the relief army led by Jagiełło's capable brother Vygantas, duke of Kernavė.

The Polish situation in Lithuania looked grim at that moment – fear of more crusader attacks, of treachery, and of Skirgaila's drunken violence – that when the Polish commander resigned, Jagiełło could not find a replacement. Eventually he persuaded Jan Oleśnicki to take the post; the new commander's first decision was to burn the city of Vilnius and build new fortifications for the castle.

Wallenrode's Diplomacy

An interregnum is necessarily a period of indecisive leadership. Acting heads of state, even grand commanders, could not commit the next administration to any policy,.When Konrad Zöllner died, Konrad of Wallenrode had summoned representatives to the general chapter and given Vytautas a residence in Barthenstein until his successor was chosen. He could not avoid making one important decision, however: Vytautas had made a marriage alliance with the grand duke of Moscow which would bring pressure on Jagiełło's rear. Therefore, Konrad of Wallenrode sent Vytautas's daughter Sophie to Moscow via Danzig and Livonia, and he allowed Ivan Olshansky to accompany her. Her husband, Basil, would become a powerful ruler.

The electors chosen by the general chapter found themselves deadlocked. This was remarkable because there was only one strong candidate, Konrad of Wallenrode himself. Perhaps the electors anticipated he would be too strong a ruler – and he had a fierce temper – but when they could put off the inevitable no longer, they accepted him. He had a reputation as a hard-bitten warrior, so heedless of priests and God that Dorothea of Montau accused him of heresy. No question he was a choleric personality. Every member of his family was.

Wallenrodes were prominent in the Teutonic Order: Konrad had been grand commander; his brother, Friedrich, was a commander; and a nephew, Johannes, became archbishop of Riga. All were strong figures. As if to confirm the worst fears of the officers, Konrad made many changes in the command structure that increased his authority, then, after establishing new rules on trade that increased tax revenues, he won support among the merchants by acting on their complaints against arrogant commanders. One chronicler remarked that he was greatly feared by all the officers, because he did not allow them to mistreat the poor. The neighbouring rulers feared him, too, but not the secular knights, native warriors, burghers, and those who lived in the countryside.

The new grandmaster conducted a complicated diplomacy that offered maximum choices for exploitation of the feud between Vytautas and Jagiełło. He encouraged Vytautas to have patience until Western crusaders came in the next summer. Meanwhile, he met Polish representatives to arrange a personal meeting with the king. He hoped to get peacefully from Jagiełło as much as he seemed likely to obtain by force of arms – Samogitia and a promise of conversion – without making Vytautas grand duke. Jagiełło would be allowed to keep the rest of Lithuania. Vytautas could hardly be excused for suspecting he was being sacrificed and that he would end up as a minor vassal, dependent on crusader support and possessing only Samogitia.

Earlier, Konrad Zöllner had sent heralds to all the great lords in Europe, inviting them to a seat at the Table of Honour in the great campaign planned for the summer of 1391. First to arrive was Friedrich the Quarrelsome of Meissen, who brought a force of 500 horsemen. He, however, only enjoyed the entertainment, then took his army home. Vast numbers of French knights came, led by Boucicaut. There were Englishmen led by Thomas of Woodstock (Bolinbroke's youngest brother) and Scots commanded by William Douglas. Prussia resembled a modern tourist centre, a fashionable resort for Europe's elite. This would have been easily endured if the aristocratic tourists had left their quarrels at home, but they did not. Despite the crusading truce, they brought their feuds with them. The French and the English got along well – they had served together before, and they were used to chivalric truces in the Hundred Years War. The Scots and English, however, hated one another too deeply to observe any truce for long. When Douglas was appointed commander of the 'Tua hundreth shippis and fiftie', of the summer expedition, the Scottish source noted that, 'Quhairat the Cliffurde had rycht grit invye, and of Ingland richt sone and suddantly Send waigit men the Douglas for to sla.'

It is not likely that the assassination was planned. English and Scottish crusaders had rioted earlier in Danzig (where Scottish chroniclers erroneously located the murder) and Clifford was unlikely to have sent assassins to Prussia. Douglas was slain on a bridge in Königsberg after defending himself manfully against four assailants. Rioting followed, the French alone taking the side of the Scots.

Konrad of Wallenrode quieted the tumult and ordered everyone to march inland immediately. The customary welcome at the Table of Honour was postponed until 1 September, when the crusaders reached Kaunas. There they enjoyed a feast never surpassed for lavishness and expense. The 'guests' then went to Trakai, only to find the castle and city reduced to ashes by Skirgaila, who had burned every field and village so that there was nothing for the horses to eat all the way to Vilnius. That made a lengthy siege of the Lithuanian capital impossible. But that would have been unimportant if Długosz was right, that Vytautas had expected to win the city by treachery. Meanwhile, the Livonian army had come within a few kilometres of the crusader camp, but they did not join forces; instead, they ravaged untouched districts to the north, then retreated. After waiting a few days, the Prussian forces retreated as well. On the return march the crusaders constructed new castles for Vytautas on the Nemunas at Ritterswerder and Kaunas and garrisoned them with Teutonic Knights.

Długosz emphasizes the importance of the Polish troops, equipment and food that were sent month after month for defending Lithuanian castles. So devastated was the country, he says, that the Lithuanians would otherwise have had to leave or starve. This so strained Polish resources that when Bohemians invaded Silesia, the king could make no effort to defend his lands there.

In November 1391 Vytautas marched up the Nemunas, accompanied by Marquard of Salzbach and 500 men, capturing Merkinė – a key point in the Lithuanian defensive system on that river – and moving on to Grodno. After three days Marshal Rabe arrived with English archers and cannon. The garrison held out for weeks, refusing offers of honourable surrender; as a result, when at last the garrison begged for terms, Rabe was against concessions. Thus, when Vytautas obtained the capitulation, Rabe treated the Poles as apostates, ordering all but one beheaded. Lithuanians, in contrast, he kept as prisoners and later gave some to Vytautas for safekeeping.

With Skirgaila's ability to communicate with Poland now limited, it seemed that Vilnius could not hold out long. When Jagiełło heard that it was likely to fall, he ordered Kaributas to hurry to the rescue.

Meanwhile, Vytautas established himself in Grodno. When crusaders joined him there in January 1392 for a raid to the east, a fearful quarrel arose over the banner of St George. English crusaders had brought their own banner and demanded that Thomas Percy (Hotspur's more capable brother) be allowed to carry it in the van of the army. This issue had arisen almost forty years earlier, and this time, as then, the Germans insisted on one of their own number bearing the banner. Only the intervention of Vytautas and his wife calmed tempers to the point where the army could march. Ultimately, the crusaders captured one of Kaributas's main strongholds, killing 2,000 of his warriors and taking his banner. The English were difficult guests, but they were also formidable warriors. They had so broken Lithuanian opposition that by early 1392 Vytautas and the crusaders met almost no further resistance.

After this Jagiełło replaced Skirgaila with Vygantas, who had been expected to be a major player in regional politics because he had married a daughter of Ladislas of Opole; this meant he could also claim lands in Masovia and Kujavia that bordered on both East and West Prussia. Now he was governor of Lithuania as well. During 1392, however, Vygantas was poisoned by his servants. Długosz suggests that Vytautas was behind the murder, noting that Vygantas was buried in the same grave as Karigaila.

When Konrad began to build castles to secure routes across the Masurian Lakes wilderness, Jagiełło realised that the game was lost unless he could pry Vytautas away from his crusader alliance. If he paid Vytautas's price, he could at least save his brothers and weaken the Teutonic Knights. He knew that Vytautas did not wish to remain subservient to the grandmaster and he could still offer more than Konrad was willing or able to deliver. He could make him supreme duke of Lithuania, with all the lands held by Algirdas and Kęstutis together, and by depriving Skirgaila of his lands, he would satisfy Vytautas's demand that Kęstutis's murder be avenged. Jagiełło had only one great problem: he had to communicate this offer secretly to Vytautas, who was constantly surrounded by crusaders.

Jagiełło resolved this difficulty by sending bishop-elect Henryk of Płock (whose mother had been the supposedly unfaithful wife of Siemowit III) as an envoy to the grandmaster, purportedly to discuss peace terms. But his real mission was to relay Jagiełło's proposition to Vytautas while the bishop was hearing Vytautas's confession. That opened the way for Vytautas to change sides again.

Vytautas Rejoins Jagiełło

Vytautas cleverly brought together all the elements necessary to outwit the watchful grandmaster. First, he asked that Anne be allowed to join him at Ritterswerder, probably arguing that she was a devout Roman Christian and could be useful for the conversion of the Lithuanians. Then he had her slip away to Lithuania to negotiate with Jagiełło. When she returned, he persuaded Konrad Zöllner to transfer many important hostages to castles along the Nemunas, holding back only Vytautas's brother, Žygimantas (1365–1440). Lastly, Vytautas offered his sister Ringailė to Bishop Henryk of Płock and promised to make him duke of territories bordering on Masovia – the marriage scandalised clerics when it became public, but it was nothing exceptional in an era when younger sons were made clerics without having to take the vow of celibacy (which, after all, was a vow not to marry; chastity was implied, but not always expected). It was no surprise when noble clerics returned to a secular life when circumstances made it possible.

Meanwhile, the grandmaster was distracted by negotiations with Sigismund of Hungary over Neumark. The king had married the Hungarian heiress, Mary, but he could not put down rebellious nobles on the border of Brandenburg without hiring mercenaries. To obtain that money, he proposed selling Neumark to the grandmaster – that would guarantee safe travel of German and French crusaders into Prussia; he also proposed selling Dobrzyń, which would block Lithuanian raids into Culm.

Beset by rebellions and nobles and Turkish incursions, Sigismund needed every penny he could raise. While he wanted to interfere in Polish affairs, he simply could not afford to do so. Therefore, he pawned Brandenburg (and Luxemburg) to a cousin, Jobst of Moravia (c. 1354–1411), for the money he needed to hire mercenary soldiers and bribe important men.

Although Jobst could have been a power in the north, he had little interest in that, preferring to watch how Wenceslaus of Bohemia handled the quarrels with his nobles, the church, and both of his wives – the first was rumoured to have been mortally attacked by his hunting dogs. Not surprisingly, Wenceslaus had no children, legitimate or otherwise; moreover, he was so slow in dealing with problems in Germany that the electors complained. Although he acquired the nickname, 'the lazy,' the problem may have been alcoholism. Jobst, like everyone else in the Luxemburg dynasty, saw himself as Wenceslaus's successor.

Jagiełło, meanwhile, was alarmed at the thought of the grandmaster acquiring the Neumark. In May 1392, just as the Hungarian representatives arrived in Marienburg, he sent messengers to Vytautas, urging him to act quickly – to break up the grandmaster's plans before it was too late.

Vytautas did as requested, acting quickly but not rashly. He first sent home the English crusaders who had just arrived at Ritterswerder, then seized the castle and burned it. Hurrying south, he surprised the garrisons at Grodno and Metenburg. In these few bold strokes Vytautas wiped out the crusader gains of two years. Moreover, his revolt so distracted the grandmaster that he was unable to prevent the Neumark from going to Johann of Görlitz (1377–96), Sigismund's younger brother.

Vytautas met Jagiełło at Astravas – about 50 km. (30 miles) north of Vilnius in August 1392. Anne acted as mediator in this historic meeting, encouraging the cousins to avoid issues which might rip their new alliance asunder – not an easy task, considering their imperious natures and their many justifiable complaints against one another. As a result of her understanding of their personalities, she brought the former best friends to lay aside their feud and concentrate on what was in everyone's interest. Her vision of what could be achieved by co-operation, and her common sense, caused her influence to grow steadily in the years to come, including attending her husband's conferences with Jagiełło and his brothers. Her brother-in-law became field commander of Vytautas's armies, even though he was Orthodox, while she was a devout Roman Catholic. The document signed at Astravas was co-signed by each man's wife and endorsed by the Lithuanian boyars. It ended ten years of brutal civil war.

Vytautas bought off Skirgaila's resistance – with the support of Jagiełło and Jadwiga – by giving him additional lands in the east, most importantly Starodub. Vytautas then strengthened his position by sharing power with his boyars, among whom were his mother's powerful Samogitian relatives; similarly, he was able to reach out to relatives such as Ivan of Pskov, whose father, Andrew, had been imprisoned by Jagiełło since 1387. Vytautas's famous temper still flared up easily, and he took revenge on traitors quickly, but he was becoming more willing to accommodate political realities. He recognised Jagiełło as supreme duke, accepting for himself the lesser title of grand duke, but titles were less important than real power – Vytautas would rule in Lithuania. As for the future, since neither man had a son, that was uncertain.

It was the autumn of 1392 before Konrad could make sense of the situation. Information came in slowly, and until the grandmaster could see what was going on, he could do little. When he was ready, he sent Marshal Rabe beyond the Masurian Lakes to attack the Bug River settlements on the Lithuanian–Polish border. After celebrating the Table of Honour at Johannisburg, Rabe moved into Masovia. He captured Bishop Henryk at Suraż, a castle on the Narew, but he missed Vytautas, who had left only the day before. The bishop's wife was soon a widow. No contemporary believed that Henryk's death was anything other than unnatural, but none really regretted his passing. Blame was placed variously on his brothers, the grandmaster, and Henryk's own wife (who was later accused of having murdered a second husband), but nobody wanted to investigate the affair too deeply.

The most important participant in the 1392 expedition was Bolingbroke, who had come to Danzig in August expecting a warm welcome – this being his second expedition and his having brought 100 men and six minstrels. However, he discovered that the ill-feelings towards Englishmen were still very much alive. His servants quarrelled with their tormentors and eventually slew a local Prussian warrior. Although not a matter for the courts (it being a clear case of self-defence), all Englishmen, and especially Bolingbroke, had to watch for revenge-seeking Germans. Bolingbroke, not being easily frightened, proceeded on to Königsberg and took up residence near the cathedral. Then, when Konrad refused to allow him to carry the banner of St George, he left

Prussia, travelled through the Holy Roman Empire to Venice, and took ship for the Holy Land. This was his last crusading venture. In 1399, Bolingbroke would overthrow Richard II and become king of England as Henry IV.

This was almost the last English participation in the Samogitian Crusade. Two years later, when an English noble wrote that he was bringing a large force to Prussia, the grandmaster discouraged him from coming. Few English pilgrims are mentioned in subsequent records. Relations between the island kingdom and Prussia grew worse as English merchants and sailors chafed at the restrictions imposed by Hanseatic merchants; and the Teutonic Knights were loyal to the Hanseatic cities.

Shortly after the incident with Bolingbroke, Marshal Rabe was demoted. This was something rare in Prussian affairs. Rabe had never been popular – though he had a strong circle of close friends, was apparently from a powerful family with lands near Eger and was famed for his military skills – and it probably did not help that Bolingbroke asked the grandmaster to reinstate him. (Bolingbroke not only knew Rabe well from the 1390 siege of Vilnius, but he was a royal who was used to getting his way.) We do not know what had happened, but Konrad and Rabe seemed to have quarrelled while their army was outside Vilnius. Rabe would understandably have considered himself the expert on how to attack the castle, but Konrad would have insisted on being in command. After the quarrel Konrad was apparently concerned that his officers would not follow orders, because he ordered the army to march home.

Once back in Prussia, Konrad explained that each office must be held by the man most competent for the duties and that the grandmaster was the best judge of that competence. The order needed new men at its head, Konrad decided, so he made a sweeping reorganisation of the officers, removing Rabe's supporters from their commands, most importantly from Balga, Brandenburg and Ragnit. For marshal he selected Werner of Tettingen (*c.* 1350–1413), a man well known for competence and loyalty to all the grandmasters he served.

Negotiations over Masovia

Konrad continued to avoid direct conflict with Poland. Essential to this policy were the dukes in Masovia, for their lands formed a buffer between Prussia and King Jagiełło. The buffer had one weakness: Dobrzyń. This territory, east of Thorn and directly south of East Prussia, consisted of five strategic castles. It had been contested among the Piast dukes of

Masovia, but Ladislas of Opole had obtained it partly as dowry, partly as security for a loan to King Louis. Although Jagiełło tried to persuade him to give Dobrzyń to his brother Vygantas as dowry when he married Ladislas's daughter, Konrad made a better offer, to loan Ladislas 50,000 *Gulden*, with the Teutonic Knights to hold the territory until he could repay it. This was the same arrangement by which Konrad was holding Wizna and would hardly have invalidated the Polish claims. Since Ladislas was not interested in a vulnerable territory far from Silesia, Konrad next sought to persuade him to transfer Dobrzyń to the duke of Stolp. This infuriated the royal council, who objected to even the slightest loss of national lands, and it ended any chance Konrad had for a treaty with Jagiełło. Nevertheless, Konrad's policy was successful in holding on to Dobrzyń until 1404 and helped keep Masovia independent. A detailed account of this complicated negotiation – in Middle High German – can be found in a memorandum in the 1392 *Urkundenbuch*.

Meanwhile, amid formal pageantry, Vytautas declared himself a subject of Jagiełło and was endowed with Rus'ian territories that Poland claimed. Most of Jagiełło's brothers accepted this settlement, but not Kaributas and Švitrigaila. In a show of strength, Vytautas sent them in chains to Jagiełło. In return, Vytautas, knowing that Jagiełło's eldest half-brother might be useful in the future, obtained Andrew's release from prison.

For the next few years Vytautas was occupied in the Rus'ian provinces, consolidating his power. He had to bring order into the government, so that when the time came to take on the Teutonic Knights or any other foe, he would be ready.

With Vytautas fighting on distant frontiers, the Samogitians were unable to keep the crusaders at bay. In January 1393 Marshal Werner of Tettingen brought an imposing army of Dutch and French knights led by Wilhelm of Geldern to besiege Grodno. So fierce was their bombardment that after three days the crusaders were able to assault the damaged walls, kill 1,000 defenders, and capture 3,000 others. The marshal made no effort to rebuild and garrison the badly damaged fortress because Vytautas would have little difficulty retaking it. What was important, anyway, was to eliminate Grodno as a Lithuanian base so that crusaders could range freely into the countryside. The Teutonic Knights now knew how to bring forces by boat through the Masurian Lakes to the upper Nemunas, bypassing the rapids on the river, increasing the range of their incursions, and carrying supplies with them.

Not long afterwards the marshal heard that Vytautas was building a new castle at Złotoria on the Drewenz River near its junction with the Vistula, not far from Thorn. Deciding to strike quickly, he sent the commander of Balga, who found the castle being constructed under the direction of Hans of Riga, one of those Livonian Germans who had a close association with the Lithuanian grand duke. The Balga commander was unable to capture any of the fleeing workmen, but he took Janusz of Masovia prisoner – perhaps when he came to ask what the crusaders were doing in his land. The commander tied Janusz to a horse in a ridiculous fashion and paraded him around, then finally released him on his word of honour to present himself later in Marienburg. No question about it, the duke had been working with the Lithuanians.

There was another attempt to capture Vytautas in the spring of 1394, while he was in Volhynia. It failed, but the raiders brought back 300 captives and immense booty.

The impressive number of crusaders coming to Prussia in 1393–4 demonstrated how few people of importance were asking why it was, with Vytautas a Christian, the crusade was continuing. The Poles, of course, were making this very argument everywhere they could – once the crusade ended, they argued, the Church could get on with its mission of conversion.

Konrad agreed with this to the extent of allowing a papal legate to arrange for him to meet Jagiełło. Konrad and Jagiełło were together in Thorn for ten days of feasting and talking, then suddenly, apparently without giving any warning, Jagiełło left. Although the legate arranged another meeting in the late summer, Konrad died unexpectedly just before it was to take place. (We need not take seriously Dorothea of Montau's dire predictions about his fate. No contemporary associated him with her visions.) It was asserted that he had died of apoplexy. Given his record of violent outbursts, this is a plausible explanation.

Konrad's place at the conference was taken by Marshal Tettingen, who was successful in ransoming many prisoners, some of whom had been in captivity for eight years. In late November 1393, the general chapter's electors chose Konrad of Jungingen (1355–1407) as grand-master, then selected a new German master. The assembled knights and representatives also inducted the newly appointed archbishop of Riga, Johannes of Wallenrode (1370–1419), into the Teutonic Order, hoping that this would result in taming the rebellious citizens of that powerful city. But they were soon disappointed. Johannes had been the Order's procurator in Rome, too young for that post and very young to become an archbishop, but a high birth justified almost everything. Intimidated by riots in Riga, offended by the Livonian master's trying to give him orders, and unable to improve his impossible financial situation, after four years Johannes accepted a stipend on the condition that he leave the country. He then went to Germany to work for Ruprecht of the Rhine (1352–1410), the weak Holy Roman Emperor-elect. Afterwards a brilliant career lay ahead of him – the title of archbishop meant little in Riga, but it was very important in Rome, where efforts were being made to end the Great Schism.

Konrad of Jungingen, like his predecessor, was a military leader who had little respect for priests and nuns but was nevertheless seriously concerned about discipline and religious observation. His rise to prominence had been swift – from commander of a border post to treasurer in Marienburg – but never had the electors chosen such an inexperienced man as grandmaster. Among his first acts was to name his brother Ulrich (1360–1410) as advocate of Sambia – it was the first step on the ladder of his spectacular career.

Konrad moved quickly to raise the largest number of crusaders in the history of his order. He planned not just one large expedition in 1394, but one invasion after another. In January, the marshal took French, German and English crusaders to Kaunas, then turned along the Nemunas to Merkinė, where he left a large body of knights to plunder the countryside and secure his line of retreat; he left a second body of knights 100 km. (60 miles) east of Grodno and led the main force to Navahrudak, deep inside Lithuania, where they found the castle in ashes. The crusaders were running wild through the country, seemingly unstoppable.

The Lithuanians resisted only with guerilla tactics, ambushing small groups of marauders, and making night-time assaults on camps, and by holding Vilnius. Długosz reported that the war was a drain on the Polish treasury. The war had become a test of endurance, each side straining to the utmost to prevail.

The Second Siege of Vilnius

When Konrad of Jungingen conferred with his commanders and advocates about employing the French and German crusaders who were expected in July 1394, he announced that the duke of Burgundy, then perhaps the most powerful ruler in Europe, was sending 150 of his famous Genoese crossbowmen. The council recommended that Konrad bring together all available forces to build a castle at Ritterswerder which could serve as a base for future invasions of central Lithuania.

Konrad led the forces of the Teutonic Knights to Labiau, followed by the marshal and the crusaders. After crossing the Curonian Lagoon to the Gilge mouth of the Nemunas, he sailed past Ragnit, and, after a short rest, went on to Ritterswerder. There he put his army to work on the fortifications and sent the ships back to Ragnit for the horses.

Vytautas, meanwhile, had summoned his forces. He had not known where the crusaders were going until they were practically at Ritterswerder, but he hurried there with 15,000 warriors as quickly as he could. The crusaders were surprised when the Lithuanians and Poles opened fire on their camps from across the river. The gunners blew apart the tents of the grandmaster, the marshal and the commander of Balga so quickly that Konrad suspended work on the castle and ordered shelters dug for his troops.

Once the crusaders had built their fortifications facing Vytautas, they were able to give more punishment than they received – bowmen killed two of Vytautas's nobles, the stone throwers killed two more in boats, and the Genoese trained a cannon upon their opponents with deadly effect. The most serious crusader casualties came from an accident when the master of the guns blew himself up. When the horses arrived, Konrad ordered his 400 knights to mount their steeds for combat. As the knights advanced across the shallow water, Vytautas ordered a withdrawal to the Neris. Many of his men failed to escape in time and ended up in chains.

For nine days Konrad pondered his choices. Then he stopped work on the castle, loaded the building materials onto the ships and sent them back to Ragnit. After leading the army to Kaunas, he rested his men and sent out scouts. Learning that the duke had blocked the direct route to his capital by erecting cannon-filled forts and felling trees across the roads, he gave instructions to use a poorly guarded path farther up the Neris. Konrad distributed supplies to last five weeks and proposed a quick march on Vilnius. His suggestion met with loud approval.

Screening his movement from Vytautas's scouts as much as possible, Konrad led his army inland and crossed the swamps on hastily constructed bridges. When he emerged from the woods near Kernavė, 55 km. (35 miles) from Vilnius, he defeated a small Lithuanian unit watching the roads there. Among the prisoners was one from Vytautas's retinue, Sudimantas, perhaps a brother-in-law, but certainly a noble who had once been a guide for the Teutonic Knights. The grandmaster called his council to discuss what he should do and then hanged him as a traitor. The following day the crusaders fought their way past an ambush and captured yet another of Vytautas's relatives. The remainder of the march was quiet. This disturbed the crusaders almost as much as continual attacks because everyone knew that Vytautas would not let them reach Vilnius unopposed.

The crusaders came upon Vytautas's ambush at the edge of a swamp. The advance guard was composed of French crusaders riding heavily armoured horses, and although few were injured by the long spears and arrows showered on them from the swamp, they hardly knew what to do. They could not stand and fight a missile battle, and they could not retreat because the rest of the army filled the road behind them. They were almost equally unwilling to charge into the swamp, which could be a death trap for armoured horsemen. When the knights did charge, they found that the bottom was not as deep as they had feared. Routing the defenders, they opened the way to Vilnius.

The grandmaster crossed the river and camped south and east of the city, then on 29 August opened the attack with a bombardment.

Kaributas, who was commanding the garrison while Vytautas collected a relief force, ordered his Polish cavalry to sally out and capture the crusader herds on the meadow. This was nearly a spectacular success, but watchmen alerted Marshal Tettingen in time to intercept them, and when the Genoese joined in, the battle became another rout.

Shortly afterwards news arrived that Vytautas was approaching from the east with an army which the scouts estimated to outnumber the crusaders ten-fold. Leaving some forces to continue the siege, Konrad went to meet this new threat. When he blocked Vytautas's way at a bridge across a swamp, the grand duke asked him to pull back so he could bring his Rus'ians and Lithuanians over and form a line of battle. Konrad cautiously declined to do so. That must have frustrated the French, who loved extravagant and foolish gestures. The grandmaster, however, had more to answer for than his reputation, and he took no risks.

The situation was bad for everyone. Neither army had unlimited supplies, nor could anyone see through the fog. Konrad took advantage of the fact that Vytautas's troops were as frightened as his. He sent Marquard of Salzbach to cross the swamps to ascertain the enemy dispositions. At first Salzbach's Sambians hesitated to enter the fog-covered marsh, but when they saw the opposing forces, their morale soared. Salzbach located where Vytautas had positioned himself, then made his attack against the other wing. Vytautas had stationed Samogitians among his Rus'ian warriors because he knew that, while Rus'ians were formidable on their home ground, they lacked enthusiasm for this war. They fled after only a short fight. When other crusader units heard cries of victory, they charged towards Vytautas's men, who were now discouraged and properly worried about being surrounded. They fought desperately until Vytautas escaped, then sought safety themselves.

The crusaders pursued relentlessly. Later they counted 500 bodies where Vytautas's banner had stood and more where the Rus'ians and Samogitians had been. They took Ivan Olshansky prisoner and captured six banners belonging to Lithuanian and Rus'ian princes. That night some Lithuanians, probably Samogitians, tried to raid the crusader camp, but cannon fire dispersed them. The crusaders lost only sleep.

Not long afterwards the Livonian master arrived. The grandmaster entertained his guests with a huge feast, serving meat from herds captured by foragers. Then he ordered the Livonian army to build two bridges and raid north of the river. There were some desperate combats in the next days, but thereafter the Livonians roamed freely wherever they wished. Konrad's first assaults had revealed how strong the southern defences of the city were. Therefore, he decided to attack on the north, at the watergate, which was sheltered by a fortified bridge. He had his men build ten wooden towers and push them forward towards the wall. The closer they came, the more effective the crusader batteries became. One week's bombardment stripped the bridge of its protective covering, but the crusaders could still not bring the towers close enough for an assault. Some towers had been damaged, some tipped into the water, and some burned. Those which did reach the wall came under such intense missile fire that the crusaders broke off the attack.

Afterwards, when Kaributas's men set the French and Flemish camp aflame, destroying valuable supplies, the grandmaster shifted his attack to a wall that had been reduced to rubble by cannon fire. The artificial moat being still too wide and deep to cross, he ordered the Prussians to dig a ditch so that the water would empty into the river. However, Lithuanian archers shot down so many workers that nothing was achieved. After the defenders had repaired the damaged wall, they sallied out to destroy gun positions, making the besiegers into the besieged. When the Livonian master announced that he was taking his men home, the grandmaster knew he was beaten.

The French knights proposed a joust with the Polish knights before they retreated, but the grandmaster forbade it, saying that no Christian could honourably enter the lists against knights who fought for pagans. The French were satisfied with challenging the Poles to come to Prague in the next summer, to fight against six of their number.

The problem then remained of getting safely out of Lithuania. Konrad knew that Vytautas had been burning all the pastures west of Vilnius and that he was collecting every available man to block the roads. Therefore, he suggested a truce by which Vytautas would promise not to burn the fields, while he would restrain his crusaders from foraging. The truce apparently held for two days, during which time the army marched away through unburned countryside. When some Samogitians attempted to block the way through a forest near Trakai, Konrad ordered the Genoese to test the enemy strength, then sent his Teutonic Knights to take the position. They did so, killing 250 defenders. Since it was not clear whether this ambush was planned by Vytautas or was a spontaneous gesture, Konrad did not regard it as a violation of the truce, but went on to Kaunas, where he and some knights boarded vessels to sail back to Prussia. The rest of the cavalry rode down the north bank of the Nemunas to Georgenburg, where they were brought over to safety.

Though the siege was a failure, it was a success in persuading the king and grand duke to seek peace. The Teutonic Knights could congratulate themselves on having demonstrated that military pressure could persuade the Lithuanians to make a clear break with their past – peace would come only at the price of eradicating the last vestiges of Lithuanian paganism, meaning the surrender of Samogitia.

The Poles and Lithuanians had differing views, of course.

Anticlimactic Aftermath

Peace talks began in the summer of 1395, the result of changing circumstances. It was irrelevant that Emperor Wenceslaus had ordered the Teutonic Knights to stop the war. Notoriously unpredictable, his drunken excesses were multiplying the results of political incompetence; his subjects were constantly denouncing him, and even his closest relatives had joined the Czech nobles in imprisoning him until he promised to make reforms. But nothing changed. Wenceslaus's every action seemed motivated by the most short-sighted of motives. The call for ending the crusade, for instance, seemed to be a repayment for Jagiełło sending troops to put down Wenceslaus's unhappy Bohemian vassals. In short, the emperor's policies seemed to be like his marriages – unhappy and without children.

The Teutonic Knights worried about this situation sufficiently to send representatives to imperial diets, where the electors debated what should be done. The grandmaster dared not make too strong a stand, however, for fear that Wenceslaus might confiscate the Order's holdings in Bohemia and encourage others to follow his example. Already rumours abounded that the pope was considering confiscating the Order's Italian possessions.

Peace talks came from a combination of motives: the winter of 1395/96 was too warm for an expedition; the duke of Stolp arrested three high officials of the Teutonic Order as they crossed his territories in Pomerania; and Sigismund of Hungary announced plans for a crusade of Germans, French and Hungarians in September 1396 to drive the Turks back into Asia, thereby saving Serbia, Bulgaria and the Byzantine Empire for Christendom. That would attract many of the crusaders who might have considered going to Prussia or Livonia. In short, the prospects for conducting military operations against Lithuania were not good.

The Battle of Nicopolis

It had never been easy to recruit volunteers for the holy war in the Baltic. In addition to apathy and cost, there were expeditions to the eastern Mediterranean, Tunis, and Spain that attracted bold, adventurous warriors. Then there were the campaigns of the Hundred Years War and the desperate struggles between English kings and Scots. But nothing disrupted the crusading effort in Samogitia as much as the great French–Hungarian crusade of 1396 to Nicopolis on the Danube River.

Seven years before this great effort in the Balkans, in 1389, there had been a great battle between Turks and Serbs on the field of blackbirds, the battle of Kosovo. While modern scholars see this battle as a decisive turning point in Balkan history, one which opened the way for a Turkish advance north, few contemporaries did. Some saluted the assassination of the sultan on the very day of his triumph as a Christian victory more important than the loss of the Serbian king and his best warriors. These optimistic analysts believed that the Turkish hold on the Balkans was very weak. Surely, if a crusading army could be raised quickly, the Serbs would rise again, and this time they would defeat their new Turkish lords.

It was six years before an expedition could be organised, because it took that long for Sigismund of Hungary to make himself master of his unruly kingdom. In the meantime, his borders had been penetrated repeatedly by Turkish raiders.

Sigismund believed that if he could raise a large army in the Holy Roman Empire, then ruled by his half-brother, Wenceslaus, and from his own subjects and allies, he could drive the Turks back, thereby liberating Serbia and Bulgaria. If he could persuade French nobles to join his crusade, he asserted, success would be almost guaranteed. Indeed, many French knights did volunteer, thinking that they would earn eternal fame by driving the Turks out of Europe, then, after having rescued the Greek Orthodox Christians, bringing them all into the Roman Catholic fold. Even a few Polish knights took the Cross. In all, according to David Nicolle's estimate, the Christian forces who marched to battle in late September 1396 numbered about 16,000. The Turks had slightly fewer men, though contemporary figures gave them many, many more.

A national army is hard to control, an international one almost impossible. Sigismund was loath to believe this, even when he could see how arrogantly the foreign crusaders behaved and how rudely his allies questioned his advice. This proud ruler, whose strong personality was to drive German politics for the next four decades, had great faith in his own judgement, but his French allies dismissed him as immature. The Burgundians, who made up much of the French force, insisted that command be given to Enguerrand VII de Coucy (1340– 97), a prominent lord who was the son-in-law of the English king. Coucy knew war well, but he was better as a courtier, famed for his singing and dancing – in short, he was such a personification of the era that Barbara Tuchman made him the central figure of her best-selling book *A Distant Mirror*, one that pleased general readers but annoyed knowledgeable historians.

Sigismund tried to warn the French that the Turks were a formidable foe, but they ignored him. Instead of waiting until the Turkish attack had worn out, then counter-attacking, the French charged at the first sight of the enemy. After exhausting themselves slaughtering second-rate infantry, Coucy tried to give his men and horses a moment to catch their breath, but the young knights insisted on pursuing the enemy up a steep slope. Everyone followed, only suddenly to find themselves facing the fresh forces of the main enemy army. The battle quickly became a massacre. The rest of the Christian army fled when they saw the French defeated, and Sigismund, who had joined in the wild charge, barely escaped the battlefield alive.

After the disaster there were very few French volunteers for the campaigns organised by the Teutonic Knights. The list of nobles who died on the battlefield or were held for ransom reads like an honour roll of crusaders who fought in Samogitia and Lithuania. Thus, the Teutonic Knights, who did not participate in the great expedition, must be listed high among those who suffered from the defeat. Yet this was not immediately obvious, because the crusade was winding down for other reasons.

Distractions Interrupt the Crusade

Had the Poles and Lithuanians chosen to concentrate on the war along the Nemunas River, the grandmaster would have been hard pressed to defend his castles there. But Jagiełło and Vytautas had decided they would do better by making peace and persuading the grandmaster to join them in fighting the Muslim and Orthodox enemies of Western Christendom on Lithuania's eastern and southern frontiers. This was not the moment for Roman Catholics to be fighting one another.

Although the Teutonic Knights were not persuaded that the Poles had made the Lithuanians into reliable converts and doubted that the Samogitians would abandon their ancient religion, there was no thirst for war with Poland. The backstory for this decision is complicated. Historians have pieced it together, but there is enough left unfinished to keep doctoral candidates busy for years. *The Chronicle of Wigand of Marburg*, the best source for the preceding years – thanks to Długosz having ordered parts of it to be translated into Latin – is largely missing and the grandmaster's correspondence tells us the what of routine activities but not the why.

The grandmaster had other matters to worry about now. The most important was the demise in 1396 of Johann of Görlitz, the controversial younger brother of Wenceslaus and Sigismund, who died on his way to Prussia from Brandenburg to participate in the Order's crusade. Poison was suspected – while staying overnight in a Cistercian abbey the 25-year-old prince had gone to bed healthy but was dead before morning. Wenceslaus was the chief suspect. This was awkward because Johann had been among the emperor's strongest supporters, despite Wenceslaus's increasingly erratic behaviour; after Johann had rescued him from captivity by his cousin Jobst of Moravia, Wenceslaus had rudely told him to leave Prague immediately. The grandmaster was concerned, firstly, because the apparent murder involved a crusader, and secondly, the Neumark might again be for sale. As it happened, the territory went to Jobst, who in 1402 transferred the Neumark to the Teutonic Order, thus guaranteeing that crusaders could ride from Brandenburg to West Prussia in safety.

Then there was the conspiracy organised by Bishop Dietrich Damerow of Dorpat in combination with Vytautas, Rus'ian princes, nobles in the archdiocese of Riga, and a group of Baltic pirates known as Vitalien Brethren. To combat this, Konrad II had to send the Livonian master reinforcements who remained in the north until 1397. Luckily for the grandmaster, Vytautas had been busy removing Jagiełło's brothers one by one from their principalities in the north and south; and intervening in disputes among the northern Rus'ian princes. Then his hated enemy Skirgaila had died – some rumours blamed the plague, but Długosz, always eager to disparage Orthodox churchmen, reported that poison was administered by a Rus'ian monk who dipped his finger into the wine after it had been tasted, thereby releasing the poison from his ring. Skirgaila had the reputation of a cruel and drunken ruler, but Jagiełło prized him for the military and diplomatic skills that his surviving younger brother lacked – Švitrigaila had escaped from captivity and fled to Hungary, then to Sigismund, who put him in contact with the Teutonic Knights.

This is another of those episodes clouded by the mysteries of time. Długosz believed that Švitrigaila had participated in the crusader campaigns but was apparently in error. Švitrigaila had been a dangerous man – impulsive, active, and untrustworthy – but Vytautas saw that he could be bought off by offering him Novgorodok, which Švitrigaila could imagine expanding into a larger Orthodox duchy encompassing Podolia and Kyiv.

This left Vytautas the undisputed master of Lithuania, ready to talk peace from a position of strength. By July 1396 the grandmaster had brought the bishops of Pomesania and Ermland to speak with him, and in September he sent several officials to meet with four of Vytautas's vassals. However, Jagiełło prevented the conclusion of peace at this time, objecting to a requirement that Vytautas swear allegiance to the Holy Roman Empire. It seems that he was afraid that an end to hostilities would allow Vytautas and Konrad to interfere with his own plans for the eastern territories. All that emerged was a truce.

Despite the last-minute failure of negotiations, Konrad continued his effort for a permanent peace through 1397. He brought the Livonian leaders together in Danzig and sought to persuade the Hanseatic cities to act against pirates on Gotland (actions that would help resolve the dangerous situation in Dorpat) and he continued sending representatives to Vytautas. An effort to work through Wenceslaus failed when the emperor insisted that Konrad give him Vytautas's brother Žygimantas, the Order's prize hostage. In June, Queen Jadwiga met the grandmaster in Old Leslau (Włocławek) on the Vistula to discuss the possession of Dobrzyń. Konrad expressed his willingness to return Dobrzyń whenever the queen redeemed the loan, and the two parted after exchanging friendly words.

Jadwiga's policies ran counter to her husband's wishes, but she was the monarch, and he was only her consort. In July Konrad's hand was strengthened when a representative from Sigismund of Hungary came to Marienburg to offer his services. Sigismund needed help. His crusade against the Turks had been a disaster. Moreover, his wife (Mary, Jadwiga's sister) had died when her horse had fallen during a hunt when she was heavily pregnant. Therefore, he needed allies who could help forestall Jadwiga from making a claim on his throne as the surviving daughter of Louis the Great. The Teutonic Knights were well placed to do this. Negotiations speeded up on all fronts. Letters flew back and forth, with the issues intermixed (Samogitia, Livonia, Dobrzyń, Novgorod), There was noticeable progress because everyone recognised that diplomacy, frustrating as it was, was less expensive in resolving disputes than was war, and less risky.

The only important combat in this year was on the Ukrainian steppe where Vytautas – the truce with the grandmaster securing him from fear of attack during his absence – led a force of Lithuanians, Rus'ians and rebellious Tatars against the Tatar khan in the Crimea. He won a smashing victory and extended his power right to the Black Sea – the memory of Vytautas wading his horse into the surf was to endure for many years.

The grand duke brought back thousands of Tatar captives. Those he sent to Jagiełło were Christianised and integrated into Polish society; those he kept for himself he settled near Trakai and allowed to retain their Muslim faith – they later became his devoted bodyguards.

The battlefield victory fed Vytautas's ambition. If he could defeat the khan of the Golden Horde as well and replace him with a willing puppet, he would become the most powerful ruler in Eastern Europe, superior to Moscow and far superior to the minor rulers of Rus' who still paid tribute to the khan.

The situation was highly favourable for Vytautas to return to the steppe. The khan of the Golden Horde, Tokhtamysh, had come to power after the 1380 defeat by Dmitri of Moscow. In the years to follow he had forced most of the princes of Rus' back into tributary status. This success had tempted him to abandon his subservience to Timur, but his efforts to make himself independent provoked the khan. When Timur sent his armies to capture Sarai and reclaim the steppe, Tokhtamysh fled into Lithuania and asked Vytautas for aid. He promised the grand duke much, of course, though what exactly was not clear. This was not what Tokhtamysh would have preferred, and it is unlikely that he would have kept his promises long, but making the humiliating bargain was far preferable to dying.

Vytautas knew that defeating Timur's new khan would not be easy, but it might be done if he could obtain Western aid. This was less easy than one might image. First, Jadwiga was not in favour of the expedition. She wanted peace on all frontiers, but especially with the Teutonic Order. In 1398 she pointedly reminded Vytautas that he owed a large payment to the crown. Instead of paying what could become an annual tax, Vytautas turned to the grandmaster to open peace talks.

What the grand duke wanted was to persuade the crusaders to loan him their highly effective artillery. Cannons were not yet mounted on gun carriages, but the Teutonic Knights could carry them on wagons, and the wagons could be used as a mobile barrier against Tatar cavalry – a tactic that proved highly effective later when employed by Czech Hussites. Vytautas also believed that he could recruit Rus'ian troops, especially from those states ruled by Lithuanian princes, and from Wallachia and Moldavia too. Some Polish reinforcement was possible, but it would not be significant; nor would Moscow join the alliance – although Basil was Vytautas's son-in-law, he considered himself the rightful head of all the Russias and he was unwilling to offend his Tatar overlord.

Vytautas had requested a crusading bull from Pope Boniface IX, but it arrived too late to make a difference. Nevertheless, no Western Christian monarch – neither Polish nor Hungarian – dared oppose his expedition. It was the opportunity of a lifetime.

Konrad of Jungingen had his reasons to support the expedition. First, there had been a long-term decline in enlistment. There was no shortage of knights in Prussia yet, but the reserves in Germany were becoming too thin to provide significant help for future expeditions. According to Udo Arnold, the foremost scholar of the Order's history, the agrarian crisis caused by climate change and the plague had affected the Order's economic base significantly, so that its membership in Germany would decline by two-thirds over the next two centuries. The grandmaster also worried about Gotland, which pirates had taken over; and about Livonia, where a combination of threats existed; and he was aware that not only had many former crusaders to Prussia died in Sigismund's disaster at Nicopolis, but that it had thrown France and Burgundy into turmoil, demoralised French chivalry, and eliminated any possibility that a Hungarian king would ever again take the field against the Lithuanians. Paravicini, in *Preussenreisen*, noted that the Table of Honour was suspended the following year for lack of Western participants.

Nor was the war in Samogitia going well. Marquard of Salzbach had lost 200 men and 500 horses in an ambush, then warm weather again frustrated the winter expedition, so that only the Livonian master was able to raid Samogitia. If the grandmaster could get even part of what he wanted without fighting, he was ready to talk.

Negotiations with Vytautas

There was only one obstacle to peace – Jagiełło. When Queen Jadwiga had demanded that Vytautas pay her an annual tax from his Rus'ian lands, she was saying that parts of western Rus' had belonged to Poland because Casimir the Great had led his armies there and because Jagiełło had promised her the remaining territories as a bridal gift. Though it is difficult to obtain insights into motivation in this era, Jagiełło may have been behind the demand, worrying that Vytautas might soon be able to declare himself independent. If so, a good humiliation was in order, and it did not seem likely that Vytautas could say no to the queen because he could not survive without Polish support. Vytautas, however, surprised her by obtaining from his nobles an assurance that they would never pay taxes to a Polish ruler.

If Vytautas had the crusaders' army behind him, he could dispense with Polish help against the Tatars and defy Jagiełło. Without much question, Anne's influence was important in his reaching this decision. She was a devout Christian who had been favourably impressed by the Teutonic Order during her two stays in Prussia, and she seems to have had some linguistic talent that aided in the negotiations. Understanding the crusader mentality better than most of her countrymen, she believed that their goals were compatible with Vytautas's ambitions. The price for Konrad's aid would be high – Samogitia and possibly missionary activity in Lithuania in competition with the Poles (or in their place). However, Vytautas could afford it. After all, the Samogitians were refusing to obey him, and it would be useful for his vassals to see how he dealt with rebels.

Sending secretly to Prussia to secure a truce, Vytautas received a delegation of Teutonic Knights in Grodno in April 1398. The crusaders were led by the grand commander, the master of the robes, and the Ragnit commander, Marquard of Salzbach. Anne was probably present, as she was at later meetings. Concluding a six months' truce so that the grand duke and the grandmaster could meet formally, they also came to a general agreement on the terms of a future peace treaty:

- Vytautas would surrender all claims to Samogitia, with the borders to be marked by a commission composed of the grand duke and his nobles on one side and by the grandmaster and his advisors on the other;
- the grand duke would seek to obtain Jagiełło's adherence to the treaty, thereby eliminating possible future Polish objections;

- the grand duke would assist in building two or three castles at convenient locations along the borders, replacing castles burned in 1392;
- the grandmaster would, for his part, free Žygimantas and all other captives, and Vytautas would release his prisoners;
- they would seek to resolve overlapping claims regarding Novgorod and Pskov.

A summer meeting prepared the way for a formal peace conference in October 1398. As before, Marquard of Salzbach was the intermediary, employing his knowledge of the Lithuanian language and his friendship with Vytautas. The grandmaster made certain that his entourage was impressive – the Livonian master, 21 officers, 54 nobles, 5 court officers. In total 566 people, to which must be added the bishops of Sambia and Ermland and their entourages, and the representatives of the secular nobility and the cities, Vytautas and Anne were present, with many of the most prominent nobles and some Poles. No doubt the Samogitians who would have been invited to witness the event must have gone home certain that their fate had been signed and sealed.

The Sallinwerder Treaty (Treaty of Salynas) was first a permanent peace, with promises not to join in any war against the other party. Second, it ceded much of Samogitia to the Teutonic Knights! There were additional cessions of unsettled lands south of the Nemunas. Third, it established the borders with Livonia and Prussia – on the Nevėžis River, just west of Kaunas – and with Masovia. In return, the crusaders abandoned all claims on Novgorod, while Vytautas abandoned Pskov. Fourth, it provided for free trade. Fifth, neither side would give refuge to rebels. Sixth (first in the document), Vytautas promised to support the spread of Roman Catholicism inside and outside his realm. Lastly, the two sides agreed on the division of booty from future wars. By this they meant the invasion of the steppe to crush the Golden Horde.

The End of Samogitian Independence

Konrad of Jungingen moved quickly, ordering several commanders to hurry to Gotteswerder, where Vytautas was waiting with workmen. Within four weeks they built two castles. The marshal also rebuilt the long-destroyed castle at Angerburg, and the commander of Balga built a castle at Lyck.

In February 1399 Marshal Tettingen struck into central Samogitia in co-operation with Livonian forces. While the pagans tried to concentrate on the Livonian forces, the Prussians ravaged without resistance, and when the pagans shifted their attention to the Prussians, the Livonians had a free hand. The degree to which the Samogitians lacked effective leadership became even more apparent in the early summer, when the grandmaster led an army into the country and remained there eleven days, moving from region to region, burning the grain. Although it was a large army, it was raised almost entirely in Prussia. The grandmaster gave fourteen squires the accolade of knighthood. It was obvious to all what Konrad would be able to do with a force of Western crusaders.

The Samogitians doubtlessly called on Vytautas to help them against the rampaging Christians, but they received no encouragement. Vytautas was far away, wading his horse in the waters of the Black Sea and trying to find some way to govern and defend southern Rus'. He had much to do there, because although the Tatars were seemingly weak, they had reserves of strength that could not be ignored. Still, his confidence was high in the summer 1399 when he led a large army to the mouth of the Dnieper River, where he built a stone and earth castle and named it Saint John's. Very likely the Teutonic Knights who accompanied the expedition were his architects, for the castle resembled those they had built so expertly along the Nemunas.

Konrad's policy was succeeding beyond his wildest hopes. Then, in the summer of 1399, twin disasters struck. Neither could have been prevented, and one alone would not have been fatal, but together they determined that the fate of Samogitia would be decided eleven years later on a battlefield in the Prussian wilderness – a battle so famous that its name is recognised even by people who have no idea who was fighting, or why, or where: Tannenberg.

The first was that Queen Jadwiga died after giving birth to a daughter who lingered only a few days. All power went to Jagiełło, whose authority was enhanced by the brief survival of the infant heiress, and his attempts to follow Jadwiga's last advice, to look for a bride with Piast ancestry. That must have pleased many who still had doubts about him, but the king must have been unhappy – he put off the ceremony as long as possible because the proposed bride was extremely unattractive – then he complied. Following the wishes of his nobles, the king made no immediate changes in policy. He kept the peace with the Teutonic Knights, but he ended royal co-operation and efforts to seek a permanent peace.

The second event was in August, after Vytautas had moved from his base at Kyiv down the Dnieper River to where the Vorskla flowed into it. He had a large army, bringing in addition to his own Lithuanians, 100 knights with men-at-arms from Prussia, 12 from the Teutonic

Order, 400 knights from Poland, over 50 minor Rus'ian and Lithuanian princes, and allied Tatars under Tokhtamysh. How large the force was is a matter of conjecture, but it must have been the most formidable army raised for centuries, equal at least to the Mongol–Tatar forces brought by Timur's general, Edigei (Edigu, 1352–1419), though those numbers are often estimated to be three times as large. There was also the matter of revenge, since Edigei's father had been killed by Tokhtamysh, and Tokhtamysh had been driven from his lands the previous year.

Our knowledge of the campaign was expanded in 2017 by Mykola Zharkikh, a prolific Ukrainian independent scholar. Ruthless in dismissing most traditional tales as reflecting later events rather than what contemporaries knew, he has called Długosz's narrative 'historical fiction'. In the end, although he argues for revision of some details, the basic outline of events remains the same.

Vytautas chose to assemble his multi-national army at this stretch of the Dnieper because it was convenient for units coming from the south, the west, and the north. Although there were woods on both sides of the river, there were open areas where armies could easily deploy. When Vytautas learned that Tatar forces were approaching, he moved to meet them, then unwisely agreed to a three-day truce. Perhaps he was setting up the wagon fort and placing the Teutonic Knights' cannon on the wagons, but the delay allowed Tatar reinforcements to arrive.

When the battle had raged for a short while, his cavalry, elated by the apparent retreat of the Tatar horsemen, set out in pursuit. Once beyond reinforcement from the infantry, they were ambushed by the enemy reserves. The Tatars then fell on the main army, showering the men huddled behind the wagons with a hail of arrows until nightfall. Vytautas and Žygimantas escaped in the darkness, followed by Marquard of Salzbach, two other Teutonic Knights, and many of the surviving warriors, leaving behind heaps of dead, among whom were the grandmaster's best diplomats, the Surville brothers, and two of Vytautas's close relatives, Andrew of Polotsk and Dmitri of Briansk. This military disaster ended Lithuanian hopes of ruling the southern steppe.

Vytautas hurried to Cracow and swore a very vague oath of loyalty to Jagiełło; meanwhile, because he wanted the help of the Order's knights in Livonia against Novgorod, he steadfastly maintained the Treaty of Sallinwerder.

The collapse of Samogitian resistance came more quickly than expected – that winter. The combination of crusader arms and the grand duke was more than the pagans could withstand. The dukes of Geldern and Lorraine had brought armies. Winter conditions were perfect. The marshal led one force from Ragnit, and Marquard of Salzbach led another to join Vytautas. When the pagans saw Lithuanian warriors in the company of Teutonic Knights, they offered to surrender to Vytautas. He, however, refused to meet their representatives – he sent them to Marshal Tettingen, a gesture that signified his renunciation of authority over Samogitia.

An Order chronicler, Polsige, summed it up, saying:

> In this time all the people of Samogitia united in surrendering to the Order, and they sent many hostages from the nobility of the land who had never bowed to the Order. And the Grandmaster built a castle in the land and set a lord of the Order there as an advocate, and he established officers who should judge and advisors, and he set laws by which they should give justice and govern.

The last recorded Table of Honour was held in 1400 at the new fortress of Friedeburg, which was to be the administrative centre for Samogitia.

Chapter Twelve

Summary and Preview

The *de facto* End of the Crusade

The year 1399 saw the end of serious recruiting for the Samogitian Crusade. Historians have traditionally preferred to describe the crusade against Lithuania as lasting until 1410, because the battle of Tannenberg (Grunwald in Polish, Žalgiris in Lithuanian) was a memorable event they could use to mark the end of an era. For Poles especially, 1410 implies that Grunwald was the culmination of Polish and Lithuanian resistance to German aggression and that everything which took place previously was an unimportant prelude to the victory by Jagiełło and Vytautas. In contrast, in German historiography, 1410 long marked the moment when history went off course, ending in effect the German domination of Central Europe. Henceforth, until 1870, Germany was the battleground of foreign armies, the victim of every ambitious tyrant in France and Scandinavia. Thus, revenge for Tannenberg was a rallying cry for German nationalists.

Traditional histories often ignore the 1343 Peace of Kalisz, the grand-masters' efforts to work with one or another of various Lithuanian dukes, the semi-myth that the Lithuanians would have been converted easily if there had been no crusade, and the reluctance to admit that paganism overlaid a militant way of life that seriously threatened Christians in Prussia, Livonia and Poland. Moreover, nationalist interpretations distorted the significance of the decade 1399–1410, when Jagiełło and Vytautas were warily watching one another, and the Teutonic Order ruled in Samogitia.

Most of the time Jagiełło and Vytautas were working together well enough for bishops and priests to introduce Roman Catholicism into the Lithuanian highlands, even though it was not clear that the official conversion would last – too much depended on those two men not dying by disease, accident or assassination. During that period of uncertainty, the Teutonic Order was attempting to understand its role in the changed situation. How could it justify its existence in either Prussia or Livonia if the Lithuanians had indeed become Christians? Of course, the knights represented a standing warning to the former pagans that the Church Militant would not permit, as a favourite phrase of the era put it, the dogs to return to their vomit. Moreover, it was argued, someone had to watch over Samogitia, which still lacked a church organisation and was periodically in revolt. All in all, those justifications were insufficient to support the continued existence of a military order that prided itself on traditions of battlefield prowess and political indispensability. From 1399 on the Teutonic Knights wrestled with a problem we would call existential: what was their reason for being?

One answer was to serve local communities in Germany and assist the Holy Roman emperor in his endeavours, especially in restoring order in Italy and ending the Great Schism. This was the view of the German master, the powerful Konrad von Egloffstein, who in 1396–1416 represented the 400 knights and 300 priests in Germany. The knights in Prussia and the grandmaster disagreed with this argument and mistrusted those who advanced it. Their answer was to continue as before, as if nothing had changed.

It appeared that there were diplomatic breakthroughs in 1404, when truces with Vytautas were signed and the grandmaster and the king held formal meetings. The most important conference, in Raciąż in Masovia, resulted in the Poles and Lithuanians agreeing to cede Samogitia to the Teutonic Knights, while the grandmaster agreed to sell Dobrzyń to the king for 40,000 florins; both sides promised to free all prisoners and not to give refuge to any exile – this was apparently aimed at Švitrigaila, Jagiełło's youngest brother. With Podolia worth less after the battle on the Vorskla, Švitrigaila's hatred of Vytautas became too intense to be quieted. Vytautas, of course, was a man who bore grudges, too, and now easily flew into rages. The days of quiet circumspection were over.

To overcome differences, the grandmaster hosted the king at memorable meeting in Thorn that was marked by three days of jousting. Although the knights of the Teutonic Order were forbidden by their rules from participating, visiting crusaders and local knights took part. At first the Polish knights were all beaten, but then the Polish champion began dismounting his challengers one by one until they were all unhorsed. Afterwards the grandmaster led Jagiełło around the city to see the magnificent brick churches, public buildings, and homes of the citizens. A scandal arose when a local woman dumped slops from her window onto the king, hitting no one else. The grandmaster had her arrested, then sentenced to death by drowning. But, according to Długosz, Jagiełło intervened and arranged for her release.

Jagiełło immediately rode to Great Poland to raise the money to purchase Dobrzyń. The nobles volunteered a special tax for this purpose, raising thereby 100,000 marks. Then he moved to Wrocław to meet with the ineffectual Holy Roman emperor, Wenceslaus of Bohemia, coming away with a treaty of friendship.

Is this important? Probably not. The great battle at Tannenberg in the summer of 1410 resolved all questions about which state would be supreme. Afterwards it was impossible to resume the crusade. Although the Teutonic Order survived in Prussia for more than another century, it never recovered.

There is also a larger question – a subsequent antagonism between Germans, Lithuanians, and Poles (a triangular relationship, one should remember) poisoned regional politics until quite recently. Its slow disappearance is a welcome sign.

Obviously, the very existence of Belarus and Ukraine owes much to the events described in this book.

Nationalism and History

There are other ways in which this volume's interpretation of the events does not correspond with patriotic accounts written by various German, Polish and Lithuanian historians long ago (but not forgotten). This book argues that an effort to make dynastic rulers into national patriots is essentially misleading and that attributing modern ambitions to medieval crusaders and monarchs reflects outdated nineteenth- and twentieth-century propaganda. It is equally wrong to divide the actors in this drama into heroes and villains. There were a few praiseworthy men on each side, a great many whose character was a mixture of good and bad (as one might expect in cultures based on military prowess), but no major figure was without some redeeming virtues.

Some historians also have, as one scholar has noted, a fear of the blank space. That is, whenever the sources do not tell us what happened or why, the historian tries to fill the gap with guesses or probable explanations. London subways warn 'Mind the gap,' but many of us put a foot there anyway.

We should not try to understand medieval culture and history in modern terms. In contrast to the 1918 Treaty of Brest-Litovsk or the plans of Hitler, the crusades were not a means of dominating Eastern Europe. To impose their religious beliefs on everyone: yes, they wanted that. However, again and again the crusaders stopped their attacks when the Lithuanian dukes offered hope for their conversion. This would be odd behaviour for real imperialists. Uniformly Roman Christians referred to Rus'ians as schismatics (those who create division and disharmony), but the Western demand for religious conformity did not equate with territorial expansionism. Moreover, there is an odd inconsistency in the way that historians condemn the Teutonic Order for seizing lands but excuse Polish kings and Lithuanian grand dukes for making conquests on a far grander scale.

Similarly, though we are familiar with the concept of holy war in the Muslim world today, we forget that medieval Christians believed in it with equal fervour. One cannot study the crusades as though the participants thought with twenty-first-century minds and emotions.

Also, cults of victimisation affect even proud and creative modern peoples. No doubt individuals, groups and nations have been victims. But only God is capable of rendering complete justice. Mortals must decide whether to succumb to anger and self-pity, or to demand compensation, or to move on. Not to forget. That is asking too much for any generation. Perhaps to forgive, for that brings peace of mind to those who forgive and may even influence the descendants of those who offended. Certainly, we should avoid blaming children for the sins of their fathers. Equally, we should not hold grudges dating from the Middle Ages.

Alternatively, one can see this era as an aspect of what Nils Blomkvist calls the spread of the Catholic World-System, a Europeanisation which could be no more easily resisted than today's globalisation. One survival strategy was for peoples on the periphery of Europe to create their own Christian states which incorporated Western institutions of the state, the church and commerce. They were able to retain what made them distinct inwardly by changing outwardly.

There is no fault in seeking to make a successful accommodation with the demands of the modern world, even when that 'modern world' was the fourteenth century. For Lithuanians to defend themselves and their acquired territories, they needed more than guns (though they undoubtedly needed those, too) – they had to modernise. In those days modernisation in Europe involved joining the Roman Catholic world, with its mercantile associations, universities, artistic tastes and literature. Anything less was an illusion.

The Illusion of Modernity

In spite of ourselves, we tend to see the 'other' as reflections of our familiar modern world, and to judge the actions of those 'others' by our own standards. This can be overcome, or else there is no point to education. It must be overcome. A sensitive modern reader, unacquainted with the subtleties and contradictions of medieval life, may recoil in disbelief at the passion and excitability of fourteenth-century men and women, but Huizinga tells us that hatred, revenge and pride drove individuals and groups into unrestrained violence, absolutely convinced of the justice of their cause. This view of the past presents problems for patriots and poets who seek heroes in their national past – how do they handle their shortcomings and contradictions?

This is especially true for the moody combination of anger and ambition that drove Vytautas, contrasting with Jagiełło's love of the deepest forests, his wandering by night to listen to a nightingale, and his reluctance to share his thoughts with anyone. One was passionate and social, the other moody and solitary. Should we see them as oriental despots, with little in common with French dandies, Italian sophisticates or untamed Scots? Or, as Huizinga could be understood to say, were they cut from the same fashionable cloth as the dukes of Burgundy? The exotic manners of the Burgundian court, were they so different from those in Vilnius and Cracow? Certainly, differences were there: we are more familiar with medieval Italians, Englishmen, Germans and Frenchmen than with the Rus'ians and Tatars who visited Vytautas. But that was a relative difference with Lithuanians and Poles, who were sufficiently exotic themselves to attract Western travellers, but neither primitive nor beyond comprehension. For example, we have contemporary portraits of the Western monarchs of this era, but none of Vytautas. Why?

We can nod our heads in agreement when Huizinga writes, 'At the end of the fourteenth century . . . the political stages of Europe had become so crowded with fierce and tragic conflicts that the people could not help seeing all that regards royalty as a succession of sanguinary and romantic events.'

As for the Teutonic Order, we should be able to understand that knights who chose to enter a military order were not aberrations from the normal but reflected widely accepted beliefs as to how all Christians, and especially all noblemen, should behave; these beliefs were not based on economics, a hunger for the pleasures of the world, or psychological dysfunctions. Huizinga wrote that there were three paths to the ideal life:

- to forsake the world,
- to make the world better,
- to dream, to follow the illusion of heroism, honour, and courtesy.

Entry into a military order combined the three paths into a highway to glory and salvation.

The members of the Teutonic Order, especially those with sufficient education and experience to reflect on the human condition, may, in fact, have had fewer illusions than many of us. They could look at their pretensions to power and glory, their protestations of humility and self-sacrifices . . . and smile. But they would smile only to themselves. From outsiders they would tolerate no supercilious airs of superiority.

Eric Christiansen has written eloquently about the various illusions that drove this crusade. The Teutonic Knights had to pretend that the Lithuanians were 'Saracens' or their equivalent, the kings of Poland had to pretend that they properly exercised sovereignty over any territory ruled by their predecessors or claimed by them, Vytautas had to pretend that each time he switched sides, he was acting on selfless motives. Christiansen concluded: 'The real question was, which illusion had the strongest army?'

This was an age of illusions. Huizinga's famous analysis of the age of chivalry contains many fine lines, but none more pertinent to the Samogitian Crusade than, 'Thus a blasé aristocracy laughs at its own ideals. After having adorned its dream of heroism with all the resources of fantasy, art and wealth, it bethinks itself that life is not so fine – and smiles.'

The modern illusion, stated and refined in the nineteenth century, was that the wars associated with this crusade were struggles of nations. This required ignoring or diminishing the personal and dynastic elements of the history. The truth was more complicated: Polish armies contained German knights and Hungarian and Bohemian mercenaries; the Teutonic Knights had Polish-speaking vassals, Bohemian and Silesian mercenaries, native Prussian knights and militia, German vassals, and an international cast of crusaders; Lithuanians had Tatars, Rus'ians and Moldavians. Important officers of the Teutonic Order had Polish ancestors; Poles had Germans. By the early twenty-first century scholars everywhere are aware that the crusade was more complex than textbooks used to portray it. Yet, textbooks and lectures must be short, and should be entertaining – just as books on the northern crusades should be entertaining, while being informative and throwing light on the contemporary world as well as the medieval. Since no scholar can be simultaneously concise, comprehensive, and universally perceived as completely fair, this is, alas, also an illusion.

This is not to say that the fine scholars in Lithuania, Poland, Germany and elsewhere are doomed to failure. But they might look around at the audience at any one of the excellent conferences on this topic, reflect comfortably that they have just given a stimulating lecture that will surely change the way that newspapers and tourist guides present the story of the glorious (or ghastly) fourteenth century, and smile.

Aftermath

The apparent success of the Samogitian Crusade in 1399 was deceiving: The Samogitians were not reconciled to their fate, and the Teutonic Order did not send missionaries among them. The grandmaster marked time, building some castles along the Nemunas River to protect his officials and to serve as centres for trade, but in appointing an advocate rather than bishops or commanders to govern for him, he was reassuring the inhabitants that he cared for their local traditions and sensibilities.

Ours is not an era that values salvation highly. If one believes that all religions are equally valid (and especially if one believes that none has much intrinsic worth), then efforts to spread one's 'belief system' are simply wrong. The historian who has reservations about this relativism can only note that this debate is not new – it reflects the opinions of learned men at the time of the crusades as well as today.

In the nineteenth century the *Deutscher Orden* became the focus of extreme views by German and Polish nationalists; in the first half of the twentieth century this became worse, and little changed during the communist rule in Poland. In the 1980s Udo Arnold joined with Polish colleagues to rectify this. By establishing a joint commission, mainly of German and Polish scholars (with William Urban as the lone American), they proposed textbook reforms. Germans tended to comply, preferring to forget the entire history, lest right-wing parties use it to come back to power, but as late as 2019, as Krzysztof Kwiatkowski noted in *Sapientia,* stereotypes of the Teutonic Order still appeared in Polish classrooms and the mass media.

One of the great achievements of Western civilisation is the ability to criticise oneself and one's institutions. We would not have it otherwise. But the public tends to swing from one excessive moral judgement of the past to its opposite, often without wondering why it does so.

The end of the fourteenth century marked more than the end of this crusade. It saw the end of crusading enthusiasm as well. Secular knights seemingly lost interest in crusades after the failed expeditions to Alexandria, Tunis and Nicopolis. Crusading was going out of style, except in Spain, where the enemy was just across the hills (and that enemy occasionally crossed those very hills to pay unfriendly visits). Chaucer's knight was almost the last of his type, a memory of a glorious past that was worth honouring (perhaps), but not worth emulating. The 'perhaps' comes from Terry Jones, who realised that the military world of the fourteenth century was changing just as Chaucer's knight began his career. Jones – a member of the *Monty Python* troupe, but nevertheless a serious thinker – caught the anti-war mood of 1980 perfectly and later adapted it enthusiastically for a television series on the crusades. Critics guardedly declared his comments stimulating, then moved on.

The implications of the changing attitude towards crusading were not recognised immediately by the Teutonic Knights, because the Samogitian surrender had eliminated the need for annual expeditions. As the chivalrous expeditions from Prussia came to an end, Western knights apparently talked less and less about defending Christendom in the Baltic; and the recruiting techniques became as rusty as the captured weapons in armorial displays. For the Teutonic Order to raise a great army in the future, it would have to call on mercenaries. The grand-master understood this better than his contemporaries and some of his officers. Within a few years Konrad of Jungingen would write to one of his fire-eating commanders who was urging an attack on Lithuania and Poland:

> War is quickly begun, but ended slowly. Better to lose a horse or four than an entire territory. We can fight one enemy better than two. Both [Lithuania and Poland] have great, expansive territories, while we have but a small land filled with people inexperienced in war.

In short, Konrad of Jungingen saw the future of the Teutonic Order as that of a regional peacekeeper that could suppress piracy on Gotland, hold down stubborn pagans in Samogitia, and develop friendly relations with the rulers of Poland and Lithuania. Not all Teutonic Knights agreed with this: some pointed to unrest in Samogitia as proof that the forces of evil were working through Vytautas and Jagiełło to undermine the Church and its defenders.

The reluctance of the grandmasters to recognise the conversion of the Lithuanian princes in 1387 is usually ascribed to the Order's insatiable land hunger. Hopefully, readers will remember the many times that the Lithuanian princes played upon the crusaders' pious wishes and papal hopes; this should remind us why the grandmasters were sceptical and determined not to be played for fools again.

Konrad of Jungingen, distracted by wars in Livonia and on Gotland, by disputes about who would be emperor and who would be pope, and by religious controversies, adopted a policy of waiting until the older generation of pagans had died off. His brother and successor, Ulrich of Jungingen, in contrast, seems to have welcomed the apparently inevitable conflict with Jagiełło so that he could give him the military humiliation he deserved. If this was the essence of the plan for conversion of Samogitia, the Teutonic Knights did not have much of a plan at all.

Peace had its price, too. The 'guests' had brought vast amounts of money into Prussia, money that made its way into the pockets of Prussian merchants, then into general circulation and taxes, and to Hanseatic cities too. As the campaigns began to wind down after 1394 and essentially ceased after Sallinwerder, the economic impact on Prussia was significant. By 1400 there was an economic depression, with many bankruptcies. Communities accustomed to seeing large sums of money spent by crusaders annually now complained about the failure of the Order's economic policies – taxes still had to be paid, but citizens found it ever more difficult to raise the money.

Already during the era of chivalry, the Teutonic Knights had become arrogant and overbearing. By 1400 their subjects were complaining bitterly. The burghers and knights still accepted the grandmaster's rule because his reputation was undimmed and his regime considerably milder than the local rulers in nearby Poland; and many could remember the days when they considered the crusade worthwhile. This was to change after 1410, after the battle of Tannenberg. But that is another book, *The Last Years of the Teutonic Knights: Lithuania, Poland and the Teutonic Order* (London: Greenhill, 2018).

Bibliography

Original Sources

Akten der Ständetage Preussens unter der Herrschaft des Deutschen Ordens. 5 v. Ed. Max Toeppen, 1878. New printing: Aalen: Scientia, 1973.

'*Die Ältere Hochmeisterchronik*', ed. Max Toeppen, in: *Scriptores rerum Prussicarum*, Bd. 3, Leipzig 1866, 519–72

Bartholomew the Englishman, '*On the Properties of Things* – Wikipedia of the Middle Ages – Psychiatry in literature'. Published online by Cambridge University Press: 25 October 2019

Beiträge zur Geschichte des Deutschen Ordens. Ed. Udo Arnold. Marburg: Elwert, 1993. [*Quellen und Studien zur Geschichte des Deutschen Ordens, 49.*]

Die Berichte der Generalprokuratoren des Deutschen Ordens an der Kurie. Ed. Kurt Forstreuter et al. Göttingen: Vandenhoeck und Ruprecht, 1961–2006.

Chartularium Lithuaniae res gestas magni ducis Gedeminne illustrans. Gedimino laiškai. Ed. S. C. Rowell. Vilnius: Vaga 2003.

The Chronicle of Prussia by Nicholas von Jeroschin: A History of the Teutonic Knights in Prussia 1190–1331. Trans. Mary Fisher. Farnham: Ashgate, 2010.

The Chronicle of Novgorod, 1016–1471. Trans. Robert Michell & Nevil Forbes. Vol. 25, Camden Third Series. London Offices of the Society, 1914.

Codex Mednicensis seu Samogitiae Dioecesis, I. (1416–1609). Rome: Academia Lituana Catholica Scientiarium, 1984. [*Fontes Historiae Lituaniae, 3.*]

Constantine Porphyrogenitus, *De Administrando Imperio.* Ed. and trans. G. Moravcsik & R. J. H. Jenkins. Washington DC, 1967, n.e. 2006. [Dumbarton Oaks Texts, I. *Corpus Fontium Historiae Byzantinae, I.*]

Hermann von Wartberge, *Chronicon Livoniae.* Ed. Ernst Strehlke, *Scriptores rerum Prussicarum* 2 (1863).

Joannis Dlugossii, *Historiae Polonicae in Opera Omnia.* Vols. 10–14. Ed. Alexander Przezdziecki. Cracow: CZAS, 1876–1878. Available in an abridged translation by Maurice Michael, *The Annals of Jan Długosz.* Chichester: IM Publications, 1997.

John Froissart, *Chronicles of England, France, Spain and the Adjoining Countries.* New York: Leavitt, Trow, 1848.

The Hypatian Codex, II: The Galician-Volhynian Chronicle. Trans. G. Perfecky. Munich, 1973.

'Die Litauischen Wegeberichte', Ed. Theodor Hirsch, *Scriptores rerum Prussicarum*, 1863.

Lites ac res gestae inter Polonos Ordinemque Cruciferorum. 3 v. Poznań: nakładem Biblioteki Kórnickiej, 1892.

Liv-, esth- und curländisches Urkundenbuch, nebst Regesten. 6 v. Ed. Friedrich Georg von Bunge. Reval–Riga, 1853–71.

Monumenta Poloniae Historica. 6 v. Ed. August Bielowski. Lviv–Cracow, 1864–93.

The Nikonian Chronicle. Vol. IV: *From the Year 1382 to the Year 1425*; Vol. V: *From the Year 1425 to the Year 1520.* Princeton, NJ: Darwin, 1988, 1989.

Peter of Dusburg, 'Chronicon terrae Prussiae', *Scriptores rerum Prussicarum* 1. Leipzig. Hirzel, 1861.

Plano Carpini, *The Story of the Mongols Whom We Call the Tartars by Friar Giovanni di Plano Carpini.* Trans. E. Hildinger. Boston, MA: Branden, 1996.

Russisch-Livländische Urkunden. Ed. K. E. Napiersky. St Petersburg: Archäographische Commission, Buchdruckerei der Kaiserlichen Akademie der Wissenschaften, 1868.

Scriptores rerum Prussicarum Die Geschichtsquellen der preussischen Vorzeit bis zum Untergange der Ordensherrschaft. Ed. Theodor Hirsch, Max Toeppen, and Ernst Strehlke. 6 v. Frankfurt/Main: Minerva, 1963– . Reprint of 1861–74 edition and one new volume. This includes 'Petri de Dusburg', *SRP, I*; 'Peter Suchenwirt', *SRP II*, and 'Die aeltere Hochmeisterchronik', Johann von Posilge, Chronik des Landes Preussen', *SRP*, III, and others.

Die Staatsverträge des Deutschen Ordens in Preußen 1230–1449. Ed. Klaus Neitman. Köln/Wien: Böhlau, 1986. [*Neue Forschungen zur Brandenburg-Preussischen Geschichte* 6.]

Das Zeugenverhör des Franciscus de Moliano (1312). Ed. August Seraphim. Königsberg: Thomas & Oppermann, 1912.

Journals

Altpreussische Forschung. 1924–43.

Altpreussische Monatsschrift. 1864–1922.

Altpreussische Biographie. Ed. Christian Krollmann. Königsberg: Gräfe & Unzer, 1941–3. Additional volumes were edited by Klaus Bürger and Bernhart Jähnig.

Journal of Baltic Studies. Published by the Association for the Advancement of Baltic Studies.

Ostdeutsche Gedenktage. Persönlichkeiten und Historische Ereignisse. Published annually in Bonn by the Kulturstiftung der deutschen Vertriebenen.

Ruthenica, Annual of East European Medieval History and Archeology. Published by the Ukrainian Institute of History.

Quellen und Studien zur Geschichte des Deutschen Ordens. Individual volumes supported by the Teutonic Order, published by Elwert in Marburg/Lahn.

Zapiski Historyczne. Polish journal produced by the TNT scientific society in Toruń.

Zeitschrift für Ostforschung; since 1995 *Zeitschrift für Ostmitteleuropa Forschung.* German journal produced at the Johann-Gottfried-Herder-Institut in Marburg/Lahn.

Secondary Sources

Arnold, Udo, ed., *Die Hochmeister des Deutschen Ordens 1190–1994.* Marburg: Elwert, 1998. [*Quellen und Studien zur Geschichte des Deutschen Ordens* 6.]

——, *Das Verhältnis des Deutschen Ordens zu den Städten in Livland, Preußen und im Deutschen Reich.* Marburg: Elwert, 1993. [*Quellen und Studien zur Geschichte des Deutschen Ordens* 44.]

——, *Zur Wirtschaftsentwicklung des Deutschen Ordens im Mittelalter.* Marburg: Elwert, 1989. [*Quellen und Studien zur Geschichte des Deutschen Ordens* 38.]

———, & Marian Biskup (eds), *Der Deutschordensstaat Preussen in der polnischen Geschichtsschreibung der Gegenwart.* Marburg: Elwert, 1982.

Avižonis, Konstantinas, *Die Entstehung und Entwicklung des litauischen Adels bis zur litauisch-polnischen Union im Jahre 1385.* Berlin: Eberling, 1932.

Backus, Oswald, *Motives of West Russian Nobles in Deserting Lithuania for Moscow 1377–1514.* Lawrence, KS: University of Kansas Press, 1957.

Barber, Malcolm, ed., *The Military Orders: Fighting for the Faith and Caring for the Sick.* Brookfield, VT: Variorum (Ashgate), 1994.

Barber, Richard, *The Knight and Chivalry.* Rev. edn. Rochester, NY: Boydell, 1995.

Baronas, Darius, 'The Lithuanians and the Tatars: confrontation from a safe distance and vested interests in the common ground', in *The Routledge Handbook of the Mongols and Central–Eastern Europe: Political, Economic, and Cultural Relations,* ed. A. V. Maiorov, R. Hautala. London, New York: Routledge, 2021, 311–20.

———, 'Sebastiano Münsterio Žemaitija: įvaizdis ir jo ištakos [Sebastian Münster's Samogitia: the Image and its Sources]', in *Žemaitija/Samogitia,* Vilnius: Vilnius Academy of Arts Press, 2020.

———, 'The River Nemunas during the war between the Teutonic Order and Lithuanians: a border and a corridor (1283–1410)', in *Homini, qui in honore fuit. Księga pamiątkowa poświęcona śp. Profesorowi Grzegorzowi Białuńskiemu,* Olsztyn: Towarzystwo Naukowe Pruthenia, 2020

———, 'The year 1009: St Bruno of Querfurt between Poland and Rus", *Journal of Medieval History* 34 (2008), 1–22.

———, & Artūras Dubonis, Rimvydas Petrauskas, *Lietuvos istorija,* t. 3: XIII a. – 1385 m. *Valstybės iškilimas tarp Rytų ir Vakarų.* Vilnius: Baltos lankos, 2011.

———, & Stephen C. Rowell, *The Conversion of Lithuania: from Pagan Barbarians to Late Medieval Christians.* Vilnius: Institute of Lithuanian Literature and Folklore, 2015.

Benninghoven, Friedrich. *Unter Kreuz und Adler: Der Deutsche Orden im Mittelalter: Ausstellung des Geheimen Staatsarchivs Preussischer Kulturbesitz anlässlich des 800 jährigen Bestehens des Deutschen Ordens.* Mainz: Hase & Koehler, 1990.

Biermann, Felix, with Christofer Herrman, Arkadiusz Koperkiewicz, & Edvinas Ubis, 'Burning Alt-Wartenburg. Archaelogical Evidence for the Conflicts between the Teutonic Order and the Grand Duchy of Lithuania from a deserted medieval town near Barczewko (Warmia, Poland)', *Lietuvos Archeologija* (2019), 265–93.

Biskup, Marian, & Gerard Labuda, *Dzieje Zakonu Krzyżackiego w Prusach. Gospodarka – Społeczeństwo – Państwo – Ideologia.* Gdańsk: Wydawnictwo Morskie, 1986.

Blomkvist, Nils, *The Discovery of the Baltic. The Reception of a Catholic World-System in the European North (AD 1075–1225).* Boston: Brill, 2005. [*The Northern World* 15.]

Bojtár, Endre, *Foreword to the Past. A Cultural History of the Baltic People.* Budapest: Central European University Press, 1999.

Boockmann, Hartmut, *Der Deutsche Orden, Zwölf Kapitel aus seiner Geschichte.* Munich: Beck, 1981.

Brundage, James A., *Medieval Canon Law and the Crusader*. Madison: University of Wisconsin Press. 1969.

Butterwick-Pawlikowski, Richard, ed,, *Central Europe* 8, (Nov. 2010).

Christiansen, Eric, *The Northern Crusades. The Baltic and the Catholic Frontier 1100–1525*. Minneapolis: University of Minnesota, 1980; 2nd edn.: New York: Penguin, 1998.

Curta, Florin, *Eastern Europe in the Middle Ages (500–1300)*. Leiden/Boston: Brill, 2019. 2v.

Davies, Norman, *God's Playground. A History of Poland in two volumes*. New York: Columbia, 1982.

Дубонис, Артурас, 'Две модели литовской экспансии на Руси (XIII – начало XIV века)', in *Исторический Вестник*, vol. 7: *Литва, Русь и Польша XIII–XVI вв.*, 2014, 54–85.

Duczko, Wladyslaw, 'Viking Rus: Studies on the Presence of Scandinavians in Eastern Europe', in *The Northern World. North Europe and the Baltic c. 400–1700 AD*, in *Peoples, Economies and Cultures* 12. Leiden/Boston: Brill, 2004.

Ekdahl, Sven, 'The treatment of prisoners of war during the fighting between the Teutonic Order and Lithuania', in *The Military Orders. Fighting for the Faith and Caring for the Sick*, ed. Malcolm Barber, Aldershot: Variorum, 1994, 263–9.

Engel, Pál, *The Realm of St Stephen: A History of Medieval Hungary, 895–1526*. ed. Andrew Ayton. I. Taurus, 2001.

Epstein, S. R., ed., *Town and Country in Europe, 1300–1800*. Cambridge, 2001.

Fischer, Mary, *'Die Himels Rote': The Idea of Christian Chivalry in the Chronicles of the Teutonic Order*. Göppingen: Kümmerle, 1991. [*Göppinger Arbeiten zur Germanistik* 525.]

Forstreuter, Kurt, *Deutschland und Litauen im Mittelalter*. Köln/Graz: Böhlau, 1962.

Franklin, Simon, and Jonathan Shepard, *The Emergence of Rus, 750–1200*. London, New York: Longman, 1996.

Friedman, John Block, & Kristen Mossler Figg, eds., *Trade, Travel and Exploration in the Middle Ages: An Encyclopedia*. New York: Garland, 2000.

Friedrich, Walter, *Der Deutsche Ritterorden und die Kurie 1300–1330* (diss.) Albertus Universität, Königsberg/Pr., 1915.

Gersdorf, Harro, *Der Deutsche Orden im Zeitalter der Polnisch–Litauischen Union. Die Amtszeit des Hochmeisters Konrad Zöllner von Rotenstein (1382–1390)*. Marburg/Lahn: J. G. Herder, 1957. [*Wissenschaftliche Beiträge zur Geschichte und Landeskunde Ost-Mitteleuropa 29*.]

Gimbutas, Marija, *The Balts*. London: Thames & Hudson, 1963.

Goenner, Mary Ellen, *Mary-Verse of the Teutonic Knights*. New York: AMS, 1944. [*Catholic University of America Studies in German XIX*.]

Goldfrank, David M., 'From butcher to saint: The improbable life and fate of Vaišvilkas/Vojšelk/Lavryš/Elisej of Lithuania and Black Rus' (?–1267)', in *Portraits of Medieval Eastern Europe, 900–1400*, ed. Donald Ostrowski & Christian Raffensperger. Abingdon/New York: Routledge, 2018, 50–8.

Górski, Karol, *L'Ordine Teutonico: alle origini dello stato prussiano*. Turin: Einaudi, 2007.

Grünberg, Walter, 'Der Ausgang der pommerellischen Selbstständigkeit', *Historische Studien*, 128 (1915).

Gulevych, Vladyslav, 'Expansion of the Grand Duchy of Lithuania in the middle and the second half of the fourteenth century and its relations with the Horde', in *Routledge Handbook of the Mongols and Central-Eastern Europe: Political, Economic, and Cultural Relations*, ed. A. V. Maiorov, R. Hautala. London/New York: Routledge, 2021, 340–67.

Gündisch, Gustav, 'Die Türkeneinfälle in Siebenbürgen bis zur Mitte des 15. Jahrhunderts', in *Jahrbücher für Geschichte Osteuropas*, 2 (1937), 393–412.

Halecki, Oscar, *Jadwiga of Anjou and the rise of East Central Europe*. Ed. Thaddeus Gromada. Boulder, CO: Social Science Monographs, 1991. [*East European Monographs* 308]

——, *Borderlands of Western Civilization. A History of East Central Europe*. New York: Ronald, 1952.

Hall, Bert, *Weapons and Warfare in Renaissance Europe. Gunpowder, Technology and Tactics*. Baltimore/London: Johns Hopkins, 1997.

Halperin, Charles J., *The Tatar Yoke*. Columbus, OH: Slavica, 1986.

Hartog, Leo de, *Russia and the Mongol Yoke. The History of the Russian Principalities and the Golden Horde, 1221–1502*. London/New York: British Academic Press, 1996.

Heinl, Karl. *Fürst Witold von Litauen in seinem Verhältnis zum Deutschen Orden in Preußen während der Zeit seines Kampfes um sein litauisches Erbe: 1382–1401*. Berlin: Eberling, 1925.

Hermann, Christofer. *Hochmeisterpalast auf der Marienburg. Konzeption, Bau und Nutzung der modernsten europäischen Fürstenresidenz um 1400*. Petersberg: Michael Imhof Verlag, 2019. [*Berliner Beiträge zur Bauforschung und Denkmalpflege* 17.]

——, *Mittelalterliche Architektur im Preussenland: Untersuchungen zur Frage der Kunstlandschaft und -Geographie*. Petersberg: Mihael Imhof Verlag, 2007.

Hoensch, Jörg K., 'König/Kaiser Sigismund, der Deutsche Orden und Polen-Litauen. Stationen einer problembeladenen Beziehung', in *Zeitschrift für Ostmitteleuropa* 46/2 (1997), 1–44.

——, 'Verlobungen und Ehen Kaiser Sigismund of Luxemburg', in *Herrschaft, Kirche, Kultur: Beiträge zur Geschichte des Mittelalters: Festschrift für Friedrich Prinz zu seinem 65. Geburtstag*. Stuttgart: Hiersemann, 1993. [*Monographien zur Geschichte des Mittelalters* 37.]

Housley, Norman, 'King Louis the Great of Hungary and the Crusades, 1342–1382', *Slavonic and East European Review* 72 (1984), 192–208.

Howard, Michael, *The Causes of Wars and Other Essays*. Cambridge, Mass.: Harvard University Press, 1983.

Huizinga, Johan, *The Waning of the Middle Ages*. London: Edward Arnold, 1924.

Hunyadi, Zsolt, & József Laszlovsky, eds., *The Crusades and the Military Orders. Expanding the Frontiers of Medieval Latin Christianity*. Budapest: Central European University, 2001.

Ivinskis, Zenonas, *Geschichte des Bauernstandes in Litauen. Von den ältesten Zeiten bis zum Anfang des 16. Jahrhunderts. Beiträge zur sozialen und wirtschaftlichten Entwicklung des Bauernstandes in Litauen im Mittelalter.* Berlin: Eberling, 1933.

Jablonowski, Horst, *Westrussland zwischen Wilna und Moskau. Die politische Stellung und die politischen Tendenzen der russischen Bevölkerung des Grossfürstentums Litauen im 15. Jht.* Leiden: Brill, 1961.

Jähnig, Bernhart, & Georg Michels, eds., *Das Preußenland als Forschungsaufgabe. Festschrift für Udo Arnold zum 60. Geburtstag.* Lüneburg: Nordostdeutsches Kulturwerk, 2000. [*Einzelschriften der Historischen Kommission für ost- und westpreußische Landesforschung 20.*]

Jakštas, Juozas, 'Das Baltikum in der Kreuzzugsbewegung des 14. Jhr; die Nachrichten Philipps de Mézières über die baltischen Gebiete', *Commentationes Balticae* 6–7 (1959), 141–83.

Jasienica, Pawel, *Piast Poland.* Trans. Alexander Jordan. Miami: American Institute of Polish Culture, & New York: Hippocrene, 1985.

Johnson, Lonnie, *Central Europe. Enemies, Neighbors, Friends.* Oxford: Oxford University Press, 1996.

Jones, Terry, *Chaucer's Knight: The Portrait of a Medieval Mercenary.* Baton Rouge: Louisiana State University Press, 1980; rev. edn. London: Methuen 2017.

Jonynas, Ignas, *Istorijos baruose.* Vilnius: Mokslas, 1984.

Kavka, František, 'Zum Plan der Luxemburgischen Thronfolge in Polen (1368–1382). Strittige Forschungsfragen', *Zeitschrift für Historische Forschung,* 3 (1986), 257–83.

Keen, Maurice, *Chivalry.* New Haven and London: Yale University Press, 1984.

Кибинь, Алексей Сергеевич, *От Ятвязи до Литвы: Русское пограничье с ятвягами и литвой в X–XIII веках.* Москва: Квадрига, 2014.

Knoll, Paul, *The Rise of the Polish Monarchy: Piast Poland in East Central Europe, 1320–1370.* Chicago/London: University of Chicago Press, 1972.

Köhler, Gustav, *Die Entwicklung des Kriegswesen und der Kriegsführung in der Ritterzeit.* Breslau, 1886.

Končius, Joseph, *Vytautas the Great, Grand Duke of Lithuania.* Miami, FL: Franklin, 1964.

Krollmann, Christian, *Politische Geschichte des Deutschen Ordens in Preussen.* Königsberg: Grafe & Unzer, 1932.

Krumbholtz, Robert, 'Samaiten und der Deutsche Orden bis zum Frieden am Melno-See', *Altpreussische Monatsschrift* 26 (1889).

Kuczyński, Stefan, *Król Jagiełło ok. 1351–1354.* Warsaw: Wydawnictwo Ministerstwa Obrony Narodowej, 1987.

Kwiatkowski, Krzystof, 'The relations of the Teutonic Order in Prussia with the local nobility in the 13th–early 16th century. Scope of issues, research state and research perspectives', *Cahiers de la Mediterranée* 104 (2022), 111–46.

——, *Wojska Zakonu Niemieckiego w Prusach 1230–1525.* Toruń: Wydawnictwo Naukowe UMK, 2016.

——, 'Die Belagerung Kauens 1362 in der Beschreibung Wigands von Marburg', *Zeitschrift für Ostmitteleuropa* 57 (2008), 238–54.

——, 'Christ ist erstanden . . . und die Christen siegen!' YUMPU.com.

Labuda, Gerard, ed., *Historia Pomorza.* Vol. 1 in two parts: *do roku 1466.* Poznań: Wydawnictwo Poznańskie, 1972.

Leighton, Gregory, *Ideology and Holy Landscape in the Baltic Crusades*. Leeds: Arc Humanities Press, 2022.

Lewicki, Anatol, 'Über das staatsrechtliche Verhältniss Litauens zu Polen unter Jagiełło und Witold', *Altpreussische Monatsschrift* (1894), 1–94.

Łowmiański, Henryk, *Studia nad dziejami Wielkiego Księstwa Lietwskiego*. Poznań: UAM, 1983.

Macek, Josef, et al., *Sigismund of Luxemburg, Kaiser und König im Mitteleuropa 1387–1437. Beiträge zur Herrschaft Kaiser Sigismunds und der europäischen Geschichte um 1400*. Warendorf: Fahlbusch, 1994.

Mályusz, Elemér, *Kaiser Sigismund in Ungarn*. Budapest: Kiadó, 1990.

Mannhardt, Wilhelm. *Letto-Preußische Götterlehre*. Riga 1936 (reprint 1971). [*Magazin der Lettisch-Literärischen Gesellschaft* 21]

Martin, Janet, *Medieval Russia 980–1584*. Cambridge: Cambridge University Press, 1995.

Maschke, Erich, *Domus Hospitalis Theutonicorum. Europäische Verbindungslinien der Deutschordensgeschichte. Gesammelte Aufsätze aus den Jahren 1931–1963*. Bonn-Bad Godesberg: Verlag Wiss. Archiv, 1970.

Mažeika, Rasa, & Loïc Chollet, 'Familiar Marvels? French and German Crusaders and Chroniclers Confront Baltic Pagan Religions'. *Francia, Forschungen zur westeuropäischen Geschichte* 43 (2016), 41–62.

Militzer, Klaus, 'Die Übersiedlung Siegfrieds von Feuchtwangen in die Marienburg', *Ordines Militares. Colloquia Torunensia Historica* 16 (2011), 47–61.

Muldoon, James, *Popes, Lawyers and Infidels*. Philadelphia: University of Pennsylvania, 1979.

Müller-Wille, Michael, ed., *Rom und Byzanz im Nordern. Mission und Glaubenswechsel im Ostseeraum während des 8.-14. Jahrhunderts*. 2 v. Stuttgart: Franz Steiner, 1997, 1999.

Murray, Alan V., ed., *The North-Eastern Frontiers of Medieval Europe: The Expansion of Latin Christendom into the Baltic Lands*. Farnham: Ashgate, 2014.

——, *Crusade and Conversion on the Baltic Frontier 1150–1500*. Aldershot: Ashgate, 2001.

Назаренко, Александр В., *Древняя Русь на международных путях: Междисциплинарные очерки культурных, торговых, политических связей IX–XII вв.* Москва: Языки Русской Культуры, 2001.

Neitmann, Klaus, *Der Hochmeister des Deutschen Ordens in Preußen ein Residenzherrscher unterwegs. Untersuchungen zu den Hochmeisteritineraren im 14. und 15. Jahrhundert*. Köln, Wien: Böhlau, 1990. [*Veröffentlichungen aus der Archiven Preussischer Kulturbesitz*, 30.]

Nicholson, Helen, *Medieval Warfare: Theory and Practice of War in Europe, 300–1500*. New York: Palgrave, 2004.

——, ed., *The Military Orders*. vol. 2. Aldershot etc.: Ashgate, 1998.

———, ed., *Die Rolle der Ritterorden in der Christianisierung und Kolonisierung des Ostseegebietes*. Toruń: Uniwersytet Mikołaja Kopernika, 1983.

Nicolle, David, with Graham Turner, *Teutonic Knights: 1190–1561*, Oxford: Osprey, 2007.

——, with Christa Hook, *Nicopolis 1396: The Last Crusade*. Oxford: Osprey, 1999.

Niess, Ulrich, *Hochmeister Karl von Trier (1311–1324). Stationen einer Karriere im Deutschen Orden.* Marburg: Elwert, 1992. [*Quellen und Studien zur Geschichte des Deutschen Ordens 47.*]

Nöbel, Wilhelm, *Michael Küchmeister, Hochmeister des Deutschen Orders 1414–1422.* Bad Godesberg: Wissenschaftliches Archiv, 1969.

Norkus, Zenonas, *An Unproclaimed Empire: The Grand Duchy of Lithuania from the Viewpoint of Comparative Historical Sociology of Empires.* London, New York: Routledge, 2018.

Nowak, Zenon Hubert, ed., *Ritterorden und Kirche im Mittelalter.* Toruń: Wydawnictwo Uniwersytetu Mikołaja Kopernika, 1997. [*Ordines Militares. Colloquia Torunensia Historica, IX.*]

——, 'Kaiser Siegmund und die polnische Monarchie (1387–1437)', *Zeitschrift für Historische Forschung* 15 (1988), 423–36.

——, ed., *Werkstatt des Historikers der mittelalterlichen Ritterorden. Quellen- kundliche Probleme und Forschungsmethode.* Toruń: Uniwersytet Mikołaja Kopernika, 1987.

Ostrowski, Donald, *Muscovy and the Mongols: Cross-Cultural Influences on the Steppe Frontier, 1304–1589.* Cambridge: Cambridge University Press, 1998.

Paravicini, Werner, *Die Preussenreisen des europäischen Adels.* Part 1 and 2, Sigmaringen 1989 and 1995. Part 3, Göttingen: V. & R. unipress, 2020. [*Beihefte der Francia 17, 1–2*].

——, ed. et al., *Mare Balticum: Beiträge zur Geschichte des Ostseeraums in Mittelalter und Neuzeit: Festschrift zum 65. Geburtstag von Erich Hoffmann.* Sigmaringen: Jan Thorbecke Verlag, 1992. [*Kieler historische Studien* 36.]

Paszkiewicz, H., *The Making of the Russian Nation.* London: Longman, 1963.

——, *The Origin of Russia.* London: Allen & Unwin, 1954.

——, *Jagiellonowie a Moskwa,* vol. 1: *Litwa a Moskwa w XIII i XIV wieku.* Warszawa: Z zasiłku Funduszu Kultury Narodowej, 1933.

Plano Carpini, *The Story of the Mongols Whom We Call the Tartars by Friar Giovanni di Plano Carpini,* trans. E. Hildinger, Boston, MA: Branden, 1996.

Plokhy, Serhii, *The Origins of the Slavic Nations: Premodern Identities in Russia, Ukraine, and Belarus.* Cambridge: Cambridge University Press, 2006.

Pluskowski, Aleksander, ed., *Ecologies of Crusading, Colonization, and Religious Conversion in the Medieval Baltic: Terra Sacra II.* Series: Environmental Histories of the North Atlantic World. Turnhout: Brepols, 2019.

——, *The Archaeology of the Prussian Crusade, Holy War and Colonisation.* London: Routledge, 2012.

Presniakov, Alexander, *The Tsardom of Muscovy.* Ed. and trans. Robert Price. Gulf Breeze, FL: Academic International, 1978.

Prochaska, Antoni, *Dzieje Witołda w. Księcia Litwy.* Wilno: Rutkowski, 1914.

——, *Król Władysław Jagiełło.* 2 v. Cracow: Akademia Umiejętności, 1908.

Purc, Jerzy, 'Itinerarium Witolda Wielkiego Księcia Litwy', *Historia* 11 (1971), 71–115. [*Studia z Dziejów Wielkiego Księstwa Litewskiego XIV–XVIII Wieku.*]

Raffensperger, Christian. *Reimagining Europe: Kievan Rus' in the Medieval World.* Cambridge, Mass.: Harvard University Press, 2012.

Rautenberg, Wilhelm. 'Einwirkungen Böhmens auf die Geschichte des Ordenslandes Preußen im späten Mittelalter', *Zeitschrift für Ostforschung* 22 (1973), 626–95.

Rhode, Gotthold, *Die Ostgrenze Polens. Politische Entwicklung, kulturelle Bedeutung und geistige Auswirkung*, Köln/Graz: Böhlau, 1955. [*Ostmitteleuropa in Vergangenheit und Gegenwart 2/1.*]

Röhrich, Victor, *Geschichte des Fürstbistums Ermland*. Braunsberg: Ermländische Zeitungs- und Verlagsdruckerei, 1925.

Rowell, Stephen C., 'Swords for Sale? Aspects of Gediminas' Diplomacy (1323–1341)', *Lituanistica* 2 (1997), 3–19.

——, *Lithuania Ascending: A Pagan Empire within East-Central Europe, 1294–1345*. Cambridge: Cambridge University Press, 1994.

——, 'Pious Princesses or the Daughters of Belial: Pagan Lithuanian Dynastic Diplomacy, 1279–1423', *Medieval Prosopography* 15/1 (Spring 1994), 3–79.

——, 'The Letters of Gediminas, 'Gemachte Lüge'? Notes on a Controversy', *Jahrbücher für Geschichte Osteuropas* 41 (1993), 321–60.

——, 'Of Men and Monsters: Sources for the History of Lithuania in the Time of Gediminas (*ca.* 1315–1342)', *Journal of Baltic History* 24/1 (Spring 1993), 73–112.

——, 'A Pagan's Word: Lithuanian diplomatic procedure 1200–1385', *Journal of Medieval History* 18 (1992), 145–60.

Rudling, Odeta, 'The Cult of the Balts: Mythological Impulses and Neo-Pagan Practices in the Touristic Clubs of the Lithuanian SSR of the 1960s and 1970s', in *Regional Studies of Russia, Eastern Europe, and Central Asia* 6/1 (2017), 87–108.

Русина, Олена, *Студії з історії Києва та київської землі*. Київ: Національна Академія Наук Україні, 2005.

——, *Сіверська земля у складі Великого Князівства Литовського*. Київ: Національна Академія Наук Україні, 1998.

Salys, Anton, *Die žemaitischen Mundarten. I: Geschichte des žemaitischen Sprachgebietes*. Kaunas: 'Spindulio' b-vės spaustuvė, 1930.

Samalačius, Stasys, 'Vilnius Cathedral Square from the Fourteenth to the Nineteenth Centuries. Part One', *Lituanus* 67/2 (2021), 28–55.

Samerski, Stefan, ed., *Cura animarum. Seelsorge im Deutschordensland Preußen*. Köln/Weimar/Wien: Böhlau, 2013.

Sarnowsky, Jürgen, *On the Military Orders in Medieval Europe: Structures and Perceptions*. Farnham/Burlington: Ashgate, 2011. [Variorum Collected Studies Series, vol. 992.]

Schumacher, Bruno, *Geschichte Ost- und Westpreussens*. 6th edn. Würzburg: Holzner, 1977.

Sedlar, Jean, *East Central Europe in the Middle Ages, 1000–1500*. Seattle/London: University of Washington Press, 1994.

Selart, Anti, *Livonia, Rus' and the Baltic Crusades in the Thirteenth Century*, trans. Fiona Robb. Leiden/Boston: Brill 2015. [*East Central and Eastern Europe in the Middle Ages, 450–1450*, vol. 29.]

Paul Srodecki & Norbert Kersken, *The Expansion of the Faith: Crusading on the Frontiers of Latin Christendom in the High Middle Ages*. Turnhout: Brepols 2022.

Sieradzan, Wiesław, ed., *Arguments and Counterarguments: The Political Thought of the 14th and 15th Centuries during the Polish–Teutonic Order Trials and*

Disputes. Toruń: Wydawnictwo Naukowe Uniwersytetu Mikołaja Kopernika, 2012.

Stone, Daniel Z., *The Polish–Lithuanian State, 1386–1795*. Seattle: University of Washington Press, 2001.

Trupinda, Janusz, ed., *Sapientia Aedificavit Sibi Domum*. Malbork: Muzeum Zamkowe w Malborku, 2019.

——, & Krzysztof Ożóg, ed., *Conflictus Magnus apud Grunwald 1410. Między Historią a Tradycją*. Proceedings of the Grunwald Conference 2010. Malbork: Muzeum Zamkowe 2013.

Tuchman, Barbara, *A Distant Mirror: The Calamitous 14th Century*. New York: Alfred A. Knopf, 1978.

Tumler, Marian, *Der Deutsche Orden: Werden, Wachsen, und Wirkung*. Bonn-Bad Godesberg: Wissenschaftliches Archiv, 1974.

——, & Udo Arnold. *Von Akkon bis Wien: Studien zur Deutschordensgeschichte vom 13. bis zum 20. Jahrhundert: Festschrift zum 90. Geburtstag von Althochmeister P. Dr. Marian Tumler O.T. am 21. Oktober 1977*. Marburg: Elwert, 1978.

Turnbull, Stephen, illus. Peter Dennis, *Crusader Castles of the Teutonic Knights*, vol. 1, *The Red-Brick Castles of Prussia 1230–1466*. Oxford: Osprey, 2003; Vol. 2: *The Stone Castles of Latvia and Estonia, 1185–1560*. Oxford: Osprey, 2004.

Urban, William. *The Last Years of the Teutonic Knights: The Teutonic Knights, Poland and Lithuania*. London: Greenhill, 2018.

——, *The Livonian Crusade*. 2nd edn. Chicago: Lithuanian Research and Studies Center, 2004.

——, 'The Organization of the Defence of the Livonian Frontier', *Speculum* 48 (July 1973), 525–32.

Vernadsky, George, *The Mongols and Russia*. New Haven/London: Yale University Press, 1953. [Vol. III of *A History of Russia*.]

Voigt, Johannes, *Geschichte Preussens von den ältesten Zeiten bis zum Untergange des Deutschen Ordens*. 9 v. Königsberg: Borntäager, 1827–1839; repr. Hildesheim: Georg Olms, 1968.

Waschinski, Emil, 'Die Münz- und Währungspolitik des deutschen Ordens in Preussen ihre historischen Probleme und seltenen Gepräge', *Der Göttinger Arbeitskreis*, 60, 1952.

Wenta, Jarosław, ed., *Sacred Space in the State of the Teutonic Order in Prussia*. Toruń: Wydawnictwo Naukowe Uniwersytetu Mikołaja Kopernika, 2013.

Żabiński, Grzegorz, 'Broń palna w państwie Zakonu Niemieckiego w Prusach – stan wiedzy i perspektywy badawcze', *Zeszyty Historyczne*, 15 (2016), 35–56.

Zharkikh, Mykola, *Push to the South, Three Years Vytautas' policy (1397–1399)*. Personal website, 2017.

Index